SHAKESPEARE
and Others

Shakespeare and Others

S. Schoenbaum

Folger Books
Washington: The Folger Shakespeare Library
London: Scolar Press

© 1985 by Associated University Presses, Inc.

Associated University Presses
440 Forsgate Drive
Cranbury, NJ 08512

Associated University Presses
2133 Royal Windsor Drive
Unit 1
Mississauga, Ontario
Canada L5J 1K5

Scolar Press
13 Brunswick Centre
London WC1N 1AF

Library of Congress Cataloging in Publication Data

Schoenbaum, S. (Samuel), 1927–
  Shakespeare and others.

  "Folger books."

  Includes bibliographical references.
  1. Shakespeare, William, 1564–1616—Addresses, essays,
lectures.   2. English drama—17th century—History and
criticism—Addresses, essays, lectures.   3. Dramatists,
English—Early modern, 1500–1700—Biography—Addresses,
essays, lectures.   I. Title.
PR2899.S314   1984   822.3'3   83-49009
ISBN 0-918016-67-3

British Library Cataloguing in Publication Data

Schoenbaum, S.
  Shakespeare and others.
  1. Shakespeare, William—Criticism and interpretation
  I. Title
  822.3'3   PR2976

  ISBN 0-85967-691-9

Printed in the United States of America

To
Shirley Strum Kenny

Contents

Preface

This book brings together selected essays, lectures, and reviews—those that I feel most worth preserving—of the past quarter of a century. Not all the items included are elsewhere readily accessible, or even available at all. "The Presence of the Past" has not been previously printed and "A Question of Decadence," published in French ("Peut-on parler d'une 'décadence' du théâtre au temps des premiers Stuart?"), in *Dramaturgie et société, XVIe et XVIIe siècles* (Paris, 1968), has not appeared in English. Relatively few, I expect, in the English-speaking world have caught "The Ireland Forgeries: An Unpublished Contemporary Account," which had a place in the *Festschrift* honoring Professor Jiro Ozu, published in Tokyo in 1980. Some pieces are here offered in fuller versions—for example, "A National Religion Established," which, mindful of journalistic constraints of space, I abridged, not without a pang, before dispatching it to the editor of the *Times Literary Supplement.*

Here and there I have corrected errors—e.g. the description of the hands present in the Caroline manuscript comedy, *Wit's Triumvirate*—but I have resisted the temptation to wholesale updating of my early essays in order to take into account subsequent contributions, for that would have been, in effect, to falsify the record. These pieces, as they stand, reflect the state of my knowledge and sensibility at the time they were written. In preparing copy for the press I have, however, so far consulted the reader's convenience as to normalize the *i-j* and *u-v* equations in old-spelling quotations, and to expand abbreviations. For quotations from Shakespeare I have used the Peter Alexander edition of *The Complete Works,* 1951.

The writer of a Preface has the happy privilege of being able to express his gratitude to those who facilitated his task. Mrs. Diane Clark uncomplainingly typed my sometimes untidy scripts. Quotations were conscientiously checked by Mr. Michael Selmon. Miss Nora Tracy helped with the proofs. Miss Jane Apple very generously offered to prepare the Index. In Dr. John Andrews the Folger has an exemplary executive director for its academic programs. My wife Marilyn kept the home fires burning.

It is an article of my faith that scholarship and criticism should be fun for the practitioner. Else why forgo the rewards of indolence? I hope that the delight I have taken, over the years, in the exercise of my far from sullen craft shows through.

S. S.

Acknowledgments

For permission to reprint I am obliged to the following (the number of each item is given in round brackets): AMS Press, Inc., for "Old-Spelling Editions: The State of the Art" (19); Cambridge University Press for "Shakespeare's Dark Lady: A Question of Identity" (4) and "*Richard II* and the Realities of Power" (5); Centre National de la Recherche Scientifique for "A Question of Decadence" (18); Kinokuniya Company Limited for "The Ireland Forgeries: An Unpublished Contemporary Account" (10); Henry E. Huntington Library and Art Gallery, San Marino, Calif., for "*The Widow's Tears* and the Other Chapman" (16); Macmillan Press Ltd for "Shakespeare and Jonson: Fact and Myth" (13) and "The Humorous Jonson" (14); New York University Press for "*A Chaste Maid in Cheapside* and Middleton's City Comedy," in *Studies in the English Renaissance,* ed. Josephine W. Bennett, Oscar Cargill, and Vernon Hall (15); Rice University Press for "*Wit's Triumvirate:* A Caroline Comedy Recovered," in *SEL* (17); Smithsonian Associates for "The Folger at Fifty" ["The World's Finest Shakespeare Library Is This Side of Atlantic"], in *Smithsonian* (12); Southern Illinois Press for "Looking for Shakespeare" (2); Times Newspapers Limited for "William Bott, the Widow's Portion, and Shakespearean Biography," "New Light on a Dark Lady," "Dark Secrets," "Looking at the Underside of the Time," "The Studied and the Spontaneous," "In Mercurial Guise," "A National Religion Established," "To Sendai for Shakespeare," "Shakespeare Shanghaied," "Shakespeare Wallahs," "Seeing Shakespeare Plain," "Alternative Shakespeare," and "Shakespeare Played Out, or Much Ado about *Nada*," in the *Times Literary Supplement* (3, 4 [I–III], 7, 8, 9, 11, respectively).

SHAKESPEARE
and Others

PART I
Shakespearean Themes

1
Shakespeare and the Book

The inspiration for this paper derives from a widely reported recent birthday party: the five-hundredth anniversary of printing in Oxford, marked by exhibitions in London, New York, Washington, and elsewhere, and celebrated with a birthday cake requiring Aeolus to blow out the candles, for there were—you guessed it—five hundred of them. When an Oxford printer in 1478 published the book which provided the occasion for that splendid celebration, Caxton had only lately introduced printing into England. The birth of William Shakespeare lay almost a century ahead. By then a silent revolution had permanently transformed learning and letters. Without printed books Shakespeare's art, shaped by his reading, could not have come to pass, at least in the form in which we know it. Without the book, his plays and poems most likely would have perished; none indeed survives in autograph except possibly one much debated fragment of three leaves. But, as things worked out, those plays and poems have become the most widely disseminated writings—Holy Writ excepted—in the history of man. Certain mysteries attend Shakespeare's relationship with the book, while the preservation of his own corpus has an aspect of the miraculous. My subject is the mystery and the miracle.[1]

So vast a topic is best given a local habitation at the outset. Let that habitation be the town in which Shakespeare made his acquaintance with the book. In the sixteenth century the population of Stratford-upon-Avon stood at less than two thousand, but in some ways this provincial market town must have looked very much as it does today. The handsome Collegiate Church of the Holy Trinity, where Shakespeare was baptized and buried, had already graced the Avon's bank for centuries. Clopton Bridge spanned the river with its fourteen massive stone arches and pointed the traveller the way to London; Shakespeare himself crossed this bridge when he first struck out on the road to the capital. The bridge still stands. So does his birthplace, more or less intact, in Henley Street. The Guild Chapel, now badly in need of repair, stood just a stone's throw from the great house of New Place, with its ten fireplaces, the house Shakespeare bought after he had established himself as the preeminently popular playwright of the

London stage. At New Place a previous owner, one William Bott, purportedly poisoned his daughter with ratsbane, whereupon she swelled to death; his malevolent influence demonstrates—if any demonstration is needed—that in those days life in Stratford was less tranquil than now. The town then had no printing press, and has never been a publishing hub; but of course, unlike Oxford, it is not a university center, and so is entitled to its cheerful philistinism. Nor did Stratford boast a theatre in Shakespeare's time, although the professional London companies included it in their provincial itineraries.

How, in such a setting, did Shakespeare get to know books in his formative years? Did he get to know books? Let me offer two opposing pictures, both sketched by eminent Victorians, and both influential. The first we owe to Charles Knight. As publisher, author, and editor, he was a tireless champion of Victorian humanitarianism who endeavored to uplift the Lower Orders by means of wholesome, instructive, and attractive literature that was cheap enough for them to afford. Knight's portrait of the young Shakespeare among his books is nothing if not wholesome, instructive, and attractive.

> [Shakespeare] speaks always with reverence of the teachers of the highest wisdom, by whatever name denominated. He has learnt, then, at his mother's knee the cardinal doctrines of Christianity; he can read. His was an age of few books. Yet, believing, as we do, that his father and mother were well-educated persons, there would be volumes in their house capable of exciting the interest of an inquiring boy—volumes now rarely seen and very precious. Some of the first books of the English press might be there; . . . Caxton's Catalogue was rich in romantic and poetical lore. . . . Here were legends of faith and love, of knightly deeds and painful perils,—glimpses of history through the wildest romance—enough to fill the mind of a boy-poet with visions of unutterable loveliness and splendour. . . . What dim thoughts of earthly mutations, unknown to the quiet town of Stratford, must the young Shakspere have received, as he looked upon the pictures of 'the boke of John Bochas, describing the fall of princes, princesses, and other nobles,' and especially as he beheld the portrait of John Lydgate, the translator, kneeling in a long black cloak, admiring the vicissitude of the wheel of fortune, the divinity being represented by a male figure, in a robe, with expanded wings![2]

Then there were the books of "traditional lore"—"Were there not in every house 'Christmas Carols,'—perhaps not the edition of Wynkyn de Worde in 1521, but reprints out of number?" Now the great thing about this sort of exercise is that it can go on for pages, and thus flesh out meager information about Shakespeare's childhood. In Knight, it does go on for pages. So we are conducted on a tour of ancient songs and gestes, the early interludes of the Tudor wandering players, and the metrical version of the Psalms by Sternhold and Hopkins. He says: "Sure we are that the child William Shakspere had his memory stored with its vigorous and idiomatic

English." And finally we arrive at the "one book which it was the especial happiness of that contemplative boy to be familiar with": the English Bible. "We believe that the home education of William Shakspere was grounded upon this Book; and that, if this Book had been sealed to his childhood, he might have been the poet of nature, of passion, . . . but that he would not have been the poet of the most profound as well as the most tolerant philosophy."[3]

Thus Knight, in his 1843 biography of Shakespeare, which went through a number of editions, and still holds the reader's interest. On the other hand, we have Knight's colleague, J. O. Halliwell-Phillipps to remind us that Shakespeare's Stratford was, in addition to being unsanitary (Shakespeare's father was once fined for having a dungheap in front of his Henley Street homestead), an illiterate and bookless neighborhood. Halliwell-Phillipps observes:

> The best authorities unite in telling us that the poet imbibed a certain amount of Latin at school, but that his acquaintance with that language was, throughout his life, of a very limited character. It is not probable that scholastic learning was ever congenial to his tastes, and it should be recollected that books in most parts of the country were then of very rare occurrence. Lilly's Grammar and a few classical works, chained to the desks of the Free School, were probably the only volumes of the kind to be found at Stratford-on-Avon. Exclusive of Bibles, Church Services, Psalters, and education manuals, there were certainly not more than two or three dozen books, if so many, in the whole town. The copy of the black-letter English history, so often depicted as well thumbed by Shakespeare in his father's parlour, never existed out of the imagination. Fortunately for us, the youthful dramatist had, excepting in the schoolroom, little opportunity of studying any but a grander volume, the infinite book of nature, the pages of which were ready to be unfolded to him in the lane and field, amongst the copses of Snitterfield, by the side of the river or that of his uncle's hedgerows.[4]

Behind the Halliwell-Phillipps picture lurks a tradition going back to Shakespeare's own lifetime; according to his contemporary, Francis Beaumont, preachers in their sermons might point to Shakespeare for proof of "how farr sometimes a mortall man may goe / by the dimme light of Nature." Milton makes the point more elegantly in his "L'Allegro," with its evocation of "sweetest Shakespeare, fancy's child, / Warbl[ing] his native wood-notes wild." Illiteracy in great ones is not necessarily a minus. As an eighteenth-century physician and naturalist, John Berkenhout, wrote in his *Biographia Literaria; or, a Biographical History of Literature:*

> They say Shakespeare was illiterate. The supposition implies more than Panegyric with a hundred tongues could have expressed. If he was unlearned, he was the only instance of a human being to whom learning was unnecessary; the favorite child of Nature, produced and educated

entirely by herself; but so educated, that the pedant Art had nothing new to add.[5]

This piercing insight made so powerful an impression that later encyclopedists cribbed it word for word.

Today we would not make the point in quite the same way, but the view expressed dies hard. William Empson has referred to "the assertively unlearned Shakespeare"; and in one of his numerous biographies of Shakespeare, Dr. A. L. Rowse has stated that his subject was no intellectual. Maybe he has a point; Shakespeare was not so formidably learned as Milton. But, then, who was? Still it seems a trifle odd to size up the author of *Hamlet, Troilus and Cressida,* and *The Tempest* as unintellectual. However this may be, the received view of Shakespeare as inspired ignoramus has served to fuel anti-Stratfordian fires. Could a man hailing from darkest Stratford, born into a family of illiterates, and bred with yokels, become the supreme poet-playwright whose image has been carved out for us by reverence in the Mount Rushmore of bardolatry? After all, Shakespeare warbled more than woodnotes. Granted that he may have had superior natural gifts; they would have served merely to make him the best of the bumpkins. If so, he might have challenged Bottom with a *Pyramus and Thisbe* of his own, but he could scarcely have awakened from *A Midsummer Night's Dream.*

The alternative—that Shakespeare's parents nourished their young son's intellect by reading aloud at the family hearth—is in fact unlikely. A deed that Mary Shakespeare, his mother, witnessed in 1579 was executed with her mark. Her husband John witnessed the same document with *his* mark, a cross. Sometimes he used instead a pair of glover's compasses for his sign-manual, for he was by occupation a glover. Now, learned authorities have pointed out that a cross on a legal instrument symbolized the holy cross, and therefore possibly betokened the piety of the subscriber; in other words, it qualified as a kind of oath. Maybe the glover's compasses had some other, more arcane significance, such as "God Encompasseth Us." It is also true that literate Elizabethans occasionally chose to sign with a mark, as we today sometimes use initials in place of a full signature. But by and large the use of a mark carries the presumption of illiteracy, a presumption reinforced by the fact that we haven't a single signature by John Shakespeare, and that he was brought up as a tenant farmer's son in a rural hamlet (Snitterfield) which, lacking a single school, must have offered severely limited educational opportunities. An historian's recent survey shows that, by the end of the sixteenth century, almost fifty percent of tradesmen and artisans were illiterate, as were three quarters of the farming population, and eighty-nine percent of all women.[6] In John Shakespeare's childhood, a half century earlier, an even bleaker situation obtained, for the Elizabethan educational revolution had not yet raised the general standard of literacy. A teasing reference (in this context) appears in relation to a suit brought in 1596 by the widow Margaret Young against another Stratford widow, Joan Perott, for deceitful appropriation of sundry items, including (according to the inventory) "Mr. Shaxpere, one book." It isn't certain which Shakespeare this document cites, but even if it was—as is likely—the poet's father, possession of a book would not demonstrate the capacity to read it; some owners are no users. (I pass over the interesting question of whether inability to write necessarily implies inability to read.) William Shakespeare's own elder daughter Susanna was characterized in her epitaph as "Witty above her sexe." She could indeed sign her name, but when confronted with some of her late physician-husband's casebooks, she failed to recognize his hand. Shakespeare's younger daughter Judith used a mark. Stratford bred few Rosalinds and Beatrices, although Juliet's nurse no doubt would have felt at home.

The conditions I have been sketching may seem discouraging; at least until we pause to remind ourselves that it is not all that unusual for immensely gifted children to come from uneducated households. Thomas Hardy, for example, had "only marginally literate" parents. In our great modern melting pots, the offspring of unlettered immigrants have time and again made extraordinary contributions to literature and the arts. But we enjoy the matchless advantages (as well as the problems) of the twentieth-century metropolis. What did Elizabethan Stratford have to offer? Was it in truth a bookless neighborhood?

The answer is no; Halliwell-Phillipps and his school are wrong. Let me give just one example. The vicar who christened William Shakespeare was Master John Bretchgirdle, who had come to Stratford from Witton, Northwich. A bachelor, he was looked after by his sister, maybe two sisters. On June 20, 1565, as he lay "visited with the hand of God," Bretchgirdle signed his will, in which he made bequests of books in his library, which was valued at half his estate. The next day he died. Bretchgirdle's books included Aesop's *Fables* (in Latin), Tully's *Offices*, Sallust, Vergil, and Horace, Withals' *Short Dictionary for Young Beginners,* and Erasmus' *Manual of a Christian Knight,* not to mention *The Acts of the Apostles, translated into English Metre, and dedicated to the King's most excellent Majesty by Christofer Tye, doctor in music and one of the gentlemen of his Grace's most honorable Chapel, with notes to each chapter, to sing and also to play upon the lute, very necessary for students after their study, to file their wits, and also for Christians that cannot sing, to read the good and godly stories of the lives of Christ his Apostles,* printed in London, 1553. Bretchgirdle bequeathed a number of his books to the five sons of Alderman Smith in the High Street. His Eliot-Cooper Latin Dictionary he left "to the common use of the scholars" at the King's New School in Stratford-upon-Avon. Young William Smith, remembered by Bretchgirdle with books and a shilling, is the only one of the twenty-six male children baptized in the same year as Shakespeare to go on to the university. After taking his B.A. from Exeter College, Oxford, he eventually became a schoolmaster in Essex. This Smith was the most promising pupil of Shakespeare's class.

I mentioned the grammar school. The rosters of pupil enrollment in Elizabethan times have long since disappeared, but the reasonable assumption that Shakespeare attended (without tuition charges, as was his right) is confirmed by his first biographer, Nicholas Rowe. Writing early in the eighteenth century, Rowe remarks that the poet's father "had bred him, 'tis true, for some time at a Free-School." Many have marvelled that a writer who demonstrates in his work such wide and varied learning with respect to literature, rhetoric, music and the law, as well as British and Roman history—quite apart from his profound comprehension of the human heart—should have succeeded so astonishingly without the advantages of a university education. However, patient modern investigation of the sixteenth-century grammar-school curriculum has revealed how broad and thorough a grounding the young scholars received in the classroom. Lessons began at six or seven in the morning and continued, with recesses for breakfast and lunch, until five or six at night. Allusions scattered through Shakespeare's plays ruefully recall the exquisite tedium of the experience. "Love goes toward love as school-boys from their books," Romeo groans beneath Juliet's balcony; "But love from love, toward school with heavy looks."[7] And in *The Taming of the Shrew* Gremio returns from Petruchio's madcap wedding "As willingly as e'er I came from school" (3.2.146). Lord Say, in *2 Henry VI*, goes off to execution for having "most traitorously corrupted the youth of the realm in erecting a grammar school" (4.7.28–30). But we remember best the second of Jaques' Seven Ages of Man, with its evocation of

> the whining school-boy, with his satchel
> And shining morning face, creeping like snail
> Unwillingly to school.
>
> (2.7.145–47)

In the early forms the pupils memorized by rote their Latin grammar, and no doubt endured the sort of interrogation to which the bumbling parson-pedagogue Sir Hugh Evans put little master William before his mother and Mistress Quickly in *The Merry Wives of Windsor.* Having painfully mastered his Latin fundamentals, Shakespeare would have gone on to acquire the small Latin and less Greek with which Ben Jonson credits him, although the Latin at least was far from small by today's standards.

Ovid's *Metamorphoses* would remain Shakespeare's favorite classic. He not only uses this work as a source but actually brings it on-stage as an essential prop in *Titus Andronicus,* his most violent and bookish play. In a crucial scene of revelation, Lucius' schoolboy son runs across the stage, books under his arms, with Lavinia in pursuit. Frightened, he drops his school-texts, and Lavinia, who has been brutally raped and mutilated, turns the leaves with her handless stumps. "Lucius, what book is that she tosseth so?" demands Titus; and the boy: "Grandsire, 'tis Ovid's *Metamorphoses*; / My mother gave it me" (4.1.41–43). Unable to speak—her tongue has been cut out—Lavinia is nevertheless able to point to "the tragic tale of Philomel" that treats of Tereus' treason and his rape, and in this way reveals to her father the circumstances and enormity of her violation.

Titus Andronicus came early in Shakespeare's career, but the spell cast by Ovid never faded. Near the time of his retirement from the stage, with *The Tempest*, Shakespeare returned to the *Metamorphoses*, consulting it both in the Latin and in Golding's translation, for his most poignant echo—the speech, often thought to have the autobiographical resonance of the play-wright's farewell to the stage, in which Prospero renounces his magic; the passage that ends:

> and, when I have requir'd
> Some heavenly music—which even now I do—
> To work mine end upon their senses that
> This airy charm is for, I'll break my staff,
> Bury it certain fathoms in the earth,
> And deeper than did ever plummet sound
> I'll drown my book.
>
> (5.1.51–57)

Whether behind this speech hover bittersweet recollections of Shakespeare's years with his acting company at the Globe playhouse, we can only doubtfully say; but there is no question that for Prospero's farewell he drew upon Medea's incantation in the seventh book of the *Metamorphoses*.

How much classical learning Shakespeare actually achieved is a matter that has been alluded to or debated almost from his own day. One learned authority has gone so far as to trace the First Murderer's remark in *Macbeth*, "We are men, my liege"—a reasonably innocuous line—to Terence's *Heauton Timorumenos* ("homo sum: humani nil a me alienum puto"). But conceivably Shakespeare might have dreamt up this line on his own. I suppose most ordinary folk go through life unaware that they are learnedly quoting Shakespeare every time they repeat the first line of *Hamlet*. The first line of *Hamlet* is, "Who's there?" However this may be, an education beyond that offered by the King's New School of Stratford-upon-Avon would not in those days have necessarily better equipped a young man for a career in letters. We do well not to confuse the modern university, with its enlightened liberal arts curriculum, with the altogether narrower course of study, inherited from the Middle Ages, of an English university in the sixteenth century. The formidably learned Jonson never took a degree either. What Shakespeare did acquire in his youth was a taste for reading, an interest in ideas, and a quick and retentive memory. His own genius and the bookstalls of St. Paul's Churchyard—center for the London book trade—furnished the rest.

In Stratford, Shakespeare laid the groundwork for another, more practical, association with the world of the book. One of his schoolfellows was Richard Field, although, three years the poet's senior, he would have been in a more advanced form. This lad was the son of a tanner, Henry Field, in Bridge Street. When the latter died in 1592, John Shakespeare, as his friend and good neighbor, helped to price the old bedsteads and other household goods that made up the tanner's modest estate, and then duly subscribed the inventory with his cross. While hardly prosperous himself, Henry had given his son the chance to master a trade by apprenticing him to a London stationer. Before long, Richard Field transferred to the Blackfriars shop of an exceptionally able Huguenot printer, Thomas Vautrollier. When this printer died, his widow Jacqueline married their only apprentice. Thus Richard found himself, at the age of twenty-seven, master of his own thriving printing establishment.

That was in 'eighty-eight, the Armada year. Some time afterward, a young newcomer from the provinces came to Field's shop with the manuscript of a narrative poem which the author describes, in his dedication, as the first heir of his invention. That was in the spring of 1593, when the plague raged in London, forcing the theatres to shut their doors and those who could afford to do so to flee to the purer air of the country. But Field kept his presses running, and in April (or thereabouts) printed Shakespeare's first book, *Venus and Adonis,* which the poet himself graced with a dedication to his patron, the Earl of Southampton. *The Rape of Lucrece,* similarly although more warmly dedicated, followed the next year, and was also set by Field. Maybe Shakespeare checked the proofs himself in the Blackfriars shop, for both poems are carefully printed, which cannot be said with any confidence about any of the other writings published in his own lifetime. But, equally possible, the accuracy reflects not the author's supervision but the pains taken by his accomplished printer.

He never worked with Field again. Nor did he ever again seek publication.[8] Publication came anyway. *Titus Andronicus,* in 1594, was Shakespeare's first play to be printed. There followed, in the same year, *2 Henry VI,* under the title of *The First part of the Contention betwixt the two famous Houses of York and Lancaster,* a text so debased that for centuries the authorities thought it was another play which Shakespeare had revised as his source. The experts are still arguing about whether *The Taming of A Shrew* (also of 1594) was the knockabout source comedy or—more likely—a corrupt version of *The Taming of the Shrew.* On the title pages of these quarto editions the author receives no credit for works published presumably without his consent or knowledge. Not until 1598 did a play appear with "W. Shakespere" under the title. This was *Love's Labour's Lost,* and the second editions of *Richard II* and *Richard III* in the same year made amends by featuring Shakespeare's name. Evidently he had found a reading public to complement the audience that flocked to his plays in the theatre.

What they read may sometimes, when examined closely, seem peculiar. Here, in language worthy of the Duke in *Huckleberry Finn,* is Hamlet pondering the great issue of whether life is worth enduring:

> To be, or not to be, I there's the point,
> To Die, to sleepe, is that all? I all:
> No, to sleepe, to dreame, I mary there it goes,
> For in that dreame of death, when wee awake,
> And borne before an everlasting Judge,
> From whence no passenger ever retur'nd,
> The undiscovered country, at whose sight
> The happy smile, and the accursed damn'd.[9]

These lines (and more of similar eloquence) appear in the so-called Bad Quarto of *Hamlet,* thus designated for reasons which here require no explanation. That was in 1603. Another, much better, quarto edition followed on its heels. This version, which the company authorized, in turn differs from that of the 1623 Folio collection of Shakespeare's plays. The *Hamlet* shelves in our libraries bulge with such titles as *The Question of Hamlet, The Mystery of Hamlet, The Problem of Hamlet: A Solution,* and *The Riddle of Hamlet: The Newest Answers,* already unfortunately left behind by newer answers. The transmission of the text of *Hamlet,* no less than the personality of its protagonist, poses questions, problems, mysteries, and riddles; so, similarly, do other Shakespeare plays. A whole flourishing cottage industry has grown up to furnish solutions. Shakespeare himself seems to have remained indifferent to the fortunes of his plays in the printing house.

He was not indifferent to the books of others. Almost everybody, I suppose, knows in a general way about the literary sources Shakespeare consulted: Raphael Holinshed's *Chronicles of England, Scotland, and Ireland,* in the 1587 edition, for the English history plays, *Macbeth, Cymbeline,* and maybe *Lear;* Thomas North's translation (from a previous French translation) of Plutarch's *Lives of the Noble Grecians and Romans* for the Roman tragedies and *Timon of Athens.* But as soon as we begin to poke beneath the surface we are astonished by the range of Shakespeare's reading. To prepare himself for his play on the reign of Richard II he seems to have delved not only into Holinshed, but also into Edward Hall's vast *Union of the Two Noble and Illustre Families of Lancaster and York;* Samuel Daniel's *First Four Books of the Civil Wars;* an anonymous drama known as *Thomas of Woodstock,* which was published in this century; Jean Froissart's *Chroniques* in Lord Berner's translation; two accounts in French, *La Chronique de la traison et mort de Richart Deux Roi d'Angleterre* and the metrical *Histoire du roi d'Angleterre Richard II,* by Jean Creton; and perhaps also *The Mirror for Magis-*

trates. How Shakespeare came by the more esoteric of these sources is not that hard to sort out; marginal notes in Holinshed would have directed him to two of the French sources, the *Traison* and Creton, then available as pamphlets in London. The mystery, however, is not one of accessibility, but that he should have bothered in the first instance. Shakespeare could have written a splendid play about Richard II without looking beyond Holinshed for characters and events. He chose to do more. But then he could have been the most popular playwright of the Elizabethan stage without turning out plays as good as the ones he gave to his company. Where did Shakespeare find the strange mouth-filling names for Edgar's devils in *Lear:* Flibbertigibbet, Frateretto, Hopdance, Smulkin, Modo, Mahu, and Obidicut; names that appear once in this play, and never again in the whole canon? Diligent scholarship has traced their source to Dr. Samuel Harsnett, chaplain to the Bishop of London, and his famous exposé of the Jesuit exorcists, *A Declaration of Egregious Popish Impostures,* published in 1603. This tome has been described as a pamphlet, but it comes to almost three hundred pages. Did Shakespeare plough through the whole lot? More likely that, here as elsewhere, he dipped into the book or skimmed rapidly, although it is a fact that a number of other echoes from the *Egregious Popish Plot* found their way into *Lear.* Like other subjects, Shakespeare's use of sources may be mechanically studied; but, imaginatively explored, they furnish passageways to the subterranean springs of the creative process itself.

Recalling the past to Miranda, Prospero speaks of the kindness of a noble Neapolitan.

> so, of his gentleness,
> Knowing I lov'd my books, he furnish'd me
> From mine own library with volumes that
> I prize above my dukedom.
>
> (*The Tempest*, 1.2.165–68)

We would ourselves prize above a dukedom the library of Prospero's creator, could we put our hands on it; nor would we protest if the dog-eared volumes were defaced with their owner's marginalia. From time to time books turn up with Shakespeare's name on title page or flyleaf, and sometimes notations supposedly in his hand; but these are in most cases patent forgeries, and the rest dubious: we haven't a single book we can, with full confidence, say once formed part of Shakespeare's working library. Nor does he mention books in his will, an omission that has raised some anti-Stratfordian eyebrows. Normally, however, books would not have been itemized in the will but separately listed in the inventory post-mortem; Rev. Bretchgirdle, with his bequests of books, is exceptional. Shakespeare's inventory has never surfaced, although I don't doubt it once existed. Should it ever turn up, a possibility unlikely but not inconceivable, it would constitute a great prize.

Shakespeare doesn't include any play manuscripts in his will either, and this apparent oversight too has puzzled some. We first hear of Shakespeare's papers a century later, when (in 1729) one John Roberts, "a Strolling Player," reported that *"Two* large *Chests* full of this GREAT MAN's *loose Papers* and *Manuscripts,* in the Hands of an ignorant *Baker* of WARWICK, (who married one of the Descendants from *Shakespear*) were carelesly scatter'd and thrown about, as Garret Lumber and Litter, to the particular Knowledge of the late *Sir William Bishop,* till they were all consum'd in the general Fire and Destruction of that Town."[10] This account is more circumstantial than probable. In any event, the inestimable value such literary remains would hold for us reflects an attitude that evolved, with the rise of bardolatry, in the centuries following Shakespeare's death. The play manuscripts were not his to dispose of. They belonged to the acting company, and would have been kept, along with the playbooks of Jonson and the rest, in the Globe storehouse. On St. Peter's day, June 29, 1613, during a performance of Shakespeare's *Henry VIII,* when cannons went off as part of the spectacular stage effects, the thatched roof of the Globe caught fire, a sudden wind fanned the flames, and within a short while the great Globe itself was consumed, leaving not a wrack behind. That afternoon on the Bankside more than timber and thatch went up in smoke.

Still Shakespeare's plays—all, or almost all, of them—have survived. That is the miracle to which I alluded at the outset of my paper. They survive because seven years after his death two fellow-actors in the King's men, John Heminges and Henry Condell, with the cooperation of the company, brought together thirty-six of Shakespeare's plays, "these trifles" (so they describe them in their dedication), as "an office to the dead, . . . without ambition, either of self-profit, or fame: only to keep the memory of so worthy a friend and fellow alive, as was our Shakespeare, by humble offer of his plays." In this volume, the First Folio, there appear in print for the first time about half of Shakespeare's comedies, histories, and tragedies, including some of the most celebrated: *Julius Caesar, Macbeth, Antony and Cleopatra.* It may strike us as (to say the least) strange that Shakespeare went to his grave apparently indifferent as to whether the works which have given him immortality would be preserved. But it could scarcely have been otherwise. Plays in this period achieved publication either some years after composition, when they no longer held any great commercial value, or when the company, hard pressed for one reason or another—the plague, for example, or official displeasure—parted with them, or when they were surreptitiously obtained without the players' consent. I rather doubt that Shakespeare felt any very acute sense of deprivation because he was denied the opportunity to print his plays—despite the eloquence with which, in his *Sonnets,* he proclaims again and again the

power of his art to outlast marble and the gilded monuments of princes. As
a dramatist, he wrote not with readers in mind, only for the applause of
audiences moved to laughter and tears in the playhouse. In performance
he found his fulfillment. The surviving records testify to the breadth and
depth of his theatrical commitment, first to the Lord Chamberlain's men,
and, after the accession of James I, to the King's men. That the troupe
came to enjoy royal patronage is a measure of its preeminence. For this
company Shakespeare was, in the jargon of the time, the "ordinary poet,"
that is, its regular playwright called upon to provide new plays twice a year.
Shakespeare also acted in these plays as well as in those of other dramatists
who wrote for his company. He must have participated in other aspects of
stage production, and as a principal shareholder he had a voice in matters
of policy. Other playwrights in this period also acted. The same is true
today—I think of Pinter. But the extent and variety of Shakespeare's engagement to the professional stage have few parallels in world drama.

His plays have come to be even more widely read and studied than they
are performed, often as that is. The 1623 Folio went through three more
editions before being replaced, early in the next century, by a new edition
more convenient to the hand, and catering to rather different reader pref-
erences. This was Nicholas Rowe's 1709 *Shakespeare*. Like all the earlier
editions, whether quarto or folio, it was published in London. So too was
Alexander Pope's edition in 1725, and Lewis Theobald's in 1733. Sir
Thomas Hanmer's *Shakespeare*, which came next in this apostolic succession
of eighteenth-century editions, was the first to be published by the Oxford
University Press. Expectation then ran high. An anonymous Gentleman of
Oxford, lately admitted to the Bachelor's degree, greeted the great occasion with *Verses Humbly Address'd to Sir Thomas Hanmer on his Edition of
Shakespear's Works*. These verses, the quality of which is less than Shakespearean, express confidence that Hanmer had settled, once and for all,
the textual question in Shakespeare.

> Those *Sibyl*-Leaves, the Sport of ev'ry Wind,
> (For Poets ever were a careless Kind)
> By thee dispos'd, no farther Toil demand,
> But, just to Nature, own thy forming Hand.

The gentleman's confidence, it must be said, was premature. As a politician
Sir Thomas had gifts which, in 1715, enabled him to become the speaker of
the House of Commons. His literary talents were less exceptional. In a
lovely little Oxford book, *Shakespeare in the Eighteenth Century*, David Nichol
Smith has thus temperately summed up Hanmer's achievement as the
editor of Shakespeare:

> Hanmer had good taste, but his toil was not exacting, and he did not in
> any way ease the labours of his successors. He is not even in the tradition,

by which I mean that whereas every editor so far had formed his text on the text that was last printed, the next editor did not use Hanmer's.[11]

Like others of his day, Hanmer was capable of taking unconscionable liberties with his text. These included degrading to the bottom of the page such "low stuff" (Hanmer's expression) as he rejected as spurious, most notably the entire scene of Princess Katherine's English lesson in *Henry V*—"that wretched piece of ribaldry . . . [so Hanmer fumes in his Preface], improper enough as it is all in *French* and not intelligible to an *English* audience, and yet that perhaps is the best thing that can be said of it." But, whatever its editorial deficiencies, Hanmer's *Shakespeare* was the most splendidly produced that had ever appeared, and, adorned as it was with numerous engravings by Gravelot after drawings by Francis Hayman, an altogether remarkable example of Oxford bookmaking. Later Oxford editions, while less sumptuous, have been more scholarly, and they have carried Shakespeare's works into millions of households round the world. There is every reason to believe that they will continue to do so in the sixth century of Oxford publishing, not only in the English-speaking world, but also in India, Japan, and other exotic outposts.

Now the Oxford University Press has established, for the first time, a fully staffed Shakespeare Department, charged with producing (among other projects) a new Oxford Standard Authors edition of Shakespeare, an undertaking with which I have the honor of being associated. Cambridge University Press also has a new Shakespeare in the works. Other publishers have editions on the drawing boards. So long as a definitive edition of Shakespeare's works remains a Platonic ideal rather than an achievable goal, so long will there be new editions; scholarship, after all, is process. The book shaped Shakespeare, and all future generations have been and no doubt will continue to be shaped by Shakespeare's book.

NOTES

1. In revising for publication a paper intended originally for oral delivery, I have furnished essential documentation and made minor adjustments; but I have not sought to change its essential character. Inevitably, I have traversed some ground I have previously explored elsewhere, but I have looked at the material afresh.

2. Charles Knight, *William Shakspere: A Biography* (1843; rpt. New York: AMS Press, 1971), pp. 39–40.

3. Knight, pp. 42–43.

4. *Outlines of the Life of Shakespeare* (1882; rpt. New York: AMS Press, 1966), pp. 41–42.

5. John Berkenhout, *Biographia Literaria; or a Biographical History of Literature* (London, 1777), p. 401.

6. These figures, kindly provided by Professor David Cressy, are cited in the Postscript to my *William Shakespeare: A Compact Documentary Life* (2nd printing; Oxford: Oxford Univ. Press, 1977), p. 321.

7. *William Shakespeare: The Complete Works*, ed. Peter Alexander (London: Collins, 1951), II.ii.156–57. Subsequent quotations are from this edition.

8. Except for *The Phoenix and the Turtle,* signed "William Shake-speare" and appended to Robert Chester's *Love's Martyr* (1601).

9. *Hamlet, First Quarto, 1603,* ed. W. W. Greg, Shakespeare Quarto Facsimiles, No. 7 (London: The Shakespeare Association, 1951).

10. *An Answer to Mr. Pope's Preface to Shakespear,* Popeiana, 5 (1729; facsimile rpt. New York and London: Garland Pub., Inc., 1974), pp. 45–46.

11. David Nichol Smith, *Shakespeare in the Eighteenth Century* (Oxford: Clarendon Press, 1928), pp. 43–44. Smith quotes the humbly addressed verses cited above.

(1981)

2
Looking for Shakespeare

One scholar in his life gives many lectures. The series in which I have the honor tonight to participate is, however, quite different from what a speaker usually encounters on the circuit. It is sponsored not by public grants but by the personal donations of former students and colleagues who have chosen in this way to pay tribute to so worthy a friend and teacher as was Fred Tupper. The audience enlisted for these occasions is not limited to fellow specialists—there are enough such gatherings—but draws upon the larger university community and lay citizens of this capital city. Few subjects besides Shakespeare could hope to accomplish that ecumenical end.

I first heard of the Tupper lectures some years back when I lived in the Midwest, and the editor of a literary paper invited me to review *Shakespeare's Art*, which brought together the first set of lectures. Tonight the occasion is special in another way, for I cannot but be conscious that my address brings to a close the second cycle of eight lectures. Such an event, like the prospect of being hanged (to apply Dr. Johnson's remark), concentrates a man's mind wonderfully. In anticipation of it I have lately once again taken down from my shelf the volume edited by Milton Crane. Alfred Harbage gave the first of these lectures in the spring of 1965. Professor Harbage was my mentor when I was a callow graduate student at Columbia University during the handful of years he passed there before his translation to Harvard. By him I was initiated into the more removed mysteries of literary scholarship. He cautioned the novice not to cut his teeth on Shakespeare; he hadn't, himself. It was good advice, which I followed. Harbage left Columbia before I had completed my dissertation but invited me to send along the remaining chapters to him for evaluation, even though he would no longer serve on my committee. Only much later, when I had myself become a beleaguered director of dissertations, did I fully appreciate how generous he had been. His Tupper lecture, "Shakespeare and the Professions," conveys the flavor of this humanist's personality.

Professor Harbage has since passed from the scene. So too has the wittily urbane Terence Spencer, who followed him a few years later on this platform and spoke with polished care on Shakespeare's careless art. Clifford Leech, who lived his humanism, is also gone; he explored the dark theme of the invulnerability of evil. Other speakers—James McManaway, Madeleine Doran, and Maynard Mack—have since retired, laden with honors, from their academic or library posts.* Were I to pick a personal favorite from among those Tupper lectures I know, it would, I suppose, be Professor Mack's subtly argued *"Antony and Cleopatra:* The Stillness and the Dance," with its closing burst of felicitous comparisons invoking Erasmus, Dante, Spenser, Keats, and Joyce, and its likening, as inspired as it is unexpected, of Shakespeare's Antony, "ever attracted by the sweeping magnanimity of his nature to an imagined literary world of perfect devotion between man and woman," with Cervantes' Don Quixote de la Mancha, suffering deeply yet a trifle comically "from the incongruities between the code he is attracted to and that world's demands."

All the speakers I have mentioned it has been my good fortune to know personally, some more than superficially, and that will perhaps account for my beginning with a backward glance. Another, more central, reason is that I have in mind a more familiar discourse than that usually inspired by a public forum such as this. Guided by memory and association, I propose to traverse some familiar paths. These are littered with artifacts: the perishable paper, parchment, and stone, which it is the historian's task to locate, examine, interpret, and then reinterpret. Those who have preceded me on this platform were, like me, looking for Shakespeare, and each in his own way found him. My own quest over the past fifteen years has been largely biographical. With the publication next year of *William Shakespeare: Records and Images,* the sequel volume to my 1975 *William Shakespeare: A Documentary Life,* I shall reach the conclusion of that phase of my scholarly pilgrimage. Bear with the infirmity of middle age, for I have, sometime since, slipped into my anecdotage. Yet I trust that some more general points about the persistence of the past will emerge to give a degree of impersonal substance to my personal remarks.

I

Let me begin my address proper by turning with you to a well-known and often reproduced ikon. I suppose just about everyone who has visited Stratford-upon-Avon has strolled over from the Birthplace or the Royal Shakespeare Theatre to the Collegiate Church of the Holy Trinity picturesquely situated on the Avon's banks and there stood before the Shakespeare monument executed by the Netherlandish stonemason, Gheerart Janssen, in Jacobean Renaissance style. The monument, situated in the

---

*Dr. McManaway died in 1980. He is keenly missed.

north wall of the chancel, has a skull—a *memento mori*—at the apex, cherubs on either side of the cornice, and, between two columns, an effigy of the poet himself, plump of cheek and ruddy of complexion, looking for all the world like a burgher of Stratford such as a latter-day Rodin might with infinitely greater skill have depicted.

If the bust (more precisely, a half-length statue) commands little admiration for its aesthetic qualities, it presumably satisfied the expectations of those yet living who knew the dramatist and worshiped in Holy Trinity; more especially the surviving members of his immediate family: his widow Anne, who was eight years his senior and outlived him by another six; his daughters Susanna and Judith; and their husbands, Dr. John Hall and the ne'er-do-well Thomas Quiney. The Shakespeare in the chancel no doubt fails to confirm our romantic yearnings about what a poet should look like; but of course Shakespeare lived before Keats and Shelley and other Romantics had helped by their example to formulate that image. Some, indeed, have asked whether Shakespeare peers out from his niche in Holy Trinity not so much because of his artistic achievement as for the fact that he had become a man of property, owner of the second largest house in Stratford, not to mention 107 acres of arable land in Old Stratford. The Janssen who fashioned the Shakespeare memorial also executed, for installation in the same chancel, the monument, with recumbent effigy, of wealthy John Combe, old Ten-in-the-Hundred, as he was nicknamed for his usurious dealings. It was a Combe who occupied the biggest house in town. Or was Shakespeare memorialized, as others have suggested, because, having invested in Stratford titles, he was appropriately interred in the church as (in effect) a lay rector?

These are no doubt intriguing speculations, but the monument itself furnishes an answer to the question. The figure there, in his sleeveless gown over a doublet, has a pen in his right hand and a quire of paper under the left. He is not tending his accounts but is in the act of creation; for his mouth is open, apparently in the act of declaiming. The clumsy epitaph beneath, by who knows whom, confirms the symbolic posture, for the memorialist praises all "that he hath writ" as leaving "living art, but page, to serve his wit." And if Janssen's stonemason's shop was known to affluent Stratfordians such as the Combes, it must have also been familiar to Shakespeare's old fellow actors at the Globe, for it was situated only a short walk away on Bankside.

The bust in Holy Trinity is one of but two unquestionably authenticated likenesses, the other being the engraving, even clumsier, made by Martin Droeshout for the title-page of the First Folio. As such it holds a special interest for the biographer, who must, along with so much else, form an impression of what his subject looked like. Now, in studying the history of the monument, I came to the realization, which I must confess fascinates me, that the impersonal materials of biography have themselves biographies. In his eternizing sonnets Shakespeare more than once proclaims the power of his mighty verse to outlast material glories, whether these be tyrants' crests, gates of steel, or tombs of brass. The triumph of art over artifacts is a haunting commonplace and one which a minor poet, Leonard Digges, uses to wonderful effect when, in a commendatory poem to the First Folio, he prophesies that Shakespeare's works would outlast his own monument:

> when that stone is rent,
> And time dissolves thy Stratford monument,
> Here we alive shall view thee still. This book,
> When brass and marble fade, shall make thee look
> Fresh to all ages . . .

Digges's prediction may one day well prove true, but meanwhile we have both book and bust. The survival of Shakespeare's plays, despite the fact that their creator took no pains to ensure their preservation and that fully half remained unpublished when he died, must be reckoned little short of miraculous. So, in its own way, is the survival of his bust carved from soft limestone. Like the other evidences of Shakespeare's life, it has undergone vicissitudes since its installation.

That must have been by 1623, when the Folio was published; so much we know from Digges's poem. Our first record of a sightseer's impression was noted down a little over a decade later; a Lieutenant Hammond in 1634 refers to viewing in Stratford church "a neat monument of that famous English poet, Mr. William Shakespeare, who was born here."

In time the lively colors with which Janssen (in keeping with a long established tradition of funerary sculpture) had painted the bust faded, as the cold damp of Holy Trinity took its inevitable toll. The monument decayed. Fingers fell off; the alabaster achitraves broke to bits. In 1746 re-beautification was commissioned and executed. Some years later a young gentleman who had "just emerged from Oxford"—he would less mischievously have stayed there—casually removed the stone pen from the poet's hand and, dithering, let it fall, upon which it shattered. Shakespeare has ever since held a replaceable quill. Before the century was out, Edmond Malone, the greatest Shakespeare scholar of his day, committed an act of singular folly when he arranged for the bust to be painted white, in keeping with his own neoclassical canons of taste. Eventually the paint was removed with solvents, and the bust repainted with colors suggested by recovered vestiges of the earlier paint. In 1973 vandals, entering the church by nocturnal stealth, displaced the bust from its niche and perpetrated some minor damage to the monument. The police, understandably baffled, thought the intruders may have been looking for manuscripts by Shakespeare or one of the impostors to whom the plays are credited. If so, these malefactors seem to have gone unrewarded. So too have others who have slipped into Holy Trinity by night, armed with shovel and pail, seeking (like pirates after buried treasure) the poet's bones or cryptic messages or elusive manuscripts.

With most of this history I was unacquainted when I paid my first visit to Holy Trinity Church. That was in 1964, the quatercentenary year, when I was invited to take part in the International Shakespeare Conference in Stratford. Late one afternoon I took some time out from the scholarly papers to visit the church. That occasion, to which I have alluded elsewhere, was for me unforgettable. In fact it amounted to what I can only describe as a quasi-mystical experience. The bust may not be much as a piece of sculpture but its setting is something else—there in the monument surmounted by the skull, in the chancel wall just a few yards from where Shakespeare lies buried under a slab with its famous malediction. One is overcome by strange emotions in the presence of the great and honored dead. One also feels, in this shrine at once holy and secular, a sense of the continuity in the veneration of so many pilgrims who have made this journey between the Shakespearean moment and our own. In any event, this adventure led me to set aside the work I then had in hand on Shakespeare's contemporaries to devote my energies to the biographical pursuit.

That quest has taken the form of a protracted odyssey, as I set myself the task of examining, firsthand, all the evidences for the study of Shakespeare's life—manuscripts, books, and artist's impressions—wherever these evidences are to be found. So, living in the Midwest, I was carried to both coasts, to the Folger Library here in Washington and the Huntington Library in San Marino, California; to the British Museum, the Public Record Office, the Guildhall Library, and Stationers' Hall in London; and in nearby Surrey to the College of God's Gift, which was founded by Edward Alleyn, who was (with Richard Burbage) one of the two great tragedians of Shakespeare's day. I visited the Kent County Archives Office in Maidstone, the Bodleian Library in Oxford, and the curious little repository known as the Plume Library in Maldon in Essex, founded by Thomas Plume, Archdeacon of Rochester, early in the eighteenth century. The Birthplace Records Office in Stratford-upon-Avon of course figured prominently in my itinerary, as did the Shakespeare properties there. I visited churches: in addition to Holy Trinity in Stratford, Worcester Cathedral, some twenty miles to the west, where in the muniments room one may still consult the documents relating to William's marriage to Anne Hathaway; St. Saviour's, where the playwright's brother Edmund, himself a player, was buried in 1607 with a forenoon tolling of the great bell, an event recorded in the parish register and fee book. Farthest afield was the University Library of Utrecht, with its unique contemporary sketch of the interior of an Elizabethan theatre and unique copy of a panorama of Shakespeare's London, for such contextual materials also constituted part of my quest. A few items remain in private hands: a unique Elizabethan sketch of *Titus Andronicus* in performance, in the library of the Marquess of Bath at his stately home at Longleat; an account book entry, curious in nature, of a payment to Shakespeare for devising an *impresa*—an insignia with motto, to be painted on a paper shield for the sixth Earl of Rutland, and carried by him as he rode on horseback for a tourney at Court on the King's Accession Day in 1613—a record still at Belvoir Castle, seat of the Rutlands, in the Peak District of Derbyshire.

These remains and others I personally examined not once but on two separate occasions, first when I was gathering my materials and then again when I was provided with proof copies of facsimiles to check against the originals for fidelity of reproduction. My obsessive-compulsive undertaking, then, has been a long one.

What conclusions may in retrospection—for my humor tonight is retrospective—be drawn from the long obsessive-compulsive pursuit? The first is that one's naïve sense of awe, which five years back I savored in a preface, dies hard. These sometimes fragile artifacts have survived the accidents of history—neglect, burial, collective amnesia, wars, fires, flood, and pestilence, the depredations of miscreants, and the misguided ministrations of would-be preservers. One may still hold the paper or vellum in the hand. They both satisfy and stimulate curiosity.

Thus we have Shakespeare's will, brought to light over a century after he passed from the scene. It has been endlessly studied, but we still puzzle over the significance of omissions: no mention of the Earl of Southampton, to whom Shakespeare dedicated two youthful poems and who was still alive when the poet died, or for that matter any other noble lord; no mention of any Hathaways, members of his wife's tribe. Above all, students debate the notorious bequest of the second-best bed to the widow. We study the three Shakespeare signatures, one at the bottom of each of the three sheets, and ponder the actual condition of the testator who declares, in the conventional phraseology of such instruments, "In the name of God, amen, I William Shakespeare . . . in perfect health and memory, God be praised, do make and ordain this my last will and testament."

Or to take a less celebrated example. A single letter addressed to Shakespeare survives. It surfaced in 1793 when Malone came upon it in a bundle among thousands of documents in the Stratford archive. It is today in the Birthplace Trust Records Office. The letter was addressed by Richard Quiney to his "loving good friend and countryman Mr. Wm. Shakespeare" in October 1598. By occupation a mercer, Quiney was the scion of a respected Stratford family, the essence of the solid citizen. What manner of business had he with the playwright who had not long since given the London stage *Romeo and Juliet, The Merchant of Venice,* and *Henry IV* with Prince Hal and Falstaff? The gist of the communication is an appeal for a loan of £30 on good security. In a time when a skilled artisan pulled down sixpence for a day's labor and an ordinary schoolmaster might earn £10 in a year, £30 represented a considerable sum. So Richard Quiney's letter, while anything but poetical, tells us something of interest, for it makes clear that by late 1598, when Shakespeare was thirty-four, he impressed his well-placed Stratford neighbor as being himself sufficiently well placed to be a likely target for a far from trifling loan. In the annals of versifying, how many poets anywhere have been so regarded by their mid-thirties? At any age? (I am reminded of a skit some years back on *Monty Python's Flying Circus* celebrating the career of a Scottish poet. One of this bard's early epics began something like, "O, can ye let me have a fiver?" Later, having established himself, another epic began. "Can you let me have ten pounds?") Quiney now and then found himself in London, so we can speculate on whether he knew Shakespeare as the darling of stage-land. Maybe the mercer did, but I rather doubt it. More likely he was aware that Shakespeare had lately bought a mansion house in Stratford.

Thus far clear sailing as we ponder Richard Quiney's letter. But as so often with the Shakespeare records, a tantalizing question presents itself. Why was this rapidly set-down document—so we gather from the hand—found among the Quiney papers in Stratford? He must then not have dispatched it. Why not? Did he decide against the overture? Or did he have a personal encounter with the dramatist and accomplish his business then? Your guess is as good as mine. The paper at once presents and withholds information. This is the Shakespeare biographer's constant vexation.

The Quiney letter, fragile and in its own way mysterious, illustrates the miracle of preservation. My next sample reflects some of the vagaries which may attend the miracle, and I have chosen this particular one because I myself had a supporting role in the dénouement. My Shakespearean quest early took me to the Folger Library. I don't remember precisely when my visit took place, nor who it was I encountered behind the reference desk in the Reading Room. But I recall this amiable young librarian's responding with surprise when I explained that I had come to see the Blackfriars Gate-house conveyance. Now, this gate-house, situated in a fashionable residential district not far from the Blackfriars Theatre which Shakespeare's company, the King's men, used from 1609 as their winter playhouse, represents, so far as we know, the last investment made by the dramatist before his death. He bought the property in March 1613, very likely after he had retired from the stage to pass his twilight days in his native Stratford. Once again a Shakespeare record raises questions, for the financial arrangements would seem to have excluded the widow's hereditary claim on the Blackfriars Gate-house. As elsewhere, alternative interpretations are available; but the matter is too complicated to explore here. I am concerned now merely with the physical existence of this legal instrument. Two copies survive. One, bearing Shakespeare's signature, is in the Guildhall Library in London. This was no doubt the seller's copy. Its counterpart at the

Folger does not bear Shakespeare's signature, presumably because it was the copy retained by the purchaser, whose own signature on the document in his possession would serve no useful legal purpose. The Folger version of the conveyance therefore has a special interest as being one of the few existing documents we can reasonably assume to have once been in Shakespeare's own possession. Probably he kept it at New Place, for the Blackfriars Gate-house seems to have been acquired as an investment rather than to serve as his residence.

James Orchard Halliwell-Phillipps, arguably the greatest of Victorian Shakespeare scholars, obtained the purchaser's counterpart in 1872. Eventually, after Halliwell-Phillipps' death, it passed into the collection of Henry Clay Folger and thus found a place in the library that bears his name. The librarian having recovered from my request, the conveyance was brought to me in the quaint wooden box in which, I suppose, Halliwell-Phillipps had kept it in his equally quaint Shakespearean wigwam at Hollingbury Copse. The box was very small but the document, as is the nature of such instruments, very large; so evidently it had been folded many times before insertion. "How very nice!" I exclaimed. "And now may I see this curiosity?" But the box was locked. Where, then, had the key gone? A frantic search took place. No key. Finally a locksmith was fetched. He scratched his head. His services had frequently been sought after burglaries or fits of absentmindedness, but he had never encountered such a box with so tiny a Victorian lock. After some desultory efforts the locksmith gave up. Finally, with a sweepingly impatient gesture, my benefactress behind the Reading Room desk removed a bobby pin from her neatly coiffed hair, inserted in the lock, and—presto!—the box delivered its contents. "Splendid!" I said, not for the first time that day. I removed the precious vellum and began to unfold it. Alarm. Was it safe, after the passage of God knows how many years, to tamper with the configuration of the document? Might it not possibly fall to bits? I pointed out that a record, even a unique one, that could not be studied was of little use to anyone. And so I was allowed to go ahead. I unfolded it without incident and examined the corrugated surface. "Let us now photograph it," I suggested. Silence, and again consternation. To photograph it, somehow we would have to contrive to make it lie flat and maybe even have to stick pins in the four corners. This too we accomplished, apparently without pins, and the Folger photographic department produced a picture of superlative quality. Whatever else might in future happen, we now had a permanent and consultable record.

As far as I know, the Blackfriars Gate-house conveyance once in Shakespeare's hands has never been returned to Halliwell-Phillipps' box, although I am informed that the library has retained that curiosity. Right now the conveyance has temporarily migrated to Kansas City, where it forms part of the great Folger traveling exhibition, "Shakespeare: The Globe and the World," at the Nelson Gallery. When in Kansas City I mosied over to have a peek. The Blackfriars Gate-house conveyance has never, I suspect, looked better at any time since when it was first drawn up. For to prepare it for display, the wonderfully able Folger conservator, Frank Mowery, had the document benevolently stretched on the rack. Visitors to the Nelson Gallery cluster round and gape at the apparently pristine surface.

Not every story has a similarly happy ending. Time, like Shelley's west wind, is destroyer as well as preserver. Two Quiney letters, not addressed to Shakespeare but referring to him, have for long been well known to students. These, like the one from Richard to his loving countryman, are in the Birthplace Records Office. On one of my visits to that hospitable archive I discovered with alarm that these Quiney letters had suffered irreparable damage during the last war. Because of the bombing of nearby Coventry, the custodians had placed them, as a protective measure, in the basement of the Records Office, which is a few steps down from the Birthplace in Henley Street. There a water leak developed which, by a remarkable stroke of bad luck, singled out these two papers from among the many bound together in a thick volume. As a result these documents were rendered illegible. The ultra-violet lamp helped a bit in bringing out some of the properties of the ink, but not enough to make the writing legible. I suggested infra-red examination, which possibly would reveal other properties; but the nearest lamp was some miles away in Oxford, and the Birthplace authorities were understandably reluctant to risk additional calamity by having the volume transported. No earlier photographs of these Quiney letters were on file in the Records Office, nor did the staff have any information that photographs had been taken. Some time later, when back at the Folger, I came quite by chance upon one of those collections published in the last century in limited editions by the indefatigable Halliwell-Phillipps; it contained a facsimile, made from a tracing, of a key passage from one of the two letters. Not much of a consolation, but surely better than nothing.

To cite another, more crucial, example, six signatures by Shakespeare survive, three of them in the will, plus two short monosyllables, "By me," also in the will; that is all we have with certainty in the poet's own hand, although many today believe (partly on paleographical grounds) that three pages from the manuscript play of *Sir Thomas More* in the British Library are Shakespeare holograph. The signature on the second sheet of the will is badly eroded and has been for some time. A facsimile, also made from a tracing, was published in the eighteenth century, when the signature was more legible, and this is of some limited help. But I made an unsettling discovery when I compared the bottom of this second sheet in a photographic facsimile published in 1916 with a more recent photograph. This comparison revealed that at least a half inch of the precious document has disappeared from the bottom. If time is the west wind, it is also (to vary the figure) a mouse, and documents are the cheese it nibbles.

An obvious moral may be drawn from these cautionary tales. Every collector, private or institutional, should safeguard the historical record—I am not now speaking about the artifacts themselves—by having whatever is unique photographed. And not only the self-evidently precious items, because who knows for sure what will stir, as unexpected revelation, the historian of the future? As for the artifacts, it goes without saying that we must avail ourselves of the most sophisticated technology when it comes to temperature and humidity control. The Folger Shakespeare Library last year closed its doors and will remain shut for at least a year longer as renovation proceeds. Readers will find the new facilities more comfortable than the old, but it was mainly the comfort of the manuscripts and books that was being consulted when plans were approved. It was with their comfort uppermost in mind that I, as a trustee of the Folger, voted in favor of the rebuilding program, although I knew that that program would deprive me of the materials for my research at a crucial time, materials for access to which I had lately transplanted myself to Washington. First things first.

Thus far my examples, while endlessly discussable, are familiar to most students. What, we may ask, is the shape of things to come? Will the future yield further documentary discoveries to elucidate Shakespeare's life, or have we reached the end of the line? If we haven't, what form are new findings likely to take? Prognostication is an uncertain art, and I can claim no special powers as a seer, but I believe I can answer with reasonable confidence, yes, we will add to the store, although I doubt that the revelations to come will be of the magnitude of the marriage license bond or the will. "The picture of Shakespeare's life in Warwickshire," Mark Eccles has written, "is a mosaic with most of the pieces missing." What we can hope to do is to recover some of the pieces—for the London as well as the Warwickshire mosaic—and make the picture a little more complete.

II

So we have lots of Shakespeare records. Yet popular opinion insists that we know almost nothing about Shakespeare, that a postcard will sum up knowledge, with plenty of room left for the address. I hear this sort of thing all the time as part of academic or theatrical chitchat, chitchat which demonstrates that small-talk can approach the infinitesimal. Popular opinion, then, is wrong. Or maybe it is wrong in one sense but in another, more profound, way correct. For what we know about Shakespeare the man belongs almost entirely to the public record of formal occasions. He required certain documents in order to marry. His christening and burial were duly entered in his church's parish registers. So too were the baptisms of his three children, the marriages of the two daughters, and the burial of all three offspring, most poignantly that of his son Hamnet at the age of eleven. They do not tell us whether the London playwright attended the

Stratford funeral of his only boy, let alone how he felt about this real-life tragedy. Other records chronicle Shakespeare's professional life: his connections with his acting company, the printing—or not printing—in his lifetime of his plays and poems. The rest have mostly to do with the acquisition of houses and property and the prudent provision made for the estate after Shakespeare's decease. They show no concern about what would become of his achievement as an artist. In a collection of short stories and other writings entitled *Labyrinths,* Jorge Luis Borges calls his meditation on Shakespeare "Everything and Nothing." In his life he seems to have been nothing, at least not anybody very special, although he was materially much more successful than most.

The life record thus seems to offer no insight into how the transient stuff of life was metamorphosed into transcendent achievements of art. We know that some successful writers have sought to discourage prying inquiry into their happy or sullen craft. Somerset Maugham is a recent instance. In his will he took pains—of course unsuccessful—to ban any biographies and asked that his letters be destroyed. Shakespeare did not even bother to do that. That aloofness—or, more probably, indifference—has served only to whet all the more the appetite for letters or diaries. These we have been sometimes offered.

There is time here tonight for only one example. In 1811 "A Barrister"— that is how the author's name appeared on the title page—published *A Tour in Quest of Genealogy, through several parts of Wales, Somersetshire, and Wiltshire, in a Series of Letters to a Friend in Dublin; interspersed with a Description of Stourhead and Stonehenge; together with Various Anecdotes, and Curious Fragments from a Manuscript Collection Ascribed to Shakespeare.* I will not trouble you with the barrister's description of Stonehenge, but the manuscript collection invites notice. "The most interesting portion of it [the author tells us] consists of letters that passed between him, Sir Christopher Hatton, Sir Philip Sidney, Lord Southampton, Richard Sadleir, Henry Cuffe, &c.; part of a journal, like most journals, carried on for a month together, then suspended during a period of four or five years; and memoirs of his own time written by himself. Some of the items are uncommonly curious, as they give you not only the costume [*sic*] of the age he lived in, but let you into his private and domestic life, and the rudiments of his vast conception."

A couple of diary items must here suffice. One tells us how Shakespeare was almost tempted to excise a celebrated passage from one of his most celebrated plays: "Att the requeste of a ladie of honore, noe less a parsonage than the Countesse of Pembrok, I had dropped the grave sceane in mie Hamlett, butt the poppulece grew outragiouse, and threatted to bury us all unlesse theire favorit parte was restorid." Another purports to reveal how Shakespeare took up language study: "Having an ernest desier to lerne forraine tonges, it was mie goode happ to have in mie fathere's howse an

Ittalian, one Girolamo Albergi, tho he went bye the name of Francesco Manzini, a dier of woole; but he was not what he wished to passe for; he had the breedinge of a gentilman, and was a righte sounde scholer. It was he tought me the littel Italian I know, and rubbid up my Latin; we redd Bandello's Novells togither, from the which I getherid some delliceous flowres to stick in mie dramattick poseys. He was nevew to Battisto Tibaldi, who made a translacion of the Greek poete, Homar, into Ittalian, he showed me a coppy of it givin him by hys kinsman, Ercolo Tibaldi." There are others: How flea infestation presented its problems, how the Earl of Southampton spoke of *Richard III* with high praise when he returned the unfinished tragedy in April 1595—a date that would enforce some changes in our received ideas about the Shakespeare chronology.

The barrister author of the *Tour in Quest of Genealogy* was, we know from other sources, Richard Fenton, and, although he tells us that he toyed with the idea of publishing the whole of Shakespeare's memoirs, he produced no more than bits and pieces of "this curious farrago." Others besides Fenton have beguiled readers with purported revelations. Some, like William-Henry Ireland and John Payne Collier, sent shock waves through the literary establishments of their day. But the Ireland forgeries—the love letter to dearest Anna; the deed by which Shakespeare bequeathed his manuscript plays to (with wonder let it be said!) an Elizabethan William Henry Ireland, his chum; and the rest—these forgeries were no more than the rationalized fantasies of an emotionally retarded youth not yet twenty. The Collier impostures offered "evidence" in support of pet theories which otherwise he would have had difficulty in proving, because they were wrong. The Fenton fabrications caused scarcely a ripple. Even were any of these contributions genuine, they would not begin to answer the overwhelming question posed to the biographer of Shakespeare: How could this apparently ordinary man have created these supreme works?

To such a question no answer is really possible. How, under the most ideal circumstances, could biography render the inconceivable comprehensible? True, biography has its own art, but it is, by and large, a prosaic endeavor. When imaginative artists have made Shakespeare a character in their plays and novels—and many have done so—they have taken full advantage of the liberty of interpretation offered them and given free reign to intuitive invention; but although their creations sometimes have an interest of their own (I think, for example, of Anthony Burgess' *Nothing Like the Sun*) they do not in any profound way furnish the illumination we crave.

So we have to make do with what we have. Surely it is the seemingly antipodean contrast between the man, as we know him, and the work that lies at the source of the anti-Stratfordian heresies: the theories offering Lord Francis Bacon or the seventeenth Earl of Oxford or the sixth Earl of Derby or any of the rest as an alternative to the grammar-school-educated glover's son from Stratford—as though a university degree and blue blood explained anything. The very term *heresy* implies, as its converse, unquestioning religious faith; the biographer must contend with the added burden of generations of bardolatry. Were we by some miracle to recover the original script, rough draft or fair copy, of *Hamlet* in Shakespeare's own hand, how many of us would, like Rossini confronted with the holograph of Mozart's *Don Giovanni,* fall weeping to our knees, and kissing the yellowed pages, cry out, "He was God Himself."

Be that as it may, there is ample precedent for the god becoming vulnerably mortal. For godlike politicians that is usually the prudent course. A feature in *Time* magazine (February 4) analyzes Ronald Reagan's also-ran finish on the Iowa Republican primary. When the governor was leading in the polls, he kept aloof from the battle. John Sears, "his highly touted strategist," explained, "It won't do any good to have Reagan going to coffees and shaking hands like the others. People would get the idea that he's an ordinary man like the rest of us."

An ordinary man like the rest of us. Reagan has since learned his lesson well. Shakespeare never needed to learn it. In him the ordinary becomes extraordinary, the extraordinary ordinary. Does not that paradox yield its own interpretive clue to the mystery we are exploring? Is not much of what is fundamental to Shakespeare's art the ordinary—the bread and cheese of life—hugely, astonishingly magnified by his unique gifts? *Romeo and Juliet* is an obvious example: young love, parental disapproval, the generation gap. We've heard it all before; we'll hear it all again. But in *Romeo and Juliet* the parents are locked into a murderous ancient feud, the sources of which have long since become obscure even to the antagonists. The divisions between the families and between young and old exact their fearful price. If the conflicts are a staple of popular romance, the degree—the magnification—is exceptional, as is the lyricism and incandescence with which it is realized. The ordinary has become extraordinary. Such is the alchemy of art.

We see an analogous alchemy operating everywhere in Shakespearean tragedy. Bear with me if my examples appear outrageous. How many domestic dramas and sit-coms draw upon comings and goings among gray-flanneled corporate types in executive suites, the Madison Avenue annex to the corridors of power? The power-seekers compete and bring their problems home to their spouses; indigestion and insomnia result. The hero is a middle-level executive. He is ambitious, his wife even more so and keen to lord it over her social inferiors. Now the boss is coming to dinner. The evening will be a success or failure, comedy or tragedy, depending upon the scriptwriter's imperatives; the protagonists will enjoy, lose, or find illusory the rewards of ambition. Is not some such recurring human predicament to be found, again enormously magnified, at the core of *Macbeth*? The middle-level executive has become a brave general. His wife is ambitious. The boss is not only his guest but also his king and kinsman. Promotion, it seems, can be achieved only by murder. The Macbeths' castle becomes an emblem of hell. Good digestion and sleep go by the boards. The everyday in *Macbeth* is pushed, with fierce poetic and dramatic concentration, to a tragic ultimate. But the essential human substance remains a constant.

Or take *King Lear.* It is not my game tonight to gainsay the vastness of Shakespeare's design, at once awesomely cosmic and finitely human, or the intensity with which that design is executed. Again and again, critics marvel at the intensity. "So powerful is the current of the poet's imagination," Dr. Johnson wrote, "that the mind, which once ventures within it, is hurried irresistibly along. . . ." In a celebrated passage of his correspondence John Keats observed: "the excellence of every Art is its intensity, capable of making all disagreeables evaporate, from their being in close relationship with Beauty & Truth—Examine King Lear & you will find this exemplified throughout." When that storm breaks on the heath, none of us—spectators or readers—can scramble for cover. I have sometimes toyed with the notion that in Elizabethan tragedy all roads lead to *Lear.* But that is the subject for another evening and another lecture. My concern now is not with the grandeur of the play but with its irreducible human substance, not with its poetry but with the prose of its dilemma.

King Lear is Shakespeare's play about retirement. We all know, from our elders or from approaching that stage ourselves, what problems are presented by letting go. At the same time that we give up, we want to hold on. Then there are the children. More often than not, we have already given them up to matrimony and therefore to leading their own lives. Now if, after retirement, we decide to live with them—an extreme solution—or to spend long periods under their roofs, such arrangements can present problems. How will the children accept the domestic burden of the visit? And how will they measure up to parental expectation? Somewhere down the pike after retirement awaits death, and for many that is an inevitability too fearful to contemplate. It is all in *Lear.* The protagonist has reached that stage of life's journey when he must (as Freud puts it) "renounce love, choose death, and make friends with the necessity of dying." This is ordinary; but of course Lear is very special. The job he is vacating is the kingship, and the children whose affections mean so much to him are either monstrously cruel or capable of redemptive love.

Separated from Shakespeare's transfiguring genius and reduced to bedrock, *Lear* is everywhere around us. My point is that the play owes much to the bedrock, just as it owes so much to the genius. Let me remind you of one recent version. Many of you have, I expect, seen Paul Mazursky's film *Harry and Tonto,* released six years ago to friendly notices and widespread popular acclaim. Art Carney won the Academy Award for best actor that year for his portrayal of Harry Combs, a seventy-two-year-old New York widower and retired high-school teacher who is forcibly evicted from his Upper West Side apartment building, which is scheduled for demolition. Harry embarks on a long odyssey which takes him to his three children—a son in New Jersey, a daughter in Chicago, another son in Los Angeles. Accompanying him is Tonto, a large ginger cat. The encounters with family prove in various ways unsatisfactory. Harry ends up alone in Santa Monica, wiser in a stoical sort of way, watching the surf break upon the glistening beach and children playing in the sand. It isn't Shakespeare.

Or isn't it? I have talked with colleagues who have a special interest in Shakespeare and film, or Shakespeare on film, and I must confess that they haven't seen *Harry and Tonto* as Mazursky's *Lear.* After all, the arts are filled with accidental parallels, just as life is, and for the critic, armed with his leveling bulldozer, these pose problems. But I am right about *Harry and Tonto.* To validate interpretation, and in anticipation of my address tonight, I managed to put my hands on the novelization of the script, by Mazursky and Josh Greenfeld, published in the same year that the movie was exhibited. Here is Harry being carried out of the house in his easy chair (I have not tampered with small lapses in his quotations):

> The crowd roared when they saw Harry and Tonto, perched on the rocker as if it were a palanquin, being carried out of the building by two grunting cops. ' "Blow, winds, and crack your cheeks! Rage! Blow!" ' they heard Harry bellowing.
> 'Pop!' Burt called out.
> ' "You cataracts and hurricanes, spout till you have drench'd our stee ples, drown'd the cocks!" '
> 'Drown the cocks! Drown the cocks!' echoed a teenager.
> 'Pop!' Burt implored. 'Act your age!'
> 'I am,' said Harry, and resumed his histrionic raging:
>
> > You sulphurous and thought-executing fires
> > Vaunt-couriers to oak-cleaving thunderbolts,
> > Singe my white head!
>
> 'You tell him, man!' someone shouted.

Later, when he is with his son Burt, these exchanges take place:

> 'You were thinking about Lear.'
> 'Lear who?'
> 'I don't know.'
> 'King Lear!' Harry exploded. 'He gave up his real estate, too. And what did they do to him? They foreclosed. That's life. . . .'

In Chicago, with his daughter Shirley, four times married but still childless, he is visibly upset:

'You'll never have kids,' he breathed out.

'I doubt it,' said Shirley.

' "I loved her most and thought to set my rest on her kind nursery," '
Harry quoted.

'Sorry, Harry,' Shirley said sharply, 'I spent eighteen years listening to
Shakespeare.'

Harry exploded. 'What's wrong with Shakespeare? He was the greatest
writer this world will ever know.'

Shirley smiled. 'But he wasn't my father.'

Harry gave up. 'I'm tired.' he said.

Tonto, the cat, is Mazursky's equivalent to Shakespeare's Fool. His presence
and companionship, however limited by his feline status, enable Harry to
express what would otherwise go unverbalized. The Fool disappears from
Lear, although Shakespeare does not tell us what has happened to him. At
around the same point in the film Tonto dies.

It is curious that the movie's antecedents went mostly unnoticed by well-
informed viewers, but that merely testifies to the skill of the translation and
the universal accessibility of the dramatic material. Which is the point I
have been making. *Harry and Tonto* is not filmed tragedy but picaresque
domestic drama which skates on the thin ice of sentimentality and sometimes falls through but never wallows in maudlin emotion. *King Lear*
achieves heights to which Mazursky's modest film sensibly never aspires.
But the human predicaments underlying both share points of reference.

Superior genius and bourgeois ordinariness make not so strange bedfel-
lows. It is astonishing that anybody could have written *Macbeth* and *Lear*
and the rest, but not, per se, that they should have been written by a son of
Stratford who married young, fathered three children, became the grandest box-office success of his age (afterwards of any age), and retired to the
town of his birth, where—according to an early biographer—he spent his
last days "as all Men of Good Sense will wish theirs may be, in Ease, Retirement, and the Conversation of his Friends."[1]

NOTE

1. I have not revised this paper to reduce its essentially oral character, nor furnished
documentation of sources, which are self-evident.

(1980)

3
William Bott, the Widow's Portion, and Shakespearean Biography

Can we hope that new information bearing, even peripherally, on Shakespeare's life, may still turn up? The last great discovery was made early in the century by Charles William Wallace and his wife Hulda: the poet's signed deposition in the Belott–Mountjoy suit, revealing him as a lodger in Cripplegate ward, and drawn into the sort of domestic imbroglio of which Elizabethan comedies were made. To land their prize the Wallaces claimed to have worked their way through several million documents in the Public Record Office. The spirit quails at the prospect of stirring all that archival dust again, in the fragile hope of finding something they missed. But how carefully could the Wallaces have studied all those records? Meanwhile, the pursuit goes on, bringing its unsensational rewards. At the same time revisionism proceeds, affecting our understanding of the crucial life records we already possess. In this article I can offer examples of both processes.

The new information first. In his preface to *Shakespeare in Warwickshire* (1961) Mark Eccles noted that he had paid special attention "to friends and associates of Shakespeare, because knowledge of their lives may some day lead to more knowledge of Shakespeare." This is justly observed, although the perimeter of useful investigation may be extended (and is by Eccles) to anyone who might have had contact with any member of Shakespeare's family. Just such inquiry was being conducted by E. Tangye Lean when he died suddenly in October 1974. Not long afterwards his widow, Mrs. Doreen Lean, graciously invited me to examine his papers, and last year I visited London to do so. The papers, which are voluminous, consist mainly of photocopies and transcriptions of documents, correspondence and the like, and an unfinished draft chapter on Shakespeare's Stratford. Among these materials I found a document naming a Richard Shakespeare who may be the dramatist's grandfather. But my most intriguing find concerned William Bott.

Bott is a villainous figure, well enough known to biographers of Shakespeare. His impact on his community was literally, as well as figuratively, poisonous. He gives a local habitation and a name to a malevolence, sinister in its dimensions, that fascinated Shakespeare in his major tragedies. We may, for want of a better word, describe the phenomenon as Bottulism.

He hailed from the Wold at Snitterfield, the part of Warwickshire where Shakespeare's grandfather lived. The two men were acquainted. Twice they together appraised (with others) the estates of lately deceased locals—the office of good neighbors. So far as I know, the first investigator to take an interest in Bott was J.C.M. Bellew, over a century ago, in *Shakespere's Home at New Place, Stratford-upon-Avon*. Bellew early smelled a rat, and concluded, from the character that oozed out of the records (his phrase) that "Bott must have been a thoroughly unprincipled, pettifogging attorney, doing all the dirty work of Stratford and its neighbourhood." Others generally assume Bott was a lawyer, but although he willingly gave legal advice when that served his interests, he was not himself an attorney, if one may accept the testimony of William Conyers; he speaks of "one William Bott of Stratford-upon-Avon" as "being sometime suspected for felony and burglary, and a person who, by reason he was sometime undersheriff of the county of Warwick taketh upon him knowledge and to give counsel in matters concerning the law, and doth daily procure and stir up much quarrelling, sedition, and strife."

Others shared Conyers' unflattering opinion of Bott. They had cause. The deputy steward of Stratford accused Bott of dishonesty, and the latter countered with a slander action, claiming that, because of the charges, he had been deprived of "magna ineffabilia lucra." Bott similarly sued Roland Wheler for denouncing him thus at the Swan Inn at Stratford: "William Bott, thou art a false harlot, a false villain, and a rebellion, and I will make thee to be set on the pillory." Another witness confirms this characterization: "Let every man beware of him, for he is counted the craftiest merchant in all our country . . . and it is said that if Bott had had his right he had been hanged long ago." To such testimony may be added that of John Harper of Henley-in-Arden. He describes Bott as "a man clearly void of all honesty, fidelity, or fear of God, and openly detected of divers great and notorious crimes, as, namely, felony, adultery, whoredom, falsehood, and forging, a procurer of the disinherison of divers gentlemen your Majesty's subjects, a common barrator, and stirrer of sedition amongst your Majesty's poor subjects." Harper knew whereof he spoke. He was Bott's son-in-law.

By a curious irony this man of evil reputation rose to civic dignity in Stratford. Although he had no record of previous service to the corporation—say, as burgess—that body in 1564 made him an alderman. That August, when pestilence afflicted the town, Bott contributed 4s for the relief of plague-victims; more than anybody, including the bailiff, and four times what John Shakespeare gave. The following spring, in May 1565, Bott was expelled from the corporation for allowing that "there was never a honest man of the council or the body of the corporation of Stratford." The outburst which cost Bott his post gave the poet's father his opportunity, for John Shakespeare was elected to the office vacated by the expulsion. The two men knew one another.

Bott had earlier secured a marriage between his daughter Isabel and the Harper already mentioned. This Harper "being himself a plain and simple-minded man," and still a minor, was over his head in debt, and to avoid the forfeiture of his inherited lands, he followed his father-in-law's advice and entered into a conveyance. That was in April 1563. Bott's machinations, worthy of an Edmund, are too complicated to be detailed here, but they involve substituted deeds and names, and a seal surreptitiously obtained for Bott by his daughter. In effect, the Botts by such "policy" assured themselves of Harper's lands should Isabel die without issue.

The stage was now set for the murder which Roland Wheler describes in a volume of depositions, "together with numerous letters, briefs, informations, answers, replications &c, on both sides" of Lodowick Greville and William Porter, defendants, *v* Francis Alford, plaintiff; "this confused and intricate suit," as the calendar describes it. The volume (LXXIX), dated June 1571, is in the Public Record Office. I came upon a transcription of the deposition among the Lean papers, and have since consulted the original (SP 12/79) at the Record Office. It is always dangerous to claim novelty where any aspect of Shakespeare studies is concerned, such is the magnitude of the available scholarship; but I have been able to find no previous reference to this document in the relevant authorities—Bellew, Chambers, Fripp, Eccles, and others.[1]

In his testimony Wheler, who had now and then performed services for Bott in return for some odd shillings and a cow, provides an eye-witness account of the murder, none the less harrowing for the dry legal phraseology:

> the said Bott having in this wise forged the said deed and so conveyed the said lands, the said Bott's daughter, wife of the said John Harper, did die suddenly and was poisoned with ratsbane, and therewith swelled to death. And this deponent knoweth the same to be true, for that he did see the wife of the said Bott in the presence of the same Bott deliver to the said Harper's wife in a spoon mixed with drink the said poison of ratsbane to drink, which poison she did drink in this deponent's presence, the same William Bott by and at that time leaning to the bed's feet. And this deponent saith that the said William Bott did see this when it was done. And this deponent saith that after the wife of the said William Bott had so given the said drink to the said Harper's wife, the said Harper and this deponent did see her lay a thing under a green carpet.

This "thing" Harper offered to taste, thinking it brimstone (sulphur, we would say), "but by the persuasion of this deponent, who suspected it to be ratsbane, he did forbear."

It is curious, assuming the accusation to be true, that Bott never stood trial for murder, although "divers persons" knew of the crime; but Wheler deposes that it was hushed up because, were Bott hanged, "Mr. Clopton and the said John Harper should both lose all their lands, which the said Bott had beguiled them of." The Stratford parish register records the burial, on May 7, 1563, of "Isabella, uxor Johannis Harper de Henleyarden." (Incidentally, Wheler gives her name as Lettice, but variant or alternative Christian names are not uncommon in any age, and he was testifying eight years after the event he describes.)

A special interest attaches to the house that contained the green carpet under which the ratsbane was allegedly secreted. For in 1563 William Clopton, a young man newly come into his patrimony and pressed for cash, gave up the title of New Place to William Bott. The next year this Clopton accused Bott of withholding rents from him and forging a deed related to Clopton lands; the charges have a familiar ring. By reason of his connection with the property, Bott makes a fleeting appearance in *An Historical Account of the New Place, Stratford-upon-Avon,* by the eminent Victorian Shakespeare scholar, J. O. Halliwell[-Phillipps], who describes him—rather oddly—as "a friendly capitalist." Bott resided at New Place for several years before acquiring it. If Wheler's is a true account, the murder—a murder of kin, by poison, for the estate—likely enough took place there. This was the handsome house of five gables, the second finest in Stratford, that William Shakespeare, a playwright of rising prosperity, bought some thirty years afterwards for £60, according to the foot of fine recording the transaction. The sum has puzzled some biographers by reason of its modesty. Quite possibly the foot of fine record is a legal fiction.

The conveyance took place in 1597. New Place had by then long since passed from Bott to the Underhill family. In July the vendor, William Underhill—described as "a subtle, covetous, and crafty man"—died mysteriously at Fillongley, near Coventry, after orally bequeathing "all his lands" to his first born, Fulke. In 1599 this Underhill, still a minor, was hanged at Warwick for poisoning his father. Thus, associated with the fortunes of New Place, either in fact or allegation, we twice have murder of kin—a father of his daughter, and a son of his father—by poison for the estate.

Shakespeare's own father was buried in the churchyard of Holy Trinity on September 8, 1601. We don't know precisely when *Hamlet* was written, but it was around this time. According to Aubrey, in his *Brief Lives,* Shakespeare "was wont to go to his native country once a year." There he owned houses, invested prudently in lands and tithes, and participated in the mundane affairs of his small town. Bott had long since expired of natural causes, with felony in his heart: he was buried at Snitterfield on November 1, 1582. His career is far removed from the larger spheres of the Court and national politics that usually attract investigators seeking topical contexts for Shakespeare; but even the most exalted achievements of the literary imagination may take on an unexpected dimension from the circumstances of such obscure provincials. So one wonders: during one of those periodic flights from the capital to Stratford, as he tended the Great Garden of New Place with its flourishing vines, and *Hamlet* was percolating subliminally in his brain, did Shakespeare ever pause to think of his house and its heritage?

Roland Wheler's deposition is the kind of contextually illuminating record that chance or diligence (more often the latter) sometimes yields in the Record Office. But the responsible biographer has as his chief task to interpret anew the central documents already available. In doing so, he must cope with an enormous body of commentary, and resist the easy path of uncritically accepting received opinion. Shakespeare's notorious bequest to his wife may serve to illustrate the pitfalls: "Item. I give unto my wife my second-best bed with the furniture" (i.e., the hangings, valance, bed linens, etc.). This provision drew Edmond Malone's famous outburst in the eighteenth century: "His wife had not wholly escaped his memory; he had forgot her—he had recollected her—but so recollected her, as more strongly to mark how little he esteemed her; he had already (as is vulgarly expressed) cut her off, not indeed with a shilling, but with an old bed." The bequest appears as an interlineation—hence Malone's reference to forgetfulness and recollection. Biographers often interpret the clause as an afterthought. But Shakespeare's will contains other interlineations: William Reynolds, a Stratford neighbor, and the dramatist's beloved fellowsharers in the King's men—John Heminges, Richard Burbage, and Henry Condell—are thus assured their memorial rings. Failure of memory? Maybe. But, at least as likely, the lawyer setting down the will, and writing rapidly, inadvertently missed these bequests, and backtracked to insert them.[2]

Whether an oversight or no, the bed presents a problem. Is this provision, as Malone assumed, derisive? Many have thought so. Or was it sentimental, this being the matrimonial bed, with the best bed reserved for overnight guests at New Place? Needless to say, students have ransacked Elizabethan and Jacobean wills for analogous bequests, and their pursuit has not proved fruitless. Most recently, Elaine W. Fowler has pointed out that when Francis Russell, second Earl of Bedford, died in London in 1585, he willed his "best bed of cloth of gold and silver," embellished with King Henry VIII's arms, not to his wife but to his youngest and favorite daughter; in similar fashion Susanna, Shakespeare's favorite child, presumably received the best bed. More directly to the point is the testament of William Palmer of Leamington, Warwickshire, a manifestly affectionate husband, who in 1573 left his wife Elizabeth "all her wearing apparel" and his "second best featherbed for herself furnished." It is also the case that a testator might deliberately deprive a spouse of a bed simply because of its associations: "Leave thy wife more than of necessity thou must, but only during her widowhood," Sir Walter Raleigh enjoined his son; "for if she love again,

let her not enjoy her second love in the same bed wherein she loved thee."
Others must have experienced similar anxieties. But Anne's age—she was
then sixty or thereabouts—renders it unlikely that apprehension about a
second love influenced this particular bequest.

An expensive article of furniture such as the best bed qualified as an
heirloom, and normally passed to the principal legatee. Borough custom,
perhaps not sufficiently consulted in this connection, furnishes a clue to
practice. Thus, in fourteenth-century Torksey an heir was entitled to the
better bed with counterpane and sheets ("meliorem lectum cum tapeto et
linthiaminis"); in Archinfield in 1663 custom provided that the eldest took
possession of "the best bed and furniture."[3] Disposal of the beds must,
however, be seen against the larger—and complicating—issue of a widow's
rights in the early seventeenth century. Over a century ago the Victorian
popularizer Charles Knight triumphantly disclosed that the English common law guaranteed the widow a life interest of one third in her husband's
estate, as well as residence in the family domicile. Many subsequent biographers have assumed that Anne was so protected; the point is confidently
made by our most distinguished living historian of the early stage: "By law
the widow during her lifetime received the income from one-third of her
husband's estate."[4] I have myself subscribed to this view in my *William
Shakespeare: A Documentary Life* (1975). It is an attractive option, but I have
had to reconsider it.

Certainly what is sometimes called the widow's portion, or legitim, did
exist, and is traceable back to the thirteenth century. If the common law
gives the male partner, upon matrimony, all his wife's goods and chattels,
"shall not the husband," the anonymous author of *A Brief Discourse* asks in
1584,

> be bound by semblable obligation of reason to leave his wife the third
> part of his goods, and if the law be in that respect defective (as what law
> in the world, except the law of God, is without his imperfections?) shall
> not the custom supply it in such sort that no barbarous and uncharitable
> or cautelous [i.e., deceitful], and unkind practices by deed or gift, or
> otherwise, shall disappoint or defraud the same?

But the writer here extols the special virtues of London, and the problem
with local customs is that they are local. A widow's portion comprised both
land and chattels. With respect to land, custom appears to have operated
fairly uniformly, the widow's right being recognized from early until modern times (the Law of Property Act of 1925 converted common law dower
of land into an equitable interest). As regards chattels, custom fluctuated
from borough to borough. One would like to know more about Stratford
practice. Wills do not provide the answer, for custom functions when the
wills are silent. Of course, Shakespeare may have figured that his daughter
and son-in-law, the Halls—reliable types—would tend to Anne's needs.

Some have so assumed, and it is a reasonable guess; but we do not actually know what he figured. It may be added that most Stratford testaments of the period look after the wife, provision being covered by some such catch-all phrase as "the residue of my estate." With Shakespeare we have only a will with a bed in it.

On the history of English law I can claim no special expertise, only an amateur's curiosity. Perhaps readers of the *TLS* better informed in such matters than I can help to fill in the picture. Meanwhile an agnostic conclusion as to Shakespeare's intentions seems the most reasonable. That is not excitingly novel or satisfyingly conclusive, but is to be preferred to a specious certainty.

I have incorporated my revised views on the will, as well as the Wheler deposition and other tidbits of new information, in my *William Shakespeare: A Compact Documentary Life,* to be published later this year by the Oxford University Press. Mrs. Lean has, since I saw them, donated her husband's papers to the Shakespeare Birthplace Trust; interested students may consult this valuable resource at the Shakespeare Centre in Stratford-upon-Avon. I understand from Mr. Robert Bearman, Senior Archivist of the Shakespeare Birthplace Trust, that the possibility is being explored "of printing 'in extenso' some of the more important documents he [Lean] unearthed relating to the history of Stratford in the late sixteenth century."[5]

NOTES

1. On Bott see, especially, *Minutes and Accounts of the Corporation of Stratford upon Avon,* Richard Savage and Edgar I. Fripp (Publications of the Dugdale Society; 1921–30), I, lvii–lx, and Mark Eccles, *Shakespeare in Warwickshire* (Madison, Wis., 1961), pp. 87–88, 90.

2. This possibility, long ago suggested by Charles Severn in his edition of the *Diary of the Rev. John Ward* (London, 1839), p. 56, has been insufficiently considered—by myself as well as others.

3. *Borough Customs,* Mary Bateson (Publications of the Selden Society, 21; London, 1906), ii. 142–3, 144.

4. Gerald Eades Bentley, *Shakespeare: A Biographical Handbook* (New Haven, 1961), p. 63. There are earlier biographers, e.g. Roland Lewis and Marchette Chute, who deny that such a custom obtained in Shakespeare's Stratford; but their assessment of the evidence is not entirely reliable, although Lewis is amply detailed.

5. I wish to thank Mrs. Doreen Lean for allowing me to make use of the Lean papers, Mr. Michael Feltovic for drawing my attention again to the widow's portion, the Rev. Eric McDermott, S.J., for wise counsel on the legal considerations, and Mr. Robert Bearman for answering my queries about Elizabethan Stratford.

(1977)

4

Shakespeare, Dr. Forman, and Dr. Rowse

I. NEW LIGHT ON A DARK LADY*

Of the welcome for A. L. Rowse's first biography of Shakespeare the memory is yet green. The advance articles in *The Times* announcing answers to perennial questions posed by the Sonnets, the spirited exchanges that followed in the correspondence columns (had he really come up with the final solution?), the publication of the book on the eve of the quatercentennial celebrations, the blasts from reviewers and counter-blasts from the author—can all this have taken place a full decade ago? To be sure Dr. Rowse has himself occasionally raked the embers of debate by forays into *The Times;* for a while he even contemplated writing a book about the reception of his book. Now he has chosen instead to favor the world with another life of the Bard. Like Sam in *Casablanca,* Dr. Rowse is playing it again, and if his tune is not quite so beguiling as Bogey's it has, thanks to its haunting Dark Lady theme, already set the Shakespearean world humming.

This biography is like the previous one, and also different. Inevitably the author follows in his own footsteps. Once again we perambulate Stratford. The story of the Sonnets, taken as fourteen-line rhymed installments in an intimate autobiography, becomes a twice-told tale. Phrases are repeated, paragraphs lightly recast. Surely the procedure is perfectly understandable and appropriate; previous biographers of Shakespeare have followed the same course, and anyway most readers will not have the 1963 *Shakespeare* under their belt. Tone and substance suggest that Dr. Rowse is this time round casting his net to capture an even more popular kind of readership than that for which his earlier best-selling biography catered. Fair enough—he has the touch, and the popularizing tradition is an honorable one—but it is at least debatable whether a work addressed to an essentially uncritical readership is the most suitable vehicle for a new and controversial thesis. That thesis concerns Emilia Lanier, née Bassano.

Dr. Rowse found Emilia in the Bodleian Library, in Simon Forman's casebooks, where for centuries her indiscretions had lain covered by the kindly dust of oblivion. For being apparently the first to tackle the mass of Forman papers Dr. Rowse has earned our admiration; it is one of those

---

*On A. L. Rowse, *Shakespeare the Man* (London: Macmillan, 1973).

scholarly inspirations that appear perfectly obvious after the fact. In Forman, for Dr. Rowse, the dark mistress of the Sonnets becomes visible. Was she the seductress who led the poet his last—or was it his last?—tango in London? . . .

Dr. Rowse professes scorn for "absurd conjectures and guesses *in vacuo*," and extols certainty, rigor, and method. These are no doubt virtues, but they here assume a talismanic potency, as though their invocation by itself constituted rigorous method. This is mystical scholarship. In effect we are being invited to accept on faith the authority of, in Dr. Rowse's words, "the foremost historian of the society of Shakespeare's Age." But no authority, however eminent, holds the laws of evidence at his commandment. Dr. Rowse has said that, for this period, we cannot expect to find corroborative letters and the like; we must content ourselves with a chain of plausible circumstance. It is no doubt true that documentary records are often scant, but this frustrating state of affairs does not entitle us to settle for less than adequate proof. It means, rather, that fewer things can get proved. In his preface Dr. Rowse claims that his critics will find it "quite impossible to impugn" his findings. The burden, however, rests not with the critics, but with the historian. It is a pity that Dr. Rowse should regard speculation in much the same way as nature esteems the vacuum, for there is a place in scholarship for conjecture, and he has come up with rather an intriguing one. Other investigators—or perhaps even Dr. Rowse himself—may one day prove it right or wrong. If he is right, the world will applaud his intuition and tenacity, while not necessarily attaching to the discovery the immense significance claimed for it. Meanwhile one suspects one hasn't heard the last of Emilia.

She is only one ingredient in a book which makes for a better read than its predecessor. For one thing it is only a little more than half as long. To achieve his drastic economies Dr. Rowse has had to suppress ruthlessly his urge to expatiate on topics that interest him, and evidence of the struggle surfaces in such poignant formulas as, "We must resist the temptation to go into this appealing play. . . ." Mainly he has sacrificed critical commentary; a wise decision, for his genius does not lie that way. As he confessed himself in *The English Spirit,* "Heaven forfend that I should be a critic." What remains of literary interpretation even novices may find excessively elementary: "The subject of *Othello,* innocent love injured and destroyed, inspired Shakespeare to one of his highest flights of imagination and poetry"; or: "His [Shakespeare's] knowledge of human beings, of the human condition, has never been surpassed." True. So uninformed are readers presumed to be that they must be told that the *Henry IV* plays come after *Richard II* and before *Henry V,* and that the whole lot make up a sequence. Dr. Rowse does better when he sticks to dates and sources.

Style, robust without elegance, befits content. The author does not disdain cliché or such colloquialisms as "family-wise" or "fell for." He keeps footnotes to a minimum out of regard for the reader's comfort, but why such frugality should make for greater rather than less convenience is not clear: even the non-scholarly enthusiast may occasionally wish to follow up a point. The practical result is that authorities quoted and documented in the 1963 life—Eccles or Fripp or Spurgeon—here go paraphrased without acknowledgment. If this be an improvement, it is one that the fastidious will disrelish.

Dr. Rowse is now keen to see Shakespeare as a writer whose primary allegiance was to the theatre. Thus we have such chapter headings as "The Player Becomes Playwright" or "At the Globe" or "The King's Men." The strategy is unexceptionable but Dr. Rowse is no stage historian, and what he has to say comes at second hand and tends to be superficial. A couple of sentences do to sum up the characteristics of the Elizabethan playhouse, with the vexed question of the existence or non-existence of an inner stage by-passed in a phrase. Mostly, Dr. Rowse depends on G. E. Bentley—a good choice, surely, but it is a pity that the latter's *Profession of Dramatist in Shakespeare's Time* appeared too late for the biographer to draw upon it. Still the new bias is salutary.

Here and there the author has changed his mind or taken advantage of later work. In 1963 Dr. Rowse thought Shakespeare no intellectual; now he is prepared to concede that the creator of *Hamlet* and *Troilus and Cressida* had egghead proclivities. We are also told that he was equipped with a "sexy nose," no doubt an appropriate appendage for the "sexiest writer in the language." Dr. Rowse has written more extensively on this stimulating topic in *The Times,* but it remains unclear how the sexiness of writers may be quantitatively ascertained. He takes into account K. B. McFarlane on the riotous youth of Henry V. He has, however, unaccountably missed Hugh Hanley's important article in the *TLS* (May 21, 1964) with its revelations, from the Sackville manuscripts, about Susanna Shakespeare and Thomas Quiney. . . . These records, which are not without interesting implications for the biographer, have provided matter for E.R.C. Brinkworth's recent book, *Shakespeare and the Bawdy Court of Stratford.* In another quarter, Warren Austin has lately sought to demonstrate, through computer-assembled data, that Robert Greene's notorious death-bed slander of Shakespeare was in fact composed by the same Chettle who afterwards apologized for it. This challenge to biographical orthodoxy may not convert the skeptical, but Professor Austin presents his thesis responsibly enough for the biographer to have to reckon with it. Dr. Rowse does not reckon with it.

A distinguished historian becomes a public figure in his own right, so the present book has a Rowsean as well as Shakespearean interest. The author's mood, exuberant as regards his subject, otherwise waxes melancholy. "Shakespeare scholarship has long reached a dead end," he proclaims. (Is he so readily dismissing the new direction given to imagistic criticism by R. A. Foakes and Maurice Charney? Or the contributions to knowledge of Shakespeare's text we owe to Charlton Hinman and Fredson Bowers? Probably not—he is thinking of biography, which has indeed grown moribund of late. But surely it is careless to equate the part with the whole.) The golden age, represented by the England of Elizabeth, is past, and worse and worse days have succeeded the former. Our speech is "etiolated," "half-baked intellectuals" control the mass media, dons suck up to press-lords and television, honey comes home diluted in a jar. It is a democratic illusion—specifically the illusion of "superficial liberal intellectuals"—that they may be trusted to govern themselves well. Dr. Rowse's outburst against the common man has its unintended irony, coming as it does in a book which will exercise its greatest appeal to unsophisticated readers.

At the end what chiefly impresses us is the powerful force of the author's personality. We can only admire the unflagging energy which during the past two years has given us two sweeping volumes of social and cultural history, an illustrated account of the Tower of London, a book of poems, and the present biography, and which promises us a life of Forman next year. No wonder Dr. Rowse detects symptoms of exhaustion in the Shake-speare Establishment. With his energy, and also his flair, he has certainly enlivened the scholarly scene. Who else could have made a conjecture about the Dark Lady matter for feature articles in newspapers throughout the world? In this respect Dr. Rowse may remind us of the brilliant and controversial young American chess expert who turned a sedentary com-petition, the preserve of a staid élite, on its heels, and attracted reporters from the four corners of the globe to an obscure hall in Reykjavik. But of course Bobby Fischer defeated the Russian grandmaster, whereas Dr. Rowse has declared a victory without checkmate.

(1963)

II. DARK SECRETS*

A. L. Rowse, as Shakespeare's biographer, has most prided himself on his elucidation of the problems of the Sonnets. He has demonstrated to his own satisfaction that Shakespeare wrote the sequence between 1592 and 1594–95; that the Fair Youth is the third Earl of Southampton; that Mr. W. H. is Sir William Harvey, the third husband of the Earl's mother; and that the Rival Poet is Marlowe. On these matters Dr. Rowse's views are not unfamiliar, for he has been reminding us of them for a decade in his two lives of Shakespeare, his biographies of Southampton and Marlowe, and in newspaper articles, interviews, and letters to the editor; not to mention his first edition of the Sonnets in 1964. In his introduction to that edition Dr. Rowse was pessimistic about the identity of the Dark Lady ever coming to light. Almost a decade later he has (as the world well knows) found his candidate, Emilia Lanier, née Bassano. He made her acquaintance only last year in the Bodleian Library, where, like the young Lana Turner in a drug

---

*On A. L. Rowse, *Shakespeare's Sonnets: The Problems Solved* (London: Macmillan, 1973).

store at Hollywood and Vine, she was awaiting discovery and fame in the obscure pages of Simon Forman's case-books. The resurfacing of Emilia provides justification for Dr. Rowse's second edition of the Sonnets. He has rewritten and enlarged his introduction, shifting emphasis to the Dark Lady, and revised his commentary on the affected poems. He has also tinkered with some of his prose versions (e.g., Sonnets 135 and 141). The present edition thus conveniently sets forth the full scope—well, almost the full scope—of Dr. Rowse's current thinking about the Sonnets.

Dr. Rowse has added an assertive new subtitle, "The Problems Solved." In his introduction Dr. Rowse urges his special qualifications as an historian with a poet's feeling for his subject. He adopts his well-known stance, dismissing "generations of vague conjecture," and proffering instead "common sense" and "correct interpretation," "definiteness and finality," and "simple and rigorous historical method." This is the vocabulary of confidence which makes facts of possibilities; it is likely to seduce the unsophisticated reader to whom this book will appeal. Close students may, however, hold views different from Dr. Rowse's about the secrets of the Sonnets, as the correspondence columns of the *TLS* have recently demonstrated, not for the first time.

He is on shakiest ground in his identification of the Dark Lady. Despite blows to his theory, Dr. Rowse remains undaunted, and, like the valiant Joe Bugner, presses the fight, which at the moment he looks like losing on points. Meanwhile Emilia, revealed as a minor poetess, becomes daily more appealing. Perhaps we may look forward to having in due course from Dr. Rowse a revised version of his revised essay.

A principal feature of this edition is Dr. Rowse's prose versions of the Sonnets, printed on facing pages, as though the poems required translation from a foreign language. Dr. Rowse says he has striven to give "the meaning and sense of the text." But the exercise is by its nature reductive, the meaning of a poem not being something apart from diction, metaphor, cadence and rhythm. Sonnet 119 opens, "What potions have I drunk of Siren tears," which Dr. Rowse renders, "What potions have I drunk of woman's tears." The alteration performs a questionable service. No doubt motivated by the best popularizing intentions, the editor has succeeded in transforming each poem into (to adapt the Houyhnhnm's phrase) the thing which it is not.

Two miscellaneous points. Dr. Rowse repeats a blunder made in the preface to his Southampton biography, in calling Malone the first supporter of Southampton as the young man of the Sonnets. Not so; Malone thought that he might be William Hughes. Southampton was first proposed by Nathan Drake in *Shakespeare and his Times* (1817). And, lastly, perhaps the most appealing novelty of Dr. Rowse's revised edition is that he has a kind word for our "more open, permissive society."

(1973)

III. LOOKING AT THE UNDERSIDE OF THE TIME*

Only last spring A. L. Rowse promised us a life of Simon Forman, the Elizabethan astrologer and physician, and this season it has arrived. The titles of Dr. Rowse's other books fill a whole page in *Simon Forman*—twenty-five items in all and the list is incomplete, lacking, for example, *The Tower of London in the History of the Nation.* There is an Elizabethan prodigality about Dr. Rowse's energy, which is sustained by an enthusiasm undimmed by all the scholarly campaigns he has weathered. That enthusiasm is much in evidence in *Simon Forman*. Of the Forman papers he declares in his penultimate paragraph: "What a portrait, in depth, of the time!—what an exposure of the underside usually covered up by conventions, pretenses, humbug, social decorum; of the miseries and squalors, the ardors and passions, the fears and expectations, the sadnesses and tragedies!" The purple excesses of the rhetoric, better suited to the blurb-writer than to the historian, should not deter us from recognizing that he is right. And Dr. Rowse has legitimate cause to crow; for the mass of Forman papers at the Bodleian Library has been freely accessible all along, but he is the first tenacious enough to mine them for a biography.

It is just that he should sympathize with the "old reprobate" who is his subject. In his own time Forman, who never had formal medical training, was hounded by the Royal College of Physicians, which refused to license him; his memorialist, in the *Dictionary of National Biography,* labeled him a quack, and others have followed Sidney Lee's lead. Yet Forman probably killed no more patients than did properly qualified doctors, and perhaps fewer, for he was no great bleeder; eventually Cambridge, recognizing Forman's "long exercise and experience," granted him a license to practice. Dr. Rowse succeeds in showing that by the standards of the day, Forman was no charlatan.

Posthumously his name has been blackened because he had the misfortune to be sought out by Frances Howard, the young Countess of Essex, who was keen to compel the affection of Robert Carr, the King's favorite (Forman dealt in love philtres and the like). The squalid aftermath, involving the poisoning of Overbury, is well known; but although Forman was named at the trial, he could have had nothing to do with the murder, which took place two years after his death. Here, too, Dr. Rowse is effective in exculpating his hero, although it is difficult to resist the judgment (early expressed on him in this context) that Forman was "a very silly fellow."

Dr. Rowse is less successful at amateur psychoanalysis. He sees Forman as an obsessive-compulsive, tending to paranoia, and suffering from an inferiority complex. Mainly, Dr. Rowse harps on the inferiority complex, but elementary Adler does not get us very far. Anyway Forman's crippled psyche is not much in evidence in these pages: he led a far too active,

---

*On A. L. Rowse, *Simon Forman: Sex and Society in Shakespeare's Age* (London: Weidenfeld and Nicolson, 1974).

satisfying, and (ultimately) materially rewarding a career. If he fretted about persecutors, they were real, not imagined. When Forman visits Sir William Monson and notes that he found the knight "lame on his bed," Dr. Rowse sniffs symptoms of "compulsive exactitude." Why *compulsive?* It seems normal enough that a physician should remark on a client's condition. Dr. Rowse also describes Forman as "abnormally heterosexual." This means that he was a strenuous enthusiast of sexual intercourse with women, an activity to which, in his private papers, he gave the code term "halek." A diary entry reads: "9 July, halek 8 a.m. Hester Sharp, et halek at 3 p.m. Anne Wiseman, and 9 p.m. halek tronco." (Tronco was his pet name for his wife.) A busy day. That was in 1607, when Forman was fifty-five.

He had by then a flourishing practice in Lambeth. All sorts—high, low, and in-between—came to him, the single common denominator being their credulity. Forman cast horoscopes, set geomantic figures, and analyzed urine. He predicted the future and prescribed purges. His clients included Hugh Broughton, the learned divine to whom mere reference is enough to bring on Doll Common's feigned mad fit in *The Alchemist*. Broughton consulted Forman about his prospects, and was keen to know when the stars favored delivering a petition for preferment. The other Frances Howard, daughter of Viscount Howard of Bindon, visited Forman too. A single consultation sufficed for him to predict that "she shall change her estate three times." As it turned out Frances married first a rich alderman's son; then, early widowed but happily unchilded, she set her sights on the Earl of Southampton, Shakespeare's patron, but settled for the Earl of Hertford, and (after his death) the Duke of Lennox, the most eligible suitor in the kingdom. So Forman's prophecy proved uncannily correct: Frances was a three-time winner in the matrimonial sweepstakes.

Seamen and seamen's wives and City merchants, anxious about the fortunes of ships and voyages, also knocked on the cunning man's door. He was visited by Richard Field and William Jaggard, printers with Shakespearean associations, and he mentions in one of his case-books an "Austin Phillips" who may have been the Augustine Phillips that left his fellow Shakespeare 30s in his will. Alas, no poets or playwrights seem to have consulted Forman, although he did minister to Sir Barrington Molyns, suffering from melancholy and "stinking sweet and venomous" worms in his nose. Sir Barrington was on the lookout for a wife.

Of all Forman's clients, it is Emilia Lanier who most intrigues Dr. Rowse. He has no further evidence to offer, except to suggest that it is not "surprising that Shakespeare's mistress should come to consult Forman, since his known landlady, Mrs Mountjoy, did so." There is no reason to suspect that Emilia and Mrs. Mountjoy had any connection with one another; this is Fluellen's logic. ("There is a river in Macedon; and there is also moreover a river at Monmouth; it is call'd Wye at Monmouth, but it is out of my prains what is the name of the other river; but 'tis all one, 'tis alike as my fingers is to my fingers, and there is salmons in both [*Henry V,* 4.7.25–29].) The historian should tread warily, for "Fluellenism" in Shakespeare studies has lately taken some deserved knocks.

The biographer of Forman, Dr. Rowse likes to remind us, must carry an Elizabethan "Who's Who" around in his head to identify the multifarious clients who make their entrances and exits in the case-books. The author's special expertise usually serves him well, although on one occasion, Dr. Rowse's "Who's Who" lets him down. Of Ferdinando Clutterbuck, who in 1601 paid Forman 2*s* for a purge, Dr. Rowse correctly says that a man "with so individual a name . . . is easily identifiable"; but he fails to identify him as the "fferdynando clutterbooke Draper" who was one of the two Petty Collectors that listed Shakespeare as a tax defaulter in Bishopsgate Ward in 1598.

Forman's "serious" writings on astrology, magic, alchemy and the like, get short shrift in this book. The spirit sags at the prospect of ploughing through them, and the author has exercised a humanly understandable prerogative. Dr. Rowse feels that the real interest of Forman resides in the case-books and diaries, which tell us much about the man and his times, although to claim (as the author does) that Forman surpasses in intimate self-revelation a Boswell or Casanova or Gide is perhaps to overstate the case. The rather sensational sub-title to the book fairly defines its scope. It does give a panoramic view of a society in which "halek" was a very popular diversion.

The prose style which serves as vehicle for these revelations will not invariably give pleasure to the discerning. John Richards, aged thirty-five or thirty-six, is "no chicken." James I, "a sugar-daddy to them all," dotes on his "boy-friend" Carr. Along with the breezily colloquial, some slapdash writing: Simon has "a dream which clearly reveals his unconscious sense of guilt, of which consciously he was unaware." Banalities too. "Never a dull moment: this is the Elizabethan age after all." "It is extraordinary to think that these brief entries in his case-books are the traces of such human stories, with their passions and their sufferings." A little of this sort of avuncular elbow-nudging goes a long way. Nor is much taken for granted. Thus, after quoting a passage from Emilia—

> For well you know, this world is but a stage
> Where all do play their parts and must be gone

—Dr. Rowse asks, "Where have we heard that before?" And proceeds to tell us. The popularizer's mission is not ignoble, but it requires a special tact not always in evidence in this book.

Nor will the specialist reader always feel assured that a due rigor has been exercised. Why should the author of a book on Forman owe a special debt of thanks to a collector "who came up with an engraving of a portrait of Forman, which I thought we should never find" when the portrait appears in *The Antiquarian Repertory?* Lee cited the *Repertory* in his *D.N.B.* article on Forman, and said that the original drawing was "the property of the Marquis of Bute." It would be interesting to have tracked it down.

"Ralph Agas's pictorial map of London," cited for the house in Silver Street where Shakespeare lodged for a time, was probably not by Agas, and the houses depicted thereon are conventionalized representations. Dr. Rowse conveniently gives, as an appendix, "Forman's Account of four Shakespeare Plays: April 1611," but scholars generally doubt, for good reason, that the play on Richard II he witnessed at the Globe on April 30 was Shakespeare's. Dr. Rowse does not tackle at all the thorny problems raised by these accounts (for an idea of the complexities see Leah Scragg's excellent essay, "Macbeth on Horseback," in *Shakespeare Survey 26,* 1973). Nor does he mention the suggestion, made in the *TLS* as far back as 1927 by F. L. Lucas, that Forman committed suicide. This speculation, based on a purported allusion some fourteen years later, may not amount to much; but it has been picked up by no less an eminence than Sir Edmund Chambers in his *William Shakespeare,* and as so little has been written on Forman, it should probably not be passed over in silence.

It is well for a biographer to record precisely the work of previous toilers in the same vineyard. In this case there is only one predecessor of note. In his preface Dr. Rowse says: "Halliwell-Phillips transcribed the Autobiography for the Camden Society a century ago, but Victorian prudery prevented its publication." This statement is amplified a little further along: "Halliwell-Phillips wished to publish the Autobiography, but after printing only some sixteen copies, found that he could not publish in his time." This is better, but still not the whole story.

Halliwell-Phillipps (Dr. Rowse, while upbraiding him for "absurd mistakes," persistently misspells the name) transcribed not only the autobiography but also the diary for the years 1564 to 1602, and a genealogical passage. The 1843 Camden Society publication was aborted, but, not one to waste his energy, Halliwell-Phillipps in 1849 printed the autobiography and diary "for private circulation only" in an edition of 105 copies. Thus the Forman papers have been in part available to scholars for over a century.

Dr. Rowse now makes the autobiography and early diary available to a larger public by including them with helpful notes in *Simon Forman.* In doing so he has performed a service for which both ordinary and specialist readers must be grateful. They will be even more in Dr. Rowse's debt for this first biography of a remarkable character. Although he invokes the magical name of Shakespeare in his subtitle, it is the vital and credulous world of Jonson's *Alchemist* that lives in these flawed but revealing pages.

(1974)

IV. SHAKESPEARE'S DARK LADY
A QUESTION OF IDENTITY

My mistress' eyes are nothing like the sun;
Coral is far more red than her lips' red;
If snow be white, why then her breasts are dun;
If hairs be wires, black wires grow on her head.
I have seen roses damask'd, red and white,
But no such roses see I in her cheeks;
And in some perfumes is there more delight
Than in the breath that from my mistress reeks.
I love to hear her speak, yet well I know
That music hath a far more pleasing sound;
I grant I never saw a goddess go—
My mistress when she walks treads on the ground.
   And yet, by heaven, I think my love as rare
   As any she belied with false compare.

(Sonnet 130)

It was, I believe, Aldous Huxley who once spoke of the imbecile earnestness of lust. Shakespeare can certainly be earnest on the subject; witness the tremendous sonnet (just preceding the one quoted) in which, in an explosively forceful series of self-lacerating modifiers, he excoriates a passion that post-coitally he despises, and which yet tyrannizes over body and spirit. But Sonnet 130 reflects another mood; the lover is at once clear-eyed and high spirited. His mistress' attractions can survive his own denigration of them. So she withstands the anti-Petrarchan assault of the three quartets— the reference to disagreeable breath seems especially devastating in an age of oral hygiene—to assert her allure, and attendant mystery, in a concluding couplet that draws its special force from *not* being dependent upon romantic illusion.

This is the Dark Lady who, more than three and a half centuries ago, sauntered into the best-loved sequence of lyric poems in the language. They describe with a playwright's art how she captivated the poet, against his reason, and seduced the golden youth he adored. One of the great sorceresses of literature, she has since added innumerable readers to the tally of her conquests. My subject is this intriguing personage, and especially how men have responded to her wiles, first in the imaginative achievements of art, and then in the more prosaic endeavors of scholarship, by embarking upon a quest for her real-life identity.

One may grant straightaway that the Dark Lady of the Sonnets is no Helen of Troy, and that her pursuers include among their number no Schliemann of literary excavation. This dusky phantom eludes us still, although every now and then somebody makes a stir by announcing to a momentarily attentive world that he has solved the riddle. Perhaps the

questors would have done well to apply to the mistress the malediction
carved on Shakespeare's gravestone. Yet the story of the search for the
Dark Lady, which begins with an eccentric Scottish antiquary in the late
eighteenth century, and ends (more likely pauses) with an idiosyncratic
English historian in the twentieth, brings its own rewards. If on the whole
we learn more about the seekers than the sought, such knowledge nevertheless holds an interest of its own for those who savor the vagaries of
human behavior. The story has moments of farce, and also of poignance.
Success of a sort unexpectedly emerges out of failure. For the critic this
question of identity raises the larger perennial issue of the relations between a poet's experience and the well-wrought urn that is the vehicle of
his experience. The Shakespeare life-record is no blank, as the uninformed
have supposed, but it is destitute of the intimate revelations which only
letters, diaries, and the like can furnish. In their absence, the Sonnets—
clearly more private than the plays—urge on us an autobiographical reading. Do we legitimately yield to their pressure?

I

Familiar as the poems are, it may be well to begin by piecing together what
we can about the Dark Lady from the revelations, sometimes obscure or
contradictory, that they afford. She makes her entrance obliquely, a felt
presence rather than a directly introduced member of the dramatis personae. "Base clouds" suddenly overcast a sunny day. Somehow the poet's
friend has given offense. We hear of a wound, of disgrace and shame, and
of penitent tears. The trespass, the next sonnet (35) reveals, was theft, and
the fault "sensual." Five poems later the nature of the larceny becomes
clearer, although not yet explicit. "Take all my loves, my love," the poet
cries, "yea, take them all." It seems that the friend has taken Shakespeare's
mistress.

At last, in Sonnet 41, indirections cease, the circumlocutions of tact and
poetical conceit give way; what has happened is starkly stated:

> Gentle thou art, and therefore to be won,
> Beauteous thou art, therefore to be assailed;
> And when a woman woos, what woman's son,
> Will sourly leave her till she have prevailed?

So she—whoever she is—has taken the role of aggressor, and the beauteous
friend has succumbed. It is an interesting triumph. The lovely boy is high-
born, the poet's patron, and of ambiguous masculinity. Nature has
fashioned him to be a woman, and given him a woman's face; but rather
spoilt things for the heterosexual poet by outfitting her exquisite creation
with a male organ. The emotional and psychological weight of these poems

resides in the relationship between the two men. The woman who has come between them is still only a shadow—or cloud.

Later she comes into her own. In Sonnet 127 we meet her properly and for the first time learn about the coloration that sets her apart. Black wires grow upon her head. Sonnet 130 adds, and "If snow be white, why then her breasts are dun," which the Oxford Dictionary helpfully defines as "of a dull or dingy brown colour; now *esp.* dull greyish brown, like the hair of the ass and mouse." If the Dark Lady is beautiful, hers is an unfashionable beauty; but some question emerges as to whether she is beautiful by any standard:

> In faith, I do not love thee with mine eyes,
> For they in thee a thousand errors note.

This is 141; just two sonnets earlier the poet has commended her "pretty looks." Are all these poems, one may wonder, addressed to the same woman? Or is it merely that we are witnessing a lover's varied moods? The old adage holds that beauty lies in the eye of the beholder; perhaps the report shifts, not the object reported. It is one of many puzzles.

Elsewhere we tread on firmer ground. We learn that the lady is musical, and (in Sonnet 128) catch a charming glimpse of her seated at the virginals. Perhaps she sings as she plays. Her fingers dance over the wooden keys, the jacks leaping nimbly up to kiss the inside of her hand. Her lover, envying the jacks, kisses his mistress on the lips. It is rather like a seventeenth-century Dutch genre painting.

Other poems show the Dark Lady as a *belle dame sans merci*, tyrannizing over her lover. She breaks her bed-vow—does this mean she is married, as most have assumed, or merely that she has broken a vow made to her lover when they were in bed together? About her sexual appetite and promiscuity, however, there is no question; she is "the bay where all men ride." Even when with the poet she humiliates him by eyeing other men. Older than his mistress—"my days," he laments, "are past the best"—and consequently insecure, he wearily accepts her infidelities, and deludes himself into crediting "her false-speaking tongue." The word *lies* furnishes an opportunity for rueful word-play:

> Therefore I lie with her, and she with me,
> And in our faults by lies we flattered be.

Will, another key word, could mean "carnal desire or appetite." It might also signify the male or female genitalia. And of course the poet's name was Will. He plays with all these meanings simultaneously in Sonnet 135, where (in the 1609 quarto) the word *will* is italicized—with an upper-cased *W*—seven out of the thirteen times it appears:

> Whoever hath her wish, thou hast thy Will,
> And Will to boot, and Will in over-plus;
> More than enough am I that vex thee still,
> To thy sweet will making addition thus.
> Wilt thou, whose will is large and spacious,
> Not once vouchsafe to hide my will in thine?

The only thing virginal about this lady is the musical instrument she fingers so fluently.

In an extraordinary sonnet (151) the poet contemplates her powers of conjuration over another instrument, which stands erect at the mere mention of her name: "flesh stays no farther reason, / But, rising at thy name, doth point out thee / As his triumphant prize." What are we to make of a mistress who can be thus addressed? Was she, as some have thought, a common prostitute? Standards of propriety of course vary with the times and with individuals; one man's grossness is another's refreshing candor. If we may occasionally lament the loss of past reticences, a flesh-and-blood Shakespeare is perhaps preferable to the impassive statuary of the culture-worshippers who wend their pious way to the Stratford shrines and cough through a performance at the Royal Shakespeare Theatre. We do well every now and then to remind ourselves that Shakespeare, father of three, had a penis.

The 144th Sonnet sets in perspective the complex triangle involving Poet, Fair Youth, and Dark Lady:

> Two loves I have, of comfort and despair,
> Which like two spirits do suggest me still;
> The better angel is a man right fair,
> The worser spirit a woman colour'd ill.
> . . . .
> But being both from me, both to each friend,
> I guess one angel in another's hell.
> Yet this shall I ne'er know, but live in doubt,
> Till my bad angel fire my good one out.

This seems straightforward enough: Hell fits nicely into a scheme that includes good and bad angels, saint and devil, and gains here another dimension by alluding to the game of barley-break, in which the last couple playing found itself "in hell." But hell was also a cant word for the female organ; hence the sexual innuendo of: "I guess one angel in another's hell." The last line possibly harbors a grimmer allusion. "To fire out," which meant originally, "to smoke a fox out of its den"—cf. *King Lear*, 5.3.23: "fire us hence like foxes"—also signified "to communicate a venereal disease."

A similar allusiveness may help to explain the otherwise puzzling last two poems of Shakespeare's sonnet sequence. These, as a recent critic sums up, are generally looked upon as an appendix not connected with the story, which Shakespeare or the printer added simply to enlarge the collection. Both tell a fanciful story about the origins of a medicinal spring, brought into being when a nymph extinguished Cupid's torch in a well, which 'took heat perpetual' from this fire.[1]

"I, sick withal, the help of bath desired," the poet reports, "And thither hied, a sad distemper'd guest." The Greek Anthology, the ultimate source of these poems, makes no reference to the curative powers of the waters. As early as the eighteenth century, a commentator queried, "Whether we shall read *Bath* (i.e. the city of that name)?" Bath is still celebrated for its medicinal hot springs, the fountains of the town proudly displaying the dubious motto, "Water is best." Although in Shakespeare's day it had not yet become a fashionable spa, Elizabethans sought out the waters of Bath for curative purposes: the title-page of the 1572 quarto of *The Baths of Bath's Aid,* by John Jones, physician, commends them as "wonderfull and most excellent, agaynst very many Sicknesses," and William Turner, doctor in physic, contributed an appendix on "the rare treasure of the English Bathes" to Thomas Vicary's *The Englishman's Treasure* (1587 ed.). True, the word *bath* is not capitalized, or placed in italics, in Sonnets 153 and 154 in the 1609 edition, as are other proper nouns *(Cupid, Dian's);* but one cannot expect nice distinctions to be scrupulously maintained by a typesetter unchecked by authorial supervision. A topographical identification is in any event not required: there were other spas, and the reference may point, not to natural springs, but to the sweating tubs, filled with hot water, used by the victims of venereal infection. Some such allusiveness seems to be indicated by the sexual innuendoes of these two sonnets.

"I, my mistress' thrall, / Came there for cure," Shakespeare concludes in the last lines of his last sonnet, but the waters appear to have vouchsafed no cure, only the awareness that: "Love's fire heats water, water cools not love." Thus, ingloriously does the cycle end. If this reading is correct, and underneath their fanciful surface Sonnets 153 and 154 reveal the unpleasant medical consequences of an illicit affair, they perhaps afford an autobiographical clue to the sex-nausea that so many critics have remarked on in *Hamlet, Troilus and Cressida,* and *King Lear.*

Whatever the merits of such speculation, the Dark Lady is (within the limits of lyric poetry) as vitally realized a dramatic creation as Cressida, with her wanton spirits looking out from every joint and motive of her body, and some have wondered whether both portraits were drawn to the life from the same sitter. Never mind; we have enough to occupy us with the Dark Lady on her own, although the information is not always so clear cut as either one would wish or some have surmised. To sum up: she is younger than the poet, musical, raven-haired and raven-eyed, dark-skinned (how dark is not clear), and either unattractive or unconventionally beautiful, depending upon the viewer and the viewer's mood. She is certainly seductive, gives free rein to her appetite, may be married, and is possibly infected with venereal disease. In character she is a *femme fatale:* proud, fickle, overbearing, and deceitful. No wonder scholars have sought to find for her a local habitation and a name.

II

That the quest got underway relatively late is also not surprising, in view of the early publishing history of the Sonnets. Thomas Thorpe's 1609 quarto, the copy-text followed by all modern editors, bristles with perplexities, but represents an authentic text, even if the author himself failed to proofread it. The edition published thirty years later by John Benson is another matter. This is a pirated text with which the stationer tampered by omitting the celebrated dedication to Mr. W. H., altering some of the male pronouns, and mischievously rearranging the poems, to which he gave misleading titles. Thus he destroyed their character as a sonnet cycle. The Sonnets were not included in any form in the First Folio in 1623 or in the three succeeding folios, which represented for seventeenth-century readers *the* collected edition of Shakespeare. In 1709 Nicholas Rowe called his six-volume collection *The Works of Mr William Shakespear,* but he too left out the Sonnets. These a publisher's hack supplied in an unauthorized seventh volume, unfortunately basing his text on Benson. The poems could by then be described as "these less known Works of *Shakespear.*"

Why were the Sonnets so negligently handled by their early editors? The simple answer seems to be that the literati then entertained no very high regard for them. Thus Charles Gildon, the aforementioned hack, acknowledged (while answering) current opinion that "they are not valuable enough to be reprinted, as was plain by the first Editors of his Works who wou'd otherwise have join'd them altogether."[2] Pope enshrined Gildon as a blockhead in *The Dunciad,* but he too ignored the Sonnets in his edition, leaving them to another hack, the physician George Sewell, to furnish in an appendix volume. It remained for Edmond Malone, justly described as "the prince of Sonnet editors and commentators,"[3] to bring out the first careful edition, complete with annotation. This he did in 1780. Even so, when thirteen years later George Steevens published his fifteen-volume edition, he adamantly refused to admit the Sonnets, sneering,

We have not reprinted the Sonnets, &c. of Shakspeare, because the strongest act of Parliament that could be framed, would fail to compel readers into their service . . . Had Shakspeare produced no other works than these, his name would have reached us with as little celebrity as time has conferred on that of Thomas Watson, an older and much more elegant sonnetteer.[4]

Steevens' low opinion of the sonnet form had previously been abundantly demonstrated in the notes he contributed in 1780 to Malone's *Supplement to the Edition of Shakspeare's Plays Published in 1778*. There (vol. 1, p. 682n.) he wrote: "That a few of these trifles deserving a better character may be found, I shall not venture to deny; for chance cooperating with art and genius, will occasionally produce wonders." Steevens' perversity is fully appreciated, but his opinion of sonnets in general, and of Shakespeare's in particular, provoked no contemporary outrage. I know of no more striking illustration of the changes wrought in sensibility by the whirligig of time. One should perhaps not too lightly discount the possibility one day of a Watson revival.

The great Malone resisted the temptation to speculate on the identity of the poet's mistress; a forbearance that his contemporary George Chalmers would have done well to emulate. Today pretty well forgotten, Chalmers is an interesting minor character, the early biographer of Daniel Defoe and Thomas Paine, and compiler of *Caledonia*, a notable repository of antiquarian Scottish lore. On the subject of Shakespeare's *Sonnets*, however, there befell Chalmers what has afflicted others since: his sanity deserted him. In his *Apology for the Believers in the Shakspeare-Papers* (1797), a tome swollen to over six hundred pages, Chalmers proposes in dead earnest that the Sonnets, apparently all of them, are addressed to Queen Elizabeth. That Shakespeare urges his adored friend to marry and procreate, and that Elizabeth was (by Chalmers' own reckoning) then past sixty, does not deter him. Nor is Chalmers perturbed by the tell-tale masculine pronouns in the poems. The Elizabethans did funny things with pronouns, the Queen was "often considered as a man"—that is, various writers, including Spenser and Bacon, refer to her as a prince—and anyway: "When Shakspeare draws his topics of praise from metaphysics, he is, like other metaphysicians, cold, dark, and unintelligible." Greeted with indifference or derision, Chalmers responded two years later with a six-hundred-page sequel volume, *A Supplemental Apology for the Believers in the Shakspeare-Papers*, in which he reaffirms and elaborates his position. He is one of the moral scholars, his aim being to demonstrate how Shakespeare—"a husband, a father, a moral man"—could not have "addressed a hundred and twenty, nay, a hundred and twenty-six *Amourous* Sonnets to a *male* object." Chalmers even reproduces Sonnet 20 and fails to detect a ribald pun in the concluding couplet:

> But since she [Nature] prick'd thee out for women's pleasure,
> Mine be thy love, and thy love's use their treasure.

"To *prick*," Chalmers sagaciously notes, "is often used by Shakspeare for to *mark*, as indeed the word is used sometimes at present. . . ." As Chalmers elsewhere remarks, apropos of the same issue: "It is for impure minds only, to be continually finding something obscene in objects, that convey nothing obscene, or offensive, to the chastest hearts."[5]

A similarly chaste motive impels the few critics who identify the Sonnets' enchantress with Shakespeare's wife, alternatively referred to as "poor Anne" or "the Stratford beauty." In view of the fact that the guilt-ridden sonnets about lust are even more unsettling—and certainly more puzzling—if inspired by a wife rather than a mistress, the whole endeavor has its self-defeating aspect. Still, the theory is not a dead loss, as it has at least yielded a limerick:

> Bill Shakespeare wrote many a sonnet:
> He gave one, instead of a bonnet,
>   Each Easter to Anne—
>   He gave it—then ran—
> And left her to meditate on it.[6]

More creditable than these wayward fancies are the claims of Mary Fitton, a Victorian favorite. She was one of the Queen's Maids of Honor, but notable neither for maidenhood nor honor; for she became the mistress of William Herbert, the third Earl of Pembroke, and had the mischance to bear him a short-lived son. The Earl, having taken his pleasure, declined matrimony, and the Queen, not amused, made him cool his heels for a while in the Fleet prison. Mary went on to bear Sir Richard Leveson two bastard daughters before marrying a Captain William Polwhele. A contemporary described this mettlesome minx putting off her head-dress, tucking up her clothes, taking a large white cloak, and marching off as a man to her assignation with the Earl. Mary has the right morals—or lack of conventional morals—for the Dark Lady role, but of course this particular identification depends upon acceptance of Pembroke as Fair Youth of the Sonnets. The Earl has not wanted distinguished advocates, and that his claim still thrives is shown by the publication, in 1975, of J. H. Padel's essay on the Sonnets, "That the Thought of Hearts Can Mend," in *The Times Literary Supplement.*

Whatever may be said on behalf of Mary Fitton, this whole episode in literary scholarship has its special interest less because of her than, rather, on account of the obscure individual who championed her cause. Thomas Tyler put the case in his 1890 edition of the Sonnets, which bears every appearance of having been printed at his own expense. And Tyler himself lives because, as a regular reader at the British Museum in the 1880s, he chanced to strike up an acquaintance with a writer of genius. Long afterwards, on the eve of the Great War, Bernard Shaw set down his grotesquely poignant description of this middle-aged gentleman, in a slightly shabby frock coat and tall hat, who was "of such astonishing and crushing ugliness that no one who had once seen him could ever thereafter forget him."

> His figure was rectangular, waistless, neckless, ankleless, of middle height, looking shortish because, though he was not particularly stout, there was nothing slender about him . . . Attached to his face from the left ear to the point of his chin was a monstrous goitre, which hung down to his collar bone, and was very inadequately balanced by a smaller one on his right eyelid . . . When you first met Thomas Tyler you could think of nothing else but whether surgery could really do nothing for him. But after a very brief acquaintance you never thought of his disfigurements at all, and talked to him as you might to Romeo or Lovelace; only, so many people, especially women, would not risk the preliminary ordeal, that he remained a man apart and a bachelor all his days.

A pessimist, Tyler

> delighted in a hideous conception which he called the theory of the cycles, according to which the history of mankind and the universe keeps eternally repeating itself without the slightest variation throughout all eternity; so that he had lived and died and had his goitre before and would live and die and have it again and again and again.[7]

For him Mary Fitton assumed the force of an obsession; the elaborateness and ingenuity of his arguments for her as the Dark Lady can only be suggested here. Accepting (with others) that the reference to a broken bed-vow required Shakespeare's mistress to be married, and aware that 1607, the year of Mary Fitton's wedding, is too late for the Sonnets, Tyler demonstrates, with contortions of ingenuity, that Mary had previously taken a husband, as a young girl, but that this marriage had been declared illegal and void. Tyler detects a pun on Fitton (= the fit one) in the bawdy 151st sonnet, a discovery to which one responds with an involuntary double-take, for the phrase "fit one" does not occur in the poem. He sought out Mary's tomb as Gawsworth in Cheshire, and delightedly announced that her monument, begrimed with the dust of centuries, showed traces of paint indicating her dark hair and complexion. The Tyler story illustrates one of the uses of scholarship: in the arms of this wraith he found solace; Mary Fitton became his surrogate mistress.

She deceived him, as she had misled others. "It would be very desirable," Tyler wrote in his edition, "that Shakespeare's graphic delineation in the Sonnets should be compared with a coloured portrait of Mrs. Fitton, if such could be found, and could be adequately certified."[8] That was in 1890. Seven years later Lady Newdigate-Newdegate, whose husband, Sir Edward, was Mary Fitton's great-great-great-great-great-grandson, reproduced in her *Gossip from a Muniment-Room* two portraits of Mary. They show an English beauty with brunette hair, grey eyes, and fair complexion. For Shaw and others the portraits settled the question, although Tyler continued his lonely crusade—he denounced the pictures as fakes—until he died, "sinking unnoted like a stone in the sea."

Still Tyler's advocacy has won its belated converts, most notably that scoundrel Frank Harris, and Mr. Anthony Burgess has in his *Shakespeare* respectfully cited her candidacy for the role of Dark Lady. But she has yielded to rivals. Inevitably it occurred to someone that the dusky mistress might be black in the sense in which we use that word today. The German poet and novelist, Wilhelm Jordan—author of *Demiurgos,* a work which, according to the 11th *Britannica,* "attempted to deal with the problems of human existence" but "found little favour"—first made the suggestion as early as 1861. He noted the lady's black wires; so her hair must be curly and twisting. "My mistress when she walks treads on the ground," Shakespeare wrote—aha, so she was flat-footed! There is a certain literalness about Jordan, and his preoccupation with race and blood has a dishearteningly familiar aspect. In any event, from these references, as well as other clues— her musical aptitude and "hot-blooded coquetry"—Jordan concluded that the Dark Lady hailed "from the West Indian colonies, [was] of creole descent with an admixture of African blood;" maybe a mulatto or a quadroon.[9] There the matter rested until 1933, when G. B. Harrison came up with a real-life woman from Shakespeare's London: Lucy Negro, a courtesan who plied her trade in the stews of Clerkenwell. A Gray's Inn entertainment of 1594 pays ironical tribute to Lucy as the Abbess of Clerkenwell, with her choir of nuns who, with their burning lamps, chant *placebo* to Inns of Court gallants and other young men-about-town.[10] The possibility of miscegenation involving the National Poet caused predictable unease in some quarters. Hyder Rollins, compelled to report the Black Lady theory, does so with fastidiously controlled distaste. To Edgar I. Fripp, Unitarian minister and Stratford antiquary, there is a way round the embarrassment: the Abbess of Clerkenwell is someone whose loose tongue and manners the poet perhaps observed, and around whom he amusedly wove "his strange, sometimes gross fancies;" not a woman whose dark mysteries he physically explored.[11] Mr. Burgess will have none of such prurient evasions. He takes an artist's view of the putative liaison: "Possibly Shakespeare's falling for a dark skin was no poetic eccentricity [there being no color prejudice in those days], though the initial contact may have come from poetic curiosity."[12]

It remained for Leslie Hotson to track down the Lucy Negro of London's demimonde.[13] He found she was not what her name suggests, but white: one Luce Morgan, who belonged in the late seventies and early eighties to the company of the Queen's familiar gentlewomen, and was more than once favored with gifts from her Majesty. At some time—when is not known—she quit the court in disgrace. Worse and worse days succeeded the former, and Luce Morgan made a new career for herself as madame of a brothel in St. John Street, Clerkenwell. She contracted syphilis and obligingly shared it. In 1600 the Court of Aldermen, in one of their periodic crackdowns on urban immorality, committed this "notorious and lewd woman" to Bridewell, where with other bawds she beat hemp for her hard labor. An epitaph printed in 1656 reports that she turned Catholic and died of the pox, when we don't know. Is this Shakespeare's Dark Lady? Dr. Hotson believes she is, and further (if I read him correctly) that he has removed a stain from Shakespeare's reputation. To Harrison, he declares, belongs "the discredit of believing Shakespeare's fair enslaver a blackamoor." Why discredit? Better, one gathers, that Shakespeare should take up with a syphilitic brothel-keeper than share his bed with a West Indian coquette. But, of course, once the Dark Lady is found to be fair, she ceases to be a Dark Lady, and Mistress Morgan is surely too old, being (by Hotson's calculation) some four years Shakespeare's senior; the Sonnets explore his infatuation with a younger woman. Once again the Dark Lady, seemingly ensnared, has eluded her pursuers.

Other players have drawn scattered applause, then retired to the wings. There is Jacqueline Field, championed by Charlotte Carmichael Stopes, who left it to her daughter Marie to eulogize married love, finding it distasteful herself. Jacqueline was the wife of Richard Field, a former Stratford neighbor of the Shakespeares who had set up shop as a printer in London, and who had published Shakespeare's two early narrative poems. Her sole qualification is that she was French; therefore dark-eyed, sallow complexioned, endowed with indefinable charm, and presumably an enthusiast of *amour*, married or not. It is curious the way this quest invokes the old stereotypes, racial or national. If an aristocrat is preferred to a bourgeois, one may wish to consider the daughter of the first Earl of Essex, Penelope Rich, who (in the discreet words of one memorialist) "had from the first an attenuated regard for the marriage tie." Does not Shakespeare allude to her in Sonnet 146, when he writes, "Within be fed, without be *rich* no more"? Lady Rich is of course Sir Philip Sidney's Stella, and it is doubtful that she made a double killing in the sonnet sweepstakes. She has had few supporters. In fact nobody in recent years has dominated the field. The stage was set for Dr. Rowse.

On January 29, 1973, *The Times* carried a feature article, headed "Revealed at Last, Shakespeare's Dark Lady," by A. L. Rowse. Once published, *The Times* article was summarized in newspapers and magazines the world over. For weeks afterwards the correspondence columns of the paper reverberated with responses—heated, facetious, or merely informative. Even Dame Agatha Christie entered the lists. Dr. Rowse had made a stir.

In his controversial biography of Shakespeare, Dr. Rowse claimed to have solved all the problems of the Sonnets but one; everything "except for the identity of Shakespeare's mistress, which we are never likely to know." That was in 1963. At the Bodleian Library, Dr. Rowse was then working his way through the case-books of Simon Forman. A contemporary of Shake-speare—Forman was born in 1552 and died in 1611—this remarkable indi-vidual was a physician, astrologer, and lecher, at all three of which vocations he enjoyed considerable success. He has long been known to Shakespeare scholars by reason of his manuscript *Book of Plays*, in which he gives eye witness accounts of performances at the Globe of *Macbeth, The Winter's Tale*, and *Cymbeline*. But apparently nobody before Rowse had undertaken to examine the mass of other papers. Here, in one of the case-books, among the mingle-mangle of English and Latin and diagrammed astrological fore-casts, Dr. Rowse discovered his Dark Lady.

She was Emilia Lanier, *née* Bassano, the daughter of Baptist Bassano and Margaret Johnson, who, although unmarried, lived together as man and wife. The Bassanos were a family of court musicians who had come to England from Venice to serve Henry VIII. Their descendants stayed on at court in the same capacity; Baptist's will describes him as "the Queen's musician." Emilia was only six when her father died, and by the time she was seventeen, in 1587, she was an orphan with a dowry of £100—not a negligible sum in those days when a skilled artisan earned sixpence for a day's work—but she was hardly an heiress. She mended her fortune, how-ever, by becoming the mistress of Henry Carey, 1st Lord Hunsdon, then well advanced in years. As Lord Chamberlain he supported the players in their sporadic skirmishes with the municipal authorities, and he was him-self the patron of an acting troupe; for a while, just before his death, in 1596, he sponsored Shakespeare's company, the Chamberlain's men. Find-ing herself pregnant by the noble lord, Emilia (according to Rowse) cov-ered up by taking as a husband a court minstrel, William Lanier, several years her junior. Not surprisingly, the marriage didn't go too well. Emilia told Forman, whom she visited in 1593 to have her horoscope cast, that

> she hath been favoured much of her Majesty and of many noblemen, hath had great gifts and been made much of—a nobleman that is dead hath loved her well and kept her. But her husband hath dealt hardly with her, hath spent and consumed her goods. She is now very needy, in debt and it seems for lucre's sake will be a good fellow, for necessity doth compel.

She will be a good fellow; so she was promiscuous. She was also, Dr. Rowse reported, dark: Forman describing her as "very brown in youth," with "a wart or mole in the pit of the throat or near it." Would she, Emilia asked the wizard, ever be a Lady? Forman, for his part, tried to have *halek* with her, and recorded progress in his case-book. At first she drew away—she was a coquette—but later dispatched her maid to fetch him to her. "I went with them," he records in his diary, "and stayed all night." She told him tales about the invocation of spirits. In January 1600 Emilia Lanier sent for

Forman, and he wondered "whether she intendeth any more villainy." By then he was finished with her.

This, in sum, is the story of Emilia Lanier, as it emerges from the pages of the case-books of the astrologer Simon Forman. His case established, Dr. Rowse re-wrote his 1963 biography of Shakespeare, mainly (one guesses) to give Emilia a showcase, and published it in 1973 as *Shakespeare the Man.* In the preface to the emended second printing he claims that the resurfacing of Emilia "has triumphantly vindicated the answers I have put forward all along, and the method by which they were found . . . The discovery of the Dark Lady completely corroborates, and puts the coping-stone on, my previous findings"—i.e. the chronology of the Sonnets and the identity of Fair Youth, Rival Poet, and Mr. W. H. And a page later, with breathtaking confidence:

> Perhaps I should add now merely that it will be found quite impossible to impugn any of them, for they are the definitive answers. It should be encouraging for research to think that Elizabethan problems, which have awaited their answer for centuries, can still be resolved at this late date.

In the same year Rowse brought out a revised version of his edition of the Sonnets, titled *Shakespeare's Sonnets: The Problems Solved,* complete with paraphrases for those who prefer to read their poems as prose, and with sufficient reference to Emilia in the annotations.

But is she the Dark Lady? She was promiscuous, and her dates do accord with Dr. Rowse's dating of the Sonnets. Coming as she did from a musical family, she may well have been accomplished at the virginals. Dr. Rowse observes that the husband's christian name, William, makes an admirable basis for puns, lending another dimension to the word-play of the Will sonnets:

> Whoever hath her wish, thou hast thy Will,
> And Will to boot, and Will in over-plus.

Over-plus indeed! But Rowse is wrong about the name of the lady's husband: she married Alfonso, not William, Lanier. Alfonso is not such a good name for puns. And was Emilia dark? An odd phrase, "very brown in youth," as though brownness of coloration diminished with the passage of the years. Stanley Wells was the first to look more closely at the words in Forman's diary, which Rowse conveniently reproduced in his *Shakespeare the Man.* The word, Dr. Wells noted, is not *brown* at all, but *brave:* she was very brave in youth. It is not even a very difficult reading. *Brave* here means "splendid," "fine," "showy"; no help. We cannot, then, even say on the basis of the evidence that Emilia Bassano, or Lanier, was dark. So we are left with

a promiscuous lady. There must have been others in Elizabethan London—
else why such an outcry about venereal disease? Even had Dr. Rowse got all
of his facts straight, his argument would have been no more than a tissue of
conjecture, very interesting conjecture, to be sure, but conjecture none the
less. No wonder that *The Times,* which had announced in a front-page
headline "A. L. Rowse discovers Shakespeare's Dark Lady," quickly beat a
prudent retreat, and for the correspondence which followed used the non-
committal heading, "Another Dark Lady."

This episode has a curious aftermath. The facts about Emilia and her
husband were not long in coming to light after Dr. Rowse published his
Shakespeare the Man. The next year, in 1974, he had a chance to retrace his
steps in his biography of Simon Forman. Again he tells Emilia's story. She is
now brave, not brown, and her husband's name is correctly given, in passing, as Alfonso. Nowhere does Dr. Rowse allude to past errors, and about
his thesis he remains impenitent. "I am all the more convinced," he asserts,
". . . that here in this Italianate woman we have the Dark Lady." As one item
of evidence he cites "her brief affair with the player-poet of the Company."[14] Thus what one sets out to prove becomes, almost magically, the
proof itself. In Dr. Rowse's latest life, *Shakespeare the Elizabethan,*[15] speculation is accorded the status of fact, and the dustwrapper duly hails "his
unanswerable identification of Shakespeare's Dark Lady."

III

Emilia Lanier brings to a close my selective survey of Dark Ladies; the
quest, pursued with so much energy, learning, and ingenuity, fizzles out
with yet another failure. Could it have been otherwise? Surely the puzzle
contains too many imponderables to admit of a solution. So long as scholars
continue to debate the identity of Mr. W. H. and the Fair Youth, and to
disagree about the dating of the Sonnets, so long is the Dark Lady likely to
retain her mystery; these problems are interrelated. External evidence
alone—a reference in some contemporary diary or correspondence—can
silence the sceptics, and that is the card some of us were hoping Dr. Rowse
had up his sleeve. Probably it was foolish to think such a card could ever
have existed. Rowse and the others assume that the Sonnets comprise
rhymed fourteen-line entries in a personal diary, and that their revelations
represent the raw materials of experience. But poets wear masks. May not
much of what is intimate about these poems be private and interior, and
what is exterior—derived from the world of events—transmuted and ordered by the implacable necessities of art? The opposition between Fair
Youth and Dark Lady is, after all, comprehensible in terms of poetic and
moral symbolism; whether or not Shakespeare in his own life kept a mistress of this hue, he required her services for his poetry. I wouldn't wish to

suggest a simple choice between the Sonnets as autobiographical record and the Sonnets as literary exercises, although critics have been drawn towards these polarities. Polarities are reductive. Between them exist innumerable gradations, which should wonderfully serve to encourage caution, the biographical virtue Dr. Rowse most conspicuously lacks. In conflating art with life, he and his predecessors run the risk of being no less naïve than the visitors to Verona who gaze, moved, at Juliet's balcony.

Must we then in the last resort conclude with Edward Dowden, "We shall never discover the name of that woman"?[16] Perhaps so. (Dowden's perjorative *that* is symptomatic. Commentators tend to endorse without hesitation the poet's estimate of his mistress; her whorish nature is a commonplace of criticism. But of course we see her only through the eyes of her restlessly dissatisfied lover; she is a creation of the male ego. Could she speak, the mistress' view of herself, her lover, and the affair might instructively differ.) One can appreciate J. W. Mackail's unillusioned judgment that "all the labour that has been spent upon it [her pursuit] is pure waste."[17] In his recent (1977) edition of *Shakespeare's Sonnets,* Stephen Booth takes a similar line, thus demonstrating a reticence not otherwise greatly evident in his stimulating if over-elaborate commentary. "Speculation on her identity," Booth tersely remarks, "has ranged from wanton to ludicrous and need not be illustrated."[18]

Perhaps I have unwisely failed to heed these counsels, although I would hope that something might be said in defense of my approach. A contemporary of Shakespeare speaks of "God's revenging aspect upon every particular sin to the despair and confusion of mortality." If I have sported with folly rather than sin, the theme has its Jehovan aspect: we witness the consequences of credulity and error, and are accordingly chastened. That is to emphasize the negative. The quest for the Dark Lady has brought its own scholarly rewards, although ironically these are not what the questors sought. They have recovered Mary Fitton and Luce Morgan and Emilia Lanier, and surely we should be grateful to them for retrieving from the buried past these vital and passionate women; minor personages no doubt, and ones who did not influence the sweep of public events, but such obscure lives convey some of the flavor of history which the careers of princes and prelates cannot.

There is more to it. When Dr. Rowse published his findings about Emilia, a university lecturer in Belfast, Roger Prior, pursued the trail a little further, and discovered that in 1611 she had published a slender volume of poems, *Salve Deus Rex Judaeorum.* This quarto survives in eight copies, several of them defective. As the title indicates, the temper of the poems is religious, with the authoress taking a stern line with respect to "wicked worldlings" and "the imbracements of unchaste desires." If she has had a past, she doesn't much sound like the Dark Lady, although Dr. Rowse (as he is entitled) thinks otherwise. What is pertinent is that these poems, which have gone unnoticed for three and a half centuries, have some character. An individual voice speaks, a feminist voice at that:

> Not that I Learning to my selfe assume,
> Or that I would compare with any man:
> But as they are Scholers, and by Art do write,
> So Nature yeelds my Soule a sad delight.[19]

Dr. Rowse would persuade us that Emilia is the second female poet of the Elizabethan age, after Sidney's sister, the Countess of Pembroke. Maybe so. Certainly the poems should find an editor. Thus we have looked for a Dark Lady, and instead we find a lady poet. We seek verifiable truth, and settle for the consolations of art. In a Keatsian sense we have perhaps not gone too far astray.[20]

NOTES

1. James Winny, *The Master Mistress: A Study of Shakespeare's Sonnets* (London, 1968), p. 27.

2. Charles Gildon, 'Remarks on the Poems of *Shakespear*', in William Shakespeare, *Works*, ed. Nicholas Rowe (London, 1709–10), vol. VII, p. 446. Hyder Edward Rollins puts Gildon and the legions of *Sonnets* editors and commentators in perspective in his New Variorum edition of the *Sonnets* (Philadelphia and London, 1944). Rollins's own commentary is indispensable for any study of the textual and interpretative history of these poems, although of course much (from which I have profited) has appeared since 1944. I have previously considered the identification of the personages of the *Sonnets* in the context of the history of Shakespearean biography in *Shakespeare's Lives* (Oxford, 1970); for the historian it is an agreeable luxury to re-survey some of the terrain after an interval of years, and to bring the story (at least as regards the Dark Lady) up to date.

3. John Dover Wilson, Introduction to the New Cambridge Shakespeare edition of the *Sonnets* (Cambridge, 1966), p. xi.

4. Shakespeare, *Plays*, ed. Samuel Johnson and George Steevens (London, 1793), vol. I, Advertisement, pp. vii–viii.

5. George Chalmers, *An Apology for the Believers in the Shakspeare-Papers* (London, 1797), pp. 42–66; *A Supplemental Apology for the Believers in the Shakspeare-Papers* (London, 1799), pp. 21, 55–63.

6. Brainerd McKee, *Shakespeare in Limerick* (London, 1910), no. XXXVI; cited by Rollins, *Sonnets*, vol. II, pp. 259–60n.

7. Bernard Shaw, *Misalliance, The Dark Lady of the Sonnets, and Fanny's First Play* (London, 1914), pp. 104–5.

8. Shakespeare, *Sonnets*, ed. Thomas Tyler (London, 1890), p. 80n.

9. Wilhelm Jordan, *Shakespeare's Gedichte* (Berlin, 1861), pp. 413–15; summarized (with translated extracts) by Rollins, *Sonnets*, vol. II, p. 243.

10. G. B. Harrison, *Shakespeare Under Elizabeth* (New York, 1933), pp. 64, 310n.

11. Edgar I. Fripp, *Shakespeare: Man and Artist* (London, 1938), vol. I, pp., 262–63. Rollins (*Sonnets*, vol. II, p. 272) disparagingly notes that Fripp makes no reference to Harrison; but the former, who died two years before Harrison's book was published, came up with the suggestion, somewhat laundered, on his own.

12. Anthony Burgess, *Shakespeare* (London, 1970), p. 146.

13. Leslie Hotson, *Mr. W. H.* (London, 1964), pp. 244–55.

14. A. L. Rowse, *Simon Forman: Sex and Society in Shakespeare's Age* (London, 1974), p. 117. When, in 1973, *Shakespeare the Man* was "Reprinted with alterations", Rowse corrected "brave", and Emilia is now married to "Alfonso Lanier"; but Sonnet 135 still "plays upon the fact that there are two Wills: her husband and Will Shakespeare" (p. 94).

15. London, 1977.

16. Shakespeare, *Sonnets,* ed. Edward Dowden (London, 1881), p. 17.

17. J. W. Mackail, *Lectures on Poetry* (London, 1911), p. 188; cited by Rollins, *Sonnets,* vol. II, p. 251.

18. *Shakespeare's Sonnets,* ed. Stephen Booth (New Haven and London, 1977), p. 549.

19. Emilia Lanier, *Salve Deus Rex Judaeorum* (London, 1611), sig. b1ᵛ. The title-page describes her as "Mistris *Aemilia Lanyer,* Wife to Captaine *Alfonso Lanyer* Servant to the Kings Majestie." Rowse gives an account of the poems in his *Simon Forman,* pp. 104–16.

20. I wish to thank I. A. Shapiro and am grateful to the late T.J.B. Spencer for helpful comments when this paper, in a somewhat different form, was given as a public lecture.

(1980)

5

Richard II and the Realities of Power

There is a scene in an Elizabethan play on the reign of Richard II—the play, anonymous and without title, of uncertain date and theatrical provenance, now commonly called *Woodstock* or *Thomas of Woodstock*—in which one of the caterpillars of the commonwealth enters the royal presence poring over a book. "How now, what readst thou, Bushy?" asks the King. To which his favorite replies:

> The monument of English Chronicles,
> Containing acts and memorable deeds
> Of all your famous predecessor kings.[1]

This book—is it Holinshed (a bit large for the purpose) or Stow evoked in a kind of surreal flash-forward?—holds examples, strange and wonderful, of treason and conquest applicable to Richard's own predicament. The information on which he eagerly seizes, however, is more prosaic. Bushy reads: "Upon the 3rd of April 1365 was Lord Richard, son of the Black Prince, born at Bordeaux." "1365 . . .," muses the King, "What year is this?" (This is one of those plays in which characters ask the year, presumably more for the spectators' benefit than their own; it is not dramaturgy of a Shakespearean order.) The year, it turns out, is 1387. Thus does it dawn on Richard that he has reached his majority. He can now claim his birthright, the throne of England, and set in motion the catastrophic sequence of events which will lead to his fall.

The episode illustrates the education of a prince and furnishes another instance—if one were needed—of the uses of literacy. The sequel in *Woodstock* properly reminds us of the caution we must exercise in making use of written memorials. Woodstock yields up the mace of his office of Lord Protector (an office that the historical Woodstock did not enjoy) with good grace, but not without glancing skeptically at the authority which the King has consulted:

> And yet I think I have not wronged your birthright:
> For if the times were searched, I guess your grace
> Is not so full of years till April next.[2]

In truth our source-materials are often enough ambiguous, confused, or contradictory. A note of complaint is heard early. "This tragicall example," William Baldwin remarks on Mowbray's "tragedy" in *The Mirror for Magistrates,* "was of all the cumpany well liked, how be it a doubte was founde therein, and that by meanes of the diversity of the Chronicles: for where as maister Hall whom in this storye we chiefly folowed, maketh Mowbray accuser, and Boleynbroke appellant, mayster Fabian reporteth the matter quite contrary, & that by the reporte of good authours, makyng Boleynbroke the accuser, and Mowbray the appellant."[3] What can a moral poet do? Leave such matters to the experts who have access to the documents, trust to the best authorities, and go about his proper business of discouraging vice and exalting virtue. For the modern scholar, deprived of the consolations of didacticism, the solution is not so straightforward.

I

I have turned to the reign of Richard II for the induction to my paper, and it is Shakespeare's play on Richard that is my subject here. It seemed an especially appropriate choice. In bodying-forth on the stage the *fons et origo* of the Wars of the Roses and the other tumultuous events that occupy Shakespeare through eight historical dramas, *Richard II* stands in much the same formal relation to the sequence as does the "Introduction" (and first year) of the history of Henry IV in Edward Hall's vast chronicle of *The Union of the Two Noble and Illustre Families of Lancaster and York.* The deposition of a reigning monarch is (as events in America have lately reminded us) a fearful thing, intrinsically dramatic, immense in itself, and also immense in its consequences. It invokes great themes and issues: the Divine Right of Kings, the falls of princes, and the destiny of a nation, and invites us to meditate on the mysteries of historical causation, as a later poet did in his great sonnet on Leda and the Swan.

Such a subject has its disabilities too, though, for *Richard* cannot be reckoned one of Shakespeare's more neglected plays. It has been explicated by authorities with a more profound grasp of historical and philosophical contexts than may be claimed by the present writer, who has lately concerned himself with such unprofound (indeed unliterary) matters as the number of elm-trees in Shakespeare's Stratford, when brick first came into use as a building material in Warwickshire, and how a dramatist living in Bishopsgate ward managed to escape paying his rates. Anyway, isn't it an illusion, under the best of circumstances, to hope to say anything excitingly novel about one of Shakespeare's major plays? The excitingly novel has a way of being excitingly wrong, or tendentious, or beside the point. So Ernst Kantorowicz, in his celebrated study of the mystic fiction of the King's two bodies, applied to *Richard II* a point in medieval political theology of which I—and I dare say a number of others—had hitherto been ignorant; but I remain unpersuaded that the vast erudition brought to bear really illuminates Shakespeare's drama, pleasing as is an unexpected encounter with such recondite lore.

Of course an alternative to being excitingly off-base is to be correctly dull. It is not enough, especially in such a context, to reiterate pedestrian commonplaces with minor variations. The time is propitious for something a little bolder, for fresh breezes are blowing through scholarship on Shakespeare's English histories. In a recent review-article Professor Cyrus Hoy has likened the Shakespeare canon to a modern urban landscape—"the tragic monuments have never lacked attention," Hoy observes, but "the historical business sector has in recent years become something of a critical slum."[4] This is perhaps to exaggerate a point for the sake of an ingenious metaphor; if the histories are a slum, then a number of able citizens have gone slumming. But it is true that the seminal contributions of Tillyard and Lily Bess Campbell established an orthodoxy, and accustomed a generation to view the two tetralogies as dramatic recapitulations of the Tudor myth of history, or mirrors of Elizabethan policy. Now we seem to have entered a revisionist phase, exemplified by the stimulating first chapter of Robert Ornstein's *A Kingdom for a Stage*. Tillyard has been enduring his knocks of late, and we are invited to take another, and different, view of the achievement of the history plays. Thus thesis breeds counter-thesis. This is well and good; it keeps the pot bubbling. Eventually, I expect, we shall look again at Tillyard, more disinterestedly, extrapolate what is of lasting value, and absorb it into the critical stream. Thus we have synthesis. It is what may be described as the Hegelian tendency in Shakespeare studies. Meanwhile Hoy is no doubt right to see the appearance of Ornstein's book as a liberating phenomenon.

These are large issues. My own objectives are more limited. I propose to look once again at two historical considerations that have been looked at often enough in the past: the matter of Richard, and the revival of a play about Richard II on the eve of the Essex rebellion. Finally I shall argue for a modest adjustment of interpretative emphasis as regards an aspect of Shakespeare's art that has been—dare I say it?—comparatively underestimated. My emphasis must be on *modest* and *comparatively*.

II

If Richard was not a popular king in his own time, he seems to have stirred a good deal of popular interest two centuries later. "Certainly," Dover Wilson says in his introduction to the New Cambridge edition, "*Richard II* took London by storm when it first appeared"; also that Shakespeare's tragedy had become "the talk of the town before December 1595."[5] Dangerous word, *certainly*. The Chamberlain's men had no Henslowe to record for posterity the takings at the Theatre, and the age boasted no show-biz weekly to report the latest sensation in Shoreditch or on Bankside.

If *Richard II* was the talk of the town in 1595, that talk has not been jotted down in any correspondence which has survived. Still, the play clearly made a strong impact. Three quarto editions issued from the presses in 1597 and 1598, and another two before Shakespeare's death.

Interest in Richard and his reign was of long standing, as is evidenced by the rich mix of sources, possible sources, near misses, and analogues to Shakespeare's play. In addition to the usual English chronicles—Hall and Holinshed—there are no fewer than three French accounts, including the *Chroniques* of Jean Froissart. This last, Shakespeare very likely consulted in Lord Berners' translation. There is also, in the library of Gray's Inn, a narrative in Latin of "The Deposition of Richard." Daniel's *First Four Books of the Civil Wars between the Two Houses of Lancaster and York* deal at length with Richard, setting forth "His Unckles pride, his greedie Minions gaine, / *Glosters* revolt, & death . . . ," Bolingbroke's exile and return, and the usurpation. In *The Mirror for Magistrates* the first five of the "sundrye Un-fortunate Englishe men" who deliver their laments are Richard and those around him. One learned investigator of the sources of Shakespeare's *Richard II* concluded, after duly weighing the evidence, that the playwright consulted no fewer than seven accounts.[6] The reckoning probably errs on the side of numerosity, but suggests the complexity of the task to which Professor Bullough has addressed himself with such superlative skill.

If anything emerges forcibly from the array of source-matter, it is the absence of consensus. Men and events are variously evaluated. In Dover Wilson's summation, "two legends about the character of Richard II have come down to us from the fifteenth century: that of his supporters, which represented him as a saint and a martyr, compared his sufferings and death with those of Christ himself, while they accounted for his capture by an act of base betrayal; and secondly, that of the Lancastrians which depicted him as a weak, cowardly, moody man who surrendered himself and abdicated of his own free will."[7] This ignores, however, the shades between. Opinions also differ about the men around the protagonist. To the chronicler Graf-ton, Thomas of Woodstock was an "honorable and good man miserable put to death, which for the honor of the King and wealth of the realme had taken great travayles"; but Daniel describes the same Woodstock as

> one most violent,
> Impatient of command, of peace, of rest,
> Whose brow would shew, that which his hart had ment:
> His open malice & repugnant brest
> Procurd much mischiefe by his discontent.[8]

As with narrative, so with dramatic portrayals of the reign. Richard figures in several plays. "Sir, findinge that you wer not convenientlie to be at London to morrow night," Sir Edward Hoby wrote to Sir Robert Cecil from his house in Cannon Row on December 7, 1595, "I am bold to send to knowe whether Teusdaie may be anie more in your grace to visit poore Channon rowe where as late as it shal please you a gate for your supper shal be open: & K. Richard present him selfe to your vewe."[9] Eminent authorities, Chambers among them, have assumed that Hoby is referring to a private performance of Shakespeare's *Richard II* for the delectation of the great, but Hoby doesn't mention Shakespeare, nor is it clear whether the play—if it is that—is old or new, or even whether the Richard alluded to was the second of that name, although likely enough it was. Such uncertainties should wonderfully encourage scholarly agnosticism. We are on safer ground in looking at the two extant plays (besides Shakespeare's) in which Richard appears, and the play about him witnessed by Simon Forman at the Globe.

Of unknown authorship and date, *The Life and Death of Jack Straw* (printed in 1593) limits itself to the Peasants' Revolt. The play is short, but few can have wished it longer. It has been attributed to George Peele, mainly (one guesses) on the unstated grounds that any play, mediocre or worse, from the early nineties that happens to be knocking around without an author had better be ascribed to George Peele. Still, the concept of Richard in *Jack Straw* holds interest. The young king is shown as an exemplary character, magnanimously dispensing free pardons to all but the ringleaders of unnatural rebellion; such compassion in a prince reminds the King's swordbearer of "The gladsome sunne-shine in a winters day."[10] It is not the only instance in the play of the sun imagery we associate with Richard.[11]

Another and less sympathetic Richard is presented to view in *Woodstock*. This headstrong youth neglects crown and kingdom as he gives himself up to "wild and antic habits": aping foreign manners, feasting boon companions and hangers-on at Westminster Hall while the commons starve, extorting revenues with odious blank charters, and—ultimate irresponsibility—farming out his realm, at a fixed rent, to self-serving flatterers. The pejorative most frequently attached to him is "wanton." Eventually he becomes a "wanton tyrant," although he is never seen as irredeemably committed to evil ways.[12] In contrast, his uncle Gloucester, plain Thomas of Woodstock, represents the homely English virtues. It is distinctly a minority view of Woodstock that this playwright provides. Stage imagery reinforces the thematic point. The bearded elders contrast with the spruce, clean-shaven courtiers; Green at one point proposes making it high treason for any greybeard to loiter within forty feet of the court gates. Woodstock's homespun clothing—he wears a country habit of English frieze—betokens the traditional values under assault. On the other hand, the king's favorites are fantastically tricked out in Polonian peaks, and jewelry chains that join knee with toe, and "so toeify the knee and so kneeify the toe, that between both it makes a most methodical coherence, or coherent method." Inevitably fashions, as men, collide: a foppishly attired courtier on horseback mistakes

Woodstock for a groom, and offers him sixpence to take and walk the beast. One of Woodstock's virtues is thrift, and later he claims his sixpence—"promise is a *promise.*" In the end he is conveyed to Calais, and there murdered at Richard's behest. The King in this play, unlike that of *Jack Straw,* is neither merciful nor just. When he experiences the twinges of conscience, and orders a reprieve, it comes, like Edmund's, too late.

The play on Richard II that Simon Forman saw on April 30, 1611, has not come down, but he has left a characteristic description of it in his "Book of Plays." Dr. A. L. Rowse, who in Forman has found a biographical subject worthy of his mettle, does not doubt that this performance was of Shakespeare's *Richard.*[13] But Dr. Rowse is not conspicuously given to doubt, and the play described by Forman differs in so many essentials from Shakespeare's that no theory of revision—always a dubious mode of rationalizing a conviction—can reconcile the two. The play at the Globe seems to have covered the whole of Richard's reign, for Forman refers to the overthrow of Jack Straw as well as to the triumph of Bolingbroke (events separated by nearly twenty years). Whether the play is old or new Forman does not say. In it Gaunt is a secret contriver of villainy who sets Richard and the nobles together by the ears, his aim being to make his own son king. This Gaunt is the sort who, having consulted a wise man about the future of his house, and having got his answer, "hanged him up for his labor, because he should not brute yt abrod or speke therof to others." Richard himself is not much behindhand when it comes to policy:

> Remember also, when the duke [Gloucester] and Arundell cam to London with their Army, king Richard came forth to them and met them and gave them fair wordes, and promised them fair pardon and that all should be well yf they wold discharge their Army, upon whose promises and faier Speaches they did yt, and Affter the king byd them all to A banket and soe betraid them And Cut of their heades, &c, because they had not his pardon under his hand & sealle before but his worde.[14]

This episode eerily reminds us of the ruthless equivocation of Prince John at Gaultree Forest.

Forman is an unreliable reporter, capable of confusing what he has seen with what he has read.[15] Still, from the sum of the reports, playtexts, chronicles, and other accounts comprising the matter of Richard, it is clear that he could be variously represented: we have virtuous Richard, wanton Richard, and cunning Richard; the weak king, the politic king, the would-be despot. So too with others in the *dramatis personae.* Gaunt is patriot or self-seeker; Woodstock, a loyal peer or malevolent trouble-fomenter. Such latitude of interpretation should serve to discourage the historical critic from facile generalizations about how the Elizabethans assessed their past.

If for the scholar the contradictions in the sources are at times vexatious, for the artist they must have had a liberating effect, and invited him to explore the complexities of character and motive we in fact find in Shakespeare's Richard. My point is a corollary of one made by Ornstein in his recent book when he complains of "the inherent bias of the historical method toward what is conventional and orthodox in Elizabethan culture, because any search for the 'norms' of Elizabethan thought must lead to a consensus of truisms and pieties."[16] Only here we do not even find the coveted norms.

III

Shakespeare's *Richard II* seems to have had several special performances in the author's lifetime. Sir Edward Hoby possibly refers to one in his letter already cited. Another took place on the high seas. In 1607 the *Dragon, Hector,* and *Consent,* bound for the East Indies, cast anchor off Sierra Leone. On September 30 William Keeling, captain of the *Dragon,* recorded in his journal, "Captain Hawkins [of the *Hector*] dined with me, wher my companions acted Kinge Richard the Second."[17] (On two other occasions the same thespians played *Hamlet,* once to the accompaniment of a fish dinner.) But the most celebrated revival of *Richard* was that mounted by the Lord Chamberlain's men at the Globe Playhouse on Saturday, February 7, 1601. The circumstances are described by Augustine Phillips, the actor who bore Shakespeare such affectionate regard that he bequeathed to him a thirty-shilling piece in gold. According to Phillips, some half-dozen men of position in the land—including the Percies (Sir Charles and Sir Jocelyn) and Lord Monteagle—had approached the players, offering them a reward of 40*s* "to have the play of the deposyng and kyllyng of Kyng Rychard the second to be played the Saterday next."[18] The actors hesitated, "holdyng that play of Kyng Richard to be so old & so long out of use as that they shold have small or no Company at yt," but in the end they consented. The purpose of the revival, as we all know, was to further sedition. At noon that Saturday the conspirators met for dinner, and afterwards repaired to the playhouse, where they applauded the downfall and murder of a king. "So earnest hee was," Francis Bacon said of one, Sir Gelly Meyrick, "to satisfie his eyes with the sight of that tragedie which hee thought soone after his lord should bring from the stage to the state, but that God turned it upon their owne heads." Meyrick was steward to the Earl of Essex. On Sunday the attempted coup took place. Shakespeare's troupe collected their £2. Essex and others were tried and executed. On the eve of the Earl's beheading the Lord Chamberlain's men acted before the Queen at Whitehall. We do not know which play; presumably not *Richard II.*

Most authorities agree that the performance bespoken by the conspirators was of Shakespeare's *Richard II.* It is not unusual to find this information given as a fact. We do well, however, to recognize that we are dealing not with a fact but an inference. Neither Phillips nor anyone else interviewed at the time mentions Shakespeare's name in connection with the event. Prosecutor Coke muddies the waters slightly when he speaks of "the story of *Henry IV* being set forth in a play," but as Bolingbroke becomes king before the end of *Richard II,* that is accountable. There is of course no reason why there should not have been other plays on this interesting theme which, like the one seen by Forman, failed to achieve print: and the designation of the one acted on February 7 as "old" opens up the whole vista of Elizabethan theatrical history. But the company in this instance was Shakespeare's, Phillips' description suits Shakespeare's *Richard II,* and no alternative possibility presents itself for consideration. So in what follows I shall assume that the "old" *Richard II* wheeled out for the Essex *Putsch* was by Shakespeare, while not claiming more than that this is a plausible assumption.

To do so disposes of one problem only to raise another. Why *Richard II?* After all, the play hardly comes across as an inflammatory tract in favor of deposition and regicide. Richard in his sufferings is too sympathetic, and ultimately (at Pomfret Castle) heroic, while Bolingbroke in his triumph is too ambiguous. It seems an odd choice to rouse the rabble. Scholarly unease is understandable. "I do not know the answer to the riddle," Lily B. Campbell confesses, and to Irving Ribner "Shakespeare's relation to the Essex rebellion remains a puzzling problem which has yet to be satisfactorily settled."[19] This may be so, but we do well to bear in mind that the revival in fact failed to kindle seditious sparks; if such was the conspirators' intention, it was one of many miscalculations. More likely, perhaps, that they were thinking of themselves rather than of the multitude, and sought by reviving a play about a successful deposition to buoy up their own spirits on the eve of the desperate adventure.

Yet might there not be another dimension, perilous to ignore and even more perilous to face? Many critics have fancied Shakespeare as moving about comfortably in the corridors of power, playfully taking the mickey out of the Sir Walter Raleigh set in *Love's Labor's Lost,* concocting a suitable wedding entertainment for the dowager Countess of Southampton with *A Midsummer Night's Dream,* or advising King James on the respective merits of mercy and justice in *Measure for Measure.* The list might be extended, and there are recent additions. Such speculations, showing Shakespeare hobnobbing with the mighty, represent what might be described as the Richard Ryan syndrome in Shakespeare studies. In his *Dramatic Table Talk* (in 1825) Ryan recorded an anecdote of Queen Elizabeth trying to catch Shakespeare's eye while he was acting at the playhouse, and resorting to the timeworn female ruse of dropping her glove; her favorite (we are told) picked it up and presented it to her, but not without first declaiming, "And though now bent on this high embassy, / Yet *stoop* we to take up our *Cousin's* glove!" It is not what one would describe as a very probable story. The Ryan syndrome is nevertheless very prominent in Shakespeare studies; it has enlisted some choice spirits, and has illuminated the contexts for the plays if not always the plays themselves. Now Professor Richard Levin in several essays has been casting a cold eye on the whole phenomenon, to which he gives the term "occasionalism." Skeptical reappraisal along these lines is long overdue, and we do well to pay heed to Professor Levin's home truths.

But what of *Richard II,* which was used in Shakespeare's own day as a move in a power struggle? Here the connection is direct, not fancied. Might not Richard's reign (in the dramatist's conception) stand in an analogical relation to Elizabeth's reign, and animadvert obliquely—as censorship enforced—on actual persons and events? Of course the trouble with oblique commentaries is that they are oblique; we may miss what is there and find what is not. To his *D.N.B.* biographer the content of the Elizabethan historian John Hayward's *Life and Reign of King Henry IV* looks innocent enough of veiled allusiveness, and even a contemporary, Chamberlain, wondered what all the fuss was about.

Such considerations serve only to whet pursuit, and the trail, in truth, is not an utter blank. "I am Richard II. know ye not that?" the Queen declared in Lambarde's presence, and she was not the first to make the comparison. As early as 1578 Sir Francis Knollys complained to Elizabeth's secretary that the Queen persisted in misliking safe counsel—in such circumstances "who woll not rather shrynkingly . . . play the partes of King Richard the Second's men, then to enter into the odious office of crossing of her Majesties' wylle?" (To be one of Richard's men is to be a sycophant; there are other such references.) Knollys was related to the Queen, and also the grandfather of the Earl of Essex. The latter traced his descent from Anne, daughter of Thomas of Woodstock, the Duke of Gloucester, sixth son of Edward III—the same Thomas of Woodstock who had his life snuffed out at Calais by Richard's command. And were not Elizabeth's hands, like Richard's, stained with "guilt of kindred blood?" "The slaying of kindred here [i.e., in *Richard II*] . . . was probably intended to remind Elizabethans of the execution of Mary, Queen of Scots." This suggestion was made almost half a century ago, by Evelyn May Albright, in what remains the most elaborate investigation of the Richard-Elizabethan analogy in relation to the play put on for the Essex conspiracy.[20] Miss Albright further notes that complaints about the influence of favorites, about oppressive taxes, and about the exaction of benevolences—all made in Shakespeare's *Richard II*—find their parallels in agitation about Elizabeth's government. There is even a passing reference to "the prevention of poor Bolingbroke / About his marriage" (2.1.167–68), and we all know how Elizabeth meddled in marriages. From such hints it is but an easy leap to interpreting York's speech in Act 2, scene 1—the speech about the consequences of Richard's seizure of "The royalties and rights of banish'd

Hereford"—as "a warning to Elizabeth" concerning "a popular favorite whom she is treating badly, and whose family also have been unfairly dealt with." And who might that favorite be other than Essex?

This is heady stuff for which some evidence, besides the detection of covert allusions in Shakespeare's text, would be welcome. Such evidence has been offered in the form of Hayward's history of Henry IV, to which I have already referred. His book was published with a brief Latin dedication to Essex, in which the latter is extolled as the expectancy and rose of the fair state. Hayward's title is a misnomer, presumably prudential, for his history deals mostly with Richard's reign, not Henry's. That the work deliberately exploited the Elizabeth-Richard analogy was widely believed at the time; we hear of this "seditious pamphlet" and "treasonable book." "He selecteth a storie 200 yere olde," noted Sir Edward Coke, "and publisheth it this last yere; intendinge the application of it to this tyme."[21] Elizabeth, outraged, wanted Hayward executed, and were it not for Bacon's discreet intervention, he probably would have been. As it was, not until after Elizabeth's death was Hayward released from prison to assemble the prayers and meditations of the enlarged *Sanctuary of a Troubled Soul*. Shakespeare and his fellows do not seem to have got into any trouble at all, which is odd if he was up to mischief similar to that for which Hayward was tried. Never mind; perhaps some neutral party, high up, intervened to get Shakespeare off the hook. Such a party has lately been suggested in the person of the Keeper of the Rolls; the same William Lambarde to whom Elizabeth made her famous protestation.[22]

What remains is to demonstrate that Hayward's *Henry IV* was one of Shakespeare's sources when he came to write *Richard II*. We are shown parallels as regards general ideas, groupings of ideas, echoes of words and phrases, the characterization of Bolingbroke, and a couple of specific episodes (Henry's repudiation of Piers of Exton, and Aumerle's supposed duplicity with Richard at Flint Castle). Some of these hold interest. There is a problem, however, and that is that Hayward's *Life and Reign of King Henry IV* was first published in 1599; three or four years after Shakespeare composed his play. Such a fact might ordinarily be deemed awkward, but there is a way round it, and that is to posit that the history circulated in manuscript for some years before being printed, and that Shakespeare saw and used it. Otherwise we might be tempted to account for the parallels as Hayward's borrowings from Shakespeare. There is nothing like a hypothetical manuscript to resolve an awkwardness of chronology. Only in this case the awkwardness remains, for Hayward is on record as saying that he had begun "to write this history about a year before it was published, but had intended it a dozen years before, although he acquainted no man therewith."[23] One might reckon that such a statement would successfully discourage enthusiasm for the theory of Hayward's influence on Shakespeare, but this would be to underestimate scholarly ingenuity. In the phrase *although he acquainted no man therewith,* maybe *therewith* refers to the interval but not to Hayward's materials? I think not. Yet Ribner, in what is the standard study of the English history play in Shakespeare's age, can suggest that there is "some possibility" that Shakespeare saw Hayward's *Henry IV* in manuscript—a manuscript that did not then exist.

Nor, although properly wary, does Ribner rule out the Albright thesis altogether. During the past year somebody has written that "Shakespeare's connection with the Essex affair was all too obvious through his praise of the Earl in *Henry V* and his authorship of the deposition scene in *Richard II*," and he goes on to speak of Shakespeare's "partisanship" for Essex.[24] It is one of many odd statements in a curious book. How many innocent spectators, standing at a play and caught up in the great issues of drama, would pause to reflect on Essex's descent from Gloucester's line, or apply passing references to abuses of Richard's rule to the politics of the moment? I don't see Shakespeare as a seditious playwright involved, however peripherally, in a conspiracy against his monarch, any more than I see him as a darling of the Court, a sort of minister without portfolio, sagely advising his Queen, and later his King, on how to manage the affairs of state. I expect that he had his hands full writing his plays, acting in them and in those of others, and as "housekeeper" advising his troupe about affairs in which we know he had a stake.

This is not to say that he failed to interest himself in the world of policy and power. That world was all around him. He found it chronicled in Plutarch and the Tudor historians. Machiavelli analyzed it. Perhaps Shakespeare glimpsed it, as an observant bystander, when his company performed at Court, or were called upon to fulfill some ceremonial function, as when they attended upon the new Spanish ambassador and his train at Somerset House in August 1604. These opportunities he seized upon, not for political advantage by insinuating himself into the affairs of state, but imaginatively, for the purposes of his art, in which we find depicted the world of policy and power. Here, behind the scenes of public confrontation, as likely as not another drama—concealed or only obliquely revealed—is going on. In that drama the issues may be graver than those overtly bandied about. Such moments show Shakespeare's sophisticated grasp of the workings of *Realpolitik*. So it is in *Richard II,* especially in the big public scenes of the first act.

IV

"I cannot believe," Yeats wrote, "that Shakespeare looked on his Richard II. with any but sympathetic eyes, understanding indeed how ill-fitted he was to be King, at a certain moment of history, but understanding that he was lovable and full of capricious fancy. . . ."[25] "What explains his failure to oppose Bolingbroke at all, his sudden collapse, as soon as the threat of deposition becomes real, into a state of sheer elegy, of pure poetry?" asks

Mark Van Doren. "The answer is simple. Richard is a poet, not a king."[26] These views have much in common; they are expressed by poets with an understandable sympathy for poetical characters. But of course in a blank-verse play the characters, unless they be peasants, usually speak in numbers. Mainly criticism emphasizes Richard's weakness. The position has been lately put by Robert Ornstein in the book to which I have already referred. "The first scene of *Richard II* intimates the King's shallowness and weakness. . . ." Or: "Precisely why Richard chooses to halt the joust between Bolingbroke and Mowbray at the very last moment we do not know, but we recognize the characteristic theatricality of the gesture: here is the weakling's pleasure in commanding (and humiliating) men stronger than himself."[27] Ornstein makes other remarks to the same effect, and together these restate, with more than usual eloquence and sensitivity, a dominant consensus. Now, one should very warily go about differing from views with widespread (even if less than universal) acceptance, for they are quite likely to be correct. So it is with some diffidence that I suggest that in Act 1, in the council chamber at Windsor and at the lists in Coventry, Richard displays as much political acumen as weakness, that his behavior is not capricious but calculated, and that he does not fail but achieves a success necessarily limited by the realities of his situation.[28]

It is no use trying to evaluate a man's strength or weakness without reference to the circumstances that determine the options he can exercise. Richard may prattle about Divine Right, but in his world power is wielded not divinely, but by men; those men in whose presence Richard goes through the rhetoric of public gestures. In the first scene Richard's maneuverability is limited by an episode from his past which has come back to haunt him. The past, whether in the form of an untoward incident on the road to Thebes or indiscreet conversations in the illusory privacy of the Oval Office, has a way of doing just that to men of exalted station. The problem for Richard, lovable poet and weakling, is that he is responsible for the murder of his uncle Gloucester, and everybody knows it. This fact Shakespeare chooses to treat indirectly, as befits the evasions of power struggles. Although Richard's embarrassment affects the conduct of all the principals, they remain silent on this score; it is rather as though the dramatist expected his audience to have made mental notes of *Woodstock*. No outside source is required once we get to Act 1, scene 2, however, for there we have Gaunt referring, in the presence of Gloucester's widow, to correction lying "in those hands / Which made the fault that we cannot correct," and some lines later he declares:

> God's is the quarrel; for God's substitute,
> His deputy anointed in His sight,
> Hath caus'd his death.
>
> (1.2.37–39)

This is plain enough about where the guilt resides, and should enforce retrospective revaluation of the preceding scene. It is extraordinary how many have failed to do so.

Well, in a way not so extraordinary. There is much to distract us at Windsor, and a little later at Coventry. The King sits in state with his nobles, trumpets sound as the champions—defendant and appellant—come on in armor, with their Heralds. There may be horses, or hobby-horses as in the recent notable production by the Royal Shakespeare Company, hobby-horses on which much of the whole action took place. Horses on the stage are a great distraction. But however we look at it, and however these scenes are staged, the pageantry of the chivalric tournament—for all the world like events depicted on a medieval tapestry—will leave a powerful impression.[29] Few producers can resist the temptation to make the most of the spectacle, and Shakespeare, dedicated professional that he was, has set it up that way. Nor does the declamatory mode, with its highflown rhetoric of subterfuge, make matters easier.

Despite the rhetoric, Richard is understandably nervous. When Boling-broke and Mowbray greet their sovereign with fulsome wishes for many happy days, indeed years, he reacts suspiciously: "We thank you both; yet one but flatters us . . ." (1.1.25). He will not in fact be granted many happy days. In this scene Bolingbroke levels several charges against Mowbray, but the heart of the matter is the death of Gloucester, whose blood,

> like sacrificing Abel's, cries,
> Even from the tongueless caverns of the earth,
> To me for justice and rough chastisement.
>
> (1.1.104–6)

Why to Bolingbroke in particular? As the Abel reference suggests, because he is Gloucester's kin. But Richard is equally Gloucester's nephew, and moreover the chief guardian of justice in the realm. Yet he isn't calling out for any chastisement, for reasons of which everyone present is aware.

Mowbray defends himself as best he can. "For Gloucester's death," he declares, "I slew him not, but to my own disgrace / Neglected my sworn duty in that case" (1.1.132–34). This is obscure, deliberately so. What is he saying? He did not kill Gloucester with his own hands—"slew him not"— but had others do the dirty work for him? What was his neglect of sworn duty? His responsibility for a royal life, A. P. Rossiter suggests, citing *Woodstock:* "that allegiance / Thou ow'st the offspring of King Edward's house," as Woodstock puts it to Mowbray's counterpart in the anonymous play. Or was Mowbray's neglect his delay in performing the King's command? His dilatoriness, according to Holinshed, gave Richard "no small displeasure."

Bolingbroke's challenge, ostensibly directed against Mowbray, equally levels at the King. Unsurprisingly, Richard would like to forget about the whole thing as soon as possible, and so he tries to reconcile challenger and challenged. But matters have passed beyond the point of no return, under the circumstances a commission to investigate the charges is out of the question, and so the King sets up the trial by combat. In Act 1, scene 3, we go through the full panoply of chivalric ceremony, until Richard casts his warder down. There follows the council session, with its verdict of a ten-year exile for Bolingbroke and lifetime banishment for Mowbray. Cunningly, Richard makes these proud men, seemingly so hopelessly at odds with one another, swear never to patch up their differences,

> Nor never by advised purpose meet
> To plot, contrive, or complot any ill,
> 'Gainst us, our state, our subjects, or our land.
>
> (1.3.188–90)

Bolingbroke's sentence is then reduced by four years.

This episode has generally been viewed as demonstrating Richard's vacillation and caprice: more prone to poetry than rule, the irresolute King falteringly exercises his authority. I believe, instead, that Richard brilliantly demonstrates his political skill under conditions of grave disadvantage. At a single stroke he manages to rid himself of two embarrassments: his aggressive cousin Bolingbroke, who represents a direct threat, and Mowbray, to whom he owes too much and who has outlived his usefulness. Had the joust taken place, and Bolingbroke triumphed, he would be still more dangerous. If, on the other hand, Mowbray came out on top, he would have an even greater hold on his monarch; the continuing presence of such men is rarely coveted. But why is Bolingbroke, less beloved, given the lighter sentence? One senses Richard's need to placate his court. Gaunt in particular is clearly uneasy, although (we learn) he has consented to the King's plan during the council we have seen represented by condensed stage time. In his book on *Shakespeare's Historical Plays* Sen Gupta suggests that it is out of pity for Gaunt, "and not with an eye to the public . . . that King Richard reduces Bolingbroke's banishment from ten years to six."[30] But Richard has little room for pity in this steely scene, and sentimental regard for Gaunt is later conspicuously absent during the deathbed interview. The seeming clemency of the reduced sentence is a gesture of politic magnanimity that costs Richard nothing—why worry about what will happen in six years?—but serves as a sop to Gaunt.

The King and his retinue depart; the scene closes. Later we see Richard in private conference with his favorites. The masks are off. They mock "high Hereford," their speech contrasting with the fraudulent rhetoric of the public scenes that have preceded. The King can now be himself.

In this reading of Act 1 of *Richard II* my aim has been to show that Shakespeare treats in a most sophisticated way the manipulation of power in a poker game where the stakes are exceedingly high. If Richard's triumph is shortlived, that is because he overplays his hand by confiscating Gaunt's estate immediately upon the Duke's death, a blunder which gives the wronged son a pretext for his return and direct confrontation with the King. It may be alleged that, even without this blunder, the King's maneuverings, however adroit, would have gained him only a temporary respite. Perhaps so, but that is speculation. It is, however, Richard's limitation that he never grasps the significance of Gloucester's death to his own tragedy.

V

The world with which I have been concerned—labyrinthine, remorselessly unsentimental, dangerous, and ego-centered—lurks everywhere in the Shakespeare canon. The power-seekers shrewdly ferret out the hidden points of vulnerability in their rivals, and work them over with the same impersonal cruelty as the prize-fighter in the ring aiming his blows at his adversary's bleeding eye. They dissimulate. They develop sudden politic cravings for strawberries. They stage elaborate little theatricals in which, appropriately costumed, they themselves perform in a bid to manipulate opinion. A father, playing crafty-sick, withholds military support from his son, abandoning him to defeat and death on the battlefield. A commander gives up pursuit of the demoralized enemy because he is conscious that by outclassing his general he courts disfavor. A duke eloquently promotes a royal match in order to rule the Queen, and through her the King and the realm. A ragged multitude, headed by a peasant with aristocratic pretensions, create a savage spectacle in the capital; the uprising seems spontaneous but is in fact manipulated from above by an ambitious peer in the expectation that, if his creature thrives, he will "reap the harvest which that rascal sow'd" (*2 Henry VI*, 3.1.381). But the possible examples are almost limitless. No other playwright in this period treats such themes so often or with such complex variety.

Were I to choose an epigraph for my paper, it would be a familiar one. "It is a strange desire, to seek power and to lose liberty," Bacon wrote in his essay "Of Great Place": "or to seek power over others and to lose power over a man's self. The rising unto place is laborious; and by pains men come to greater pains; and it is sometimes base; and by indignities men come to dignities. The standing is slippery, and the regress is either a downfall, or at least an eclipse, which is a melancholy thing." From Bacon we expect such hard-won wisdom, but we are perhaps less prepared to find it so pervasively present in gentle Shakespeare. I am conscious that by these remarks I am placing myself in a vulnerable position, as I am only too well aware that I have but scratched the surface of a complex topic by treating it representatively. Still there may be something to be said for adding another Shakespeare to the list. The psychoanalysts have had a go at him; the

Marxists too. Criticism has given us (among others) Shakespeare the practical professional, Shakespeare the theatre poet, Shakespeare the mythmaker, and Shakespeare the Christian gentleman. He also wandered imaginatively in the corridors of power, and what he recorded of the behavior of men in those treacherous environs enables us to speak of Shakespeare the politic realist.

NOTES

1. *Woodstock: A Moral History,* ed. A. P. Rossiter (London, 1946), p. 98.
2. Ibid., p. 104.
3. *The Mirror for Magistrates,* ed. Lily B. Campbell (Cambridge, 1938), p. 110.
4. Cyrus Hoy, "Recent Shakespearian Criticism, Prefabricated and Authentic," *The Sewanee Review,* LXXXII (London, 1974), p. 363.
5. William Shakespeare, *King Richard II,* ed. John Dover Wilson (The New Shakespeare; Cambridge, 1939), introd., p. ix.
6. M. W. Black, "The Sources of Shakespeare's *Richard II,*" *Joseph Quincy Adams Memorial Studies,* ed. James G. McManaway et al. (Washington, D.C., 1948), pp. 199–216.
7. Shakespeare, *King Richard II,* ed. Wilson, p. lix.
8. Samuel Daniel, *The First Fowre Bookes of the Civile Wars . . . ,* in *Narrative and Dramatic Sources of Shakespeare,* ed. Geoffrey Bullough (London, 1957–75), III, 437.
9. E. K. Chambers, *William Shakespeare: A Study of Facts and Problems* (Oxford, 1930), II, 320–21.
10. *Jack Straw,* ed. Kenneth Muir and F. P. Wilson (Malone Society Reprints; Oxford, 1957), 1. 1014.
11. See also:

> The Sunne may sometime be eclipst with Clowds,
> But hardlie may the twinckling starres obscure,
> Or put him out of whom they borrow light.
>
> (238–40)

In such an imagistic context figures of plant growth have propriety: ". . . commaund our wealth, / But loyall harts the treasure of a Prince, / Shall growe like graines sowne in a fertill soyle" (1194–96). The sun images are remarked by Irving Ribner, *The English History Play in the Age of Shakespeare* (rev. ed.; London, 1965), p. 74.
12. I cannot go quite so far as Robert Ornstein, who describes the Richard of *Woodstock* as "thoroughly despicable and corrupt," *A Kingdom for a Stage: The Achievement of Shakespeare's History Plays* (Cambridge, Mass., 1972), p. 13.
13. A. L. Rowse, *Simon Forman* (London, 1974), pp. 13–14 and (transcript) pp. 305–6.
14. I quote from the text in Chambers, *William Shakespeare* , II, 340.
15. The problems presented by a Forman account of a Globe performance (in this case of *Macbeth*) are expertly discussed by Leah Scragg, "Macbeth on Horseback." *Shakespeare Survey 26* (Cambridge, 1973), 81–88.
16. Ornstein, *Kingdom for a Stage,* p. 4.
17. Chambers, *William Shakespeare,* II, 334.
18. Chambers conveniently prints extracts from the principal documents (II, 325).
19. L. B. Campbell, *Shakespeare's "Histories": Mirrors of Elizabethan Policy* (San Marino, 1947), pp. 211–12; Ribner, *English History Play,* p. 155 n.
20. Evelyn May Albright, "Shakespeare's *Richard II* and the Essex Conspiracy," *PMLA,* XLII (1927), 686–720. Her essay drew a rejoinder from Ray Heffner, "Shakespeare, Hayward, and Essex," *PMLA,* XLV (1930), 754–80. Undaunted, she replied in "Shakespeare's *Richard II,* Hayward's History of Henry IV, and the Essex Conspiracy," *PMLA,* XLVI (1931), 694–719.

21. Margaret Dowling prints Coke's notes on Hayward's *Henry IV* in an important article, "Sir John Hayward's Troubles over *His Life of Henry IV*," *The Library*, 4th ser., XI (1931), 212–24. For the passage cited, see p. 213.

22. W. Nicholas Knight, *Shakespeare's Hidden Life: Shakespeare at the Law 1585–1595* (New York, 1973), p. 144.

23. Quoted by Albright, "Shakespeare's *Richard II*, Haywood's History . . . ," p. 695.

24. Knight, *Shakespeare's Hidden Life*, p. 143.

25. William Butler Yeats, "At Stratford-on-Avon," *Ideas of Good and Evil*, in *Collected Works* (London, 1908), p. 123.

26. Mark Van Doren, *Shakespeare* (New York, 1939), p. 89.

27. Ornstein, *Kingdom for a Stage*, p. 110.

28. A view of these scenes very similar to my own is taken by Moody E. Prior in *The Drama of Power: Studies in Shakespeare's History Plays* (Evanston, 1973), which I had not yet seen when writing this paper abroad. Prior makes the point that "Bolingbroke's challenge to Mowbray is in effect an oblique way of attacking the king" (p. 144), and he allows the advantages to Richard of Mowbray's banishment: "The one man in whom is locked the secret of the murder of Gloucester is never to be in a position to worry the king again" (p. 145). Such a reading is indeed enforced as soon as one accepts as crucial Richard's complicity in Woodstock's murder. Prior and I do differ on a few details: he describes the murder as "an old crime," although it took place only some six months before the events at Windsor Castle dramatized in 1.1; and he takes a more qualified view than I of Richard's effectiveness when he concludes that this scene and 1.3, "Epitomize the uneasy unstable equilibrium which sustains the impressive façade of Richard's style of rule." But mostly we agree; Prior's whole carefully considered discussion— which expresses what is still a minority view—should be read.

In another recent contribution, "The Antic Disposition of Richard II," *Shakespeare Survey 27* (1974), 33–41, Lois Potter interestingly observes how in *King Richard II* rhetorically elaborated language is associated with powerlessness, and brevity with strength; and how in the early scenes it is Richard (not Bolingbroke) who displays terseness. She notes too that even late in the play Richard shows flashes of his "sharp-tongued, self-mocking and quite unresigned" self.

29. The "medievalism" of *King Richard II* can, however, be overstressed; Nicholas Brooke is surely right when he suggests that "The politics of the play were clearly contemporaneous; the jousting was Elizabethan; and the figure of Richard is far more significant to the play than a mere image of medieval man" *(Shakespeare's Early Tragedies* (London, 1968), p. 109. Brooke has a number of acute things to say about the play.

30. S. C. Sen Gupta, *Shakespeare's Historical Plays* (London, 1964), p. 116.

(1975)

6

Shakespeare's Histories: The Presence of the Past

At Stratford-upon-Avon a few years ago Terry Hands brought the *Henry VI* plays triumphantly back to theatrical life, in reasonably full texts, without reshufflings or interpolations, on the vast Royal Shakespeare Theatre stage. Considerable anticipatory anxiety must have attended the revival. All three plays! What a commitment! Would they work? Would visitors, passing through Stratford in the expectation of catching *Romeo and Juliet* or *Hamlet* or one of the others written mainly in quotations—would such audiences bite? We now know the answer. The plays worked, and audiences bit. Thus did the Royal Shakespeare Company confront the challenge of the history plays, as Shakespeare wrote them, on the stage.

How do we confront Shakespeare's histories—not just *Henry VI* (usually, I expect, unassigned), but Shakespeare's histories generally—in our college and university classrooms? What does English history from that day in April of 1398, when Richard II faced the challenge of Bolingbroke at Windsor, until August 22, 1485, when the armies of Richard III and Henry, Duke of Richmond, met near Market Bosworth in Leicestershire— what does this history, as recreated in dramatic terms almost four hundred years ago by an Elizabethan playwright, mean to our undergraduates in Lexington or Akron or College Park, or to the audience of anonymous millions who will take time out from "Barney Miller" and "Starsky and Hutch" to watch the four plays, from *Richard II* to *Henry V,* as dramatized by the Beeb on the box?

The history itself, one may hazard a reasonably safe guess, will mean very little to students in America. Some of the young I encounter haven't any very clear idea of when the Okies made their trek to California during the Great Depression, or when D-day took place, or even when John Kennedy met an assassin's bullet in Dallas. Others have vague notions of how in the Middle Ages people stumbled about in the dark, then the sun came out, and it was the Renaissance, and everybody started eating with knives and forks, and the artists began painting nudes instead of Madonnas. I know I am being unfair to reasonably well informed students; but I have myself heard the amiable Henry Tenenbaum, host of a TV program called "PM Report," announce an Elizabethan street fair in Maryland—just like a real Renaissance fair in the Middle Ages. However that may be, what are the Richards or Henries or Yorks or Exeters to them? We can—and do—refer them to Peter Saccio's wonderfully informative and readable *Shakespeare's English Kings: History, Chronicle, and Drama*. But many outside the academy will perforce make do without pedagogical guidance. What did they make of the enormous four-act drama they watched on Public Television—if they watched it? And what of the other tetralogy, when it comes along, and Young Clifford bids

> the vile world end
> And the premised flames of the last day
> Knit earth and heaven together.
>
> (*2 Henry VI*, 5.2.40–43)

On the possible meanings of such an experience I have some thoughts to share with you.

My starting point may seem oddly beside the point. Recently, I served on a university search committee charged with finding a new chairman for my department at the University of Maryland. The experience was for me, and I expect for all my colleagues, at once tedious, stressful, and filled with contending passions, stirring fewer associations with Shakespeare than with C. P. Snow. Anyway, at one meeting the merits of a prospective candidate were championed on the basis of what may be termed predictive historiography. It was noted that this individual had been in her department for just one year, was female, and came to notice just as the committee was reaching an impasse. The previous chairman, chosen six years back, was also female, a new appointment, and selected when deliberations had reached a standstill. "History repeats itself," a colleague suggested, and we should recognize our powerlessness to do anything about it. Heads gravely nodded, whether in approval or slumber I know not. But, although I like to think I have an open mind about this candidate, I was alarmed by my colleague's argument. Surely we were being offered mere parallels; in substance the two cases were entirely unlike: these were two different people with individual personalities in a department which has changed radically in recent years. So I complained about the reasoning; reasoning with which we are periodically faced when there is a national crisis, and we are forewarned of another Munich, with Chamberlain about to stalk again with his umbrella. We looked to the committee chairman, who is by profession an historian. "History doesn't repeat itself," he remarked wearily. "Only historians repeat themselves."

Only historians? Critics too, surely. But never mind that. If history doesn't repeat itself, we may nevertheless draw wholesome instruction from the past, a process facilitated by the ubiquity of parallels. The imaginative endeavors of art teem with parallels, whether in the ochestration of the double plot in *King Lear* or in the compositional arrangement of a Poussin painting. Criticism thrives on parallels. So do ordinary folk conscious of the presence of the past in their otherwise fragmented and not always coherent daily lives. Analogical modes of thought have been around for a very long time, and show no sign of relinquishing their hold. Such modes lend what I would describe as an associational resonance to artifacts of the imagination. I would submit that in the theatre and on the box and in our Shakespeare courses, such perceived resonances help to shape the impact of particular plays in particular contexts. My examples to illustrate the point take their force—if they have force—not from any novelty, but from the fact that others here might, if called upon, point to the very same instances.

Vietnam belongs to our very recent past, but for many of us that past already seems to belong to another time and another country. During those troubled years I was at Northwestern. When I first took up my post there in the early fifties, Northwestern had the reputation, not entirely undeserved, of being a smug bastion of upper middle-class privilege. The coeds were known for their Waspish beauty, the males bore the insignia of Brooks Brothers affluence. Books, beards, and blacks were out, sororities and fraternities in. But times changed, the student body became more diverse and intellectual, more inclined to take part in the political process. That metamorphosis was well under way when as a nation we sank into the Vietnam morass. Northwestern wasn't hit as badly as Wisconsin or Columbia, but it was hit. Students demonstrated, protesters manned the barricades in Sheridan Road where that artery passed alongside our handsome campus. Some students begged me to cancel classes so that they could go out and make their voices heard at anti-war assemblies. I didn't call off the classes, which I regarded it as my duty to conduct. There were no untoward consequences; most of my students came. We were, however, all conscious of a special tension in Harris Hall, where I lectured in my upper-level Shakespeare course to an audience of a couple of hundred. In previous years *Hamlet* and *Lear* were expectedly the plays which most moved my students; transiently *Romeo and Juliet,* when Zeffirelli's film, newly released, caught their imagination. But during Vietnam, the play that got to my students was one that had previously scarcely existed for them.

From isles of Greece the commanders, "their high blood chaf'd," had

> to the port of Athens sent their ships
> Fraught with the ministers and instruments
> Of cruel war.
>
> (*Troilus and Cressida,* Prologue, 3–5)

That was seven years past when *Troilus and Cressida* begins. The Greeks had pitched their brave pavilions on the Dardan plains, but Priam's six-gated city yet stood. The war was stalemated, the contending forces oppressed by a no-win situation. The whole context struck my students as—if you will permit me the great imprecise cliché of these days—relevant. But what really grabbed them was Act 2, scene 2, the great council meeting in Priam's palace, in which the overwhelming question is finally asked. Why go on? "Deliver Helen," the Greeks have urged,

> and all damage else—
> As honour, loss of time, travail, expense,
> Wounds, friends, and what else dear that is consum'd
> In hot digestion of this cormorant war—
> Shall be struck off.
>
> (2.2.3–7)

Reason urges that this be done. "What merit's in that reason which denies / The yielding of her up?" Hector asks. Troilus's reply—

> Nay, if we talk of reason,
> Let's shut our gates and sleep.
>
> (46–47)

—and Hector's rejoinder:

> Brother, she is not worth what she doth cost
> The keeping.
>
> (51–52)

—and a little further along:

> is your blood
> So madly hot that no discourse of reason,
> Nor fear of bad success in a bad cause,
> Can qualify the same?
>
> (115–18)

—these exchanges thrilled my students committed, by their very presence at the University, to the imperatives of reason, and profoundly apprehensive about a war the origins of which seemed to them obscure and which seemed also to have no foreseeable end. I am, I hasten to add, not here offering my own interpretation of events, nor do I presume to speak for all students; but that was how the articulate ones viewed things, and they included some of the best and brightest. Shakespeare's dialectic summed up their dilemma and expressed their obsession. At the scene's end, as we all know, the spokesman for reason unreasoningly throws in the sponge after Troilus' specious appeal to honor: "I am yours," Hector tells him. That conclusion for my students prefigured our own sophistries and bankruptcy. Vietnam was their Troy. History was not repeating itself, but that peculiar moment it had another rendezvous, one of innumerably many, with a poetic image of the past.

After Johnson, Nixon; but the war dragged on. We didn't associate our disgraced leader with a hero king, except for perhaps one fleeting moment which many of you will recall. Late one night in Washington, when student protestors bivouacked outside the White House after a hectic day of picketing, the President suddenly appeared unannounced, and mingled self-consciously with his detractors. He asked, one pale horn-rimmed youth later reported in bemusement, how their football team was doing. This episode did not escape the press. I remember reading the next day—was it in *The New York Times?*—an account headlined "A Little Touch of Nixon in the Night."

But when Vietnam was past and Watergate upon us, with Deep Throat and the withheld tapes and Cox and Jaworski filling the headlines, Nixon was clearly facing not another Agincourt but impeachment. Neither *Henry V* nor *Troilus and Cressida* was the play which most tellingly held the mirror up to nature, but *Richard II*. Truth to tell, Plantagenet Richard bore little resemblance to his unprincely namesake who assured us he was not a crook; that is, little apart from the fact of deposition. But that fact is momentous, and was so depicted in Shakespeare's history and so made manifest to us all as we watched, transfixed, the successive stages of the President's fall, until the televised abdication speech, and the final wave of the hand as he boarded the helicopter that whisked him out of our lives on the first stage of his self-banishment to San Clemente, where a kinder fate awaited him than the one which greeted his namesake at Sir Pierce of Exton's hands in Pomfret Castle.

The parallels are imprecisely general, except for one haunting detail which escaped nobody. When Richard in the deposition scene has divested himself of crown and sceptre, and with his own tears washed away his balm, "What more remains?" he asks his tormenters. Northumberland, implacable, presses on:

> No more; but that you read
> These accusations, and these grievous crimes
> Committed by your person and your followers
> Against the state and profit of this land;
> That, by confessing them, the souls of men
> May deem that you are worthily depos'd.

> (4.1.222–27)

This was, as you will recall, the burning issue after the other deposition. In neither instance was a confession of wrongdoing insisted upon or obtained, although Nixon had his Northumberlands. Nor need I remind you of the consequences for his successor when pardon followed.

Given the infinite variety of Shakespeare's art, we should not be startled by the way events have of presenting startling juxtapositions. One recent example. Last year, on February 14, along with untold others, I flipped on the television for the evening news, and saw shouting throngs, their arms upraised, in Tehran. They have since become a depressingly familiar sight, but then they were still novel and filled us with an apprehension which events have amply justified. A few weeks earlier the Shah had embarked on his fateful exile, the Ayatollah Ruhollah Khomeini had not yet made his fateful return from exile, and an interim government totteringly presided. We were watching a convulsion of state, of awesome dimensions and unforeseeable consequences. That's the way it was that night, as Cronkite says. A half hour later I tuned in again and saw another convulsion of state. This time there were classical columns rather than the grimy façades of Tehran, and the mob, volatile in their sympathies and vulnerable to demagogic manipulation, wore togas. The emperor fell in the Capitol. A poet with the same name as one of the conspirators wandered unluckily out of doors:

> *3. Plebeian.* Your name, sir, truly.
> *Cinna.* Truly, my name is Cinna.
> *1. Plebeian.* Tear him to pieces; he's a conspirator!
> *Cinna.* I am Cinna the poet, I am Cinna the poet. . . .
> *4. Plebeian.* It is no matter, his name's Cinna; pluck but his name out of his heart, and turn him going.
> *3. Plebeian.* Tear him, tear him! Come, brands, ho! firebrands!
> *(Julius Caesar,* 3.3.26–29, 33–36)

The modest BBC budget for *Julius Caesar* wasn't able to match Cronkite's cast of thousands; the director, Herbert Wise, had to make do with a few dozen for the crowd scene. But, then, Cronkite couldn't match the BBC when it came to language. The two programs counterpointed each other.

Through poetry and rhetoric and shaping theatrical form, *Julius Caesar* furnished a ritual reenactment of mythic events. The spirit of Caesar, hovering over the play after his assassination, suggests that Shakespeare is no less concerned with Caesarism than with Caesar. So too the spirit of Shah Mohammad Reza Pahlavi has hovered over Iran, and us all, ever since he vacated the Peacock Throne. In his first substantive television interview since his fall

> His remarks revealed a strong sense of betrayal about his final months as Iran's king of kings. Flashing a wry smile, he said it would take a Homer or a Shakespeare to describe what he obviously believes was a net of intrigue involving two close friends and U.S. Air Force Gen. Robert E. Huyser.

The report I have quoted appeared in *The Washington Post* last January 18. The Shah didn't name the close friends, nor did he cite Shakespeare's *Julius Caesar.* Did he have that play in mind?

It's tempting to toy with such a possibility, but the temptation is best resisted. Homer and Shakespeare are magical names, at once tops of the classics and tops of the pops. No one came to grips more grandly with grand themes, and the Shah is not one to underestimate the magnitude of what overtook him. The names also suggest part of his problem, for they are symptomatic of the western orientation against which his country so fiercely reacted. You don't find the Ayatollah—any Ayatollah—making a point by appealing to Shakespeare.

But what especially intrigued me in that interview were the Shah's dark references to betrayal in high places, and the machinations of trusted friends and a trusted ally. These conjure up associations with that world of power and politics, of intrigue, dissimulation, and remorseless ambition, which so powerfully appealed to Shakespeare's dramatic instincts.

In the last speech of *1 Henry VI* Suffolk, having by false eloquence persuaded his king to marry the beauteous Margaret, stands alone upon the stage and with perfect propriety of image foresees things to come:

> Thus Suffolk hath prevail'd; and thus he goes,
> As did the youthful Paris once to Greece,
> With hope to find the like event in love
> But prosper better than the Troyan did.
> Margaret shall now be queen, and rule the King;
> But I will rule both her, the King, and realm.
>
> (5.5.103–8)

In the sequel Suffolk has his inning before meeting his foreordained death, and York moves to the center of the power struggle as he manipulates from afar Jack Cade's ostensibly popular insurrection. Shakespeare's analysis of these events is as unillusioned as it is masterly.

I see that I have begun to move through the plays one by one. It would take me a long time to arrive at Shakespeare's ripest treatment of these themes in *Antony and Cleopatra,* and the wonderful little scene, usually found expendable in production, in which Ventidius, making his way in triumph through Syria, with the dead body of Pacorus the King's son borne before him, and the vanquished Parthians fleeing, decides to call it a day:

> O Silius, Silius,
> I have done enough. A lower place, note well,
> May make too great an act; for learn this, Silius:
> Better to leave undone than by our deed
> Acquire too high a fame when him we serve's away. . . .
> Who does i' th' wars more than his captain can

Becomes his captain's captain; and ambition,
The soldier's virtue, rather makes choice of loss
Than gain which darkens him.
I could do more to do Antonius good,
But 'twould offend him; and in his offense
Should my performance perish.

                                                    (3.1.11–15, 21–27)

Ventidius is not one of those destined to suffer—in Francis Bacon's terms—a melancholy eclipse.

There is no need here to multiply examples; all through the canon, Shakespeare explores the corridors of power. He is well aware that adjoining any corridor of power is a vestibule of impotence, that for a Bolingbroke there is a Richard, for a York there is a Henry. I have dealt at some length with the theme in an essay on *Richard II* and the realities of power. The subject invites a proper full-dress treatment, with due attention to the intellectual context. Not in this paper, but I venture to think that such a study would reveal Shakespeare not as a genuflecting Tudor apologist but as perhaps the greatest unsentimental politic realist in drama. He tells it as it is; not simply, but as it is.

                                                    (1980)

7
Critical Encounters

I. THE STUDIED AND THE SPONTANEOUS*

While F. P. Wilson's *Shakespearian and Other Studies,* edited by Dame Helen Gardner, will be welcomed by all admirers of excellence, its appearance must sadly remind us that Wilson did not live to finish any of his three great undertakings: the volume on the Elizabethan drama for the "Oxford History of English Literature," the edition of Dekker's non-dramatic writings, and the revised and enlarged *Oxford Dictionary of English Proverbs.* Of these the first was to have been his magnum opus. A completed segment of it, *The English Drama 1485–1585,* has received separate publication, and was reviewed here on July 3, 1969. Now we are given two additional long chapters, on the history play and on Shakespeare's comedies, from the same work. There will be no more.

These essays display Wilson's wonted authority and elegance of style, as well as his gentle and civilized humor. Sometimes all these qualities converge in a single fine sentence, as when he distils the essence of Holinshed:

> He did not look the gift-horses of the middle ages in the mouth, accepted the Trojan ancestry of Britain (according to Hayward a senseless fiction invented by Geoffrey of Monmouth), eked out the few facts known about Macbeth with a circumstantial romance composed by Hector Boece, and side by side with the death of kings, the carnage of war, the evolution of laws, he told of apparitions seen in the air, murders of private gentlemen like Arden of Faversham, disastrous fires, strange fish caught upon the coast, and the ingenious blacksmith who put about a flea's neck a golden chain of forty-three links with lock and key, which it drew with ease.

An introductory section defining the English history-play makes that vexed question look easy; but Wilson always wore his immense learning lightly. His work has also the considerable merit (in a literary history) of eschewing polemics. A special weight attaches to the judgment of such a critic; the

---

*On F. P. Wilson, *Shakespearian and Other Studies,* ed. Helen Gardner (Oxford: Clarendon Press, 1969), and M. C. Bradbrook, *Shakespeare the Craftsman,* The Clark Lectures, 1968 (London: Chatto & Windus, 1969).

scholar will not lightly pass over Wilson's remarks on the possibility of Shakespeare's hand in *Edward III,* or on the date of the *Merry Wives of Windsor,* or on the relation of the anonymous *Troublesome Reign* to Shakespeare's *King John,* or that of *A Shrew* to *The Shrew.*

What of ordinary readers? These will find themselves in the hands of a wise and humane guide, one who resists the critical ingenuity that would make a Vice of Falstaff or have us see *Love's Labour's Lost* as a coterie comedy built round a School of Night which perhaps never existed. They will obtain many shrewd insights into Shakespeare's characters (never mind that some are repeated from Wilson's other writings), and they will come away with a heightened appreciation of the function of rhetorical figures in his style.

These are good things. Yet, if ripeness is much, it is not in this context all. One has at times an uneasy sense that the writer's imagination is not operating at full stretch, that not all his resources of intellect and sensibility are concentrated upon the object. Did Wilson, one wonders, give so much of himself to his lectures and travels and exertions on behalf of others during his last years when his health was failing, that he sometimes turned with weariness to his main task? Literary history is often less adventurous than other kinds of criticism, yet it need not be so, as companion volumes in the Oxford History, notably those by Lewis and Bush, testify. But the virtues of sanity and grace must not be underestimated. One may recommend these chapters to the undergraduate with an easy conscience.

So too the non-specialist reader will profit from the reprinted papers on "Shakespeare and the Diction of Common Life," "Shakespeare's Reading," and "The Elizabethan Theatre." Some of the remaining essays, such as those on mock-prognostications and seventeenth-century jest-books, have more restricted appeal. A paper on ana, or table talk, is slighter than these, but amusing. All (except for memoirs of Chambers and Greg) originated as lectures, and suffer at times from the inhibitions imposed by the genre. "I begin with some remarks on the public stages," Wilson says at one point, "but in the time at my disposal I must make the most drastic omissions."

There are a few slips (it is not a fact but a speculation that Middleton wrote *The Puritan,* Greg's edition of *The Second Maiden's Tragedy* is misdated, some names are spelled inconsistently, etc.), but these are all trifling. The editor has performed her difficult task with exemplary skill. A good deal of surgery, she tells us, was required to make self-contained essays of what were intended as part of a larger canvas. Even the eight previously published papers offered problems, for although Wilson had not formally revised them, he had incorporated additional matter, and it was left to the editor to determine the mode of presentation. All students of Elizabethan literature owe Dame Helen a debt of gratitude for her selfless labors.

Shakespeare the Craftsman offers a study in contrast. Wilson, one feels, deeply meditated every statement before putting pen to paper; Professor

Bradbrook gives the impression of spontaneity. She is blithely uneven, offering a scrappy survey of the history and organization of Shakespeare's company and a fully orchestrated chapter on *Timon* (the latter being her inaugural lecture at Cambridge).

The mode of discourse matches the content: heterogeneous ideas are without transition yoked together in short, sometimes bitty, paragraphs, as Professor Bradbrook hops birdlike from topic to topic. Not infrequently, however, she comes up with a juicy worm of an idea.

Few others, surely, can have thought of seeking a common pattern that unites *King John* and *Henry VIII*, plays which would appear to be alike only in standing apart from the two historical tetralogies. If Professor Bradbrook fails to make a prima-facie case, the juxtaposition nevertheless invites fresh insights. So too she has something original to say about Sonnets 85 and 86, which she relates to the competition of the poets at the Great Festival of the Piu, London's foreign merchants. The writings of Robert Armin, Shakespeare's clown, had been unaccountably ignored; Professor Bradbrook remedies the deficiency in an informative vignette. Unintimidated by prevailing orthodoxies, she will have none of the view that *Timon* is an unfinished and (in Shakespeare's day) unperformed play. Rather she sees it as

> *A Dramatick Shew of the Life of Timon of Athens, wherein his progress through the Four Seasons, as also through the Four Humours in an earthly Zodiack is set forth, together with the City Vice of Usury in diverse Senators, the snarling asperity of prideful Scholars, and the mercenary decline of Poetry and Painting in this latter age. All displayed in sundry variety of dramatick utterance, chiefly by way of Paradoxes.*

This is good fun as well as being significant criticism.

When it comes to scholarly rigor, however, Professor Bradbrook lets us down. She mars names, dates, and quotations in the relating. O. B. Hardison appears disguised as J. O. Hardison; Van Doren, as Van Doran; Panofsky, as Panovsky. There are other misspellings. Manningham's contemporary anecdote about the rivalry of Shakespeare and Burbage for a citizen's favors is improbably misdated 1662. Some lines from Sonnet 144 are attributed to 194 (there are only 154). She can make a comical hash of quotations: words drop out, are substituted, or misplaced. A couplet in *Timon*, described as jingling like false money, jingles the more falsely for having a word omitted. One would not know from her reproduction of Antony's speech, "Sometimes we see a cloud that's dragonish . . ." (*Antony and Cleopatra*, 4.14.3), that it is twice interrupted, and the inadvertent omission of half-a-dozen words wrecks the sense.

This carelessness unfortunately extends to interpretative issues. Shakespeare, we are quaintly informed, "seems to have acted a sort of banker and general agent for his Stratford friends when he was in London." Presumably Professor Bradbrook is thinking of the Quiney letter asking the poet for a loan of £30, but this is to say the least inadequate evidence for her conclusion. Elsewhere she speaks of the "atmospheric intensities" of Kyd's *Hamlet;* but it is not certain that Kyd wrote the lost *Hamlet,* and one cannot safely talk about its atmosphere on the basis of an eighteenth-century German text of a Hamlet play. The author sees reflected in the *Merry Wives* Shakespeare's matchmaking efforts when he lodged with a Huguenot family in London; but the dramatist did not know the Mountjoys until after his play was written. In this chapter, called "Royal Command," much is made of the "very early" tradition that the comedy was written in a fortnight at the Queen's request. This tradition is less implausible than most, but it is not "very early," having been first recorded in 1702, a full century after the fact.

Yet there are good things in the discussion of *Merry Wives.* Professor Bradbrook sets herself against a formidable body of critical opposition to the play (Wilson regards it as the least worthy of Shakespeare's comedies), as she emphasizes the craft virtues of a farce with "the crowded vivacity of a Breughel painting." She has a point, and one which receives independent affirmation from the success of the recent Royal Shakespeare Company production.

In "The New Clown" Professor Bradbrook treats the impact upon Shakespeare's art of Armin's presence in the company, her chief exhibit being *Twelfth Night.* But we cannot be sure that Armin had joined the Chamberlain's men by the time this play was written. The problem is summed up, in usual masterly fashion, by Wilson in the essay on jest-books in *Shakespearian and Other Studies.*

Professor Bradbrook has as one of her purposes to relate Shakespeare's craftsmanship to the particular circumstances that gave rise to an individual play. Thus *Henry VIII* is a craft-pageant intended by the King's players "to give the select audience of their expensive theatre the Blackfriars a spectacular triumph." But can we really speak of it as a Blackfriars play? The earliest reference to production is at the Globe, and in fact the theatrical provenance of Shakespeare's last plays is uncertain (see Seltzer's essay in *Later Shakespeare,* 1967). The same problem occurs in more acute form in the chapter on *Timon,* which, Professor Bradbrook argues, was also performed at Blackfriars. She assumes that actual music for the masque in Act 1 is preserved in a British Museum manuscript containing an air called "The Amazonians' Masque." But, the title excepted, is there any evidence that the reference is to *Timon?* It is not the only stage-work of the period to feature Amazons: a "Maske of Amasones" was given at Court in 1579, and another, in which Lady Hay was to have appeared as the Queen of the Amazons, was intended for performance in January 1618, but canceled. It is not even certain that all the tunes in the manuscript actually belong to masques. Nor is this reviewer convinced that, as Professor Bradbrook maintains, the anonymous *Comedy of Timon* parodies Shakespeare's play. Her hypothesis of the Blackfriars performance is intriguing but remains unproved.

Yet the essay as a whole is brilliant. Professor Bradbrook makes the striking point that the plotting of *Timon* is emblematic rather than dramatic, and she discerns two patterns throughout, the theatrical and the cosmic. As a result of her discussion our understanding of a deeply puzzling work is permanently enriched. One may quarrel with some of her views, one may wish that she attended more carefully to her transcriptions and to the marshaling of evidence; but she is always stimulating. In these days especially, when the academic mills grind so remorselessly and often so dully, that is a quality greatly to be valued.

(1970)

II. IN MERCURIAL GUISE*

The young man—perhaps in his mid-twenties, maybe a trifle older—is richly but not gaudily dressed. An unostentatious collar of lace cutwork lies flat on his sober slashed doublet. He wears a sugarloaf beaver ornamented with a feathered brooch and jewelled hatband. His upraised right hand clasps a left (it looks more female than male) strangely issuing from a bank of clouds. The hands have an unearthly white pallor, contrasting with the lively flesh tones of the sitter's face and neck. His auburn hair caresses the hat brim in curly ringlets; he sports a neat beard and full moustaches. The wide eyes arrest our own, suggesting mysterious recesses of thought. In all, he cuts a handsome aristocratic figure, this young sitter. Leslie Hotson, as the title of his new book proclaims, is persuaded that he is William Shakespeare. Could this indeed be Shakespeare of Warwickshire, aged twenty-four, son of a decayed former bailiff of Stratford? With some effort we remind ourselves that true nobleness does not necessarily presuppose blueness of blood.

Nicholas Hilliard, portrait painter *par excellence* to the court of Queen Elizabeth I, executed the oval miniature in the Armada year. So much we know because he inscribed "Anno · Domini · 1588" in gold letters against the blue backdrop. He also included, between the clasped hands and his subject's face, a puzzling motto, *"Attici amoris ergo,"* which has in the past been translated, none too confidently, as "And therefore of Attic love." Whatever does the phrase mean? In catalogues the portrait is entitled "Unknown Man clasping a Hand issuing from a Cloud."

The miniature exists in two versions, almost, but not quite, identical. One is on display at the Victoria and Albert Museum. The other, in better

---

*On Leslie Hotson, *Shakespeare by Hilliard* (London: Chatto & Windus, 1977).

preservation and if anything more exquisite (so far as one may judge from the excellent color reproduction) in former times adorned the collection at Castle Howard in Yorkshire. Today it belongs to Dr. Hotson, who bought it in 1961 from a private collector. He tells us that it cost him more than he could well afford, but I doubt that he has for one moment regretted his extravagance. The picture has haunted him, "exciting" (as he says, quoting Samuel Johnson), "restless and unquenchable curiosity," and impelling him to devote "years of search for the meaning of its unique features in the light of their own time." *Shakespeare by Hilliard* relates his attempt at exorcism.

The narrative unfolds absorbingly, as Dr. Hotson pursues his quarry. With easy familiarity he draws upon Renaissance literature and art (both English and Continental), mythology, heraldry, and custom, as well as the resources of modern scholarship. His memory never lets him down, his pace never flags. In a field where so much of the secondary literature is colorlessly specialist, he writes with an assurance and panache that invite the engagement of ordinary readers. The book brims with youthful vigor. So we absorb with wonder the fact that the author has lately celebrated his eightieth birthday.

Dr. Hotson has been hailed as "the Maigret of the literary world," and clearly he enjoys thinking of himself as a detective: his text is sprinkled with references to Sherlock Holmes, the CID, Fabian of the Yard, and the like. Dr. Hotson is entitled to see himself in this light. While still in his twenties he published his celebrated account of the circumstances leading up to the violent death of Christopher Marlowe in nasty company at Deptford on a spring day in 1593. The discovery made his reputation. No fluke, it was followed by *Shelley's Lost Letters to Harriet* (1930). The next year Dr. Hotson announced his recovery of a writ of attachment of 1596 naming Shake-speare—a scholar-sleuth's biggest game—and in *Shakespeare versus Shallow* he elaborated on the significance of the laconic record. Over the years Dr. Hotson has also illuminated our understanding of the peripheral figures around Shakespeare: Thomas Russell, for example, one of the two over-seers of the dramatist's will; or William Johnson, host of the Mermaid, who participated with him in a property purchase in Blackfriars. For his many contributions we owe Dr. Hotson a great debt of gratitude.

In recent years he has diverted his incomparable investigative gift into more controversial pursuits: new arguments about the first night of *Twelfth Night*, Elizabethan staging, the dating and personages of the Sonnets. Un-like the earlier discoveries, these suggestions derive their force from inter-pretation and novel applications of Hotson's wide-ranging knowledge of the Elizabethan age. Thus the eclipse of the "mortal moon" in Sonnet 107 alludes to the defeat of the crescent-formationed Spanish Armada, and therefore helps to date the cycle. While these contributions have instigated lively debate, they have by and large met with a skeptical reception once the dust has settled. A document naming Shakespeare is one thing; analogies and inferences are something else. *Shakespeare by Hilliard* belongs in this latter category.

Dr. Hotson's initial premise is that the mode of his miniature is allegorical. If *The Faerie Queene* embodies a dark conceit, the Hilliard portrait entices us with a brightly colored one, deploying a now forgotten language of visual symbolism in which every detail of costume, ornament, and gesture contributes to a hidden, yet recoverable, meaning that is completed (as in the manner of the *impresa*) by the accompanying motto. Not all portraits of the period are allegorical, but in this one the presence of the hand issuing from the clouds by itself sufficiently indicates the game afoot. So the premise makes perfectly good sense.

The task, as Dr. Hotson stresses in his first chapter, is to see the picture as an Elizabethan would. Of course we are not Elizabethans and so cannot truly see with their eyes, any more than we can truly re-create the Globe playhouse. We must settle for approximations. Moreover, that familiar fiction of the historian, "the Elizabethan," these days arouses deserved mistrust; no two Elizabethans perceived their world with precisely the same eyes. As regards paintings, we do well to bear in mind that forms, like words, harbor alternative significances, and more than one key may seemingly unlock the cabinet of thought. Besides, the essentials of anatomy, no less than the imperatives of allegory, dictate the presence of certain elements of design: a foot will have five toes whether or not the artist is playing numerological games. So, while the elucidator's endeavor may be valid enough, he will wherever possible seek external validation of his interpretative findings.

Dr. Hotson's revelations, if not his complex arguments, may be briefly summarized. He concludes that the sitter represents Mercury. The superior god issuing from the clouds is Apollo, and the inscription is to be translated "Athenians because of love." (Citing Sir Frank Adcock, he argues that the phrase cannot mean "Because of Attic love," or the like, *Attici* being a nominative plural and not a genitive singular.) The Athenians thus joined in True Love are humans in divine guises. Apollo is to be identified as one William Hatcliffe, a Lincolnshire man who reigned as Prince of Purpoole (equated with Delphic Apollo) at the Gray's Inn Christmas revels of 1587/8. Mercury is Shakespeare.

In identifying Apollo, Dr. Hotson performs acrobatic feats without quite disarming our consciousness of the meagerness of the iconographical details—a hand, a ruff-cuff, and some clouds—he has to work with. For Mercury he produces more voluminous evidence, not all of it persuasive. Noting that the little is the "mercurial finger," Dr. Hotson makes much of the fact that this digit is separated from the others clutching Apollo's index finger: emphasis by separation points to Mercury. All right; but the index finger of the same hand is even more prominently parted from the others, a fact which does not interest Dr. Hotson until much later, when he remarks that this finger signifies Apollo. On the basis of such reasoning, the hand, with its Mercurial and Apollonian fingers, could belong to either deity. Or neither.

Mercury is associated with the number four, so that and its multiples must be remorselessly hunted down. (Apollo's number, seven, is denoted by the seven clouds from which his hand emerges, but in the damaged V and A miniature I counted only six with the aid of a flashlight—the light in the case being out that day—and I am not convinced that there were ever seven.) The year Hilliard inscribed on the picture, 1588, is a multiple of four. Dr. Hotson states, as though it were fact, "Had the date been 1587 or 1589, he would have left it out." Why? Hilliard often, though not invariably, dates his portraits; examples are the self-portrait of 1577, and his miniatures of Elizabeth I (1572), an unknown man (1572), the Earl of Leicester (1576), and Sir Henry Slingsby (1595). An artist's impulse to put a date on his work is comprehensible in other terms than those of numerical symbolism. All in all, however, even while his method stirs apprehensions, Dr. Hotson makes a sufficiently provocative case for Mercury in the picture, and to a lesser extent, for Apollo's presence, too. He has the field to himself, for nobody has ever advanced a competing interpretation.

But is the sitter Shakespeare? To that question all others lead. Dr. Hotson himself is not given to doubt. All through he employs the vocabulary of confidence: such words as "demonstrably," "unmistakable," "conclusive," and "infallibly" exert a pressure difficult to resist. But arm yourself with the Hilliard miniature and the ubiquitous Droeshout engraving (an authenticated likeness), buttonhole an innocent bystander, and say, "Look here upon this picture and on this," and the odds are that he will not leap to the conclusion that both represent the same man. Still, an interval of years, as well as a grosser disparity of technical skill, separates those two icons. Minute comparison, while normal and desirable, won't settle the matter, and Dr. Hotson doesn't trouble himself about Droeshout. Instead he draws comfort from the presence of Hilliard's "fair curling hair and beard," the "hazel eyes," and "straight nose," in the Stratford bust in Holy Trinity Church, as described by M. H. Spielmann half a century ago. The bust, however, had been painted white in the eighteenth century and afterwards restored. Here I can supply a tidbit of confirmatory information, for I have come upon a privately printed account by John Britton in 1816 of the bust as "originally painted." Britton speaks of "the eyes of a light hazel, and the hair and beard, auburn."

Dr. Hotson must somehow show that Shakespeare was popularly associated with Mercury. He points to Thomas Freeman's eulogy, in 1614, of "Shakespeare, that nimble Mercury," and the allusions to Shakespeare as both Apollo and Mercury in Jonson's celebrated tribute. But mostly Dr. Hotson must by indirections find directions out, and the indirections tend to be very indirect. Mercury has many attributes. He is, as we are reminded, poet, couturier, butler, teacher, companion, and manager of mirth; he is gentle, sweet, and a double-dealer. It therefore follows that when anybody identifies Shakespeare with any of these characteristics, he is thinking of Mercury. All those allusions to gentle Shakespeare recall his Mercurial guise. In *Eikonoklastes* Milton describes Shakespeare as "one whom we well know was the closet companion" of Charles I in his prison solitude—thus showing that Milton viewed Shakespeare as companionable Mercury. Not all readers will find Mercury in these passages, and we tend to lose sight of the fact that Hilliard painted his miniature in 1588.

Other recalcitrant problems intrude. Although Hilliard himself fought a losing battle with insolvency in his Gutter Lane house-cum-studio, he catered for the beautiful people of his day, especially the circle clustering round Leicester. Portrait-painting, he firmly believed, was not for the hoi polloi. As he tells us in his manuscript *Treatise Concerning the Art of Limning*, "it is a thing apart from all other painting or drawing, and tendeth not to common men's use," but "is for the service of noble persons very meet in small volumes in private manner for them to have the portraits and pictures of themselves."

In 1588 Shakespeare had a wife and three children in Stratford, and was (so far as the documentary record reveals) unknown to the world. He had published nothing. This is the period known in Shakespearean biography as the Lost Years. It ends in 1592 when Robert Greene, dying in envy and squalor, lashed out at "the only Shake-scene in a country." On the face of it, Shakespeare seems an unlikely client for Hilliard.

To Dr. Hotson, however, the Lost Years are less obscure. He maintains that Shakespeare had composed the main body of his Sonnets by 1589— that, as proclaimed in *Shakespeare's Sonnets Dated* (1949), *"Shakespeare's power had reached maturity by the time he was no more than twenty-five years old"* (Hotson's italics). Will Hatcliffe, the Apollo of the Gray's Inn revels, is Mr. W. H. of Thorpe's riddling dedication of the 1609 Quarto of the Sonnets, and also the adored youth of the cycle. Shakespeare wrote *Love's Labour's Lost* for the 1588–89 revels. Ferdinando Lord Strange graced that occasion as guest of honor, while his troupe, Strange's men, acted the comedy. For Dr. Hotson this reconstruction is confirmed by the clasped hands of Hilliard's miniature; for the badge worn by Strange's servants was joined hands upright.

The argument thus consists of a sequence of mutually reinforcing hypotheses. As such they must compete with opposing hypotheses. Others argue, with greater plausibility, that Shakespeare wrote his Sonnets between 1592 and 1595, and that the Fair Youth was the Earl of Southampton. Most informed commentators date *Love's Labour's Lost* some years later than 1589. Not everybody agrees that Shakespeare began his theatrical career with Strange's men, the Queen's company being a recently touted rival. All such theories are harmless enough, so long as one does not claim for them the status of truth. Establishment of the identity of the sitter for Hilliard's portrait requires evidence from outside the hermetic confines of Dr. Hotson's arguments. In the absence of such evidence he remains an "Unknown Man clasping a Hand issuing from a Cloud."

Never mind. Even voyagers unprepared to disembark when Dr. Hotson reaches port will have had their spirits refreshed by the numerous and varied pleasures along the way. He has beguiled us before without in the end winning us over. With *Shakespeare by Hilliard* Dr. Hotson should succeed in opening the eyes of the general reader, that vanishing species, to the allegorical riches of Renaissance portraiture, and to the self-sufficient excitement of the scholar's quest. He will enlighten student and specialist alike with sentences crammed with information from widely scattered sources:

> The *manus Dei* appears pictured A.D. 245 in the Synagogue at Dura-Europos on the Euphrates, in the Roman catacombs, in a medal of Constantine the Great, frequently in Christian art of the Dark and Middle Ages, and in the Bayeux Tapestry.

Even the journal-wearied professional Shakespearean will profit in unexpected ways from so learned a guide (there are some nice bits on Autolycus, "litter'd under Mercury"). The book affords a species of delight distantly akin to that of *The Anatomy of Melancholy;* we do not always accept Burton's conclusions either. In his last chapter Dr. Hotson owns to having another study of the Sonnets up his sleeve. May his youth prevail as he gets on with the task in his ninth decade.

(1977)

III. A NATIONAL RELIGION ESTABLISHED*

Did Ophelia, besides her other woes, suffer from bad breath? In Shakespearean commentary no suggestion—however trivial, *outré*, obstinately wrong-headed, or ludicrously ill-informed—is out of bounds. That is one reason Shakespeare presents such a unique challenge, at once inspiriting and depressing to the historian of criticism. As for the issue of Ophelia's breath, we find it surfacing not, as we might expect, in an age of oral hygiene, but in 1698, in Jeremy Collier's *Short View of the Immorality, and Profaneness of the English Stage.* Shakespeare should have drowned Ophelia sooner, he suggests: "To keep her alive only to sully her Reputation, and

---

*On *Shakespeare: The Critical Heritage*, ed. Brian Vickers (London: Routledge & Kegan Paul, 1974–81), Vol. 1: 1623–1692; Vol. 2: 1693–1733; Vol. 3: 1733–1752; Vol. 4: 1753–1765; Vol. 5: 1765–1774; Vol. 6: 1774–1801.

discover the Rankness of her Breath, was very cruel." Collier's heavy-handed sarcasm did not go unnoticed. The next year James Drake came to Ophelia's defense in *The Ancient and Modern Stage Survey'd:* "Nay, Mr *Collier* is so familiar with her as to make an unkind discovery of the unsavouriness of her Breath, which no Body suspected before. But it may be this is a groundless surmise, and Mr *Collier* is deceived by a bad Nose, or a rotten Tooth of his own."

Collier notices Shakespeare only passingly—the reference to Ophelia, another to Falstaff. ("He is thrown out of Favour as being a *Rake,* and dies like a rat behind the Hangings." Has Collier, one wonders, confused Falstaff with Polonius?) That Vickers should find space for snippets from a controversialist's polemic against the stage of his own day testifies to the extraordinary breadth of this *Critical Heritage* round-up. A special commitment underlies the contents of these six substantial volumes. Vickers stands at the opposite end of the spectrum from such other historians as Arthur M. Eastman, who defends his strategy thus in his brisk *Short History of Shakespearean Criticism* (1968):

In military history, said A. W. Schlegel, we do not give the name of every soldier who fought in the files of the hostile armies: "we speak only of generals, and those who performed actions of distinction." The same truth applies to the history of Shakespearean criticism.

Vickers finds space—lots of space—for the foot soldiers, and even for some guerrilla partisans. His aim was to present "an integrated picture" of the vicissitudes of Shakespeare's reception in England; one that would include, besides formal criticism, the major adaptations of Shakespeare's plays, theatrical notices (both of the original texts and of revampings), and textual criticism.

Despite this amplitude, Vickers allows himself exclusions. He gives short shrift to the abundantly documented coronation ceremonies for the National Poet at the Stratford Jubilee of 1769; even shorter shrift—a single paragraph in which he manages to confuse William-Henry Ireland with his father Samuel—to the great Shakespeare Forgery that enthralled London as the century drew to a close. Still, Vickers had to draw the line somewhere. Readers may well feel he should have drawn it more ruthlessly all along. Do we really need three pages of Samuel Badcock, dissenting minister and copious reviewer, on the 1773 Johnson-Steevens *Shakespeare?*

These volumes tend to get fatter, although not uniformly so, as the series moves along: 448 pages for Volume 1, 650 for the last installment. All told, 309 entries; God's plenty. Yet it is the reviewer's duty to note—as all users of these books cannot but be aware—that Vickers has concluded without bringing to completion an undertaking which has occupied him for a decade. In the General Editor's Preface, five times repeated, B. C. Southam remarks that the collection is intended to chronicle Shakespeare's "reception and reputation extensively, over a span of three centuries." By my arithmetic that would bring us roughly to 1923. I shrewdly suspect that that was never Vickers' expectation. Indeed, in a final personal note he ruefully confesses that he "imagined that six volumes would be enough to take the story down to 1832." Hazlitt published his *Characters of Shakespeare's Plays* in 1817, and the two essays on Shakespeare which Coleridge himself saw through the press appeared, respectively, in 1817 and 1818.

Vickers had thus hoped to end with these and other Romantic luminaries. As things stand, he concludes on a note of decrescendo at 1798–1801 with brief selections from William Richardson, Nathan Drake, and Arthur Murphy. The miscalculation, we are informed, resulted from the quantity and interest of the eighteenth-century material Vickers unexpectedly turned up. Such are the penalties and rewards of scholarship, and the editor must count himself fortunate in having had his publisher's go-ahead. Whether his readers will fully share such gratitude may be open to question. I do not myself doubt that Vickers could have come up with an entirely responsible, and probably more shapely, survey in the six volumes allotted him had he resisted temptations to critical self-indulgence; exclusion, no less than admission, is after all part of the editor's task.

The first volume surveys the period from the publication of the 1623 Folio until the performance of *The Fairy Queen,* an operatic version of *A Midsummer Night's Dream,* possibly by Elkanah Settle, with music by Purcell, in 1692. This is the longest span covered by any single installment, and critically the most barren. We begin with Ben Jonson's poem in memory of his beloved, probably the most celebrated eulogy in the language, but one which (as Vickers reminds us) Dryden would disparage as "An Insolent, Sparing, and Invidious Panegyrick." Others have taken different views in a debate which reverberates to the present day. Phrases provided touchstones for future inquiry: "Thou hadst small *Latine* and lesse *Greeke,*" for example, which sometimes became "Small Latin and little Greek"—not precisely the same thing—or even, in Samuel Johnson's 1765 Preface, "*small Latin, and no Greek.*" Vickers reproduces brief scattered comments from the commonplace book, c. 1655, of Abraham Wright, Vicar of Okeham, averring that *Hamlet* is but "an indifferent play, the lines but meane: and in nothing like *Othello*"; the gravediggers' scene has its points, but doesn't compare with a little number like Thomas Randolph's *Jealous Lovers.* Brief *Diary* entries from Pepys follow—on the way to Deptford by water on August 20, 1666, he read *Othello,* which he had "heretofore esteemed a mighty good play, but having so lately read *The Adventures of Five Hours,* it seems a mean thing." Clearly the curtain had not yet begun to rise on bardolatry; a later—and most consequential—part of Vickers' story.

In the absence of anything like formal criticism, he gives many of his early pages to theatrical adaptations. He even finds space for Dryden's *All for Love,* which, although *"Written in Imitation of Shakespeare's Stile,"* is (as Vickers grants) not properly an adaptation. All told, he gives excerpts from fourteen plays in his first volume. Of these the most significant, from the standpoint of theatrical history, is Nahum Tate's *King Lear,* in which the reviser hit upon the happy expedient of having "run through the whole A *Love* betwixt *Edgar* and *Cordelia,* that never chang'd word with each other in the Original." Tate's *Lear,* signaling the ascendancy of neoclassical prejudices, would hold the stage without rival for a century and a half.

In subsequent volumes, adaptations usurp less space. These fall off numerically, and anyway Vickers has other fish to fry. Should he have included them in the first instance? I have mixed feelings about this. Plays by their very nature tend to take lots of printed space, and the anthologist, mindful of other imperatives, will in abridging be naturally drawn to the most striking innovations. What the adapter keeps, however, is also part of the story, and all sorts of small alterations—brief excisions, transpositions, substitutions of phrase—contribute to the overall effect. Vickers himself seems a bit defensive on this score, allowing (Vol. 1, Pref.) that he would have preferred to give some adaptations entire. Perhaps he should have done so, and summarized (with illustrative quotation) the others. In any event, I would agree that the adaptations have a place here. They affected the sensibilities of critics and editors; without them the theatrical notes of Arthur Murphy, George Steevens, and others, which sometimes hold much interest, would have been reproduced *in vacuo.*

The pot comes finally to a boil over Garrick. In his version of *The Winter's Tale* he gets round the sixteen-year interval between Acts 3 and 4, so offensive to neoclassical taste, by the simple expedient of scuttling the first two acts, and summing up the antecedent action in a tedious new first scene. Garrick made musicals out of *The Tempest* and *A Midsummer Night's Dream.* For his *Romeo and Juliet* he introduces a "grand funeral dirge" for the as yet undeceased heroine, and has Juliet come to before poison ends her Romeo's life. "Oh *Juliet! Juliet!*" he whispers in his dying breath, upon which she faints on his body. This improvement won plaudits although it did not go unnoticed that Garrick had been anticipated by Otway in *his* rescension with the unlikely title, *The History and Fall of Caius Marius* (1697; item 20). But perhaps most unsettling—and certainly least generally familiar—of his popular adaptations is his *Hamlet.* Garrick torpedoes most of Act 4, scenes 5–7, and Act 5, reducing the 1,002 lines to 104, and adding 37 of his own pseudo-Shakespearean invention. Out of deference to neoclassic aversion to mixing the genres, he denies his audience those crowd-pleasers, the gravediggers. Hamlet never sails for England, so no ambassador need report that Rosencrantz and Guildenstern are dead. This adaptation dispenses with the fencing match and the poisoned rapier and wine, hence also with Osric; in the end Hamlet—so the stage direction reads—*"runs upon Laertes's sword and falls."* The Queen flees and falls into a trance. Thus did Garrick, as he boasted to an acquaintance, rescue "that noble play from all the rubbish of the 5th act." Yet otherwise he showed greater respect for the text than his stage-manager predecessors. Garrick's *Hamlet* became a box-office triumph at Drury Lane. Walpole fumed, but Voltaire applauded.

Vickers sees this castrated affair as "the most remarkable adaptation of the period, and the greatest sacrifice to contemporary taste." Accordingly, he makes it the centerpiece for his discussion of Garrick in Volume 5, and reproduces all the notices he has managed to put together. Of the adaptation itself, though, he gives only the portion from 4.5.125 (Laertes' demand to know where his father is) to the end; five pages here. It is just the second time that this text, which survives in a Folger Library manuscript, has been printed anywhere.

In his own time the charismatic Garrick inspired extraordinary adulation, although he had his detractors too. Vickers painstakingly attempts a balanced view, and I think succeeds, giving attention even to the actor's role as a collector of old plays, to which, after an assessment of the evidence, he accords unstinting praise. His handling of Garrick typifies his judicious way with his materials throughout. Vickers gives—for example—a similarly balanced estimate of Johnson's Introduction to his 1765 *Shakespeare*, on which so much scholarly ink has been spilt.

In broad outline the story these volumes chronicle is familiar enough, but here given a special resonance in the *Critical Heritage* by reason of the rich contextual framework which Vickers uses to set off the key critical exhibits. The Frenchified taste-makers of the Restoration, themselves ruled by the rules, shook their heads over Shakespeare's free-wheeling violations of the unities, decorum, and poetic justice. Thomas Rymer drew his own moral from *Othello* with savage glee:

> 1. First, This may be a caution to all Maidens of Quality how, without their Parents consent, they run away with *Blackamoors*. . . .
> 2. Secondly, This may be a warning to all good Wives that they look well to their Linnen.
> 3. Thirdly, This may be a lesson to Husbands, that before their Jealousie be Tragical the proofs may be Mathematical.

Rymer's racialist sneers prompted Charles Gildon to remonstrate that "Even here at home Ladys that have not wanted white Adorers have indulg'd their Amorous Dalliances with their Sable Lovers, without any of *Othello*'s Qualifications, which is proof enough that Nature and Custom have not put any such unpassable bar betwixt Creatures of the same kind because of different colors." Others made a similar point; "even in *England*," remarked Mrs. Lennox—a fierce neoclassicist with feminist stirrings—"we see some very handsome Women married to Blacks, where their Colour is less familiar than at *Venice*."

By and large, Rymer—that venomous insect (as Gildon saw him)—

received a respectful hearing. Still, the plays themselves did not fail to transport readers, nor to move theatre audiences to tears and laughter. And if, in general, Shakespeare paid little heed to Time and Place, did not Unity of Character, which he never failed to preserve, matter ever so much more? The most quotable passages were gathered together and popularly disseminated; William Dodd, the clergyman editor of *The Christian Magazine*, published *The Beauties of Shakespeare* in two volumes in 1752—an anthology that went through numerous editions and remained in print long after its compiler had been hanged for forgery.

Others enumerated Shakespeare's faults with equivalent relish. The tension between neoclassical theory and Shakespearean practice runs through the criticism of the period. Pope is typical: while praising Rymer as, "on the whole, one of the best critics we ever had," he can yet allow that "To judge . . . *Shakespeare* by *Aristotle*'s rules is like trying a man by the Laws of one Country who acted under those of another." Long before the century was out, the English public had rendered up its foregone verdict. "With us islanders *Shakespeare* is a kind of established religion in poetry." Thus, Arthur Murphy in 1753 admonished the most formidable anti-Shakespearean of the Enlightenment, Voltaire himself.

An established church requires an authorized version of Holy Writ. The apostolic succession of eighteenth-century editors, from Rowe in 1709 to Steevens et al. in 1793, packaged and re-packaged Shakespeare for evolving tastes, and consolidated and amplified knowledge. Similitudes—buildings and greenery appealed—express editorial sensibility. Shakespearean drama reminds Pope of "an ancient majestick piece of *Gothick* Architecture compar'd with a neat Modern building. . . . It has much the greater variety, and much the nobler apartments; tho' we are often conducted to them by dark, odd, and uncouth passages." In Shakespeare, for Theobald, "as in great Piles of Building, . . . some Parts are made stupendiously magnificent and grand, to surprize with the vast Design and Execution of the Architect; others are contracted, to amuse you with his Neatness and Elegance in little." To Johnson, Shakespeare was a forest rather than a formal garden; "oaks extend their branches and pines tower in the air, interspersed sometimes with weeds and brambles, and sometimes giving shelter to myrtles and to roses."

While unintimidated by established reputations, Vickers has his own unconventional editorial heroes—Charles Jennens, for example, who truly appreciated the importance of textual collation and exactness, and correctly took the measure of that unconscionable intimidator Steevens. Historians (myself included) have too often failed to take Jennens seriously enough—although anybody who undertakes to publish a book anonymously and embellishes it with a fulsomely appreciative dedication to himself is probably inviting mirth.

Theobald presents a weightier case. He was singularly unfortunate both in his friendships and his enmities. In *Shakespeare Restored* (here generously excerpted) he gave *a Specimen of the Many Errors, As well Committed, as Unamended, by Mr. Pope in his Late Edition of this Poet.* A dilettante who saw himself as discharging "the dull duty of an Editor," Pope vented his understandable fury by making Theobald the hero of the first *Dunciad,* yet at the same time didn't hesitate to avail himself of many of Theobald's readings when a new edition of his own *Shakespeare* was called for. Theobald's relations with another fellow Shakespeare editor, the terrible William Warburton, were psychologically more complex. Theobald deferred obsequiously to Warburton, in every way his inferior, and—in correspondence— declared gratitude for fellowship he took to be "the offspring of a truly generous mind." But Warburton's mind knew no generosity, nor did Christian charity lurk in the bosom of the clergyman who would be elevated to the see of Gloucester. His emendations, offered with breathtaking arrogance and dogmatism, made him the laughing-stock of the *cognoscenti.*

Theobald is best appreciated for such happy readings as "'a babbled [Folio: 'a Table'] of green fields" in *Henry V,* and Macbeth's "bank and shoal [Folio: 'Schoole'] of time"; but he played a grander role than these would suggest. Vickers, surely correctly, sees Theobald as a pioneering theoretician and practitioner of "total editing." His gifts did not go unrecognized in his own day, but they were not sufficiently recognized, and he had the further misfortune of suffering Johnson's terrible, and amply disseminated, censure as "a man of narrow comprehension and small acquisitions"; ignorant, faithless, and petulant. In the *Critical Heritage* the process of rehabilitation, already well underway, proceeds apace.

Edward Capell, the last of Vickers' heroes, is the one that in the end he has come most to admire "for his combination of intelligence, good sense, enormous range of learning, minute accuracy, scrupulousness of detail, and the ability to visualize a text in theatrical terms, a grasp of its totality which is rare in any age and was unique in his own." High praise indeed, from a critic not given to superlatives, and justified by the selections in this volume and the preceding. Also a judgment not easily arrived at, for Capell, like Theobald—but in a different way—was his own worst enemy.

An enthusiast of typographical excellence, he refused to disfigure his pages with notes, and so reserved them for separate publication, with other ancillary materials, in the over 1800 mostly double-column pages of his *Notes and Various Readings to Shakespeare,* which I have found, I dare say like others, a nightmare to consult. Capell's ungainly prose style also didn't help matters. "If he had come to me," Johnson remarked to his "much valued friend" Bennet Langton, "I would have endeavoured to endow his purposes with words; for, as it is, he doth gabble monstrously." Yet Capell gave of himself prodigiously to his life's work; report holds that he transcribed all of Shakespeare ten times over. At last, in our own time, recognition has belatedly come, first, some twenty years ago, in an essay by Alice Walker hailing Capell as "a neglected Shakespearian," to whom indeed we owe the very word "Shakespearean." Eastman, to be sure, fails to mention Capell, but now that he has been promoted by Vickers to general, and decorated for valor in the field, awareness of his achievement should be quickly spreading to a large, non-specialist audience.

Vickers includes a good sampling from Capell, and for the others, from Pope onwards, he supplements the editor's Introduction with some of the notes, which are in places more provocative and informative (besides being more difficult of access) than the Introductions themselves. Picking and choosing must have been a prodigious task. Vickers himself lightly annotates his own texts; too lightly maybe: not everybody can be counted on to know that Sir Paul Pliant (cited by Aaron Hill here) is a character in Congreve's *Double Dealer*. But Vickers is, I suspect, merely deferring to *Critical Heritage* policy in such matters. He translates Latin quotations, and—an especially welcome feature—cites their precise origins. (No identifications are offered of the Shakespeare portraits on the jackets. This is a pity—few readers will, I imagine, know that the one for Volume 3 (for example) reproduces the handsome Janssen likeness that now hangs at the Folger.) My spot checks of the texts themselves reveal a commendable standard of accuracy. Vickers' head-notes to the 309 selections are concisely informative.

In his six general Introductions he is never merely perfunctory, nor does he patronize the uninitiated reader, who may sometimes feel he has been given more than he bargained for: the nine generous sections of Vickers' last Introduction occupy almost 90 pages. Unfortunately, he cannot resist discursiveness in his notes, which here run to more than 20 pages. Like everybody else, Vickers makes mistakes, which he hastens to correct. Thus, he concludes Volume 4 with a notice, from the *Critical Review* (1765), which he confidently entitles, "George Steevens on restoring Shakespeare's text." It is always dangerous to ascribe ephemeral journalistic pieces on the basis of style, and here Vickers comes a cropper; in the next volume he correctly attributes the item to William Guthrie. No edifice of critical speculation collapses and has to be rebuilt as a result, but such details have their own interest—say, for the biographer of Steevens. That great and harmful eccentric deserves a biography.

A measure of a successful anthology of any kind is its capacity to tease one into looking beyond its covers. That happened to me more than once— for example, when I encountered Charlotte Lennox in Volume 4 (item 141). She is no great shakes as a critic, to be sure, but the headnote and extracts intrigued me, so I looked into her career, and laid hands on the three volumes of her *Shakespeare Illustrated* (1753, 1754). Born in Albany, New York, Mrs. Lennox took up the literary life in London. She translated from the French, wrote plays, poems, and romances, and helped edit a monthly magazine, *The Ladies' Museum*. Johnson befriended her, and crowned her with laurel at a "debauch" at the Devil Tavern; in his *Dictonary* he cites Charlotte under "Talent"—attentions which, Mrs. Thrale reports, turned her head. Johnson composed the elaborate dedication running to ten printed pages—one of half a dozen he did for her—which graces *Shakespeare Illustrated.* "My *Sex,* my *Age,*" he has her protest, "have not given me many Opportunities of mingling in the World." Still, she for a time didn't do too badly before dying in penury in 1804.

Vickers hasn't done too badly either. His *Critical Heritage* chores past, he declares an interest in picking them up again one day, should the demand exist and the publisher agree. I hope he does. Meanwhile, he has other commitments—long deferred—to get on with. In bidding *au revoir,* Vickers leaves his followers with an impressive addition to the Shakespeare shelf. Hardly anyone, I expect, will read these volumes through seriatim, but they will be frequently consulted for edification and sometimes even amusement.

(1982)

8
Three Conferences

I. TO SENDAI FOR SHAKESPEARE

It looked comfortably familiar, this gathering of middle-aged, conservatively attired donnish types, with a sprinkling of the young (junior lecturers and postgraduate students) and a few smartly dressed women. They had come together on a fine October weekend to listen to learned papers, exchange academic chitchat, and do a little sightseeing. Because I had arrived on a late train I missed the first session, a panel discussion called "What is Jacobean Drama?" but was informed, reassuringly, that the participants gave guarded answers. The next day there were papers on the consciousness of self-deception in Shakespeare's Sonnets, dramatic technique in *Macbeth,* and the tragic sense of Robert Greene; also an entry on Machiavelli and the English Renaissance. My own contribution "In Search of Shakespeare" (an examination of some of the problems of biographical research), was to be the principal paper at the conference. All these meetings, I thought as I joined the reception, were much the same, whether in Evanston or Waterloo or Stratford-upon-Avon. But I had flown almost halfway round the world for this one. It was being held in Sendai— formerly Morinomiyako, city of the forest—a provincial center (population half a million) 200 miles north of Tokyo; and the papers, all save mine, were in Japanese. This was the sixteenth annual conference of the Shakespeare Society of Japan, hosted by Tohoku University.

At the railway station I was met by Peter Hyland, a lecturer in English at Tohoku. "What brings you to Sendai, on the narrow road to the deep north?" he asked, alluding to one of Bashō's travel sketches. "Nobody comes to Sendai." But Hyland had come two years previously, a casualty of the Great Academic Famine of the 1970s: reared in Huddersfield, Ph.D. from McMaster University (thesis on disguise and role-playing in Jonson), a wife and growing family, no job. He had done time in Tabriz, in Iran, where the Martian landscape of red mountains oppressed him; *that* was the middle of nowhere. Now he was lucky to have a university post with congenial colleagues; Tohoku, he told me, received two or three applications each week from American hopefuls. Still, he longed for an English pork pie.

Sendai bustles on Saturday night, so we had trouble finding a taxi, and arrived late for the reception. Over a hundred conferees stood round rather stiffly, ignoring a table laden with food (eastern and western), excellent Japanese bottled lager, knives and forks and chopsticks; courtesy required that everybody wait until the guest of honor had first helped himself. Then after we had all wet our whistles and retreated from the trough, people came over, some rather hesitantly, as though diffident about using their English, and we talked about their projects: a commentary on Aristotle's *Poetics,* a comparative study of Shakespeare and Racine, a source investigation of *Othello.* One man had edited *The Changeling,* and reported a production on the Japanese stage somewhat the worse for *Marat-Sade* influence. Another told me about being held hostage aboard the Japan Air Lines plane hijacked out of Bombay. He described the dehydrating heat inside the craft, the brutality of the terrorists, the fear. I marvelled: "It certainly shows a lot of dedication to Shakespeare scholarship to come to the conference so soon after your ordeal." He smiled sheepishly; actually, he said, he was on the lam from reporters seeking him, as apparently the only Japanese hostage with fluent English, for an interview for a world television audience. "I think I'm safe here." Nobody comes to Sendai.

Yet it is a handsome, modern city with wide boulevards and innumerable trees; in the mountains outside, autumn leaves had already begun to fall. A short distance away is Matsushima which, with its cedars and pines, fantastic dragon ferries, and hundreds of tiny volcanic islands eroded by wind and the squid-crowded sea, is reckoned one of the three most spectacular views in Japan. The guidebooks all quote Bashō's haiku which, by the simple expedient of repeating the name, Matsushima, along with an untranslatable exclamation of rapture, celebrates such beauty as words cannot convey. But my hosts told me that the poem was not a true haiku, and that the attribution was suspect; Bashō Apocrypha, one sneered. No similar doubt attaches to Edmund Blunden. He celebrated his stay with a poem, and out of respect and gratitude the locals erected a monument in his honor. It is on a small hill somewhere in Matsushima but I never got to see it, nor had anyone I met. However, at the Plaza Hotel in Sendai, the owner, proud possessor of a holograph poem by Blunden, plans to place a memorial stone in the hotel garden. Blunden is big in Japan.

My lecture seemed to go down well enough. Cameras snapped, the recording machine taped. On the slow train back to Tokyo, as I sipped my Kirin in the restaurant car, an assistant professor from Kyoritsu Women's Junior College—she had attended the conference—alluded to some farfetched rumors she had heard about my reasons for abandoning my chair at Northwestern University. Academic gossip, I mused; it certainly gets around.

While in Japan I gave a lecture at Meisei University on the outskirts of the overwhelming urban sprawl that is modern Tokyo. In the library, with my shoes removed, I shuffled respectfully past a case displaying the First Folio. Report holds that this is the only copy in Japan. Meisei means "Bright Star," and the library staff regard this volume as the brightest star in the collection. But it forms part of a constellation that includes the other three Shakespeare Folios, as well as early quarto editions of *Henry V* and *King Lear.* Shakespeare is alive and well in Japan.

(1977)

II. SHAKESPEARE SHANGHAIED

At the International Shakespeare Conference held at Stratford-upon-Avon in 1980 Professor Philip Brockbank, lately installed as director of the University of Birmingham's Shakespeare Institute, stirred the delegates when he introduced Professor Lin Tung-chi. A rather fragile, elderly man, Lin had come from Fudan University in Shanghai. He carried a scroll, handsomely inscribed in Chinese characters, with a poem paying tribute to the Institute and its conference. Professor Lin has since died, but the Chinese connection thrives. Among the newcomers at this year's conference, the twentieth, were Professor Zhouhan Yang from Peking University and Professor Lu Gu-sun, director of the lately established Shakespeare Library at Fudan.

Some of us were a little apprehensive about the prospect of meager attendance, for only last summer Stratford had played host to the World Shakespeare Congress, which meets every fifth year in a different venue. As things worked out, 170 of the faithful turned up: from Kent and Ghent, from Tbilisi State University of Soviet Georgia and the University of Georgia in the New World Athens; from thirty countries all told. I didn't meet the delegate listed in the program as from the Polish Writers' Union, although I understand he showed up; but the East Germans were absent, including a man from Humboldt University down for an address. Those who came were impressed with the generally high standard set by the papers.

Professor Lu dwelt on the relatively recent enthusiasm for *Hamlet,* as for Shakespeare generally, in the People's Republic. After a ten-year freeze, translations and studies now abound; a China Shakespeare Society flourishes in the lakeside city of Hangzhou, and at Lhasa *Romeo and Juliet* has been successfully produced in Tibetan, with Tibetan cast. This paper, as most of the others, suited well the accommodating conference theme, "Shakespeare and the Twentieth Century."

The Nigerian playwright Wole Soyinka, from the University of Ife, talked unsolemnly about Shakespeare's hold on modern dramatists, and in doing so made the Arabic connection—the Nile must have flowed in the veins of Shayk al-Subair when he turned to *Antony and Cleopatra.* Others were occupied with the self that Auden brought to the Shakespearean mirror, or with other moderns—Stoppard, Graves, or Eliot—and Shakespeare. In a thoughtfully wrought long paper Professor Philip Edwards placed *Hamlet* in the context of modern criticism and the modern sensibility. Recent developments in textual studies had their innings when Dr. Stanley Wells challenged, with stimulating lucidity, the traditional editorial recourse to conflation of the 1608 Quarto and 1623 Folio texts of *King Lear,* characterized as a pair of legitimate—although far from identical—twins.

The RSC offered an ampler menu of evening diversions than in some recent seasons. The gorgeous and unabashedly romantic *Much Ado About Nothing*—directed by Terry Hands and designed by Ralph Koltai—and the magical *Tempest* of Ron Daniels won greatest applause, Derek Jacobi holding audiences in the palm of his hand as both Benedick and Prospero. I had several years earlier much enjoyed Michael Gambon as the dim-witted veterinary Tom in Alan Ayckbourn's *Norman Conquests,* so naturally I had great expectations of his Lear, but these alas were disappointed; Adrian Noble's gimmicky production enthralled some conferees, repelled others, and left the rest (myself included) disturbingly undisturbed. A neat idea, though, to pair *King Lear* at the large house with Edward Bond's infrequently produced *Lear* (directed by Barry Kyle) at The Other Place.

Conference innovations this year included replicas and plans connected with projected reconstructions of the Globe playhouse, one in its original Southwark habitat, the other in middle American Detroit; also an exhibition of illustrations and theatrical designs by the incomparable C. Walter Hodges. Many took advantage of the opportunity to pad about in the paddock behind Mason Croft, where our meetings were held; there Hodges had laid out, in vinyl-coated cloth strips, a ground plan, at full size, of *his* Globe reconstruction.

The first conference concert ever, conducted in Shakespeare's Guild Chapel by Colin Timms, featured the baritone Christopher Underwood and that fine soprano Elizabeth Lane, along with nine instrumentalists, in a program of rarely performed eighteenth-century pieces inspired by Shakespeare. William Boyce's "Ode to the Memory of Shakespeare"—a beguiling item—was given for only the second time in this century, and was enthusiastically received, as were the others.

Let the late Professor Lin have the last word. His translation of his own poem of praise includes this passage:

> Galaxies of worthies forgather here,
> Heritage vitalized as winged thoughts fly.
> The cherished dream of the Orchid Pavilion
> Beckons all smiles in my mind's eye.

(1982)

III. SHAKESPEARE WALLAHS

In *Shakespeare Turned East,* offered by the University Press of Mysore in 1976 as "A monument to hands and hearts across the seas," east and west met in both authorship and content. Written by Professor H. H. Anniah Gowda, Director of the Centre for Commonwealth Literature and Research at Mysore, together with Dr. Henry W. Wells, Curator of the Brander Matthews Dramatic Museum of Columbia University, it explored analogues between Shakespeare's late romances and the classic theatre of India: the Sanskrit plays of the school of Kalidasa. Wells has since died, but his collaborator continues to use the Shakespearean connection to bridge two cultures. In January in semitropical Mysore, with its palm trees, bullocks, coconuts, and University clientele, Professor Gowda brought together twenty-five or so of us for a seminar on "Shakespeare in the Commonwealth."

From near and far they came: from Sri Venkateswara University in Tirupathi and the Punjab University in Patiala; from Hyderabad, Dharwar, Calcutta, and Madras; even from the North-Eastern Hill University of Kohima. Professor Philip Brockbank, the Director of the Shakespeare Institute at Birmingham, was the British delegate. It was, I understand, the most widely representative Shakespeare conference ever to be held in India. Somehow Gowda had managed to see to it that nobody had to pay his own way; even my own return booking via India Airlines from New York was looked after. No wonder his colleagues refer to him as His Highness.

At night we slept beneath mosquito nets; by day we listened to papers and discussed them. Comments were sometimes as pungent as the local curries. "We must thank Professor ———— for his concise, insightful, and beautifully presented paper, but there are one or two points with which I must differ"; and we were off. Indian themes understandably loomed large. Professor Gowda broadened his comparative inquiries to include Shakespearean middle comedy with a talk on "Likeness and Difference between *Much Ado About Nothing* and Kalidasa's *Shakuntala,*" with special reference to the estranged pairs: Hero and Claudio, Shakuntala and Dushyanta. (Others thought that maybe Hermione was a less distant kinswoman than Hero to Shakuntala.) In "Transcendental Vision: An Indian Light on Shakespeare's Last Plays," Professor T. R. Rajashekharaiah of Gulbarga discerned the Indian view of "Samyak"—wholeness or harmony—in the dramatist's last phase.

The translator's task occupied several speakers. A lively nonacademic author and journalist from Madras, Dr. D. Anjaneyulu offered "A Simple Study" of the variety of translations and adaptations in Telugu. Mostly, he felt, these failed to measure up, and traditional Indian Pandits evinced ambivalent attitudes towards Shakespeare. Dr. V. Sachithanandan of Madurai Kamaraj University examined in detail Tamil translation, giving special attention to local traditions—linguistic, religious and cultural. "Good Shakespearean scholars are not good translators," K. S. Bhagavan sadly remarked apropos of Shakespeare in Kannada, "and good translators are not good scholars."

Shakespeare's histories failed to engage a single speaker, and the comedies too got relatively short shrift. Of the tragedies, *Hamlet* attracted the lion's share of notice; not surprisingly in a country which can boast the only learned journal anywhere devoted exclusively to a single Shakespearean play, *Hamlet Studies,* ably edited from Delhi by Professor Rupin Desai. But the paper which impressed us most was Brockbank's extraordinarily wide-ranging "Blood and Wine: Patterns of Tragic Ritual from Aeschylus to Soyinka." I found Brockbank most moving on *Antony and Cleopatra,* considered in relation to the Bacchae plays of Euripides and Soyinka. "Like the Bacchae plays," Brockbank observed, "the action of *Antony and Cleopatra* is bounded by the comprehensive and inescapable catastrophic process by which we are all born, flourish and die, and the poet articulates that elemental cycle through which life reverts to the slime which breeds it ('let the water-flies / Blow me into abhorring') and then starts up again with the help of erotic agriculture ('he ploughed her, and she cropped')." I chaired this session, and it wasn't out of mere compliment that I was moved to observe that Professor Brockbank had dealt profoundly with the profundities which were his subject matter.

The arrangements for all these goings-on went forward with a sometimes exasperating, but mostly engaging, fluidity. We heard at least one speaker who was not listed in the program; ten of the twenty-eight others failed to show. Just as well, as things turned out, for there wouldn't have been time for them anyway: our four days were crammed. Rather late in the advance planning, I had been asked to come armed with "a general paper on 'Shakespeare in the Commonwealth,'" so I was prepared to talk for perhaps thirty or forty minutes about Northrop Frye, Harold Oliver, Desai, and Sen Gupta and other worthies; but when I arrived I learned that a fifteen-minute introductory address, part of the seminar inauguration, would do nicely, thank you very much. Only when I saw the program did I realize that I was also down for a full-length paper, title unspecified, later on in the proceedings. I talked about the playwright's relations with his own commonwealth—stage censorship and the like—and in the end had a good time.

A bonus was the appearance one day at our guest house of a professor on sabbatical leave from York University in Ontario. Canadian literature rather than Shakespeare was his line, and, with his wife, he was cutting a swath across India, at intervals breaking the journey at university lodgings. He was keen to repay hospitality by singing for his supper, and so requested time at our seminar to sing the praises of Canadian Stratford: the theatre, the company, the performances; a dulcet tune. He harbored, I learnt, an ulterior motive; during World War II he had served as an officer in the Indian army, and now he was keen to find his faithful batman, whom he had not seen all these years. How to accomplish this? He had no address, only some old photographs. Madras, he thought, was where the batman might be, and a newspaper advert was in order. I suggested a private eye—some Indian Lew Archer—a proposal which was politely received. Later, in Delhi, I checked the telephone directory to see whether detective agencies indeed formed part of that scene, as they did of ours. Sure enough, a number advertised their services, discretion assured. I hope one day I may find out how my new acquaintance fared in tracking down his old batman.

More than once during the seminar's deliberations anxiety was expressed over how Shakespeare—and the humanities generally—would fare in the universities amid the hardware and software bequeathed by the computer-chip revolution; for inevitably, as we all recognized, a knowledge explosion carries in its wake an ignorance explosion. As regards this concern, as well as others, east met west at Mysore. On the whole, people however troubled, didn't despair over what the future might hold, and my own overall impression, very keenly felt, was that Shakespeare is alive and well in India.

(1983)

9
Shakespeare in Performance

I. SEEING SHAKESPEARE PLAIN: THE ROYAL SHAKESPEARE COMPANY, 1977

After some doubtful experiments, including a *Much Ado* with the incomparable Sinden inviting (and getting) easy laughs against the unlikely setting of Imperial India, the Royal Shakespeare Company has lately managed more than once to achieve popular success without artistic compromise. The happier new phase calls for appreciative notice.

Last summer the company had the temerity to mount all three parts of *Henry VI*. They had last graced the Stratford repertory in the quatercentenary year, protectively disguised as *The Wars of the Roses*. Back in 1964 such free-wheeling adaptation, which included a good deal of pseudo-Shakespearean verse cooked up for the occasion, failed—with a few exceptions—to elicit the howls of execration that usually greet any tampering with a sacred text. But this was King Henry of enfeebled memory, not Prince Hamlet. A lot of ordinary playgoers had never heard of the works, they were juvenilia (although the author, father of three, was hardly a juvenile), and maybe Shakespeare—as authorities from Theobald onwards had argued—did not write all of it. Now Terry Hands was treating *Henry VI* respectfully, presenting reasonably full texts without reshufflings and interpolations; in short, Shakespeare *nature*, minus gimmicks. Not even the RSC being exempt from commercial pressures, this was an act of directorial courage.

In truth the productions had their drawbacks. The evolving part of Margaret, sustained through the three plays, made demands to which the talented Helen Mirren was unequal; Emrys James, slight of stature and musical of voice, was miscast as that rugged Machiavellian warrior York, while Alan Howard in the title role could not erase memories of the shamblingly moving David Warner. But Hands had set out to demonstrate that the trilogy was truly actable, and he achieved on the whole an outstanding success. A contemporary of Shakespeare describes the dead Talbot in Part I as being new embalmed with the tears of ten thousand spectators. Audiences today react less readily to the formalized rhetoric of grief, but Shakespeare's version of the saintly Maid of Orleans—

130

emphatically neither saint nor maid—was scandalously effective. *Henry VI, Part II* worked best, the black comedy of the Jack Cade uprising being accessible to the modern sensibility. A rabble follower's advice, "The first thing we do, let's kill all the lawyers" (4.2.73), gets a sure-fire response in this post-Watergate world.

I missed the one-shot marathon performance of all three plays, which ran from morning till midnight. That was sold out months ahead, and not even press tickets were to be had. So it is good news that the company has scheduled other marathons in Newcastle and in London. Meanwhile we can welcome the fact that these plays, with their epic dramaturgy and panoramic view of a society plunging hell-bent into anarchy and civil war, have returned to the repertory, along with *Titus Andronicus* and other previously contemned achievements of Shakespeare's so-called apprenticeship.

In Stratford the pilgrims of summer have gone now, and the tour coaches stand less thick on the Birthplace curbside. The Shakespeare season continues, however, both there and in the West End. Trevor Nunn's *Macbeth*, a sensation last year at The Other Place, the company's own bare-bones alternative to the lavishly fitted out Royal Shakespeare Theatre, has transferred to London. There, with Ian McKellen and Judi Dench still the principals, it now mesmerizes audiences at the Warehouse, a stone's throw from the echoing emptiness of the disused Covent Garden market. The house holds a mere couple of hundred, and the seats, all unreserved, are a bargain at £1.50—if you can get them. To assure myself of a good place (only the front row offers an unobstructed view) I showed up over half an hour before the doors opened on a chilly December night. I was too late, and mildly alarmed when the couple alongside politely asked me what play we were queueing for.

Inside we shivered some more on the uncushioned seats. Of the three electric fires—the sole discernible sources of heat—only one functioned. The Warehouse is a desolate box, with the lighting equipment suspended from the high ceiling, and performance taking place within a circle painted on the plank floor. Production in such surroundings enforces Aristotle's principle that, of the several elements of drama, spectacle matters least. There was no furniture to speak of (fair enough; why should the actors enjoy more comfort than the paying customers?), only up-ended wooden crates, which must do even for the banquet at Forres, where Macbeth finds himself with one guest too many.

Clothes and uniforms were a deliberate hodge-podge. Duncan, an imposing physical presence, wore a white gown and a crucifix round his neck; with white hair and beard, he cut an appropriately saintly figure. But Malcolm appeared in a turtleneck, and Macbeth kept his papers in a convenient zippered envelope. I don't know if it was an intended touch that the murderer reporting to Macbeth at the banquet wore an adhesive bandage on one finger. The only elaborate costume was the gold-embroidered vestment of royalty figured with religious iconography. It was twice briefly donned—first by Duncan, later by Macbeth—and otherwise hung empty, a symbol of the prize for which Macbeth kills. The mixture of costume, as well as the general absence of scenery, succeeded in distancing the play from any recognizable past or present.

There were other deprivations. The omission of an interval, while theatrically defensible, was cruel to middle-aged bladders on a cold night. Murdered Banquo's ghost passed up dinner, nor did we see the Show of eight Kings; it was sufficient for Macbeth to describe these incorporal realities. His enormous first soliloquy, beginning with a buried Judas-reference and opening up to a vision of Judgment Day, was thrown away without the trappings of Duncan's Last Supper, as called for by the Folio stage-direction: "Hautboys, torches. Enter a Sewer, and divers Servants with dishes and service over the stage" (1.7). But on the whole the strategy of denial worked. The effect, enhanced by audience proximity to the actors, was to enforce concentration on the language. Even the difficult long scene at the English court, with Malcolm's testing of Macduff and the recital of pious Edward's success with the King's Evil (often cut in performance), was attentively received.

Under such conditions sound effects assumed a wonderful power: the caterwauling of the Weird Sisters at the beginning, the knocking at the gate and ringing of the alarum bell, Macbeth's daggers chattering against one another as he stood trembling after Duncan's murder. Similarly effective were the spare visual effects. Never did the rolling up of a sleeve carry such weight as when Macbeth prepared to enter the chamber where the King lay sleeping. Nunn makes the most of blood. Macbeth's bloody hands looked enormous when he returned from the murder. He was slain offstage without loss of dramatic effect; we need only see Macduff's hands afterwards. Nunn spared us the sight of the tyrant's severed head. He knows the value of small effects in a small auditorium.

The acting was big, however, and not to everybody's taste. Mr. Bernard Levin, expressing a minority view, has complained about McKellen's "ranting and twitching" and Dench's veering "from improbable whispers to impossible yells." I can see his point. McKellen gave a characteristically overwrought reading. He must somehow negotiate the hero-villain's two-hour progress from valor's minion to dead butcher; but the overpowering consciousness of guilt in between most absorbs him. This Macbeth allowed himself baroque seizures of epileptic remorse; the conduits of mucus flowed at will. McKellen punctuated the most celebrated passages with strange pauses, as though haunted not only by Banquo's ghost but also the ghosts of all those other *Macbeth*s. Yet, amid all the sound and fury his blankly spoken "She should have died hereafter" (5.5.17) had great—and quiet—impact. This is an actor who achieves his best effects when under

strictest control; witness his splendid Consul Bernick in Inga-Stina Ew-
bank's felicitous new translation of *Pillars of the Community*.

He works well with Dench. Together they establish the chemistry of an
intimate relationship, evidently rooted in sexual attraction, which the deed
destroys. Her registers *were* erratic at times, rather like sophisticated
stereophonic sound equipment with a volume control going occasionally
berserk. Still her keening in the sleepwalking scene was most expressive
and in general she made a powerful impression. But this is a production
sustained by ensemble playing rather than star magnetism. John Wood-
vine's Banquo was especially well spoken, and Bob Peck as Macduff con-
vincingly expressed a manly grief too deep for tears.

Terry Hands's *Coriolanus* succeeded better than any I've seen in encom-
passing the huge dimensions of this unlovable but fascinating work. It is in
a way odd that the RSC should be having another go at it so soon after a
distinctly rum revival with Corioli a tribal settlement and the Volscians half-
naked savages, for *Coriolanus* has never rated as a stage favorite. In the era
of the common man, when "élitist" has become a pejorative, it is calculated
to give special offense.

"What is the city but the people?" demands their tribune Sicinius. "True,"
the plebs shout, "The people are the city" (3.1.199–200). But, in the complex reality of this play, the city is something greater, and different. It is
more than the lengthened shadow cast by the hero; more, too, than the
patrician class of which he is the most outspokenly right-wing representative. The city, as Menenius patiently explains (first comfortably seating
himself for a long-winded parable), is an entity comprising many mutually
dependent organs, rather like the human body. It is also an abstraction
capable of engaging powerful loyalties. Thus Coriolanus fights with extreme valor for an ungrateful Rome made up mostly of the mob he despises. Honor impels him. Later he spares the city which has dishonored
him not out of ideology but because of a mother's supplication. In yielding
he compromises the honor pledged to his new allies. The act humanizes
and destroys him. He goes back to Corioli to be slaughtered—a fate he half
expects—with the vociferous approval of a mob no less volatile than the
Romans in their loyalties. *Coriolanus* is full of irony and paradox, and rich
with the resonance of implied dialectic.

The spacious scale required the full depth (not always utilized) of the
Royal Shakespeare Theatre stage. Yet Hands kept the production simple. A
half dozen or so citizens made sufficient clamor in the big public scenes; the
assault on Corioli was choreographed rather than fought. Costumes were
(if such a thing is possible) at once severe and rich: mostly black, with some
white trim, and everywhere the glint of steel. The play *is* steel. There is a
place in the theatre for sumptuousness, but Shakespeare seems to work
best when words, rather than production values, call the tune. Less can be

more. This season, in most of its productions, the RSC seems to have fully absorbed that hard-purchased lesson.

Alan Howard showed splendid form as Coriolanus. A bloodthirsty cannibal on the battlefield—shrugging off wounds like so many shaving nicks while devouring the enemy—he melted to porridge when faced down by his even fiercer mother. Apart from gore and mom, he is fueled by vituperative tirades against the reeking multitude. When Howard stood begging votes in his ill-becoming garment of humility, his intonation took on a contemptuous sing-song that chilled. Otherwise he expressed his opinion of the masses in a voice rasping with gravelly disgust. Yet the infrequent gentler moments were tenderly realized. So, in the camp after Corioli, when the trumpets had sounded and the soldiers cheered their hero, Howard's simply delivered "I will go wash" (1.9.68) was strangely affecting.

Julian Glover, fresh from his authoritative Warwick the Kingmaker in *Henry VI,* eloquently portrayed Coriolanus' arch-adversary Aufidius. He delivered the great speech on the character of the tragic hero—the closest Shakespeare comes anywhere to setting forth a critical theory on the subject—standing almost motionless, front stage, under a bright light. During Coriolanus' reconciliation with his mother, he turned his back; one of innumerable happy touches. As Volumnia, Maxine Audley made the most of one of Shakespeare's juiciest female roles. But the company as a whole excelled. The night I went, the actor playing the Third Roman Citizen was indisposed and had to be replaced. That was a pity, but it gives me an excuse to return to Stratford to see this *Coriolanus* again.

After such austere splendors, *The Comedy of Errors* gave us the RSC in a holiday mood, and the show was in fact this year's Christmas merriment at the Aldwych. It would take a lot to dim the memory of the company's last *Comedy,* staged by Clifford Williams in 1962 and twice triumphantly revived. That production offered an Ephesus full of nimble jugglers, dark-working sorcerers, and prating mountebanks; Dr. Pinch was properly cadaverous. The spirit of commedia dell'arte reigned, and the effect was in every way magical. Reasonably, the company has not tried to top that one. Instead they have gone back with a vengeance to gimmicks. After all, *The Comedy of Errors* is minor Shakespeare, of mediocre literary quality (as somebody attached to the RSC remarked to me); so what the hell.

In Nunn's new production, Ephesus has become a modern Greek holiday town out of a package tour. The Duke is a colonel, an imposing figure with his enormous epaulets, chest beribboned with medals, and Castro beard. To make his points he bellows into a microphone amplified by loudspeakers. The disconsolate Aegeon passes round family snapshots; Antipholus of Syracuse wears a camera round his neck, and describes Ephesus with the aid of a paperback guide. His brother's house is equipped with an entrance phone which becomes the basis for an entertaining visual gag when it is angrily ripped from its mooring. The Porpentine offers postcards, sun hats, and assorted tourist rubbish. At the Tiger Taverna a band plays, *Never on Sunday* style. With its Guy Woolfenden score, this *Comedy* has been acclaimed by the West End Society of Theatre Managers as the Best Musical of the Year. The critics have raved. Pleasure-seekers make each performance a sellout.

Many, if my audience were typical, do not know the play; a great gasp went up when the Abbess disclosed that she was Aegeon's wife. So much for West End sophistication. I was not myself bowled over. In these hybrids there is an essential incongruity between the Elizabethan text, with its own idiom and references, and the modern setting and music. A stop-and-go rhythm establishes itself as the play halts for a production number, then gets started again. One cannot reasonably expect good actors also to be accomplished singers and dancers: Roger Rees (as the Syracusan Antipholus) looked acutely uncomfortable lining out a banal ballad. Such occasions invite broad miming, and the production had a sufficiency of grimaces, mincing walks, somersaults, tongue-wagging, and the like, which eventually I found fatiguing. These exercises work best when the metamorphosis is total, and the new creation becomes something rich and strange in its own right. But we cannot really look to the RSC for another *Kiss Me Kate,* and anyway Cole Porter is dead.

Still, this *Comedy* had, besides incidental felicities, two redeeming assets. Judi Dench was in superb form as Adriana, knocking down her Campari neat while splashing her servant with the soda. She was comic shrewishness incarnate, impeccable in her timing, and nicely offset by Pippa Guard as her primly bespectacled sister, prattling bookishly about a wife's proper (sexist) role. And then, after all the mediocre songs and the longueurs of the second act, including an interminable exorcism scene, suddenly, miraculously, the whole affair lifted off at the very end. "We came into the world like brother and brother," Dromio of Ephesus says to his twin with tender wonder, "And now let's go hand in hand, not one before another" (5.1.423–24). These lines, the last in the play, became the basis for Woolfenden's best number. The Dromios sang, then the whole company joined in. So did the audience, clapping away rhythmically. The elusive magic of the theatre had asserted itself, and just about everybody (it seemed), including the many children at the matinee I attended, went off with spirits refreshed. Nunn's *Comedy* may be, as an American connoisseur said in another context, a pistash, but it isn't too bad as pistashes go. If it stirs apprehensions of a future *Hamlet* with Alan Howard wailing the Elsinore blues while a jazz combo plays mournfully in the castle keep, we will face that Danish pastry when we get to it.

I caught these productions at unlike theatres. Despite recent alterations, disguising the proscenium and bringing the stage closer to the audience, the Aldwych retains its Edwardian character. It is smaller than the Royal Shakespeare Theatre, which is revised 1930s-modern, with fancy hydraulic equipment to facilitate the manipulation of playing levels. The Warehouse is scarcely a theatre at all, as that term is generally understood. Yet the plays, from early and late in the canon, happily accommodated themselves to diverse conditions, as they do when the company goes on tour to Brooklyn or Los Angeles or Newcastle. Over the centuries they have survived not only the vagaries of taste but also changing playhouse architecture. There is a lesson here for the historian who uses the evidence of dramatic texts to help reconstruct the Elizabethan theatre or to establish theatrical provenance. For the texts were always malleable. Shakespeare's company could perform them at the large open-air Globe or small enclosed Blackfriars, at court or the Inns of Court, or at whatever passing accommodation was available during provincial itineraries. The enduring stage-worthiness of the plays, demonstrated yet again this season by the RSC, may owe something to the requirements of flexibility which Shakespeare, the supreme professional, had always to bear in mind.

(1978)

II. ALTERNATIVE SHAKESPEARE: THE ROYAL SHAKESPEARE COMPANY, 1978

Last season the Royal Shakespeare Company gambled big, and won. It gave Terry Hands, on fire to do *Henry VI*, his way, and he responded by staging the plays in their original form: without massive surgery or the adapter's artificial limbs. The trilogy had been performed a few times in recorded history—most recently by Sir Barry Jackson's Birmingham Repertory Company at the Old Vic in 1953—but never, I expect, so fully or so splendidly. One should not underestimate the risks. Even a subsidized national company cannot afford half-empty houses. That is why we see so few of Shakespeare's contemporaries despite the critical success, some years back, of *The Jew of Malta* and *The Revenger's Tragedy*. This time Hands proved the skeptics wrong. At the box office his *Henry VI* has been a great success. The academic returns, now beginning to filter in, ratify the popular verdict. Speaking of this revival in the staid pages of *Shakespeare Quarterly*, Homer Swander enthuses, "No acting company since the death of Shakespeare has performed a greater service to its art." His pronouncement perhaps smacks a little of hyperbole, but the Hands achievement *was* considerable. And he followed it up later in the same season with an austerely stunning *Coriolanus*, featuring Alan Howard, which demonstrated again the drawing power of ungimmicky Shakespeare done with flair and intelligence.

The current season of comedies at Stratford shows the company in a less venturesome mood, and not always inclined to profit from its own example. I found *The Tempest* flat, *The Taming of the Shrew* perverse, and *Measure for Measure* flat and perverse. You cannot hope to win them all. But the season has also yielded a delightful *Love's Labour's Lost* in the main house and an impressive *Merchant of Venice* at The Other Place. Peter Brook's *Antony and Cleopatra,* which has just opened, I have not yet seen.

The Clifford Williams *Tempest* is enough to make one wonder, briefly, whether Lytton Strachey did not have a point when he characterized Prospero as "an unpleasantly crusty personage, in whom a twelve years' monopoly of the conversation had developed an inordinate propensity for talking," and the play as the work of a dramatist "half enchanted by visions of beauty and loveliness, and half bored to death." Then we recall other, more magical, revivals, and remind ourselves that Strachey is merely inverting, with wonted outrageousness, the pieties of Victorian biographical criticism; he must bring Shakespeare down from his Dowden heights. Down he is in the Williams production, in which the play labors under its burden of retrospection. The director never conveys a sense of imaginative engagement. When Ariel, aided by solemn music, charmed the shipwrecked Neapolitans to sleep, I noticed that some in the audience had joined them—an extension of the airy spirit's powers that his creator can scarcely have intended.

Partly Williams was defeated by the house. I have never seen the Royal Shakespeare Theatre appear so cavernous and inhospitable. Nor did Ralph Koltai's vaguely futuristic set, with its huge celestial orb and mostly useless breaking wave, help matters, looking as it did like a reject from a low-budget sequel to *Star Wars.* The Masque of Ceres featured mannequins evidently modeling gowns for a couturier's trade fair. Even the initial shipwreck, which I had always thought sure fire, was botched: the actors, disadvantageously placed upstage, fought a losing battle with the sound effects.

A seasoned veteran of excellent voice, Michael Hordern as Prospero nevertheless lacked the presence to suggest the benevolent power of the magus. The appeal which Miranda (Sheridan Fitzgerald) found in Alan Rickman's Ferdinand is perhaps best explained by the fact that she had never seen another young man; he played some lines for sniggering laughs. Only David Suchet, as Caliban, gave this becalmed *Tempest* some moments of fitful life. His bronzed skin glinting with a greenish sheen when the light caught it, he clearly hailed from the Third World, never mind which outpost.

The Victorians, assimilating Darwin, could see Caliban as the missing link; for us, still recovering from the hangover of imperialism, he is a disturbing reminder of the burden which the white man has none too gracefully set down. A special frisson attaches to his outbursts against his highminded European governor, as it does to the scene in which, seduced by firewater, he kisses his chosen master's foot, and exuberantly sings of freedom while at the same time proclaiming his new servitude. The Folio *dramatis personae* describes Caliban as "a savage and deformed slave." The only suggestion of anatomical peculiarity in Suchet's make-up was in the knobs, made of congealed porridge, sprouting from his cranium. This may be the first Caliban whose deformity is edible.

About Barry Kyle's *Measure for Measure* the less said the better. Isabella (Paola Dionisotti) never exhibits the passionate virtue capable of arousing a suppressed Puritan. Perhaps just as well, for Angelo, played by Jonathan Pryce, lacks the energy to respond: he is a mediocre bureaucrat shuffling his papers with smirks and fidgety mannerisms. His realization that we are all frail should be a piercing moment of truth, but in this production it hardly stirs a ripple. When the great confrontation scenes fail to ignite, machinery takes over, and we become irritably conscious of the huge bare bones of plot. The night I attended, a number of sufferers decamped during the interval. Had they come back for more, they would have been regaled with a Mariana hitting the bottle in her barn, a Duke prepared (as if to justify Lucio's calumnies) for a romp in the hay with her, and a stark-naked Barnardine. I do not doubt that a due sincerity governed Kyle's conception, but this *Measure for Measure* is perhaps most charitably dismissed as an intent that perished by the way.

Michael Bogdanov's *Taming of the Shrew* opens with a *coup de théâtre* by now so well publicized that it cannot come as a real surprise to many spectators; rather we look forward to it with much the same expectation of vicarious delight stirred, in times past, by the mayhem in a Laurel and Hardy film. Before the house lights dim we become aware of an uproar in the aisle. A roughly dressed man, grasping a bottle, quarrels loudly in a prole accent with the usherette, then proceeds to clamber on to the stage and wreck the set—one of those tacky, pastel-flavored, Italian Renaissance confections, complete with proscenium arch, we used to associate with touring-company Shakespeare. Much tumult accompanies the demolition: stagehands running up and down, bits and pieces of carpentry collapsing.

It is one hell of a device for getting your public's attention. Jonathan Pryce, playing the pugnacious drunk, is as energetic in this *Shrew* as he was listless in *Measure for Measure*. He is the archetypal yob, dues-paying member of the brotherhood of football hooligans who mug old ladies and tear up the upholstery in railway carriages after the match; except that they congregate in mobs, while Pryce is a one-man mob. What Bogdanov is up to has the character of a manifesto. By violently dismantling the set, he is rejecting a whole genteel heritage of Shakespeare production. We are a long way from *Kiss Me Kate*.

Pryce goes on to become the drunken Sly, and then Petruchio. Unbearded but needing a shave, he plays the suitor as a heartless mercenary in the sex wars, with more than verbal brutality. He beats Grumio unplayfully; in his country house, after the wedding, he spits out his drink and hurls his overdone mutton to the rafters. Nothing will keep this male chauvinist pig from wiving it wealthily in Padua and then breaking his wife's spirit. As the chosen sow, Kate (Paola Dinisotti again), thin-lipped, with granite jaw and permed geometric hairdo, puts up a stiff fight, but the virago is no match for the macho.

The production is, it goes without saying, in modern dress, and may be recommended to anybody who prefers his Shakespeare on motorcycles, with brass bands. I liked the band. Lucentio's man Tranio is a Scot, a fact of which I was previously unaware. The others have a big time being sporadically stage Italians. For the scene in which Bianca's suitors offer their financial credentials, Baptista sits behind a huge desk, attended by a Mafia bodyguard in tinted specs, and enters the dowry inventory on his adding machine until Tranio shorts it. Why make this harmlessly bemused father into a Godfather? Enough, I suppose, that he is Italian and a businessman. Anyway, it is only a passing gimmick to be used and then discarded in favor of other gimmicks. Petruchio's pursuit of his quarry is presented as a hunt, complete with the off-stage baying of hounds. Among other fatuities, the souvenir program offers old-spelling extracts from an early hunting treatise with the long *s* ignorantly represented as *f*.

At the end an ornate chandelier overhangs a green baize gaming-table for the wager scene. Kate's long speech of wifely submission resonates with discomfiting irony. As she clasps her husband's thigh, he nervously runs his fingers through his hair, then abruptly exits, leaving Grumio to scramble on to the table to gather up his master's winnings. The huntsman, having slain the deer and won his trophy, is filled with wordless shame.

It is a symptom of the prevailing philistinism of this production that Petruchio should be throughout mispronounced with a *k*, the Elizabethan spelling being intended as the phonetic equivalent for Petruccio. I suspect that Bogdanov despised the play for its sexist values, and felt he could come to terms with it only by exploiting to the hilt his company's unequalled resources and his own abundant invention. He mangles the script with as much abandon as he mangles his inital set, although he has the conscience to forewarn the unwary, in his program, that "Certain parts of the text have been cut or rewritten." But what troubled me most was the combination of brutality with soft-core sentiment. Petruchio's change of heart lacks any preparation. It is rather like the last-minute conversion at the end of an eighteenth-century sentimental comedy; this *Shrew* is less razzle-dazzle with-it than Bogdanov would have us believe. I found the evening pretty depressing—the more so because just about everybody else seemed to be enjoying it enormously.

"They have been at a great feast of languages and stol'n the scraps" (5.1.34), mocks Moth as Armado and Holofernes exchange salutations. I caught John Barton's *Love's Labour's Lost* twice, and both times the audience feasted merrily on language with the scraps furnishing some of the tastiest bits. Yet Hazlitt wrote of the play, "If we were to part with any of the author's comedies, it should be this." Production proves him wrong. Short on plot but prodigally endowed with word-play of a distinctively Elizabethan character, *Love's Labour's Lost* was offered, and happily received, on its own terms.

Don Armado, finely played by Michael Hordern as a moth-eaten Don Quixote dreaming his impossible dream, drew out the thread of his verbosity finer than the staple of his argument. In this play only a Dull is ever at a loss for words. Costard, an unlettered clown unable to deliver a letter properly, yet favors us with *honorificabilitudinitatibus*, which the learned have traced back to Dante and Petrus of Pisa, Charlemagne's tutor. Armado brought the house down when, twiddling his mustachio, he recalled how the king had once leant on his shoulder to dally with his excrement. I suspect that a number of those around me were unaware of the word in the sense, used here, of "that which grows out or forth . . . said *esp.* of hair, nails, feathers" *(OED)*. Nor would a modern audience be likely to recall ink-horn battles, long since fought and lost, when Holofernes complains of the "rackers of orthography" who fail to pronounce the *b* in *doubt* and *debt* or the *h* in *abhominable*—solecisms which drive him, in his own neologism, to *insanie*. The posteriors of the day (for afternoon) amused mightily, as did the curate's praise of the pedant as "learned without opinion, and strange without heresy"—even if, again, one wonders how many grasped the Elizabethan sense of opinion as "self-conceit." No matter. The lines were on the whole delivered without condescending efforts to gloss them by means of business, although Paul Brooke performed wonderful arabesques of movement with Holofernes' praise of Mantuan. Barton's production demonstrated that ordinary theatregoers can respond to the verbal pyrotechnics of a set of wit well played even when the historical dimension eludes them.

The wit game is, of course, only one strand of *Love's Labour's Lost.* In Koltai's autumnal setting of a forest glade, with masses of foliage more brown than green, and a leaf now and then fluttering down, the King of Navarre and his companion lords take their foolish vows of abstinence—no women, plenty of books—only to remind themselves of the imminent arrival of the French king's daughter. So the compact is foredoomed, although Richard Griffiths, plump and bespectacled as Navarre, with a gracious diffidence, makes the situation credible in the first instance. He is well matched with Carmen Du Sautoy, also bespectacled, as the princess. The eavesdropping scene, in which each gallant in turn betrays his apostasy, with Berowne (Michael Pennington) the last to swagger hypocritically over his fellows until Costard spoils the game with his incriminating letter, was broadly played, but with much comic brio. The broadness is perhaps inevitable in a democratic age that has lost its flair for the aristocratic style in the theatre, as elsewhere. This barefoot princess sweeps up after her picnic as though in deference to some unseen "Do Not Litter" sign.

Still, the production worked up to a splendid comic crescendo in the

Show of the Nine Worthies, with Sir Nathaniel, as Alexander, veering about dangerously on his hobby-horse with his huge spear and coming to grief to the accompaniment of derisive heckling. Holofernes, as Judas Maccabeus, suffers similar ignominy, but embarrasses the onlookers—off-stage as on—when he confronts them with their bad manners: "This is not generous, not gentle, not humble" (5.2.621). The reproach comes as a salutary shock. It is followed by the greater shock of Marcade's entry, with his clipped message of death. Meanwhile (as called for by the lines) night has fallen. Barton allows full weight to the darker side of this bright comedy. Oaths, however foolishly entered, may not be lightly dismissed; Jack must wait his year before claiming Jill. In these last moments, delicately poised between laughter and poignancy, we recognize the perfect propriety of the autumnal setting.

I have saved the best for last. The afternoon I was there, Barton's arresting production of *The Merchant of Venice* was rapturously received at The Other Place, the company's alternative house, by an audience consisting almost entirely of Shakespeare scholars: the organizers of the International Shakespeare Conference, meeting that week in Stratford, had booked the whole theatre—some two hundred seats—for the delegates. This cannot be the easiest public for actors to play to, but almost everybody I talked with afterwards felt that this *Merchant* was the high point of the current season, with *Love's Labour's Lost* a close second. Particularly striking was Barton's refusal to be seduced by what may be described as the opposing voice.

Alongside the main thrust of theme, characterization, or dramatic development in Shakespeare, we may feel the presence of a negating counter-thrust which, while kept subordinate, can have a powerfully subversive effect. Together thrust and counter-thrust may assume the dramatic force of dialectic. Is the Ghost of Hamlet's father a spirit of health or goblin damn'd? The former, most of us (including Hamlet) conclude. Yet at the crowing of the cock, the Christian significance of which Marcellus makes explicit, this majestical presence starts like a guilty thing. The text offers enough other hints to encourage a minority thesis that maybe Hamlet should have resisted the unchristian injunction to revenge. *Henry V,* celebrating a hero king and the glory of Agincourt, makes an ideal wartime morale booster, as the Olivier film demonstrated; but Pistol and his crew are less than eager to rush into the breach, there is Michael Williams with his disturbing vision of legs and arms and heads chopped off in battle, and the final coda eulogizes not conquest but the medicinable virtue of gentle Peace. Thus it is possible for the director to seize upon the opposing voice (to apply Professor Maynard Mack's pregnant phrase) and, without doing great violence to his script, produce *Henry V,* Brechtian fashion, as an anti-war play. But surely the most striking instance of this recurring feature of Shakespearean dramaturgy is to be found in *The Merchant of Venice.*

The play gives us Shylock as the Devil Jew: the usurer and paternal despot, his name synonymous with anti-Semitic opprobrium. Yet Shakespeare allows him ample scope to state his case, which he does with an intelligence and eloquence that only Portia, of the gentiles, can command. Scapegoat and outcast, Shylock is spat upon and spurned like a dog by the otherwise tender-hearted Antonio. His own daughter rejects his faith, steals his gold, and casually exchanges for a monkey the ring Leah gave him when, as a bachelor, he came courting. In that most purple of passages, when Shylock asks his Christian persecutors whether a Jew has not the same senses, affections, and passions as they, contradictory voices co-exist side by side. The speech that so movingly affirms the humanity of which we all partake serves, in the last resort, to justify an inhuman purpose: "The villainy you teach me I will execute," Shylock warns Antonio's friends; "and it shall go hard but I will better the instruction" (3.1.61–62).

After the Holocaust and the history of European Jewry in this century, what is the producer—conscious that he too partakes of common humanity—to do? Some, especially in the United States, will decide to leave well enough alone, and join the school administrators who have banished *The Merchant of Venice* from the classroom. When the play is performed, the director usually takes the easier option of harkening to the opposing voice. In the Jonathan Miller production, which was deemed sufficiently innocuous to be taped for the box and viewed by the impressionable millions, Olivier wore no beard for Antonio to void his rheum on, nor did he murderously whet his knife in the Court of Justice. Offstage, after his final exit, he harrowed his audience with a great Kaddish wail of suffering; that we should not forget Shylock in the tranquility of Belmont, Antonio and Jessica exchanged meaningful glances when left alone on stage at the end. All things considered, it was a sentimental *Merchant*. Barton, on the other hand, has had the courage to be faithful to the main thrust of the play.

Shylock may not be one of Olivier's great parts, but Patrick Stewart riveted us in the role at The Other Place. He wants us to see Shylock not as a despicable Jew but as a despicable person, so he avoids stereotypically Semitic features: no ringlets or prayer shawl or stage nose. This strategy cannot, of course, fully succeed, for the script makes Shylock's Jewishness part and parcel of his villainy. But Stewart takes advantage of such opportunities as come his way. Shylock smokes hand-rolled cigarettes—the setting is Edwardian—and saves the ends in his case: a practice that at once illustrates his meanness and distances him from even his fellow Jew Tubal, who puffs a cigar. We see Shylock weighing his gold on the same scale that is later set forth for Antonio's flesh. At home, in Shylock's only private scene, we are given Jessica's view of their domesticity: "Our house is hell" (2.3.2). In the most questionable bit of business in this production, Shylock slaps his daughter after handing over his keys to her. Why? Shylock has caught the flicker of rebellion in her eyes—she is about to elope—and chastises her for it. Thus Stewart explicates. But nothing in the dialogue explains or supports the gesture and a theatre, unlike a cinema audience, cannot read the expression in Jessica's eyes. Shylock's only overtly violent act comes across as capricious tyranny.

In public he runs the gamut of emotion. He weeps, he laughs; hands and body are energetically expressive. At one point Stewart pops a couple of pills in his mouth; tranquilizers, I thought, to bring him down a peg. With Tubal he dramatically exhibits the knife he plans to use, while his friend, who has goaded him on, shakes his head disapprovingly. In the great scene of reckoning, which I have never seen more excitingly realized, Shylock removes his boot and, ostentatiously raising it, whets his blade on the sole so all may shudder. At first he is wary of Portia—he knows, from experience, the cunning of these Christians—but, like everybody else, he is mesmerized by her rhetoric, and drops his guard. When she reminds him of his alien status, Shylock knows he is done for. He grovels on hands and knees for mercy; he throws off his yarmulka, embraces his enemy (how Christian can you get?), even laughs at Gratiano's taunting joke. He will survive. As for the Venetians, they have behaved fairly by their own standards, but it is appalling to see the power of the state extort such abject submission.

All through the performance one might hear the proverbial pin drop; so rapt were we. Unfortunately, silence also greeted the Gobbo routines. With his curly hair and battered hat, Hilton McRae intended (I suppose) to remind us of Harpo Marx, and he even had Harpo's horn, which now and then he squeezed. But his noisy efforts proved strenuously unfunny; this company is weakest when it comes to the clowns. The patronizing notion that it is hilarious for an actor merely to bob up and down and scamper about dies hard, despite the fact that such antics, employed for any other playwright, would be hooted off the stage. The Edwardian setting made an anachronistic hash of Shylock's point about the Venetians using purchased slaves but otherwise did not unduly distract. These are mere details; Barton's *Merchant* deserves the tumultuous ovation which greeted it. He is this season's hero.

Such a success has its sobering aspect. In this bare-bones playhouse, with a couple of rows of not very comfortable seats and a few rudimentary props, the RSC is on the whole achieving more exciting theatre than in its luxuriously appointed and lavishly equipped principal house. The latter does well enough by large cast spectacle, but no hydraulic machinery, however sophisticated, can match for sheer effect the special rapport that springs up between actors and audience when the two are in almost tactile proximity. Nor can the big arena match the fluidity of staging at The Other Place, where the rapid flow of action brings out juxtapositions between scenes which even brief delay may obscure. The Elizabethans knew the secret: even their epic *Tamburlaine* required only a platform. The lesson of Stratford is that we need more alternative Shakespeare.

(1978)

10

The Ireland Forgeries: An Unpublished Contemporary Account

For students of Shakespearean and eighteenth-century literary byways, the Ireland affair is, in its outlines, as familiar as it is bizarre. For fifteen months, through 1795 and the following winter, the astonishing discoveries produced by a youth not yet twenty held cultivated Londoners in thrall. Then the bubble burst, disgrace and ignominy overtook the protagonists, and the episode was soon forgotten, to be resurrected by modern scholarly inquiry.

I

William-Henry Ireland, the only begetter of the Shakespeare Papers, was the son of the artist-engraver, Samuel, collector of books, pictures, and curios (in which he conducted a discreet but profitable trade), and author of illustrated books—picturesque tours of Holland and English rivers: the Medway, Thames, Wye, and Avon—which despite their insipidity enjoyed some popularity. His son, a failure at school and lacking any apparent aptitudes, he articled to James Bingley, a conveyancer in chancery. Alone in Bingley's rooms in New Inn, and surrounded by old deeds, he embarked upon his career of forging Shakespearean documents. These he produced on genuine old paper or parchment acquired from the bookstalls, setting down his labored pseudo-antique scrawls in bookbinders' fluid, and appropriately darkening the ink by holding his handiwork over the flames. William-Henry presented his discoveries to his delighted father—an impassioned enthusiast of Shakespeare in the early day of bardolatry—explaining that he owed them to the generosity of a mysterious gentleman who had allowed him to rummage in his chest. The forger began modestly with prosaic legal documents—a mortgage deed, a promissory note—before going on to ever more daring flights of fancy: an exquisitely effusive exchange between poet and patron, a Profession of Faith, a love letter and amorous verses addressed to Anna Hatherreweaye, a Deed of Gift of his manuscript plays to his friend, Master William Henrye Ireland, who had saved him from drowning in the Thames; then the holograph manuscript of the *Tragedye of Kynge Leare,* happily purged of obscurities and vulgarities for which the players were responsible; and finally a heretofore unknown original play, *Vortigern,* inspired by the legendary history of Britain. For William-Henry the Shakespeare Papers served at once to relieve the tedium of his workaday life, to win the approval of a parent persuaded of his son's witlessness, and to demonstrate his own genius.

Esteemed elders applauded. Multitudes flocked to view the papers when Samuel put them on display in his house in the Strand. The celebrated manager of Drury Lane, Richard Brinsley Sheridan, booked a production of *Vortigern.* To disarm skeptics the Poet Laureate, Garter King-of-Arms, the Whig leader, and others, including Boswell, solemnly affixed their signatures to a Certificate of Belief. The most formidable Shakespeare scholar of the day, Edmond Malone, kept aloof until Samuel on Christmas eve of 1795 published his sumptuous folio edition of *Miscellaneous Papers and Legal Instruments under the Hand and Seal of William Shakspeare: including the Tragedy of King Lear and a Small Fragment of Hamlet, from the Original MSS in the Possession of Samuel Ireland, of Norfolk Street,* embellished throughout with facsimiles of the treasures. Malone now had all the evidence of handwriting, orthography, and the like he required. Three months later he published his four-hundred-page exercise in demolition with the deadpan title, *An Inquiry into the Authenticity of Certain Miscellaneous Papers and Legal Instruments, Published Dec. 24, M DCC XCV. and Attributed to Shakspeare, Queen Elizabeth, and Henry, Earl of Southampton: Illustrated by Fac-similes of the Genuine Hand-writing of that Nobleman, and of Her Majesty; A New Fac-simile of the Hand-writing of Shakspeare, Never before Exhibited; and Other Authentick Documents.* That was on March 31. Two nights later, before a packed house at Drury Lane, *Vortigern* had its first—and last—performance with the great John Philip Kemble in the title part. Pandemonium broke loose as the play was hooted off the boards. When at last the house quieted down, Kemble reappeared on stage to announce the withdrawal of *Vortigern* and its replacement, in the aftermath of scandal, with *The School for Scandal.* The Shakespeare Papers were finished. Samuel Ireland died, broken-hearted, in July 1800. Five years later William-Henry published his swaggering and self-justifying *Confessions.*

The episode has its antecedents in the history of literary imposture. Earlier in the century James Macpherson delighted lovers of the antique with his epic *Fingal,* attributed to the legendary third-century Irish bard Ossian, son of Finn. Next came "the marvellous boy" Thomas Chatterton, who briefly imposed upon credulity with the creations of the poet-monk Thomas Rowley, confessor to the Lord Mayor of Bristol in the fifteenth century. But both Ossian and Rowley were invented. Ireland chose as his bard *the* Bard, and actually produced, rather than merely reported, the "authentic" documents for a transiently enraptured world. The fates of the three forgers differed too. Chatterton swallowed arsenic before his eighteenth birthday and became the stuff of Romantic myth. In the same year that disaster overtook the Irelands, Macpherson expired peacefully at Belville, the estate he had acquired in his beloved native county of Inverness. Destined to become neither well-heeled nor a legend, William-Henry eked out a hand-to-mouth existence as a Grub Street hack until almost sixty.

"The Ireland forgeries have been strangely neglected by historians," John Mair wrote in 1938 in the Preface to *The Fourth Forger: William Ireland and the Shakespeare Papers.* His book is an undocumented exercise in the higher journalism, written with a precocity worthy of its subject, for Mair was only twenty-four when he published it. The overused phrase "strangely neglected" is here strangely apt, and Mair's own work remedies some of the neglect. He breaks new ground by consulting the Ireland papers among the Additional Manuscripts in the British Library, as well as pertinent letters in the Bodleian. The only other book-length overview, Bernard Grebanier's *The Great Shakespeare Forgery* (1965), reflects ample consultation of Mair and contemporary printed comment generated by the controversy. His researches seem not to have tempted him to stray from Brooklyn. Abundant manuscript materials are, however, scattered among the great libraries of the United States and England; other papers remain in private hands. Some of these I consulted for my section on the Ireland affair in *Shakepeare's Lives* (1970) and my chapter on forgeries, illustrated with facsimiles, in *William Shakespeare: Records and Images* (1981). Room remains for a comprehensive study based on all the available primary sources, of which the letter in the Folger Shakespeare Library here reproduced is of more than routine interest, for it is an account of the sensational affair by an observer close to the happenings described.

II

Addressed to a John Mander in Witney, Oxfordshire, the letter is subscribed "T.C." These initials presumably stand for Thomas Caldecott. A specimen holograph in the Folger Library—a letter from Caldecott to Dr. John Sherwen dated April 23, 1818—is, allowing for the passage of more than twenty years, compatible with the hand of the document here transcribed. Circumstantial details all point in the same direction; the author's easy skill, suggestive of legal training, in presenting the case; his personal acquaintance with the Irelands, his scholarly pretensions, and his contempt for Malone. I know of no one else with the same initials who meets all these requirements.

Born in 1744, Caldecott was educated at Winchester and at New College, Oxford, where he proceeded B.C.L. in 1770. He was called to the bar at the Middle Temple, and became a bencher. There followed his long and distinguished service as counsel on the Oxford circuit. This experience produced the two volumes (1786, 1789) of his *Reports of Cases Relative to the Duty and Office of a Justice of the Peace, from Michaelmas Term 1776, inclusive, to Trinity [and thence to Michaelmas] Term 1785, Inclusive,* a continuation of Sir James Burrow's *Reports.*

A bibliophile with a passion for earlier English literature, Caldecott fancied himself an authority on Shakespeare. He disparaged his celebrated scholarly contemporaries: Steevens was "an ass"; Malone, "a fool"; Ritson, "that scurrilous miscreant." He was, however, on terms of cordial familiarity with Thomas Warton and Bishop Percy; it helped that neither the historian of English poetry nor the editor of the *Reliques* especially concerned himself with matters Shakespearean. Caldecott himself was no more than a scholarly dilettante. In 1785 he published an edition of Milton's *Poems upon Several Occasions,* which was reissued in 1791; but Shakespeare above all tested an editor's mettle. Thus it was that in 1819 Caldecott brought out at his own expense a pilot volume, slow in the making, which offered *Hamlet* and *As You Like It* as prelude to a complete *Shakespeare.* Caldecott was then seventy-six. It was bold of him to think he still had time enough left. About that he was probably right—he died at the age of ninety—but otherwise he miscalculated. His specimen texts, with their elaborate notes, stirred little interest. "This labour of nearly half a century's meditation, no sooner made its appearance," a contemporary recalled, "than the mouse was recognized as the result of the mountain throes; and the parent was never induced to add to his still-born offspring."[1] Caldecott died in February 1833.

It was as a collector that he made his mark, specializing in rare sixteenth- and seventeenth-century books. Caldecott began at an early age. In those days he could pick up for four or five shillings apiece first editions of *Venus and Adonis* and *The Rape of Lucrece* and the 1609 *Sonnets.* Later he began to haunt the auction rooms. In an age of great eccentrics he cut a curious figure. One who observed him at the auctions recalls: "His figure and manner were at once striking. Extreme shortness of vision induced him always to carry a glass, which, in the studied absence of spectacles, was placed close to the eye. His head was slightly bent on one side during the use of this glass."[2] Shortsightedness did not prevent Caldecott from acquiring, under a feigned name, rarities which had previously graced the shelves of Steevens or Farmer or West. His quartos of Shakespeare's poems and plays Caldecott bequeathed to the Bodleian Library. There remained enough exceptional books to pack Sotheby's for six days in December of 1833, prompting the *Gentleman's Magazine* correspondent to exclaim, "The Bibliomania is alive again."

One of the books Caldecott had purchased was Ireland's *Miscellaneous Papers and Legal Instruments,* the alphabetical "List of Subscribers" included in the front matter recording "Caldecot, Thomas, Esq." (The only other sponsor with the same initials among the 122 was Thomas Coutts, the merchant banker who, with his brother James, founded the great house of Coutts & Co. in the Strand. His energies did not, however, extend to more than the encouragement of literary pursuits.) Malone knew that Caldecott knew the Irelands. When public curiosity about the Shakespeare Papers was at its height in 1795, Malone, unwilling to press in among the throng in Norfolk Street but keen to inspect the items, sought a viewing on neutral ground—maybe in Caldecott's house. Accordingly he asked his friend, the artist Ozias Humphry, who was also Caldecott's acquaintance, to intervene in his behalf. But Malone had failed to reckon on Caldecott's envious rivalry. The latter gleefully informed Humphry that the papers "would not be removed into the house of any person whatever, unless he Mr. I. should be requested to wait on his Majesty with them"—an opportunity which indeed came Ireland's way, for on December 30, 1795, he was escorted to Carlton House for an audience with the Prince of Wales. After Malone pricked the bubble, and the Irelands' world collapsed, Samuel produced, as his swan song, *An Investigation of Mr. Malone's Claim to the Character of Scholar, or Critic, Being an Examination of his Inquiry into the Authenticity of the Shakspeare Manuscripts, &c.* Ill equipped for such an examination, the distraught Ireland turned to Caldecott for the specifics of his rebuttal.

The Caldecott letter here reproduced followed hard upon the heels of dramatic events. With pregnant timing, it came just after the catastrophe wrought by Malone's exposure and ratified by the calamitous reception of *Vortigern*, but before the dénouement of Samuel Ireland's death and William-Henry's *Confessions*. In appraising Caldecott's performance one must allow for his personal connections with the principals; yet these were not so close as to be disabling, and they give his account a special immediacy.

His attitudes are generally predictable enough. He is sympathetic to the elder Ireland, hostile to Malone. But the vehemence of the loathing expressed is impressive: he characterizes the *Inquiry* as "such a specimen of Ignorance, Dulness, Incapacity & Presumption" as "was perhaps hardly ever exhibited" and goes on to demonstrate in detail the propriety of each epithet. Predictable too is his response to a peculiar by-product of this peculiar affair, George Chalmers' *An Apology for the Believers in the Shakspeare-Papers, Which Were Exhibited in Norfolk-Street.* Caldecott adds his voice to the chorus of derision which greeted the *Apology*. He mocks "the extravagant conceit," and in a postscript added to the letter after the appearance of Chalmers' *Supplemental Apology for the Believers in the Shakspeare-Papers,* published in 1799, notes the arrival of "another cumbrous & tiresome Volume" by the same author.

Like others seduced by the forgeries, Caldecott cannot bring himself to believe that William-Henry, a youth incapable (as he sees it) of writing a sentence correctly, and ignorant of the parts of speech, could have managed more than the bread-and-butter items which swelled the store. It is Samuel's view. The latter was willing to credit his son with guile but not brains. He was "strongly persuaded, that by some Artifice, Fraud or worse he [William-Henry] got possession of some antient Papers & Instruments; & that from such materials these were by somebody (some of these probably himself) manufactured." Who this "somebody" was neither Samuel nor Caldecott nor anybody else essayed to guess. But Caldecott does strongly attest to the elder Ireland's innocence at a time when many regarded him as a co-conspirator. Thus, almost two centuries after the dust has settled on the Ireland affair, does an observer with special credentials posthumously offer himself as a character witness in Samuel's behalf. It is not the last word on the subject, but it is a word deserving a place in the record.

III

The four-page letter serves as a flyleaf insert to a bound volume of nine published items, ranging from verse ephemera to substantial polemics—from G. M. Woodward's *Familiar Verses, from the Ghost of Willy Shakspeare to Sammy Ireland* to Francis Godolphin Waldron's *Free Reflections on Miscellaneous Papers*—spawned by the controversy. Samuel Ireland's investigation of Malone is expectedly included; also *Vortigern* and Wally Chamberlain Oulton's *Vortigern under Consideration;* not to mention William-Henry's first confessional exercise, the 1796 *Authentic Account of the Shakspearian Mss.* The title on the spine of the collection reads *Shakspeare Papers.* An unsigned note by J. O. Halliwell-Phillipps on the inside front cover attests, "I bought this curious volume of Willis & Sotheran for £1.14.0." Willis and Sotheran (later Henry Sotheran & Co.) were well known London booksellers. The Folger shelfmark is PR2950.B5. Copy 2. Cage.

The John Mander to whom the letter is addressed remains elusive, although we know from it that he was an acquaintance of Samuel and had, some time previous, sojourned in the Ireland house.[3] More teasing is the note at the foot of the last page referring to Chalmers' *Supplemental Apology,* which, as we have noted, did not see print until 1799. Does the Folger text then represent a draft or copy of the letter preserved by the writer as a memorial to an episode which could not but have deeply impressed him?

A few names mentioned in the letter call for brief comment. John Caley (d.1834) was a legal antiquary and keeper of the records in the Augmentation Office. Respected for his ability to decipher old hands, he became secretary to the first record commission and was in 1818 appointed keeper of the records in the ancient treasury at Westminster. Eventually Caley's highhandedness, neglect of duties, and abuse—for personal gain—of the archives entrusted to his care drew scandalized comment, but he escaped any more serious repercussions. Craven Ord (1756–1832), a respected antiquary and for several years vice president of the Society of Antiquaries, was an authority on English sepulchral monuments, and, while publishing little himself, gave valued assistance to several compilers of county histories. The "dygne Dean Milles" referred to in connection with the Chatterton affair was the dean of Exeter Cathedral, Jeremiah Milles (1714–84), whose enthusiastic advocacy of the Rowley poems prompted him in 1782 to publish an edition, with commentary, as elaborate as it was ill advised. Malone and others pounced; Milles's reputation never recovered. Coleridge is cited by the *D.N.B.* as saying of him that, "though only a dean, he was in dulness and malignity most episcopally eminent."

In transcribing I have followed the spelling, capitalization, and punctuation of the original, but for the reader's convenience I have expanded the fairly frequent abbreviations, except for such standard or untroublesome forms as "M^r" or "Q." (for "Queen").

Now, upon the cessation of all controversy respecting the authenticity of the Shakspeare Papers, you wish me to throw together my recollections upon a Subject, on which you say I must have had opportunities of seeing some parts of the conduct & process. I approve the suggestion & readily comply.

I was made acquainted with the Shakspeare papers very early, ie. soon after they were put into the hands of Mr Ireland, the possessor of them. They were few in number, viz. Some small prose compositions on paper, & two or three parchment instruments. I was no judge of the vehicles of these productions; neither could I read the scrawl of the paper MSS. Upon their authenticity therefore in this view, viz. Whether they were written upon the paper & parchment, & in the character, of the Age, to which they were ascribed, I recommended that Mr Caley should be consulted as to the Papers; & that the Parchments should be submitted to the eye of some Antiquary, or person familiarly acquainted with instruments of that sort. They were to many, to official & other competent persons; & I soon afterwards chanced to see them in company with Mr Caley & Mr Craven Ord. Caley was perfectly satisfied, & Ord generally so. The Composition was managed with dexterity; & they were certainly beautiful. Shakespeare was indeed made not to deal so much in distinct images as in his common style, but to generalize more; & yet I saw nothing that told me, they were not his Compositions. The fearless audacity with which numberless evidences of different denominations were afterwards heaped upon us (any one of which, if clearly contradicted & exposed, must have blown up the whole) seemed to bespeak & challenge Confidence. Suspicion first came across my mind upon the production of that very vapid, empty & ill composed Address of the young Bard to his Mistress. From a desire to serve this acquaintance of yours, in whose house you had been so long an inmate & in whose hands they were, & under an apprehension, that, whether genuine or not, this Trash might blow them up, I lodged a written remonstrance, as you know, against the impolity of printing or any longer producing this specimen. From an idea that it was improper to suppress any thing that had been extensively circulated & known, &, I verily believe, an honest conviction that they were genuine (for he thought it was very fine, & there were some foolish people who told him so, & he was not at all capable of judging upon the subject himself) this advice was rejected; & the opinion, which coincided with his own persuasion & his sense of duty, prevailed. But the Publication of the papers at once decided the question of their Authenticity: Till then, in the illegible state of the MSS. (for such it was to almost every one, & in consequence a translation or deciphering of the crabbed text was always placed beside it) a comparison of the mode of spelling of the several supposed writers was impracticable: but upon Publication it was seen, that not only Shakespeare, but *others,* whose writings were exhibited as Originals & not Transcripts, were made to spell in the same way, & that a way not only unknown to any particular period, but unknown to all times; & in which no one was ever known to have printed any more than to have written: &, as if this (ie. two or more persons concurring here to spell in a way in which no one ever printed wrote or spelt elswhere) were not conclusive, Q. Elizabeth was made one of this number; a Personage, who has left behind her, in every period of her life, in public repositories & in private families, numberless specimens of her epistolary & other writings, but no one having the least resemblance to this. As all these came out of the same quarter, from the same chest & made part of one & the same collection or treasure, it was not possible, that such a coincidence as this could have occurred in any other way, or could be accounted for upon any other principle, than that the whole must have been the fabrication of some one Person or Confederacy: & consequently, that, unless something that bore some affinity to these MSS. could be produced under Q. Elizabeth's hand, it was impossible, that any credulity could entertain the tale for a moment. This coincidence was first pointed out to me by the Bishop of Dromore (Percy) (for I had not then, at the time of the Publication, given myself the trouble of looking into the work, which I had lent) & I instantly recognized the very objection which "dygne Dean Milles" had supplied me with in his Vindication of Rowley, and which I had uniformly insisted upon as conclusive in that case: & I instantly admitted here to the Bishop, that it was unanswerable. Till this appeared & the Play was presented, the Papers received all the collateral support that could possibly be given them. Neither was it so much the unreserved communication & mass of the Papers &c, &c. (so many separate sources of detection) as the senseless objections industriously circulated & afterwards stupidly insisted upon in print by Malone, that with me tended to give them a favourable reception. He objected to Words as not being in use at that time (& one of them is in a Note in his own Edition of Shakespeare) for no other or better reason than that they were not to be found (where several also were found) in the meagre gleanings, the *manipuli* or handfuls, of the Vocabulary writers & Lexicographers of the day; & from this negative evidence pronounced positively, that no such words existed: & such a specimen of Ignorance, Dulness, Incapacity & Presumption was perhaps hardly ever exhibited. His Ignorance & Stupidity were *demonstrated* by one declaration only; viz. that the MSS. were a clear & clumsy Forgery, because there were many words spelt in a way used at no time whatsoever, as ande, forre, &c. His *Ignorance* (not so much, Pretender as he was to a knowlege of this lore, because a solitary instance, or possibly two or 3 instances of these words might be produced, but) because there exists no one who has the slightest knowlege on this subject & does not know, that the mode of spelling was at that time perfectly arbitrary; that Orthography was a thing unknown; that Spelling was so much, so altogether unsettled, that not only no *two* persons, but even *upon the same page* hardly *any one,* in Print or MS., spelt the

same word in the same manner; & consequently that every antient MS.,
every specimen of early Typography, must be likely to afford some such
evidences against their own authenticity, from whatever unsuspicious &
unquestionable channels they were derived: His *Stupidity;* because, as the
Forger of these Papers embarked *upon a System* (viz. that of every where
multiplying the Consonants & adding a final e) not to have adhered to
this throughout, would have been losing sight of his Polestar, a derelic-
tion of the Principle upon which he set out, & in the instances in which he
suffered it to occur, a sort of tacit admission that it would not carry him
through; & thus, by subjecting himself to suspicion, have ultimately become himself the means of his own detection. The objection raised was
therefore in the character rather of a Party to the Fraud than of a Dectec-
tor, inasmuch as it indirectly favoured the grand engine which he by
wholesale used, as a shelter for Ignorance, a security against all risque, &
a compleat discharge from all labor & investigation; & so perfect a
Panoply, so well aimed a devise it was, that, had it been confined to the
few Shakespeare MSS. first exhibited to the Public, whatever suspicions
might have remained, a full & clear conviction had been impossible. And
it was at last only had, by making several supposed originals & not
transcripts, drawn from the same source, the same chest, repository or
manufactory, spell in the same manner. Had his objection been, that the
System, thus adopted, is the very opposite of that course which common
probability would have assigned to such a writer as Shakespeare, this
would have grappled with the very Foundation & Existence of the
Forgery; for, as no man living ever possessed an Imagination so overflow-
ing, as no man's ideas ever succeeded each other in so rapid a course as
Shakespeare's, it does not seem much to correspond with our notions of
the Genius of such a Writer, that he should form, not merely adopt, a
System of Spelling; which, instead of facilitating the means of commit-
ting his ideas to paper, must impede & retard them in a most
troublesome & offensive degree. Upon the production of the Play (which
was put into my hands to weed of superfluous & improper matter & to
give some body & form to the loose disjointed, skimble skamble stuff,
which, it was pretended, was the original state of all Shakespeare's
versification) both Folly & Fraud somewhere, stared me in the face
broadly & most glaringly. At this time Mr Ireland seemed to entertain
some doubts & boggle a little, but Sheridan had bought the Play at the
price of 200 Guineas & other House profits, & had persuaded himself it
was Shakespeare's; & Mr Ireland had then advanced too far to recede; by
degrees led on by his Son, who throughout took care to keep aloof from
me, to whom he never communicated any thing & whom I scarce ever
saw. The Articles promised also were not produced, the Picture, the
uncut impressions of the first Folio & the Library; & the Son's conduct
respecting this business in several particulars wore a suspicious appearance. There existed also one strong Fact. At an early period a date upon
a paper respecting Lord Leicester, as not corresponding with historical
truth, was obliged to be torn off. This however, I am satisfied he thought
was, as he said, a mistake; & that it ought not to destroy the whole,
supported & buttressed as it was by such a mass of various other supposed indisputable testimony. For the purpose of exposing that which
sufficiently exposed itself, an Answer appeared from Mr Chalmers, entitled "An Apology &c." He is a very silly Coxcomb, & an execrably bad

Writer; but he has not spared his pains, & was possessed of extraordinary sources of Information. Preeminent above his other Follies is the extravagant conceit, that Shakespeare's Sonnets were addressed to a* Lady & that Lady, Q. Elizabeth. See his reasoning p. 59. & read sonnets 9, 20.

The real secret of this audacious & wholesale Imposture has not yet been divulged: &, tho' the world, naturally enough, will never be brought to believe, that the Son & Father were not knowingly playing into one anothers hands, I have been throughout the whole of this business, & am now, thoroughly satisfied, that Ireland, the Father, was both innocent, & intirely ignorant of the Authors as he was of the management of this Fraud. He was, I am assured, the dupe of a Son, to whom it may have been, that he had given an example & in part accomplished in Arts, which were afterwards practised against himself. The Son has published to the World, that he is the author of every thing sent out into it or exhibited in this business. This in the extent stated (ie. that he was capable of writing the small pieces first produced) no Individual throughout it ever gave the smallest credit to. His father was strongly persuaded, that by some Artifice, Fraud or† worse he got possession of some antient Papers & Instruments; & that from some such materials these were by somebody (some of them probably by himself) manufactured. Neither one or the other of them to my certain knowlege are capable of writing a sentence of English correctly, or know even the common parts of Speech.

T.C.

John Mander Esqr
Bampton
Wilney
Nov: 30. 1797. Oxfordshire.

---

*Since the above was written, another cumbrous & tiresome volume has appeared, in which this Absurdity is repeated, & laboured with a most perverse industry.

†And for such practises he lately owed to the mercy of his Prosecutor an escape from the Gallows.

NOTES

1. "The Library of Thomas Caldecott, Esq. Bencher of the Middle Temple," *The Gentleman's Magazine*, n.s., i (1834), 59n.
2. Ibid.
3. No John Mander is listed in the *D.N.B.* or, for this period, in the British Museum *General Catalogue of Printed Books. Alumni Oxonienses* records a John Mander, "solicitor to the University," as privilegiatus April 30, 1745.

(1980)

11
Shakespeare Played Out,
or Much Ado about *Nada*

"The latter Part of his Life was spent, as all Men of good Sense will wish theirs may be, in Ease, Retirement, and the Conversation of his Friends. He had the good Fortune to gather an Estate equal to his Occasion, and, in that, to his Wish; and is said to have spent some Years before his Death at his native *Stratford*." Thus, early in the eighteenth century, did Nicholas Rowe sum up the twilight years of a poet not yet decked with the laurels of bardolatry. By then Shakespeare lay dead almost a century. However, in assembling his materials for the first connected Life, Rowe took the trouble to send the celebrated Shakespearean actor Betterton, then past seventy, on a pilgrimage to Stratford, "on purpose to gather up what Remains he could of a Name for which he had so great a Value." There Betterton would have been in touch with a still living tradition. In any event, it is what we have to go on for the mood of this phase of Shakespeare's life, and the basis for subsequent biography. Edward Bond knows the tradition of Bardic tranquility well enough.

"You are serene. Serene," Jonson tells Shakespeare enviously at the Golden Cross, where the two men have met for a final binge in *Bingo,* Mr. Bond's new play about Shakespeare's last days. And later, drunk in the snow, he muses: "Serene. Serene. Is that how they see me? *(He laughs a little.)* I didn't know." The laugh is mirthless, the serenity a delusion. Shakespeare is not—in Dowden's notorious formulation—On the Heights, but In the Depths. He feels hatred and despair. At the end he swallows poison in the form of sugar-coated tablets conveniently provided by Jonson, who has no further use for them.

The suicide takes place despite Shakespeare's material success, or rather because of it. That success the biographical record amply documents. The multitudes that applauded Shakespeare's plays at the Globe made the Chamberlain's men (later the King's men) the premier troupe in the land. As a "house-keeper," their principal dramatist shared in the profits, which he invested prudently. In Stratford in 1597 he bought a pretty house of brick and timber, called New Place, with extensive gardens. (The biggest

154

house, the old College, was occupied by one of the powerful Combes.) At £60, the sum mentioned in records of the transaction, New Place was a steal, but Shakespeare may well have paid more, for such figures were customarily legal fictions. Five years later he paid £320 in cash to William Combe and his nephew for a large tract of arable in Old Stratford. Then, in 1605, he made his most ambitious investment, £440 for a half interest in a lease of tithes in Welcombe and other neighboring hamlets of Stratford. His tenants cultivated their narrow subdivisions, and his representative, Anthony Nash of Welcombe, managed the tithes, which brought Shakespeare £60 a year after rents. Near the end of his life he bought the Blackfriars Gatehouse in London, presumably as an investment rather than as a residence. Meanwhile Shakespeare pursued debtors in the courts, although whether he ever collected is not known. The Heralds' Office granted his father a coat of arms, probably at the son's instigation, and the latter is thereafter described in records as William Shakespeare, gent. A curious career, in a way, especially to those who subscribe to a romantic conception of the poet's odyssey. After all, as Dowden long ago pointed out, does not Shakespeare mock Osric as being "spacious in the possession of dirt" at just around the same time that he was himself becoming spacious in the possession of Old Stratford dirt?

If the the pattern of Shakespeare's life has puzzled some, and fueled anti-Stratfordian fires, it appealed wonderfully to Victorian Philistinism. "He must have been a close student, and a hard worker," Samuel Smiles noted with satisfaction in *Self-Help*, and (in a chapter entitled, "Business Qualities"): "It is certain . . . that he prospered in his business, and realized sufficient to enable him to retire upon a competency to his native town of Stratford-upon-Avon." He is an example for us all. In the magisterial setting of the *Dictionary of National Biography*, Sidney Lee expresses essentially the same view in his memoir of Shakespeare:

> With his literary power and sociability there clearly went the shrewd capacity of a man of business. His literary attainments and successes were chiefly valued as serving the prosaic end of providing permanently for himself and his children. His highest ambition was to restore among his fellow-townsmen the family repute which his father's misfortunes had imperilled. Ideals so homely are reckoned rare among poets, but Chaucer and Sir Walter Scott, among writers of exalted genius, vie with Shakespeare in the sobriety of their personal aims and the sanity of their mental attitude towards life's ordinary incidents.

The judgment is endorsed by another sober literary genius: ". . . he was, like all highly intelligent and conscientious people, business-like about money and appreciative of the value of respectability and the discomfort and discredit of Bohemianism." Thus Shakespeare as seen by Bernard Shaw.

Mr. Bond will have none of such comfortable doctrine. His Shakespeare is a corrupted seer; as a property-holder he supports "the Goneril-society." In *Bingo* that society is much more powerfully evoked than is Shakespeare himself. The play fairly drips with cruelty. Perhaps we should expect as much from a dramatist who has elsewhere said that he writes about violence as naturally as Jane Austen wrote about manners. The violence of *Bingo* is none the less harrowing for being recollected in disquiet, or represented by its consequences, rather than overtly enacted.

Two of the characters are mental defectives. The Old Man, employed in Shakespeare's garden, was normal once, and happily married; but the press men came and hauled him off to war. On the battlefield somebody accidentally knocked him on the head with the blunt end of an axe while butchering a man lying on the ground. In the course of the play he is shot dead by his own son while childishly frolicking in the snow. The Young Woman is a vagrant passing on her way from Coventry to Bristol. Whipping has turned her wits. She has no money and no pass; an upstanding townsman has her dragged off to be flogged in the marketplace until the blood runs. Later she sets fires (a "suddaine and terrible Fire" ravaged Stratford in 1614: Mr. Bond has done his homework) and is caught and hanged. Her body, suspended against a post on a hill, is the dominant visual image (inspired by a Rembrandt drawing) of the third scene.

One of Shakespeare's longest speeches describes the popular Elizabethan pastime of bear-baiting:

> In London they blinded a bear. Called Harry Hunks. The sport was to bait it with whips. Slash, slash. It couldn't see but it could hear. It grabbed the whips. Caught some of them. Broke them. Slashed back at the men. Slash, slash. The men stood round in a circle slashing at it. It was blind but they still chained it to the ground. Slash, slash. . . .

Not very probable as dialogue, perhaps, but the point is starkly made. Elsewhere we are fleetingly reminded of the heads of executed traitors that barbarously festooned the gatehouse of London Bridge. Jonson in his cups thinks of his days in prison, the inmates being carried out to have bits and pieces—noses, hands—lopped off, or their stomachs ripped open. In the lunatic asylums doctors whip their patients. Bond includes the lot: war, poverty, prison, torture of man and beast, madness. Most of it, of course, is also in *King Lear,* and the Shakespeare of *Bingo* sitting in his garden, with the deranged young girl and the deranged old man, cannot but remind us of Lear in the company of the Fool and mad Tom. We recall that Mr. Bond a few years back gave us his own *Lear.*

Along with misery, hatred. "Shall I tell you something about me?" Jonson confides to Shakespeare. "I hate. Yes—isn't that interesting!" He hates Shakespeare. Shakespeare's face in John Gielgud's performance is a suffering and inexpressibly sensitive mask, but he hates too. He hates his intimidating Brünnhilde of a daughter, played with statuesque authority by Gillian Martell; also his silly, obstinate wife, abandoned more than thirty years past, when her boy husband ran off to London. Like the invalid mother-monster of Ayckbourn's *Norman Conquests,* Anne keeps to her offstage bed, but in the last scene we hear her crying hysterically, and banging on Shakespeare's locked door, which he refuses to open. Mostly Shakespeare hates himself. It is rather too much of a bad thing. In *Bingo* hatred never explodes into rage; even the hysteria is fake, quickly assuaged when Shakespeare slips his will under the door. Rage may be unavailing but it does offer release—for actors and audience—as the real Shakespeare knew and expressed in *King Lear* and *Timon of Athens.* In the last resort, *Bingo* is a juiceless play, insufficiently vitalized by dramatic energy.

Still, it holds much interest. To demonstrate the corruption by participation of his protagonist Mr. Bond must seize on a particular episode as a peg for his action, and in choosing the Welcombe enclosures he has had a real inspiration, for he is able to provide imaginative answers to questions that tease biographical speculation. "Most biographies of Shakespeare," Mr. Bond says in the bibliographical note to the printed edition of the play, "barely mention the Welcombe enclosure"; but it is well enough known. There are a number of pertinent documents, the chief of which—the memoranda of the town clerk, Thomas Greene—are a palaeographer's challenge.

The facts may be quickly summarized. In the autumn of 1614 Arthur Mainwaring (or Mannering), steward to Lord Chancellor Ellesmere, in league with the prominent landholder William Combe, was seeking to enclose the common fields from which Shakespeare derived his tithe income. The conversion of arable to sheep pasture held the promise of more productive agriculture; at the same time it threatened to increase unemployment and force up prices. To protect his own interests Shakespeare entered into an agreement with Mainwaring's attorney, William Replingham, by which he was guaranteed against his loss as a result of enclosure. (In *Bingo,* for perfectly legitimate reasons of artistic economy, Combe alone represents the property-holders, and it is he who delivers the document to Shakespeare in the first scene.) The corporation of Stratford, mindful of its 700 almsfolk, opposed enclosure, and sent Combe a delegation "to present their loves & to desire he would be pleased to forbeare to inclose & to desire his love as they wilbe redy to deserve yt." Combe spurned their love and began surrounding the fields with a ditch, which the tenants surreptitiously filled in. There were incidents of violence and abuse. Eventually, at the Lent Assizes of 1616, the Chief Justice of the King's Bench, Sir Edward Coke, ruled against Combe's scheme. Enclosure was now dead in Stratford. So, soon after, was Shakespeare.

Shakespeare, Mr. Bond argues, had to side either with the landlords or with the poor who stood to lose their holdings. He chose the landlords. As a class they were not evil men, but they tolerated the human price for their material advancement. "I know this," Combe tells the potential victims of enclosure:

> there'll always be real suffering, real stupidity and greed and violence. And there can be no civilization till you've learned to live with it. I live in the real world and try to make it work. There's nothing more moral than that.

Mr. Bond sees the Replingham covenant as conclusive evidence of Shakespeare's complicity with—or, at the least, acquiescence in—the enclosures, but few things are clear-cut in Shakespearean biography. The same agreement protected Thomas Greene too; yet he doggedly opposed enclosure. Greene was related by blood or marriage to Shakespeare, referring to him as cousin, and he turned to the dramatist for advice. Greene records Shakespeare and his son-in-law, Dr. John Hall, telling him they thought nothing at all would be done. There is a mystifying entry in Greene's diary in September 1615: "W Shakespeares tellyng J Greene that I was not able to beare the encloseinge of Welcombe." Thomas had a brother John. But why should Shakespeare tell him what he would surely already know? Is "I" a slip for "he"? Or did Greene mean to write "barre" but put down "beare" instead? Such questions must go unanswered. Mr. Bond is, however, right in concluding that there is no evidence that Shakespeare actively resisted the enclosure of the Welcombe fields. His apparent detachment renders provocatively apt the large questions Mr. Bond raises about the social responsibilities of the artist in an unjust society. These are questions each reader or viewer must answer for himself.

Mr. Bond's Shakespeare allows himself humane gestures. He is reputed a generous man. He wants to help the wretched waif with money, and later with a meal and cast-off clothes. But the gestures fail, and the ice within him remains unthawed. New Place, purchased at the cost of his youth and best energy, brings no solace. It was a mistake. No consolation, either, from the achievements of his art, for like all writers he has created out of other men's blood. "Was anything done?" he asks. It is the best line in the play, and Mr. Bond milks it for all it is worth: Shakespeare asks himself the same question four times in his last speech. The final word, however, is left to Judith, after frantically searching her father's bedroom for a new will. (What she would make of one remains unclear, for she apparently could neither read nor write; her mark is preserved.) "Nothing," she cries. It is the *mot juste*, conveying as it does the void—an overwhelming sense of *nada*—at the center. *Bingo* has no winners.

Voids are dispiriting. Sir John makes the most of the part, but it offers an actor little to sink his teeth into. The suffering that Shakespeare has seen has stupefied him. One stage direction expressly forbids him to give away anything by movement or facial expression. He must sleepwalk through the play. The early scenes have him sitting on a bench in his garden and staring silently ahead. In the tavern with Jonson (robustly played by Arthur Lowe) the play flares briefly to life, but that is because of Jonson, who evokes desperately needed laughter. In this scene Shakespeare falls across the table, spilling his wine, and slumps forward; when Jonson gets up to refill his flask he is, although drunk, in control of his faculties. Later, in an open field, Shakespeare is tempted to throw a snowball, which he aims badly, but before long he is lying down in the snow, and he has to be helped to his feet and led off by his old serving-woman. He is played out; the end, when it comes, is a relief. Mr. Bond in his Introduction claims to have flattered Shakespeare: better that he should finish up thus than as "a reactionary blimp or some other fool," or slide into senility—as though the options stopped there. To others the choice may seem self-indulgent and futile, also (as at least one reviewer has remarked) sentimental. Anyway, Shakespeare can get by without flattery.

"Of course, I can't insist that my description of Shakespeare's death is true," Mr. Bond concedes, but he regards it as probable, and as following with psychological truth from the historical facts. To characterize these pretensions as doubtful would be an understatement. Mr. Bond is doing what countless others have done when confronting the enigma of a poet who was (in Borges' phrase) "many and no one": he stares into the glass of Shakespeare's life and finds the image of his own preoccupations. As a playwright, selecting and ordering his materials, and inventing imaginary dialogue, he has a better warrant than the biographer to do so. He is entitled to the license of art. And Mr. Bond does have the candor, after all, to admit that his real interest is not in the "true biography" of his subject, as an historian's would be, but in the writer's relationship to his society. In other words, in himself and us.

Still Mr. Bond exploits an historical setting and actual events and personages. With some success he manages to convey, through the servant couple's son and his mates, the reverberations of Puritan enthusiasm. Puritanism was a potent fact of life in Stratford then—John Hall had leanings that way. Shakespeare's elder daughter Susanna never enters the play, but the exclusion is deliberate, her role of her father's comforter being taken by the Old Woman. So too, for reasons of dramatic convenience, the Warwickshire poet Michael Drayton does not participate in the carouse with Jonson. No mention is made in the play of a husband for Judith, although in his introduction Mr. Bond refers to Thomas Quiney, whom she married. There is, however, an intriguing set of facts about Judith's marriage that Mr. Bond ignores altogether. They first came to light a decade ago, in an article by H. A. Hanley in the *TLS* (May 21, 1964), but, although they have been elaborated on by E.R.C. Brinkworth in *Shakespeare and the*

Bawdy Court of Stratford (1972), they are yet to seep properly into the mainstream of Shakespearean biography: A. L. Rowse overlooks them in his recent *Shakespeare the Man*. These facts are relevant to Shakespeare's last days.

Judith married Quiney on February 10, 1616, during the Lenten prohibited season. She was thirty-one, and her husband four years her junior. The previous summer Quiney had got another local girl, Margaret Wheeler, pregnant, and just a month after the wedding she gave birth. The Stratford parish register records the burial of both Margaret and her infant on March 15. Quiney was haled before the ecclesiastical court, which dealt with such offenses, and confessed to having had carnal copulation with Margaret. The court sentenced him to perform open penance in a white sheet on three successive Sundays before the whole congregation. This penalty was, however, remitted, and Quiney spared public humiliation. All this happened one month before Shakespeare's death.

One can only speculate on the effect of these developments on a dying man, but on March 25—the day before Quiney's court appearance—Shakespeare called in his lawyer to revise his will. A new first page was required, and there were a number of changes in the other two. The first sheet deals mainly with Judith. Long before the new information came to light, Sir Edmund Chambers shrewdly suspected that Shakespeare's bequests to Judith argue no great confidence in his new son-in-law.

The Margaret Wheeler episode, which is not devoid of intrinsic drama, is fact, whereas the merry meeting between Shakespeare, Jonson, and Drayton has the lesser status of tradition, having been first set down half a century after the event. These are matters to interest the biographer of Shakespeare, about whom more is known than generally supposed. Meanwhile we have Mr. Bond's play. It is more compelling than most on the subject. In limiting himself to the retirement phase, the playwright is spared any temptation, exceedingly dangerous, to depict Shakespeare in the throes of literary creation. Mercifully he is not shown chewing the cud of red-letter phrases from his plays, and the dialogue is free from *mayhaps, forsooths,* and other like archaisms, although not entirely from self-conscious artifice about white swans and dark water and writing in the snow. Theatrically undernourished *Bingo* may be, and overly explicit (as in Combe's speech to the tenants), but it is unsettling, as its author intended. If this Shakespeare serves ultimately as a vehicle for his creator's personal obsessions, with what other vehicle could the despairing protestation—"Was anything done?"—achieve an equivalent resonance?

(1974)

12
The Folger at Fifty

No easy task, but were I to select just one book expressive of the Folger Shakespeare Library in Washington, D.C.—a library filled with treasures—I suppose it would be the Vincent Folio. The first collected edition of *Mr. William Shakespeare's Comedies, Histories, and Tragedies,* published seven years after the poet's death, may not be the rarest of rare books; but it is surely one of the most precious.

Augustine Vincent, a high functionary of the Heralds' College, counted among his friends William Jaggard, who with his son Isaac printed the First Folio (as the book is called). William died while it was still being produced, but not before presenting Vincent with an early copy. The latter duly acknowledged "William Jaggard Typographer" for the gift in his bold hand on the upper right-hand corner of the title-page. (It is, so far as we know, the first copy of Shakespeare's works to be given as a present.) The volume, which preserves from the contemporary binding Vincent's device of a muzzled bear, is one of seventy-nine copies of this edition in the Folger collection. The next largest number under one roof anywhere else in the world is—expectedly—in London, in the British Library, which has five copies. These days one is especially mindful of the riches of the Folger, for in April of this year the Library celebrated, its fiftieth birthday.

The Folger is a magnet—a Shakespearean scholar's New Jerusalem—which has lured me irresistibly for a quarter of a century. In the old days, when I lived in the Midwest and taught at Northwestern University, I used to try to fly in from Chicago once or twice a month to grab a couple of days there. Now, when I reside on Capitol Hill, less than ten minutes away on foot, approaching the entrance on East Capitol Street still fills me with wonder and astonishment. What a location! Across the road you can see that noble old pile, the Library of Congress; kitty-corner stands the Supreme Court building; while at the end of the street looms the familiar dome of the Capitol of the United States. Such is the breathtaking confluence of government, jurisprudence, and the printed memorials of Western civilization, here at the nerve center of the Free World.

By Washington's monumental standards the Folger building itself is modest enough: a chaste marble rectangle without columns or pilasters.

Instead, fluted shafts separate the nine tall windows; aluminum Art Deco grills on windows and balconies lend an unexpected—and unostentatious—modern touch to the classical façade. At the base of each window a bas-relief depicts a celebrated moment from the plays: Portia lecturing Shylock on the quality of mercy, Lear raging on the heath, Julius Caesar lying assassinated in another capitol. On the grounds near the entrance an amused Puck holds up his arms; underneath, a carved inscription reads, "Lord, what fooles these mortals be": an appropriately unsolemn warning for those who cross the threshold to pursue their studies of Shakespeare, the age which produced him, or the heritage—theatrical, critical, cultural—to which he gave rise.

Within, the visitor finds himself transported at once to the Tudor past. White marble gives way to the warm tones and textures of Appalachian white oak, the materials of the New World thus being drawn upon to express the traditions of the Old. The long Exhibition Gallery, evocative of Tudor architecture on the grand scale, becomes itself an exhibition. High up on either side, running the length of the walls, hang decorative pennants bearing heraldic emblems: for (among others) Queen Elizabeth I; for Shakespeare's patron, the Earl of Southampton; for Richard Burbage, the preeminent actor who first gave stage life to Hamlet, Othello, and Lear; for the town of Stratford-upon-Avon, where the dramatist was born and died; and for the city of London, which gave him his fame and fortune. Above the door at the east end—eastward being the direction of England, where it all began—is Elizabeth's coat of arms; at the west end, looking toward the Capitol, is the American Shield and great eagle. The building itself thus represents an allegory of the sort that Shakespeare's age would have appreciated.

The Reading Room, open to qualified researchers, suggests an Elizabethan Great Hall, perhaps in a college. There are book-lined shelves, balconies, balustrades, and a hand-carved screen. At the center stands a huge stone fireplace, heaped with logs. (That is one hearth I have never seen a fire blazing in, and never hope to.) Rare books and manuscripts are fetched for readers from the vaulted Treasure Room below. At the east end of the Reading Room, beneath a replica of the memorial bust in Holy Trinity Church, where Shakespeare lies buried, are the ashes of Henry Clay Folger and his wife Emily Jordan Folger, founders of the Library and avid collectors for nearly fifty years.

How did their bequest come to pass? Henry Clay was not a Folger of mountain-grown coffee fame (although he was distantly related to that branch of the family), but the eighth lineal descendant of a transplanted Englishman who settled in Nantucket, taught school in Martha's Vineyard, and on Sundays preached to the Indians in their native tongue. Cotton Mather, who presumably knew whereof he spoke, described Peter Folger as able, godly, and "well learned in the Scripture." Peter's daughter Abiah was Benjamin Franklin's mother.

Born in Brooklyn in 1857, Henry Clay Folger was the son of a moderately well-to-do wholesale milliner. He attended Amherst College, but when his father went broke in the Panic of 1876, Henry nearly had to drop out in his sophomore year. The generosity of a classmate, Charles M. Pratt, turned the tide for him. "You are like a son to us," Pratt's father, who had an oil company, confided in Henry, "so we will finance your education, and, after graduation, you will have a job with the Pratt Company, if you want it." He wanted it.

Before then, though, he had an experience as momentous as it was unexpected. As a senior in the spring of 1879 he paid 25 cents to hear Ralph Waldo Emerson give his last address at Amherst. The great man, heavy with years, and with a daughter standing by on the platform to assist him if he faltered, seemed to be reading to himself. It didn't matter; young Folger was enormously moved. He procured Emerson's essay "On the Tercentenary of Shakespeare's Birth," and took to heart the Transcendentalist's tribute to the poet as "the consoler of our mortal condition." Six years later, Folger paid $1.25 for a collected edition of Shakespeare's works. In 1889, for $107.50 payable in installments, he bought a copy of the Fourth (and last) Folio of 1685. This was his first rarity, and the beginning of the Folger Shakespeare collection.

His business career went hand in hand with the collecting. After Amherst, Folger took a job as a lowly clerk with the Pratt Company, meanwhile pursuing a law degree at Columbia University, and passing the New York Bar. When Pratt joined forces with John D. Rockefeller, Sr., Folger made the oil connection in the predawn of the automotive age. In 1891 *Chambers's Encyclopaedia* asked him to contribute, for a fee of $30, the article on petroleum. Being an author in his own right evidently brought Folger gratification: he sent an offprint to Merrill E. Gates, the president of Amherst, who responded with an appreciative letter saying he would be glad to hear of all his alumnus' future successes. Succeed Folger did. In time he became (after the dissolution of the Standard Oil trust in 1911) President and, later, Chairman of the Board of Standard Oil of New York, as well as Secretary and a Director of Standard Oil of New Jersey. During his tenure the company's profits increased tenfold. Folger found himself a captain of industry in an age of tycoons.

Many of his confreres, suddenly flush with great wealth, collected voraciously, often indiscriminately, jewelry, books, Old Masters—you name it. They crossed the ocean in style, bedded down with their retinues in luxury hotels, and ostentatiously signaled their bids from the auction floor. Folger's was a different style. Modest and shy, this deeply religious man who loved music made the transatlantic journey eleven times by the S.S. *Min-*

nehaha—no superliner. His favorite shipboard reading was *The Tempest.* Always accompanying him on his collecting forays was his wife Emily, an enthusiastic coconspirator. They had no children; books, lovingly assembled, became their offspring. Shunning publicity, they used agents to enter their bids secretly. "If I could only find out what Folger does *not* have," a chagrined dealer remarked, "I could become the richest man in the book trade."

Folger was a passionate golfer, and the story is told of him walking off the green with (who else?) John D. Rockefeller, and being softly sounded out, "Henry, I see from the papers that you just paid $100,000 for a book!" After recovering from a sinking feeling in the pit of his stomach, Folger came back quickly, "Now, John! You know better than anybody else how newspapers exaggerate, especially about things like that. If you buy something for $10,000, it becomes $100,000 in print." Pause. "Well," said Rockefeller, "I'm glad to hear you say that, Henry. We—that is, my son and I and the Board of Directors—were disturbed. We wouldn't want to think that the president of one of our major companies would be the kind of man foolish enough to pay $100,000 for a book!"

On an undated scrap that I found among Folger's personal papers, I came upon this collector's credo hastily scrawled in pencil:

> Don't try to tell me that if you are sufficiently determined—devoted, eager to the point of making any sacrifice to attain your aim—you cannot buy the costliest treasure even though you have no means. Don't try to tell me that—I know better. I have done it—not once only, but over & over again. Nothing is *impossible* if one is sufficiently in earnest.

So it proved for Folger. Among his greatest coups was acquiring the 1594 first edition of *Titus Andronicus,* that brutal cavalcade of rape, mutilation, slaughter, and cannibalism; Shakespeare's youthful experiment with Roman tragedy, the opposite side of the coin to *The Comedy of Errors,* his youthful experiment with Roman comedy. Nobody would claim that the play is in a league with *Julius Caesar* and *Coriolanus,* but in modern times it has been revived successfully more than once—Laurence Olivier's Royal Shakespeare Company production of 1955 was one of the great occasions of my theatregoing career. The glory of Folger's purchase resides in the fact that this vulnerably delicate little book is the only copy of the 1594 edition—an edition which differs significantly from those that followed. It is an essential determinant of our idea of *Titus Andronicus.*

Recently, while in Lund, Sweden, where I lectured at the University, I was taken to the Grand Hotel for a splendid celebratory dinner. Between *skoals,* as the aquavit flowed and the piano player rendered *As Time Goes By* (my favorite grand-hotel tune), my host remarked, "You know, that copy of *Titus*—it was here in Lund once." Indeed so; it had turned up mysteriously at Malmo in 1904, in the attic of a postal clerk of Scottish descent, and was left for safekeeping with the Librarian of Lund University. Folger caught the terse announcement of the discovery in *The New York Sun,* and cabled his London agent, who had his representative show up, cash in hand, in Sweden in time to beat out the other eager bidders. It took Folger all of three hours to come up with a winning figure; within days of the purchase dealers were bidding ten times his £2,000 (some $10,000) for the book.

But what about all those seventy-nine copies of the 1623 Folio? May not the sheer number possibly reflect an inordinate greed of acquisition, the robber-baron instinct surfacing in the mildly reclusive millionaire? Not so: modern investigation of the printing and proof-reading of the First Folio— the standard study, published under that title by Charlton Hinman, was prepared at the Folger Library—has demonstrated that innumerable minute textual differences exist among the various copies; differences the responsible editor must take into account in preparing what he hopes will be an authoritative edition of a classic author. The 1623 Folio is of course an enormous book—over 110,000 lines arranged in double columns—and the collator's task correspondingly vast. Hinman answered the challenge by inventing a wonderful machine that superimposes optically one page upon another, thereby at once disclosing any variant readings. Only the Folger Library had enough examples of the First Folio to make Hinman's work possible. He collated over fifty of them there.

The Folgers, however, had passed from the scene long before the Hinman Collator was devised. Could they have had any real idea of the scholarly significance of their own collection, or did their purchases merely signify the prophetic good luck of people who were very lucky all their lifetime? In fact, Mrs. Folger did grasp the importance of multiple copies, for she was a trained student of literature. The daughter of the Solicitor of the Treasury under Abraham Lincoln (and also under President Andrew Johnson), Emily Jordan as a little girl—no more than four—met Lincoln at the White House, an experience she never got over. She was graduated from Vassar College and, some years after her marriage, returned to take a postgraduate degree there. As her thesis topic she offered "The True Text of Shakespeare"; she understood very well that during the printing of the Folio the presses were stopped from time to time to make changes possible.

Together the Folgers single-mindedly pursued their avocation; they possessed books, and books possessed them. Among Emily's papers at the Folger are draft articles posing questions that interested her—"Was Shakespeare an Aristocrat?" "Was Cleopatra a Serpent of Old Nile?"—and a privately printed paper answered in the affirmative another query, "Did Not Shakespeare Write Shakespeare?" Henry's capsule biography in *American Men of Mark* classifies him, not inaccurately, as "Capitalist," and credits him, with poignant overstatement, with having "written many monographs on Shakespeare." *Atlantic Monthly* and *Harper's* politely turned down his piece on "The Most Precious Book in the World" (the Vincent copy of the

First Folio), but Folger managed to place it in *The Outlook,* a monthly magazine. With "Shylock versus Antonio," which the curious reader may consult in typescript at the Library, he struck out altogether; even *The Outlook* said no to this one. He toyed with publishing a volume of his own Shakespearean essays, but nothing came of the idea. Instead Folger founded the great institution which exists to further the scholarly researches of countless other enthusiasts.

The choice of a site was no foregone conclusion. Folger considered his old *alma mater,* several major university campuses, and Stratford-upon-Avon. His wife's Washington ties were to play a role in the decision, as would what was happening in the city—"Forty years ago I would have said no," an advisor allowed, "but now I say yes." Folger's funeral eulogist, the Reverend Samuel Parkes Cadman, recalls asking him why not Stratford, and Folger's reply: "I did think of placing the Library at Stratford, near the home of the great man himself, but I finally concluded I would give it to Washington, for I am an American."

Accordingly, in his will he devised that, through a fund set up for the purpose, the trustees of Amherst College should install and administer his Shakespeare collection "as a permanent library in a building in the city. . . ." For that purpose Folger had prudently acquired a suitable parcel on Capitol Hill. The cornerstone of the Folger Shakespeare Library was laid in June 1930. Within two weeks, Folger was dead of heart failure following surgery; his wife would live on for another six years, long enough to attend the dedication on April 23, 1932, in the depths of the Great Depression. President Herbert Hoover, in top hat, was the guest of honor that bright sunlit afternoon. During the Library's first year, 300,000 visitors filed through the Exhibition gallery.

The items which the Folgers had examined in their home on Brooklyn Heights, or in Henry's Manhattan office, and which they both had carefully catalogued, were packed away for safekeeping in fireproof warehouses. Only they knew the scale and quality of the collection. By the time Folger died he had laid away close to 3,000 cases. Transporting them by truck, and unpacking them at the Library, took six months. They contained 93,000 rare books (including 208 early Quartos of Shakespeare's plays and poems), 50,000 prints, watercolors, and engravings, and 250,000 Shakespearean playbills—not to mention 200 oil paintings.

The inventory would not remain static; Folger had provided for subsequent growth, and additional funding would be sought to that end. In 1938 the Library's holdings were augmented by another purchase, the collection of Sir Leicester Harmsworth, a powerful British newspaper magnate, who had gathered together 9,000 titles printed before the mid-seventeenth century. Sir Leicester's widow parted with the bulk of the collection to escape death duties and because she found attractive the idea of an American home for the books. Continental, as well as English, books have since swelled the store: 1,000 Italian sixteenth-century plays and at least 950 Reformation works—most acquired as recently as 1977—including a rare first edition of Martin Luther's 95 theses.

Some years ago, when I was conducting a seminar at the Folger, I asked each student, as a weekly assignment, to come up with a wonder from the collection. Through the ten weeks the course ran, nobody complained that the assignment was unreasonable. For purposes of illustration, I here limit myself to a random gathering of Seven Wonders of the Folger. The Library holds the late medieval manuscript *The Castle of Perseverance,* a Morality play with a cast of personified abstractions including Mankind and the Seven Deadly Sins. Another unique manuscript is the anonymous Cambridge University play, c. 1603, *The Progress to Parnassus,* with its references, by name, to Shakespeare. Also in the collection is a splendid copy of William Caxton's edition of Chaucer's *Canterbury Tales,* one of the first books printed in England. Another treasure is a Book of Hours presented to Henry VIII by his fourth wife, Anne of Cleves, and inscribed by her; also a Bible once owned by Queen Elizabeth I, and decorated with silver clasps and bosses bearing her monogram, her coat of arms, and Tudor roses. There is Shakespeare's own copy of the deed to the Blackfriars Gatehouse, the London property he bought in 1613. And the Folger has sixteen volumes of *Note Books* of the Reverend John Ward, the vicar of Stratford from 1662 until his death in 1681. To Ward, who was licensed to practice medicine by the Archbishop of Canterbury, and who knew the poet's daughter Judith, we owe the report—otherwise unsubstantiated but not implausible—that "Shakespeare, Drayton and Ben Jonson had a merry meeting, and it seems drank too hard, for Shakespeare died of a fever there contracted."

All seven of these wonders, plus the Vincent Folio, the *Titus Andronicus* Quarto, and a host of other treasures, formed part of the great traveling Folger road show, "Shakespeare: The Globe and the World." It opened in San Francisco in 1979, then crossed the country to New York after intermediate stops in Kansas City, Pittsburgh, Dallas, and Atlanta: recently it completed a return California engagement in Los Angeles before having a grand windup at the Kennedy Center in Washington, D.C. The exhibition formed part of the Library's enlightened outreach program, the brainchild of its energetically humanistic director, Dr. O. B. Hardison, Jr.

The Folger Theatre, at the north end of the building, is an intimate house with a 200-plus capacity. The three-tiered gallery surrounding the pit, and the two supporting stage pillars, as well as an upper-stage, suggest the open-air playhouses of Shakespeare's age. Here the Folger Theatre Group, currently under the artistic direction of John Neville-Andrews, holds their annual season of plays. Other attractions, open to the public in the theatre and the Exhibition Gallery, include poetry readings, symposia, and lectures by world-renowned scholars, as well as concerts by the esteemed resident early music ensemble, the Folger Consort. Among the patrons of the Consort, since its inception, has been a labor union, the Marine Engineers Beneficial Association, moved by gratitude for the consolations of classical music furnished in the wee hours to lonely long-distance mariners.

"Share the fantasy," beckons a TV ad. Let me share with you a Shakespearean fantasy I have entertained. I am in Amsterdam, in a little bookshop tucked away on a side street, and come upon a little quarto copy of *Love's Labour's Won*. Such a title was included among Shakespeare's comedies in 1598 by Francis Meres in a rare little number entitled *Palladis Tamia*, of which the Folger has three copies; but the play itself has never surfaced, although it is mentioned in an old bookseller's list that turned up not too long ago. Maybe the play never really did exist, but was an alternative title for one of Shakespeare's extant comedies, in which love's labor is usually won. Never mind; in fantasy all things are possible. I buy the book for a ridiculously low sum (the dealer, poor fellow, being a foreigner doesn't realize its value—the most unlikely ingredient of this pipe dream), and slip by customs. Then I present the book anonymously—the ultimate ego trip—to the Folger Library, where it becomes another wonder of which the founder would have been exceedingly proud, for he would have appreciated its significance.

(1982)

Part II
Shakespeare and Other Playwrights

13
Shakespeare and Jonson
Fact and Myth

It is one of the curiosities of literary scholarship that the twentieth century, already two-thirds past, has not yet produced an authoritative biography of Shakespeare which synthesizes modern learning and reflects the modern temper. Chambers' two monumental volumes still dominate the scene, a mighty Everest, but although the author later referred to them as a "Life," they are better described by Chambers' own subtitle: *A Study of Facts and Problems*. That serious scholars should now shrink from attempting the authoritative biography which each age requires is understandable enough. The inadequacies of the documentary record are familiar to all. And how irritating that the traditions and legends which cluster together to form the Shakespeare mythos should show the author of *Lear* tippling with sots and greeting the dawn from beneath a crabtree's spreading canopy, poaching deer, and fornicating with an innkeeper's wife, but hardly ever reveal the supreme dramatist in the creative context of the London theatrical world. About his relations with his fellows we know little except that Heminges and Condell valued so worthy a friend, and Augustine Phillips, that stalwart of the Chamberlain's men, bequeathed him a thirty-shilling piece in gold. But what of Shakespeare's dealings with other playwrights? About this side of his professional life, rather than the acting, curiosity is after all most intense.

In his triple capacity—playwright, actor, shareholder—he must have often come into contact with other dramatists. If we can accept the conclusions of modern scholarship—still not exempt from debate—Munday, Dekker, Chettle, and possibly Heywood called on him to help salvage a play, *Sir Thomas More*, that had run afoul of the censor. But the first three men nowhere allude to Shakespeare, and the last, Heywood, mentions him briefly and uninformatively on two occasions—he praises mellifluous Shakespeare, he complains that an unscrupulous printer has included two of his poems under Shakespeare's name in *The Passionate Pilgrim*. Fletcher succeeded Shakespeare as principal dramatist for the King's men, and during the period of transition the two playwrights may have collaborated on *Henry VIII* and also on *The Two Noble Kinsmen;* yet the younger man nowhere records his impressions of the retiring master. Jonson remains; and it is fitting that we should glimpse in conjunction with one another the two colossi who bestrode the drama of the age.

I

Shakespeare and Jonson: how many themes for argument the linkage of the two names conjures up! Focus on their writings, and we may see them as representatives, the greatest in their day, of mutually exclusive conceptions of the playwright's craft: romantic versus classical, nature versus art, the theatre of a whole people versus the theatre of a côterie. These are subjects for whole papers, and indeed have been much discussed. The biographical side, however, has commanded least attention of late, and so I shall dwell on that.

For the relations between Shakespeare and Jonson, personal and professional, we have a number of records, and these are supplemented by a body of traditionary lore. But knowledge, no less than ignorance, brings its problems. What manner of coexistence obtained between the two giants of the Elizabethan stage? Were they friends, genial rivals, or adversaries? Shall we in the mind's eye see them feasting and carousing and exchanging happy specimens of tavern wit? Or shall we imagine the fell incensed points of mighty opposites towering above baser natures? Both these conceptions, as well as various intermediary gradations, are available to us. As specialists whose task it is to seek the truth, we are confronted not only with the evidence but also with a scholarly tradition which has, over the centuries, made a critical battleground of the subject, generating heat and passion and, rather less often, shedding light. It behooves us at times to examine our scholarly heritage. Such an exercise will yield consoling instances of the fallibility of our betters and furnish edifying *exempla* of the dangers of interpretation; it may also help us to achieve that sense of historical perspective which can enable us to steer clear of prejudice and to resolve contradictions.

First a word about the records. I shall, I fear, be traversing some well-ploughed terrain, but better to do so than to falsify the picture by omission; and sometimes a fresh look even at the familiar brings its rewards, not the least of these being the elimination of hereditary confusions.

In the Jonson Folio of 1616 Shakespeare's name heads the list of "principall Comoedians" in *Every Man in His Humour,* and also appears prominently among the "principall Tragoedians" who acted *Sejanus.* To the First Folio of 1623 Jonson contributed not only his celebrated eulogy of Shakespeare but also the verse accompanying the Droeshout engraving. To my mind a mood of affectionate warmth pervades these poems: we hear of "my beloved," "Soule of the Age," "my gentle *Shakespeare*," "Sweet Swan of *Avon.*" The actors had praised him for never blotting a line, but Jonson

insists that his friend (like himself) did sweat and "strike the second heat /
Upon the *Muses* anvile," and he goes on to praise

> his well torned, and true-filed lines:
> In each of which, he seemes to shake a Lance,
> As brandish't at the eyes of Ignorance.

An odd way of viewing Shakespeare's accomplishment, to be accounted for
by the irresistible Elizabethan urge to pun, which Jonson displays elsewhere in his occasional poems by his quibbles upon the names Portland,
Palmer, and Brome. Perhaps, however, it is not entirely fanciful to discern
the author's identification with his subject: these lines apply more aptly to
Jonson than they do to Shakespeare, who wages no campaigns against
ignorance. Self-congratulation is the sincerest form of compliment. When
not under encomiastic obligations, in notebooks that remained unpublished until after his death, Jonson affirms that he loved the man and
honors his memory on this side idolatry. "Hee was (indeed) honest, and of
an open, and free nature: had an excellent *Phantsie;* brave notions, and
gentle expressions. . . ." *Honest* is the most laudatory term in Jonson's
lexicon of praise.

These remarks require no super-subtle reading. What evidence from the
record, for the opposing image of Jonson the calumniating rival? In his
eulogy he speaks of Shakespeare's "small *Latine,* and Lesse *Greeke,*" a phrase
offensive to bardolatrous ears, but not necessarily patronizing. Jonson is
more openly critical in his *Discoveries,* already cited: would Shakespeare had
blotted a thousand lines! That way he might have avoided such inanities
"As when hee said in the person of *Caesar,* one speaking to him; *Caesar, thou
dost me wrong.* Hee replyed: *Caesar did never wrong, but with just cause:* and
such like. . . ." The passage does not appear in *Julius Caesar* but a half line
apparently marks the place of excision; perhaps Shakespeare heeded his
friend's advice and deleted, not an absurdity, surely, but a penetrating
paradox. Elsewhere Jonson alludes disparagingly to the *Henry VI* plays and
to *Henry V,* to *Titus Andronicus, The Tempest,* and "mouldy tales" like *Pericles.*
Drummond records Jonson's censure that "Shaksperr wanted Arte," and
his jibe at the shipwreck in Bohemia, "wher y^r is no Sea neer by some 100
Miles." In his *Essay on the Dramatique Poetry of the Last Age,* Dryden reports
that Jonson threw up his hands in horror at some bombast speeches in
Macbeth. Some have found an allusion to Shakespeare's motto in the one
proposed by Puntarvolo for Sogliardo in *Every Man out of His Humour:* "Not
without mustard"; others, however, find a favorable reference to Shakespeare as the second pen that had a good share in the stage version of
Sejanus. But such allusions belong to the conjectural rather than the factual
record and need not detain us.

About Jonson, as about all contemporary authors with the exception of
the dead shepherd Marlowe and the Rival Poet (whoever *he* may be),

Shakespeare is silent, but the University of Cambridge, around 1601, favors us with an intriguing anecdote. In the Second Part of *The Return from Parnassus,* performed at St. John's, Kempe informs us:

> Why heres our fellow *Shakespeare* puts them all downe, I and *Ben Jonson* too. O that *Ben Jonson* is a pestilent fellow, he brought up *Horace* giving the Poets a pill, but our fellow *Shakespeare* hath given him a purge that made him beray his credit.[1]

In time, commentators would make much of this purge and Shakespeare's triumph over Ben, naively failing to see that the praise in the *Parnassus* play is ironic; for the portrait of Kempe reflects the university scholar's scorn for an unlettered stage clown.

How shall we, who hopefully are not naive, evaluate the Shakespeare-Jonson record? Let us begin with the *Parnassus* allusion. If one may be allowed the collocation of metaphorical clichés, it has started many hares but upon examination turns out to be a red herring. Dekker, not Shakespeare, administered a purge to Jonson in *Satiromastix;* perhaps, as is suggested by J. B. Leishman, the able editor of the *Parnassus* trilogy, the anonymous university playwright thought of the Globe and the Chamberlain's men as Shakespeare's theatre and Shakespeare's company: guilt by association. Perhaps he was simply confused, for his information about the London theatrical scene is otherwise not very precise; Kempe was apparently no longer one of Shakespeare's fellows, having moved to a rival company.[2] As for Jonson's remarks on Shakespeare as a writer, these are such strictures as one might expect from a poet who constructed his own art on very different principles; and one must guard against confusing aesthetic with personal issues. I detect no malice in Jonson's comments, only the candor of one who prided himself above all else on his honesty. As for Drummond, he is the sort of man of whom you can say that if you have him for a friend, then you don't need an enemy. If we can believe this hostile witness, Jonson described Middleton as a base fellow, and dismissed Sharpham, Day, and Minshew as rogues; he said that Abraham Fraunce in his English hexameters was a fool and that Donne, for not keeping accent, deserved hanging. But even in Drummond, Jonson never refers to Shakespeare in such terms. So far as Dryden's report is concerned, it comes late; the two men could not have known one another personally. We may, I think, accept Jonson's statement that he loved the man, but this side of idolatry. The idolatry a later age would furnish.

II

But the story does not, of course, end with this handful of references. It is in the nature of traditions that they are more picturesque than facts; hence the image formed by posterity would in large measure be fashioned by the mythos. The chief document is the famous account of Shakespeare and Jonson in the memoir of the former that appears in the *History of the Worthies of England* (1662) by "the great Tom Fuller" (as Pepys termed him):

> Many were the *wit-combates* betwixt him and *Ben Johnson,* which two I behold like a *Spanish great Gallion* and an *English Man of War;* Master *Johnson* (like the former) was built far higher in Learning; *Solid,* but *Slow* in his performances. *Shake-spear* with the *English-man of War,* lesser in *bulk,* but lighter in *sailing,* could turn with all tides, tack about and take advantage of all winds, by the quickness of his Wit and Invention.[3]

"Which two I behold," writes Fuller. The picture he has formed is clearly in his mind's eye; this is a literary evocation, not a reminiscence derived from report. The impression is confirmed by the rest of Fuller's short biography, which is starkly devoid of concrete data. Although he combed the countryside in quest of matter for his *Worthies,* he failed to learn the year of Shakespeare's death, for which he leaves a poignant blank in his text. Yet the date is plain to see on the monument in Stratford Church.

Other sources, however, give samples of extemporaneous wit. In a mid seventeenth-century manuscript miscellany, *Merry Passages and Jests,* Sir Nicholas L'Estrange records how Jonson, after the christening of one of his infants, came upon Shakespeare, the godfather, in "a deepe study." Why so melancholy? asked Jonson. "[N]o faith *Ben:* (says he) not I, but I have beene considering a great while what should be the fittest gift for me to bestow upon my God-child, and I have resolv'd at last; I pry'the what, says he? I faith *Ben:* I'le e'en give him a douzen good Lattin Spoones, and thou shalt translate them."[4] (For modern readers this merry jest requires a gloss: *latten* was a brass or brass-like alloy.) The same story appears in the Plume manuscripts, but there it is Shakespeare's offspring that is being christened, and Jonson who delivers this devastating stroke of wit. Also in Plume we find Jonson beginning an epitaph: "Here lies Ben Johnson—who was once one—"and Shakespeare taking the pen from him to write:

> Here lies Benjamin—with short hair up*on* his Chin—
> Who w*hi*le he lived was a slow thing—& now he's b*uri*ed is no thing.[5]

An anonymous version (ca. 1650) of the same anecdote gives it a tavern setting, but not until a century later does legend place the two great men under a similar roof. In the *Town Jester,* around 1760, the following item appears:

> Ben Johnson and Shakespeare were once at a tavern-club where there were several lords from the court who went to hear their wit and conversation; Shakespeare call'd upon Ben Johnson to give a toast; he nam'd

that lord's wife that sat near him; the nobleman demanded why he nam'd her: Why not, replied the poet, she has the qualifications of a toast, being both brown and dry; which answer made them all laugh, his lordship having been obliged to marry her against his inclinations.[6]

From the notebooks of John Ward, vicar of Stratford from 1662 to 1681, we learn of the last convivial episode of Shakespeare's career and its sad aftermath. "Shakespear, Drayton, and Ben Jhonson, had a merry meeting," Ward writes, "and itt seems drank too hard, for Shakespear died of a feavour there contracted. . . ."[7] Some biographers have attached weight to this report; Drayton, a Warwickshireman, sometimes stayed in the village of Clifford Chambers nearby to Stratford. But elsewhere Ward (who had to remind himself to peruse Shakespeare's plays in order to avoid ignorance in that matter) turns out to be a less than reliable informant, for he absurdly exaggerates the dramatist's income.

None of the authorities thus far mentioned hints at sinister undercurrents of bad feeling in the relations between Jonson and Shakespeare. Not until late in the seventeenth century do we find suggested the opposing image of a malevolent Jonson, with gentle Shakespeare the innocent object of his jealousy and spite. In this connection Dryden stands at the crossroads of criticism. His attitudes towards Jonson, complex and ambivalent, might well furnish matter for another paper. We remember Dryden as expressing a high opinion of Shakespeare's rival. More than once he describes Jonson as the most judicious of poets, an English Vergil; *The Silent Woman,* examined by Dryden in the first extended critique of an Elizabethan play, he preferred before all other comedies. Yet in his own day Dryden gained a reputation as Jonson's foe, a charge he repudiated in his Preface to *An Evening's Love* (1671): *"I know I have been accus'd as an enemy of his writings; but without any other reason than that I do not admire him blindly, and without looking into his imperfections."* Elsewhere, indeed, he criticizes Jonson's faults of language and wit. He describes him as "a learned plagiary." But most fraught with consequence is a brief passage in the *Discourse Concerning the Original and Progress of Satire* (1692) in which he characterizes Jonson's tribute to Shakespeare's memory as "an insolent, sparing, and invidious panegyric"— to which Jonson might have replied in precisely the words used by Dryden in his Preface to *An Evening's Love.*[8]

Dryden may also have supplied Rowe, as he did Gildon, with the story, probably apocryphal, of a memorable meeting between Jonson, Davenant, Suckling and others, at which tempers flared and Suckling warmly defended Shakespeare from Jonson's repeated slurs about want of learning and ignorance of the ancients. The episode appears in Rowe's *Account* of Shakespeare's life, the first attempt at an authoritative memoir. In the same sketch, which prefaces his 1709 edition of Shakespeare's *Works,* Rowe describes the "remarkable piece of humanity and good Nature" with which the dramatist began his acquaintance with Jonson. The latter, as yet un-known, had offered the company a play which, after a superficial perusal, they curtly refused; but Shakespeare, happening to see the script, liked it so well that he persuaded the players to reverse their decision. In this way did Jonson make his debut as a playwright. "After this they were profess'd Friends," Rowe continues,

> tho' I don't know whether the other ever made him an equal return of Gentleness and Sincerity. *Ben* was naturally Proud and Insolent, and in the Days of his Reputation did so far take upon him the Supremacy in Wit, that he could not but look with an evil Eye upon any one that seem'd to stand in Competition with him. And if at times he has affected to commend him, it has always been with some Reserve, insinuating his Uncorrectness, a careless manner of Writing, and want of Judgment. . . ."[9]

This passage, paraphrasing and expanding Dryden, drops out of later editions of the *Account,* and it was popularly supposed that the author himself had upon second thought retracted his unflattering portrayal of Jonson. But Pope, not Rowe, deserves credit—if that is the right word—for the castration. An editor who felt no compunctions about improving upon Shakespeare would hardly regard Rowe's text as sacrosanct, nor did Pope deem it necessary to draw attention to his tamperings when he reprinted the *Account* in his 1725 *Shakespeare.*

Indeed, the laureate of Twickenham took a view different from Rowe's of Shakespeare's and Jonson's relations. Anecdotal Spence records an observation made by Pope around 1728. "It was, and is, a general opinion," he remarked, "that Ben Jonson and Shakespeare lived in enmity against one another. Betterton has assured me often that there was nothing in it, and that such a supposition was founded only on the two parties which in their lifetime listed under one, and endeavoured to lessen the character of the other mutually."[10] Note that Betterton, cited by Pope as his authority, was also Rowe's informant on the facts of Shakespeare's life. Note too that, thus early, Pope refers to the *general opinion* of enmity between Jonson and Shakespeare. This tide of opinion he attempted to reverse in his own Preface. "It is an acknowledged fact," Pope asserts, "that *Ben Johnson* was introduced upon the Stage, and his first works encouraged, by *Shakespear.* [How easily does hearsay gain acceptance as fact!] And after his death, that Author writes *To the memory of his beloved Mr.* William Shakespear, which shows as if the friendship had continued thro' life. I cannot for my own part find any thing *Invidious* or *Sparing* in those verses, but wonder Mr. *Dryden* was of that opinion."[11] Pope goes on to point out the exalted status conferred upon Shakespeare by Jonson in his eulogy; also, the note of personal kindness expressed in the *Discoveries.* But despite Pope's formidable reputation, and despite his censorship of Rowe, the darker view of relations between the two dramatists persisted, and indeed gained ground.

III

"I cannot give into the Opinion, that *Johnson's* Friendship to *Shakespear* continu'd through Life," John Roberts ("a Stroling Player") replied to Pope,

> or even was faithfully preserv'd any part of it, and therein beg Pardon, that I once more dissent from this *infallible* EDITOR: If it is an acknow-ledg'd Fact that *Ben. Johnson* was introduc'd upon the Stage, and his first Works encourag'd by *Shakespear,* How mean, how base, and malevolent does it appear in him, to pick out a single Sentence from all his Writings, and misquote it after his Friend's Decease, in order to reproach him with Weakness of Judgment, and expose him to Ridcule [*sic*] and Laughter?[12]

Roberts' outburst of indignation does not end with his rhetorical question; in a similarly prejudiced vein, he goes on to castigate Jonson for his "prej-udic'd Pen."

On April 23, 1748, *The General Advertiser* carried a letter from an anony-mous correspondent, in fact Charles Macklin the actor, on the occasion of a revival of Ford's *The Lover's Melancholy* for the benefit of Mrs. Macklin. The writer claims to have found a pamphlet entitled "Old *Ben's Light Heart* made heavy by Young *John's Melancholy Lover,*" and containing anecdotes about Jonson, Ford, and Shakespeare. The following extract will indicate the temper of Macklin's letter:

> *Ben* was by nature *splenetic and sour;* with a share of envy, (for every anxious genius has some) more than was warrantable in society. By edu-cation rather *critically* than *politely* learned; which swell'd his mind into an ostentatious pride *of his own works,* and an overbearing *inexorable* judg-ment of his *contemporaries.*
>
> This raised him many enemies, who towards the close of his life en-deavoured to dethrone *this tyrant,* as the pamphlet stiles him, out of the dominion of the theatre. And what greatly contributed to their design, was the *slights* and *malignances* which the *rigid Ben* too frequently threw out against the *lowly Shakspeare,* whose fame since his death, as appears by the pamphlet, was grown too great for *Ben's envy* either to *bear* with or *wound.*
>
> It would greatly exceed the limits of your paper to set down all the *contempts* and *invectives* which were uttered and written by *Ben,* and are collected and produced in *this pamphlet,* as unanswerable and shaming evidences to prove his *ill-nature* and *ingratitude* to *Shakspeare,* who first introduced him to the *theatre and fame.*[13]

Macklin's solicitude for an editor pressed for space does not prevent him from including a few choice samples of Ben's contempts and invectives. These, being old hat, cannot be said to swell the store, and anyway the rare pamphlet turns out to be a creature of Macklin's own imagination, invented to puff a revival from which he had expectations of pecuniary gain. So much Edmond Malone demonstrates in an essay that reads like a dry run for his celebrated unmasking of the more sensational impostures of William-Henry Ireland.

The Macklin forgery is symptomatic of a curious state of literary affairs. With the decline of Jonson's reputation and the concurrent rise of bardolatry, the poet formerly preferred to Shakespeare by the intelligentsia became a favorite target for denigration. One sees the process at work in the article on Jonson in that popular compendium, the *Biographia Britannica* (1757). The anonymous memoralist is not sparing of those slights and malignances for which Jonson was being taken to task. Ben's chosen spelling of his surname is cited as "one instance, among innumerable others, of that affectation, which so strongly marks the character of our poet." Elsewhere in the same piece we hear of his "hardy and sullen" temper, and of the "presumption and vanity" of the *Ode to Himself.* His natural disposition, we are told, was no more respectable than his corpulent and bulky physique, his hard and rocky countenance; Drummond's unflattering impressions of his guest receive prominent display. The author does not dwell upon Jonson's relations with Shakespeare, but his characterization of the latter as "that humane good-natured bard" implies a contrast between the two men which had already become a biographical commonplace.

The contrast is magnified by the commentators. Farmer is an exception; in his *Essay on the Learning of Shakespeare* (1767) he describes Jonson's eulogy as "the warmest Panegyrick, that ever was written," and concludes, "In truth the received opinion of the pride and malignity of *Jonson,* at least in the earlier part of life, is absolutely groundless." (Note, however, the phrase, "received opinion.") The others of this generation—Steevens, Malone, et al.—who deserve all honor for their contributions to our knowledge of Shakespeare, appear in a less flattering light when it comes to Jonson. They scrutinized his text with all the critical instruments at their disposal, and found imagined sneers where previously none had been suspected.

In his *Supplemental Apology* (1799), Chalmers is the first to identify Shakespeare as Jonson's target in his fifty-sixth epigram:

> Poor *Poet-Ape,* that *would be thought our chief,*
> 　Whose works are e'en the frippery of wit,
> From brokage is become so bold a thief,
> 　As we, the robb'd, leave rage, and pity it.
> At first, he made low shifts, would pick, and glean;
> 　By *the reversion of old plays,* now grown
> Into a *little wealth,* and credit in the scene,
> 　He takes up all, makes each man's wit his own. . . .[14]

There is nothing in these lines to suggest that Shakespeare is their object, apart from the presumption that he *must* be the victim of any attack directed by Jonson against any unspecified poet. Chalmers' *aperçu* perhaps does not come unexpectedly from a critic who has the distinction of being the first to propose that the Fair Youth of Shakespeare's Sonnets is the ageing Queen Elizabeth. His discussion of the Poet-Ape later threw Jonson's editor Gifford into one of those fits of apoplexy to which the imbecilities of commentators made him prone. "Mr. Chalmers," he explodes, "will *take it on his death* that the person here meant is Shakspeare! Who can doubt it? For my part, I am persuaded, that GROOM IDIOT in the next epigram is also Shakspeare; and, indeed, generally, that he is typified by the words 'fool and knave,' so exquisitely descriptive of him, wherever they occur in Jonson."[15]

The terrible scene in *Lear* of the blinding of Gloucester, and its aftermath of the servant going to fetch flax and egg whites to apply to the bleeding face, has evoked extraordinary responses from critics. An eminent psychoanalyst has suggested that the blood and bandage represent the surfacing of the poet's suppressed childhood memories of his mother's menstruation. The gloss offered by Shakespeare's eighteenth-century editor Steevens, while less sublime, deserves to be regarded with equal solemnity. He finds Jonson expressing his scorn for *Lear* in Act 2, scene 7, of *The Case Is Altered,* dated 1609 by Steevens. Here Juniper urges Martino, whose head has been broken in a fencing match, to "go, get a white of an egge, and a little flax, and close the breach of the head, it is the most conducible thing that can be." Steevens forgets to mention that flax and egg whites must have been a common Elizabethan remedy for such injuries; nor does he say that 1609 is the publication date for *The Case Is Altered,* not the year of first performance, which took place almost a decade before *Lear.* Malone exposed Steevens' error but, unwilling to part with a good thing, suggested that Jonson had interpolated his dig between the appearance of Shakespeare's play and the printing of his own.

In truth Malone, one of the great scholars of the day, did more than anyone up to his time to advance the myth of personal enmity between his idol and Jonson. Again and again in his notes he harps upon Jonson's clumsy sarcasms and malevolent reflections. "In the *Silent Woman,* 1609, Jonson perhaps pointed at Shakspeare as one whom he viewed with *scornful* yet *jealous* eyes. . . ." "In the *Devil's an Ass,* all Shakspeare's *historical plays* are obliquely *censured.*" "The Induction to the *Staple of News,* 1625, contains a *sneer* at *Julius Caesar.*" And so on; many more instances might be adduced. In his reprint of Rowe's *Account* for his 1790 *Shakespeare,* Malone resurrects in a note the passage (already mentioned) excised by Pope, and he goes on to describe Jonson's "envious disposition" as "notorious" in his own day, and to picture Ben as "pouring out against those who preferred our poet to him, a torrent of illiberal abuse."[16] Coming from so eminent an authority, Malone's illiberal abuse of Jonson carried weight. Currency too, for Rowe's *Account* with Malone's notes would be more than once reprinted.

IV

Eventually a reaction came to eighteenth-century Jonson-baiting, and this shift in the critical wind I would attribute to the newfound interest in Shakespeare's contemporaries as dramatists fascinating in their own right, and not as lesser breeds useful merely to illustrate obscure phrases of the Immortal Bard. Jonson found his first notable defender in Octavius Gilchrist, who brought out *An Examination of the Charges Maintained by Messrs. Malone, Chalmers, and Others, of Ben Jonson's Enmity, &c. towards Shakspeare* in 1808, significantly the same year that witnessed the publication of Lamb's *Specimens,* which marked a new tide in the affairs of poets. If Jonson was indeed the ungrateful libeller of his friend, Gilchrist declares, "his writings ought to be condemned to the hands of the hangman, and his name be consigned to perpetual infamy." (But why, even if Jonson were a cad, for that reason throw out *Volpone* and *The Alchemist?* This is the very ecstasy of bardolatry.)

> If, however, [Gilchrist continues] it shall appear that his fair fame has been blackened, his memory traduced, and his writings perverted, for the unworthy purpose of raising a rival poet on the ruins of his reputation; and that malevolent critics may display their sagacity and acuteness in tracing passages applicable to their favourite poet; the voice of public justice, it is to be hoped, will restore to the brow of the poet his violated honours, committing to merited shame and obloquy the "viperous critics by whom they were bereaved."[17]

Clearly Jonson had found an eloquent champion. Gilchrist proceeds to sift "the ample dunghill of antiquarian defamation," pointing out the excesses of Steevens, Malone, and Chalmers. He makes short work of the Macklin forgery and of the Poet-Ape; but excess breeds excess. In acquitting his hero of imputed girds at Shakespeare, he goes so far as to deny allusions where they indubitably exist, as in the Prologue to *Every Man in His Humour* and the Induction to *Bartholomew Fair:* Jonson's satire must always be general, and never have personal application. A similar whitewashing occurs when Gilchrist cites Jonson's passage on Shakespeare in *Discoveries*—he quotes only the favorable bits, passing over in silence honest Ben's censure of his friend's supposed lapses. An edition of Ford by Weber in 1811, reviving the discredited Macklin pamphlet and charges of "the bitterness of Ben Johnson against his too powerful rival," moved Gilchrist to buckle on his armor again in *A Letter to William Gifford, Esq.* (1811). But it is the latter who now moves to the center of the stage as Jonson's most impassioned defender.

Urbanity is not Gifford's forte, as it is Gilchrist's, but he makes up for this deficiency by the vigor of his prejudiced polemics in his edition of Jonson's *Works* (1816). Generously acknowledging his friend's pioneering contribution, Gifford devotes a whole section to rebuttal of "Proofs of Ben Jonson's Malignity, from the Commentators on Shakspeare." The introductory memoir contains many curious declarations. Gifford would have us believe that in 1598 "Jonson was as well known as Shakspeare, and perhaps, better" (so much for Meres!). He dismisses *Pericles* as "worthless." He admits to surreptitious expurgation of the text: "I know the importance of fidelity; but no considerations on earth can tempt me to the wanton or heedless propagation of impiety." (Editors please note.) But Gifford's chief contribution is to envisage, so far as I know for the first time in print, Shakespeare's participation in the happy sessions of the wits at the Mermaid Tavern:

> Sir Walter Raleigh . . . had instituted a meeting of *beaux esprits* at the Mermaid, a celebrated tavern in Friday-street. Of this Club, which combined more talent and genius, perhaps, than ever met together before or since, our author was a member; and here, for many years, he regularly repaired with Shakspeare, Beaumont, Fletcher, Selden, Cotton, Carew, Martin, Donne, and many others, whose names, even at this distant period, call up a mingled feeling of reverence and respect. Here, in the full flow and confidence of friendship, the lively and interesting "wit-combats" took place between Shakspeare and our author; and hither, in probable allusion to them, Beaumont fondly lets his thoughts wander, in his letter to Jonson, from the country.
> ————"What things have we seen,
> Done at the MERMAID! . . ."[18]

It is strange to find the haughty Raleigh presiding over tavern high-jinks attended by Shakespeare—especially when one considers that from the accession of James until after the poet's death the knight was imprisoned in the Tower. Nor, despite the fact that Shakespeare knew the landlord of the Mermaid (as is attested by a real-estate transaction of 1613), is there any evidence that he was a member of any club that met at this tavern or anywhere else. The sessions at the Mermaid conjured up by Gifford belong not to the historical record but to a nineteenth-century critic's romantic fancy; so I. A. Shapiro has conclusively shown in an important article.[19] In the pages of Gifford's *Jonson* we witness the birth of a legend, although one for which hints had been supplied by Fuller and traditionary anecdotes.

Artists would sketch Shakespeare and Jonson and the other wits with meticulous Victorian verisimilitude. Poets would furnish the scene with words. In George Willis Cooke's *Guide-book to the Poetic and Dramatic Works of Robert Browning* (1891), I find the following commentary on "At the 'Mermaid'": "In this poem the speaker is Shakespeare, to whom it has just been suggested that he is to be the next great poet. He is speaking to his literary friends, especially to Ben Jonson, gathered at 'The Mermaid' tavern, the favorite resort in London of the Elizabethan wits."[20] A scholar's sentimental romance has been canonized as fact. Inevitably the supposed fact would be fictionalized as romance. There is a delicious scene in a light modern novel in which Shakespeare, Jonson, Raleigh, Sidney, and other worthies are assembled at the Mermaid. Through the open window float the voices of prentice lads singing "Drink to me only with thine eyes. . . ." "O rare Ben Jonson," exclaims the Bard, weeping, as the voices die away. "God," Jonson nods sadly, "what genius I had then!"[21]

V

The next important development occurs later in the century, with the emergence of a rage for topical allusions, particularly as they were to be found in plays purportedly connected with the so-called War of the Theatres. In *Shakespeare and Jonson. Dramatic, versus Wit-Combats* (1864), Robert Cartwright proposed that in *Every Man in His Humour* Shakespeare is represented by both the town sophisticate Wellbred and the country gull Stephen; moreover, in *Poetaster* "there can be little doubt" that Ovid stands for Shakespeare. Cartwright makes many other ingenious suggestions: Shakespeare replied to *Every Man out of His Humour* in *Much Ado about Nothing.* He vented his wrath upon Jonson in the character of Apemantus in *Timon of Athens.* And "Who can doubt, that Iago is 'malignant Ben'?" asks Cartwright, and does not stay for an answer. An anonymous critic, probably Simpson, in *The North British Review* (1870), identified Amorphus (the Deformed) in *Cynthia's Revels* as Shakespeare who, we learn with some surprise, had been nicknamed "Deformed" because of his ignorance and plagiarisms. This is crazy stuff, and there is a lot more of it. But the Rev. Frederick Gard Fleay is someone to be taken more seriously.

In 1874 the eccentric headmaster of Skipton Grammar School took the just established New Shakspere Society by storm with a series of papers on chronology and authorship. Fleay is the first of the great modern disintegrators of Shakespeare's text. As he proceeded from instalment to instalment his views became increasingly bizarre, until they proved too much for the Society which had provided him with a forum. Turning from statistical studies, for which he was not especially well suited by reason of his inability to add, Fleay compiled annals of the stage and ferreted out topical references which, to his delight, appeared everywhere.

Only the Jonson-Shakespeare allusions here concern us. About *Twelfth Night* Fleay writes in his *Life of Shakespeare* (1886): "I believe that Sir Toby represents Jonson and Malvolio Marston; but that subject requires to be treated in a separate work from its complexity."[22] This monograph, alas, never appeared, although Fleay elsewhere elaborated somewhat his comment on *Twelfth Night.* He identifies *Troilus and Cressida* as the purge which, according to *The Return from Parnassus,* Shakespeare administered to Jonson, "Ajax representing Jonson, Achilles Chapman, and Hector Shake-speare." In his *Biographical Chronicle of the English Drama* (1891), he enlarges on this hypothesis:

> . . . whoever will take the trouble to compare the description of Crites in *Cynthia's Revels*, ii.1, with that of Ajax in *Troylus and Cressida*, i.2, will see that Ajax is Jonson: slow as the Elephant crowded by Nature with "humors," valiant as the Lion, churlish as the Bear, melancholy without cause (compare Macilente). Hardly a word is spoken of or by Ajax in ii.3, iii.3, which does not apply literally to Jonson; and in ii.1 he beats Ther-sites of the "mastic jaws," i.3, 73 (Histriomastix, Theriomastix), as Jonson "beat Marston," *Drum. Conv.*, 11.[23]

And how did the unknown Cambridge playwright find out that Shake-speare had administered a purge to Jonson in a play never clapper-clawed by the palms of the vulgar? He saw it in production when the Chamber-lain's men visited the university in 1601. Q.E.D.

Fleay's work, highly influential in its own day, left a mark on Josiah H. Penniman's *The War of the Theatres* (1897), and also on Roscoe Addison Small's *The Stage-Quarrel Between Ben Jonson and the So-called Poetasters* (1899), which however is more critical. Still, Small can say that "No Elizabethan audience could hear Alexander's description of Ajax [*Troilus and Cressida*, 1.2] without at once thinking of Jonson."[24] This just goes to show, I suppose, the advantage that an Elizabethan audience had over a modern one.

What inferences are we to draw from this selective and no doubt superficial survey? My last remark, about Penniman and Small, may serve to illustrate the hold that the past has upon the present: these mouldy dissertations, seventy years old, must still be cited as the latest authorities on the War of the Theaters, and Shakespeare's and Jonson's roles therein.[25] But our scholarly inheritance is everywhere about us. A presumed sneer at Shakespeare in *Every Man out of His Humour*, first detected by Steevens in the eighteenth century and effectively countered by Gifford in 1816, has in recent years been exhumed. A gifted researcher like Leslie Hotson can blandly assume the existence of a Mermaid Club with a membership in-cluding Shakespeare and other *beaux esprits*. Despite Gilchrist and Gifford there are twentieth-century students who insist that Shakespeare is Jon-son's Poet-Ape, and that old Ben felt evil in his heart towards benevolent Will.[26]

Old ghosts, then, haunt biography and criticism. It has been my purpose in this paper to exorcise a few of them, and to help restore the picture, overlaid with the dust of centuries, of two excellent playwrights who some-times labored for the same company, and who took a lively interest in one another's work: Shakespeare by acting in *Every Man in His Humour* and in *Sejanus*, Jonson by his scattered remarks, not always approving, on his great colleague's writings. How intimate were the terms of their relationship, what tensions (if any) underlay the surface, we cannot at this remove of time ascertain. But we may rest assured that Heminges and Condell would not have invited Jonson to contribute the principal eulogy of the First Folio if he were not their fellow's friend, and Jonson would not have penned so noble a tribute if he did not esteem Shakespeare as an artist and colleague. Nor would he have, in the privacy of his study, described Shakespeare with a warmth that he expressed for no other poet. We may believe that he loved the man; to be sure, on this side idolatry. That is not an unpleasant note on which to end.

NOTES

1. *The Three Parnassus Plays*, ed. J. B. Leishman (London, 1949), p. 337.
2. See Leishman's discussion, pp. 59–60, 336n.
3. Fuller, *Worthies*, Warwick-Shire, p. 126.
4. E. K. Chambers, *William Shakespeare: A Study of Facts and Problems* (Oxford, 1930), II, 243.
5. Ibid., p. 247.
6. Ibid., p. 286.
7. Ibid., p. 250.
8. The extremely influential remark made in the *Discourse Concerning Satire* has received insufficient notice. Aden does not include it in his dictionary of *The Critical Opinions of John Dryden;* Chambers omits it from the Dryden references in the second volume of his *Shakespeare,* as do Herford and Simpson from the ampler body of Dryden extracts in Vol. XI of their edition of Jonson.
9. Shakespeare, *Works*, ed. Rowe (London, 1709), I, xiii.
10. Joseph Spence, *Observations, Anecdotes, and Characters of Books and Men*, ed. James M. Osborn (Oxford, 1966), I, 23.
11. Shakespeare, *Works*, ed. Pope (London, 1725), I, xii.
12. [John Roberts], *An Answer to Mr. Pope's Preface to Shakespear* (London, 1729), pp. 10–11.
13. The letter is reproduced by Malone (Shakespeare, *Plays and Poems* [London, 1790], Vol. I, Pt. i, 203), from whose text I quote.
14. See Chalmers, *Supplemental Apology*, pp. 235–42.
15. Jonson, *Works*, ed. Gifford (London, 1816), VIII, 181, n.4.
16. Shakespeare, *Plays and Poems*, ed. Malone, Vol. I, Pt. i, pp. 111–13, n.3.
17. Gilchrist, *Examination*, pp. 6–7.
18. Jonson, *Works*, ed. Gifford, I, lxv–lxvi.
19. "The 'Mermaid Club'," *MLR*, XLV (1950), 6–17.
20. Pp. 41–42.
21. Caryl Brahms and S. J. Simon, *No Bed for Bacon* (London, 1941), pp. 133–34.
22. *A Chronicle History of the Life and Work of William Shakespeare* (London, 1886), p. 220.
23. I, 366.
24. P. 169.
25. Re-evaluation is, however, at last underway; since this paper was written, Stuart B. Omans has completed a Northwestern University dissertation, "The War of the Theatres: An Approach to Its Origins, Development, and Meaning."
26. Inimitably misinformed, Colin Wilson has recently remarked, in the fictional context of *The Philosopher's Stone* (1969), "Jonson referred to Shakespeare as a 'Poet-ape' in *The Return from Parnassus*."

(1970)

14
The Humorous Jonson

I hope my gracious hosts, who have invited me back for a return engagement at this select conference in pleasant Waterloo, won't account me ungrateful or, worse, discourteous, if I preface my remarks with a few frank comments on anniversary rites for the renowned dead. I expect I am not alone in being of two minds about such occasions. We all know what an orgy of celebration—a weariness to the Gordon Ross Smiths of this world—1964 produced. Such rifling of bottom desk-drawers! Such laborious efforts to restate for the occasion what one had already said, more freshly, without artificial pressure. Suddenly, for a year, Shakespearean scholarship became, as it were, one massive *Festschrift*. "Much of the book is fluffed out with the author's comments on all the individual plays," remarked the *Times Literary Supplement* reviewer of an anniversary biography. "He has to say something, but he has nothing to say." Now, it seems, in 1972 we are confronted with the same phenomenon on a smaller scale. But fortunately there is another side to the picture; I am not thinking merely of the small rewards of conferences—the renewals of friendships, the chance to meet colleagues for the first time, the transitory pleasures of a booze-up. The commemorative urge, of which literary biography is an eloquent expression, is not ignoble. If, after 1964, Jonson were to be ignored this year, we would deservedly feel some shame. More significant for criticism, a conference such as this allows for a certain stock-taking. We can pause to examine ideas and attitudes that have a general interest rather than confining ourselves exclusively to the specialized contributions which are the usual staple of learned gatherings.

At least that is how I have interpreted my brief today. There are dangers, however, which I cannot claim to have successfully avoided. I am afraid that my theme, when in my circuitous fashion I have finally got round to it, will impress you as having an obviousness which is positively blinding. Moreover, some of you may feel that, in addition to being simplistic and platitudinous, I have taken an anti-intellectual position, or at least one that is unappreciative of the accomplishments of academic investigation. That I would regret, for such is not my intention. About my obviousness I am unrepentant.

I

After these preliminaries let us turn to goose-turds in Jonson. In Act 4, scene 4, of *The Alchemist*, Dame Pliant is hustled before Subtle by her brother the angry boy, and Face. Together they urge upon her the desirability of being a Spanish Countess. "Why? is that better than an *English Countesse?*" the pliant heiress asks, and they explain why it is, by enumerating all the advantages which will be hers: pages, ushers, footmen, coaches. "Yes," interjects Face,

> and have
> The citizens gape at her, and praise her tyres!
> And my-lords goose-turd bands, that rides with her!
>
> (4.4.48–50)

Goose-turd bands. "Yellowish-green" is Herford and Simpson's gloss for *goose-turd*. A more recent commentator, F. H. Mares, in his text for the Revels Plays, is not satisfied:

> goose-turd bands] collars in the fashionable colour of goose-turd green, usually described as a yellowish green. However, to my observation, goose turds are a very dark green.[1]

This interesting intelligence has inspired a poem. By Jeannie Robison, and entitled "On Editing Jonson," the verses (somewhat defectious in the rhyme) go like this:

> What stares you must have caused
> When armed with spectrum and glass,
> You searched the English countryside
> For what the geese had passed.
>
> Perhaps you only shoe'd the pile,
> Convinced of its darker green.
> Or bending down, gently turned
> And checked the side unseen.
>
> For judgments must be closely wrought;
> Knowledge's end is truth.
> And even Jonson must be taught:
> Give turds their proper hue.[2]

Much ado about goose-turds. No dramatist in English, surely (always excepting Shakespeare), comes to us laboring under so heavy a freight of learned exegesis. Such a burden must have interesting consequences for criticism.

I am afraid I cannot resist one or two more examples from commentaries on *The Alchemist*. In Act 2, scene 2, Sir Epicure Mammon luxuriates in a vision of voluptuous rewards that make, for him, actual possession of the Philosophers' Stone almost superfluous. "My mere fooles," he foresees,

> Eloquent burgesses, and then my poets,
> The same that writ so subtly of the *fart*.
>
> (2.2.61–63)

For which the obliging Mares furnishes this annotation:

> *the fart*] In *Musarum Deliciae or The Muses Recreation* (1656) are several poems on this subject. One—"The Fart Censured in the Parliament House"—refers to an event of 1607, was written before 1610, and is to be found in the Harleian MS. 5191, f.17, so that it cannot be original to Sir John Mennis and James Smith, who put out the 1656 volume. That this poem is referred to seems more probable if we take *burgesses* (62) in its old sense of members of parliament, since it contains "about forty stanzas of the most wretched doggerel, conveying the opinion of as many members of parliament, on the subject" (G[ifford]).[3]

What other English dramatist can have inspired learned dissertations on so unprepossessing a subject?

But my favorite is the note on *chiaus* in the magisterial Clarendon edition. "What doe you thinke of me," protests Dapper, "That I am a *Chiause?*" "What's that?", asks Face, to which Herford and Simpson obligingly reply:

> *Chiause.* The word is an imperfect adaptation of the Turkish *chāush*, "messenger," "herald." On 13 October 1611 the King gave £ 30 to "Two Chiaus or Messengers from yᵉ Turke" (Exchequer accounts, E 403/2731, f.9). W. R. Chetwood, whom Gifford took over without acknowledgement, first traced its English origin in *Memoirs of the Life and Times of Ben. Jonson, Esq.*, 1756, p.15n., but he blundered over the facts and the date. The true story was given for the first time in Sir William Foster's edition of *The Travels of John Sanderson*, a Levantine merchant, published by the Hakluyt Society in 1930, pages xxiii–xxxv.
>
> A Turk named Mustafa reached England towards the end of July 1607, announcing that he was an ambassador from the Sultan, though he took no higher title than that of *Chāush*. He had left Constantinople in 1605 as a courier in attendance on the French ambassador, but he had procured from the Sultan letters to the kings of France and England. The secretary of the Levant Company warned the authorities about him. But he had been received by the French king, and they were nervous about offending the Sultan. The Levant merchants had to entertain him at a cost of £5 a day, and paid all his expenses; he made them even find the thread to mend his clothes. In September 1607 he was received at Windsor, and presented a letter complaining of the depredations in the Mediterranean of pirates sailing under English colours. He departed in November 1607.
>
> He added a new word to the English language, "to chouse," to cheat, because of the way he had fooled the Levant merchants. Chetwood's

form of the story that Sir Robert Shirley had sent Mustafa as his agent from the Grand Signior and that he had decamped after having "chiaused" the Turkish and Persian merchants of £4,000 is untrue.[4]

From its exposition learned to put-down supercilious, with sidethrust dismissive along the way, I know of no more masterly exemplar of the one-upmanship of footnoting. It is to be recommended to all thesis writers.

Erudite exegesis is one manifestation, and an important one, of the academic way with Jonson. There are many others. We study his sources, his verse imagery and prose style, his classical ideal of form and how he succeeds in living up to it or fails to live up to it. We are at pains to place him in his proper historical context as creator of comical satire after Archbishop Whitgift's prohibition of verse-satire, as purveyor of masques to the Stuart court, and as burly literary dictator at the Mermaid Tavern. We use him as a whipping-boy to demonstrate the incalculable superiority of Shakespeare. My aim today is not to belittle the fruits of scholarly inquiry into Jonson, although for the last sort I have little patience. More often than not, Jonson commands the full deployment of the critical intelligence. One may say of him what his namesake said of the race of metaphysical poets: to write on Jonson, it is at least necessary to read and think. Anybody can write on Shakespeare, and everybody does.

The vice of erudition is pedantry, and it is by their pedantries that Jonson's commentators make themselves fair game for the wits. Now the pedantry that lurks in the footnotes may be symptomatic of the more dangerous vice of over-solemnity, which will surface in the critical introductions and have a baleful effect on readers, and perhaps ultimately on producers. Yet if Jonson is, as I believe, a great dramatist, he is great as a comic master. His triumph resides not primarily in his comical satires, or in the two Roman tragedies that were jeered off his own stage, or in the masques whose temporal glories we cannot recreate without his scenes and machines; not in these, but in the astonishing series of comedies to which *Every Man in His Humour* is dazzling prologue. And central to these plays is laughter: rude, boisterous laughter, more often derisive than genial, but laughter nonetheless. Jonson can be a very funny writer; that is my simple theme today. This truism has not had the critical attention it deserves. In a book promisingly entitled *Jonson and the Comic Truth*, John J. Enck has a chapter which he calls "The Streame of Humour." But Enck's stream flows through a narrow and well-worn channel; he has in mind our old and tiresome friends the humours. Humor (in the unclinical sense of the term) he would banish to the suburbs of comedy; "one has no choice," Enck informs us in his concluding summation, "but to relegate laughter itself to a marginal position."[5] I submit that too many of us, as critics and pedagogues, have submitted to this unnecessary necessity and relegated laughter to a marginal position in pursuing the humours at the expense of the humor. The former, so long as I can remember, have made matter for the set questions we put to our students; we have less frequently asked them to explore Jonson's comic mode.

The study of Jonson should warn us away from overstressing a point, lest we become, like one of his *dramatis personae*, the victims of an *idée fixe*. Our ablest critics, the majority of them anyway, have not sat frozen-faced in the presence of the great comedies. It is a matter of emphasis, of priorities.[6]

Still I do feel that it is appropriate—even incumbent upon us—to celebrate Jonson's humor these days when (it seems) criticism has lost all its mirth. In Jonson studies, solemnity takes varied forms. We do not run the risk of underestimating the importance of the didactic elements in his art; indeed, we have a whole treatise on the subject. When the dean of American literary critics, the late Edmund Wilson, applied his formidable powers to Jonson, the dramatist emerged as an anal-erotic. This proctoscopic critique is not one of Wilson's happier efforts. In *Volpone*, Mares remarks, "Virtue survives (as in *King Lear*) only because vice destroys itself. . . ." That vice destroys itself is an old story, at least as old as the Book of Proverbs, and has provided a *peripeteia* for innumerable comedies and tragedies. It should be possible to discuss this phenomenon in *Volpone* without hauling in *Lear* and thus invoking shades of apocalypse. Vice and virtue mean different things in different contexts; Volpone is no Edmund, and Celia no Cordelia.

The malaise of criticism has extended to production. Two recent instances. I expect that some in this audience were here in Waterloo in 1969 for the Second Elizabethan Theatre Conference, when the Stratford Festival season included a production of *The Alchemist*. It was reckoned successful enough to go on tour—this play can withstand punishment—and, although there was much bustle and noise, this viewer at least discerned little evidence of directorial conviction that the play was really uproarious. The miscasting of Sir Epicure Mammon was symptomatic. It was rather as though, in an accident of repertory, the actor playing Cassius in *Julius Caesar* mistook Tuesday for Thursday, and wandered into the alchemist's premises. The Stratford Sir Epicure had a lean and hungry look, and we could not for a moment believe that this sensualist—described by his creator as "the fat knight"—would dream of having his bed blown up, not stuffed, down being too hard. The only comic inspiration I recall in the production was the cunning doctor's marvelous machine which, with its pulsations and gyrations, did credit to the memory of Rube Goldberg. This contraption was periodically wheeled out, to the general delight of the spectators, although in Jonson's text it is of course kept off-stage throughout. The most recent production I have seen of Jonson was the National Theatre's *Bartholomew Fair* a few seasons back at the Aldwych in London. The hues—and I am thinking literally of costumes, sets, etcetera—were somber and the production as a whole seemed to belong to the Brechtian twilight that had for so long kept possession of the British stage, and was at last (none too soon) departing. A reviewer in one posh Sunday paper labeled his notice "Bartholomew Foul." This was an exaggeration—the pig woman is indomitable and the puppet play survives directorial perversity— but I can understand his reaction.

The current state of criticism and performance is one reason for my concern with the humorous Jonson. There is a second. We do well to emphasize Jonson's laughter, which is a manifestation of the popular in his art, because his reputation, at least outside the academy, is precarious, and has been for some time. He has a capacity unique among the classic English writers of arousing the displeasure, sometimes pungently expressed, of his more articulate readers.

As we all know, the Romantic revival of interest in the Elizabethans, a revival sparked by Lamb's *Specimens* in 1808, brought back into favor playwrights previously in eclipse. Dekker, Heywood and Webster benefited handsomely, I expect in part because their art is in some respects "Shakespearean." Jonson fared less well. Lamb included eight specimens from (among other titles) *The Case Is Altered, Sejanus, The Poetaster,* and *The New Inn:* "serious extracts," in Lamb's own phrase, in which the humorous Jonson is little evident. These the anthologist followed, for variety, with Sir Epicure Mammon's spectacular opening dialogue with Surly. Here is exhibited, according to Lamb, Jonson's "talent for comic humour," but the reader's appreciation of this winning trait is doubtfully enhanced by Lamb's postscript; for he sees Sir Epicure as "the most determined offspring of the author." Mammon's "lying overbearing character" is "just such a swaggerer as contemporaries have described old Ben to be."[7] For Lamb's contemporary, Coleridge, Jonson has become a specimen of another sort: a palaeontological exhibit in a museum of critical curiosities:

> He [Jonson] could not but be a Species of himself: tho' like the Mammoth and Megatherion fitted & destined to live only during a given Period, and then to exist a Skeleton, hard, dry, uncouth perhaps, yet massive and not to be contemplated without that mixture of Wonder and Admiration, or more accurately, that middle somewhat between both for which we want a term—not quite even with the latter, but far above the mere former.

To Hazlitt this playwright was an acquired taste, like that for olives, and one which, despite effort, he failed to acquire; Jonson's power remained for him "of a repulsive and unamiable kind." To Swinburne he was "as a rule,—a rule which is proved by the exception . . . one of the singers who could not sing."[8] So it goes.

This critical heritage was memorably summed up in the next century by

T. S. Eliot. "The reputation of Jonson," Eliot begins his essay on the dramatist, "has been of the most deadly kind that can be compelled upon the
memory of a great poet. To be universally accepted; to be damned by the
praise that quenches all desire to read the book; to be afflicted by the
imputation of the virtues which excite the least pleasure; and to be read
only by historians and antiquaries—this is the most perfect conspiracy of
approval."[9] (The approval, we have seen, is more qualified than Eliot suggests, and it is significant that throughout his essay he refers to Jonson as a
writer to be read, not a dramatist to be played.) Twenty years after Eliot
wrote, things hadn't changed very much, if we may judge from Harry
Levin's introduction to a volume of Jonson's *Selected Writings:* "Ben Jonson's position, three hundred years after his death is more than secure; it
might almost be called impregnable. He is still the greatest unread English
author. . . . Jonson has always had more attention from antiquarians than
from critics, and has too often served as a cadaver over which to read a
lecture on the lore of language and custom."[10]

Since 1938, when Levin's edition appeared, the cadaver has evidenced
some twitchings of life. In 1952, more than twenty-five years after the
appearance of the first volume, the Clarendon edition reached its majestic
conclusion; a monument, if not of the new bibliography, then of an older
and still valued tradition of humanistic learning. There has been a spate of
important books since, among them (to name just a few from which this
reader has especially profited) Edward Partridge's *Broken Compass* and
Jonas Barish's *Ben Jonson and the Language of Prose Comedy,* more recently
Stephen Orgel's *The Jonsonian Masque,* and very lately Alan Dessen's *Jonson's
Moral Comedy,* tracing the dramatist's native roots in the early Tudor hybrid
moralities. Yale University Press has given us excellently edited texts of
individual plays for students. What year does not bring a new edition of
Volpone? This is no doubt progress, much of it a revaluation stimulated by
the completion of Herford and Simpson. Yet I cannot help feeling that the
Jonson industry is on the whole a specialized one, academicians talking to
one another; not a movement that has made any very deep impression on
the common understanding. Just a couple of months back the *Times Literary
Supplement* commended as excellent a new edition of *Every Man in His
Humour,* but described the play itself as "patently unreadable" (not, please
note, patently unactable; performance has not even crossed the mind of
this reviewer). In his recent excellent chapter on Jonson for the Sphere
History of Literature in the English Language, Ian Donaldson is a trifle
stingy in limiting to a handful the excellent studies of the past half-century,
but I am not inclined to question his conclusion that Eliot's judgment still
holds. "For the common reader and playgoer," Donaldson says, "Jonson
still seems to stand as the most daunting and formidable of English classics,
an author one would gladlier walk round about to avoid than walk in
company with."[11]

II

Perhaps we should hesitate to assume too readily that such ought not to be the case. He became his admirers, Auden says of the dead Yeats in his great poem. So all writers become their admirers, and Jonson's reputation may well reflect what he is. Did he ever actually court the universal audience that Shakespeare has always enjoyed? Does surly Ben really want us to laugh?

It is certainly true that in his criticism Jonson powerfully espouses the corrective role of comedy as reformer of men and manners; the comedian no less than the tragedian is, he insists, a teacher. And, as for laughter, in his *Discoveries* he goes so far as to declare:

> Nor, is the moving of laughter alwaies the end of *Comedy*, that is rather a fowling for the peoples delight, or their fooling. For, as *Aristotle* saies rightly, the moving of laughter is a fault in Comedie, a kind of turpitude, that depraves some part of a mans nature without a disease. (2629–33)

This is harsh doctrine, but not without its escape clause (the word *always*); and if laughter depraves, one can only say that it is a form of turpitude to which Jonson in his less austere moments succumbs. So, too, it is well to note that if he plumps strongly for the didactic function of art, he does not ignore the other pillar of the Horatian dictum. His true scope, as he says in his Prologue to *Volpone*,

> if you would know it,
> In all his *poemes*, stil, hath been this measure,
> To mixe profit, with your pleasure.
>
> (6–8)

An artist wears more than one mask. To Alfred Harbage, whose *Shakespeare and the Rival Traditions* is, for our period, the most influential work of criticism embodying the moral ideal of democracy, Jonson is the presiding genius of coterie drama. Again and again this dramatist heaps scorn upon that beast, the multitude. "*Expectation* of the *Vulgar* is more drawne, and held with newnesse, then goodnesse," he grumbles in the *Discoveries;*

> wee see it in *Fencers*, in *Players*, in *Poets*, in *Preachers*, in all, where *Fame* promiseth any thing; so it be new, though never so naught, and depraved, they run to it, and are taken. Which shewes, that the only decay, or hurt of the best mens *reputation* with the people, is, their wits have out-liv'd the peoples palats. They have beene too much, or too long a feast. (405–12)

The recurring metaphor of feasting appears also in Macilente's revised conclusion to *Every Man Out*, where Jonson addresses himself to those who can judge:

> The Cates that you have tasted were not season'd
> For every vulgar Pallat, but prepar'd
> To banket pure and apprehensive eares:
> Let then their Voices speake for our desert.
>
> (10–13)

He contemns (in the Prologue to *Poetaster*) "base detractors, and illiterate apes." "If it were put to the question of theirs, and mine," he muses in his preface to *The Alchemist*, "the worse would finde more suffrages: because the most favour common errors." Looking about his audience, Jonson casts a disdainful eye on the civet-wits in their new suits, knowing no more than the price of satin and velvet; the mustachioed lisping gallant swearing down all who sit about him; the bottle-headed spectator with a cork brain who squeezes out a pitiful-learned face and is silent. And finally, after the failure of *The New Inn*, we have the bitter "Ode to Himself," in which Jonson heaps abuse on the loathed stage—"They were not made for thee, lesse, thou for them"—and sees himself literally as casting pearls before swine.

In better days he could address the select audiences of the private theatres more amiably. So, in the Prologue to *Cynthia's Revels*, acted by the Children of the Chapel, he is positively flattering:

> If gracious silence, sweet attention,
> Quicke sight, and quicker apprehension,
> (The lights of judgement's throne) shine any where;
> Our doubtfull authour hopes this is their sphere.
>
> (1–4)

Whatever Jonson's elitist tendencies, however, it is a fact (as Harbage is well aware) that he wrote almost as much for the popular as for the select playhouses. He furnished Shakespeare's company, the Chamberlain's men, with *Every Man In* and *Every Man Out,* and then gave *Cynthia's Revels* and *Poetaster* to the Chapel Children. But in June 1602 Henslowe (who had previously paid him for additions to the quintessentially popular *Spanish Tragedy*), was lending Jonson money for a book called *Richard Crookback* to be acted by the Admiral's men, who catered for the masses. With *Sejanus* he was back with Shakespeare's troupe, and the association was continued with *Volpone* and *The Alchemist. Bartholomew Fair* is another popular play, produced by the Lady Elizabeth's men at the Hope Theatre. So it goes. Harbage gets round the problem by suggesting that Jonson's "inclinations and influence" linked him with the coterie.

Elsewhere Harbage acknowledges that, in Jonson's case, genius "complicates the pattern as genius always must." Perhaps we may more properly understand Jonson not so much as an exemplar of either of the rival dramatic traditions, but rather as an archetype of the independent artist;

some such fabulous voyager as James Joyce in our own century, embarked on his own creative odyssey, steering his lonely course between the Scylla of applause and Charybdis of derision. Jonson is, like Joyce, an experimenter:

> In this alone, his MUSE her sweetnesse hath,
> Shee shunnes the print of any beaten path;
> And proves new wayes to come to learned eares.
> (*Cynthia's Revels,* Prol., 9–11)

But even this attractive view of Jonson must be qualified; for the playwright does not enjoy the same independence as the novelist, and the theatre offers a very different forum from that of the little magazines. The dramatist is forced to please even where he loathes, and the comic dramatist must provoke the laughter of those he seeks to improve. As a professional, Jonson knew as much. "It had another *Catastrophe* or Conclusion, at the first playing," he writes of *Every Man Out:* "which . . . many seem'd not to relish it; and therefore 'twas since alter'd." And in the remarkably genial Prologue to *Epicoene,* Jonson accepts without protest the unyielding condition of his art: that the drama's laws the drama's patrons give. He writes:

> Truth sayes, of old, the art of making plaies
>   Was to content the people; & their praise
>   Was to the *Poet* money, wine, and bayes.
> But in this age, a sect of writers are,
>   That, onely, for particular likings care,
>   And will taste nothing that is populare.
> With such we mingle neither braines, nor brests;
>   Our wishes, like to those (make publique feasts)
>   Are not to please the cookes tastes, but the guests.
> (1–9)

Jonson's theory is not without its contradictions, nor does it uniformly square with his practice. Despite the *Discoveries,* we may seek laughter in his comedy, and despite his scorn for the multitude, his greatest plays may yet find a wider audience than the academy.

III

Of these great plays, in the minutes remaining to me, I can but discuss one or two in any detail. It is only fair that I should confront straightaway the work which exposes my position at its most vulnerable, and so I turn to *Volpone.* For some would not only deny laughter to *Volpone* but also question its proper status as comedy. In his undistinguished but still consulted handbook, *An Introduction to Stuart Drama,* Frederick Boas describes the play as "in its lurid colouring . . . more akin to tragedy than to comedy."[12] This judgment echoes Herford and Simpson:

. . . in its whole conception and conduct, in the lurid atmosphere which pervades it from beginning to end, in the appalling and menacing character of the principal movers of the plot, it approaches, not indeed the profound and human-hearted tragedies of Shakespeare, but, very obviously and significantly, his own grandiose and terrible tragedy of two years before.[13]

These respected authorities can, moreover, appeal to the authority of Jonson himself. Did he not equip his play with a noble dedicatory epistle to the two famous universities; an epistle in which he vows to "raise the despis'd head of *poetrie* againe, and stripping her out of those rotten and base rags, wherwith the Times have adulterated her form, restore her to her primitive habit, feature, and majesty, and render her worthy to be imbraced, and kist, of all the great and master-*spirits* of our world." (This in 1607, just after *Lear* and *Macbeth*.) In the same preface Jonson admits that his catastrophe may, in "the strict rigour of *comick* law, meet with censure"; but his special aim has always been "to put the snaffle in their mouths, that crie out, we never punish vice in our *enterludes*, &c." Never mind that elsewhere he insists that comedy should "sport with humane follies, not with crimes"—the corrective mission takes precedence over the niceties of aesthetic criteria. This playwright will instruct and amend licentious spirits; for, after all, "the principall end of *poesie*" is the doctrine, "to informe men, in the best reason of living." Here Jonson sees eye to eye with his sympathetic interpreter, Professor L. C. Knights, who applies to *Volpone* the words of a modern writer not celebrated for his humorous disposition. "The essential function of art is moral," D. H. Lawrence proclaimed. "Not aesthetic, not decorative, not pastime and recreation, but moral."[14]

Do we dare, then, turn for pastime and recreation (ignoble pursuits) to this most sardonic of Jonson's masterpieces? There is certainly much to support the view of Herford and Simpson: from the stunningly blasphemous opening scene in which Volpone, an anchorite after the new fashion, invokes the language of Genesis as he makes his obeisance before his altar of dross; to the fierce punishments meted out at the end—Mosca to be whipped and made perpetual prisoner in the galleys, Volpone, his fortune confiscated, to lie cramped with irons until he has experienced the ailments and lameness he feigned. The *dramatis personae* belong not to humanity but to some monstrous zoo, and behave accordingly. For no other reason than greed, a father with one foot already in the grave disinherits and denies the legitimacy of his virtuous son; a husband, known for his morbid jealousy, makes haste to pimp for his wife; a lawyer debases his noble profession, and would for a few small coins plead against his Maker. The protagonist presides over a deformed household of dwarf, eunuch and hermaphrodite. Are they fruit of the fox's loins, or is he as sterile as is his pursuit of gold? The question is raised, glancingly, and left unanswered. Fittingly the word *unnatural* echoes through the play. We may well be tempted to con-

clude that the comic spirit is allowed to frolic only in the underplot of the
Would-be's, she with her voluble vanity, he with his onions and red her-
rings, their innocent English follies contrasting with (to use the critic's
term) lurid Italianate vice; comic relief, if you will. Surely Jonson must have
been in a ruthless mood during the five weeks that he burned his way
through the composition of *Volpone*.

Yet his Prologue suggests another dimension. Jonson describes his play
as "quick comedy":

> All gall, and coppresse, from his inke, he drayneth,
> 　Onely, a little salt remayneth;
> Wherewith, he'll rub your cheeks, til (red with laughter)
> 　They shall looke fresh, a weeke after.
>
> 　　　　　　　　　　　　　　　　(33–36)

We are meant to laugh after all. And examined closely, with the doctrine
for once not uppermost, *Volpone* is rich in mirth-provoking comic invention
and detail. There is always the serviceable humor of deafness, with its
mistaking of the word. So Corbaccio inquires after Volpone's health:

> *Mosca.*　　His speech is broken, and his eyes are set,
> 　　　　　His face drawne longer, then 't was wont ——
> *Corbaccio.*　　　　　　　　　　How? How?
> 　　　　　Stronger, then he was wont?
> *Mosca.*　　　　　　　　　　　No, sir: his face
> 　　　　　Drawne longer, then 't was wont.
> *Corbaccio.*　　　　　　　　　O, good.
>
> 　　　　　　　　　　　　　　　(1.4.38–41)

Or:

> *Corbaccio.*　How do's he? will he die shortly, think'st thou?
> *Mosca.*　　　　　　　　　　　　　　I feare,
> 　　　　　He'll out-last *May*.
> *Corbaccio.*　　　　　　To day?
> *Mosca.*　　　　　　　　　No, last-out *May*, sir.
>
> 　　　　　　　　　　　　　　　(3.9.12–13)

Take our spruce merchant Corvino. The first comic touch is likely to be
missed in the study, for it is merely the direction for his exit, made precipi-
tously, without a word, at the mere mention of his "gallant wife." True,
Corvino mistreats the long-suffering Celia barbarously, but cruelty is
mitigated by timely double entendre:

> And, now I thinke on't, I will keepe thee backe-wards;
> Thy lodging shall be backe-wards; thy walkes back-wards;
> Thy prospect—all be backe-wards; and no pleasure,
> That thou shalt know, but backe-wards.
>
> 　　　　　　　　　　　　　　　(2.5.58–61)

This tirade is put in perspective by Corvino's abrupt volte face when informed that Volpone requires a lusty wench, "full of juice, to sleepe by him," a remedy presumably more efficacious than that recommended by the College of Physicians of having a flayed ape clapped to his breast; Corvino is now all husbandly solicitude. Later the third suitor, Voltore, is called upon to perform an about-face of a different kind in the Scrutineo; faced with the necessity for a sudden reversal of tactics, he simply topples over as if possessed (*"Voltore falls,"* reads the stage direction):

> God blesse the man!
> (Stop your wind hard, and swell) see, see, see, see!
> He vomits crooked pinnes.
>
> (5.12.23–25)

This particular bit of business I have seen brilliantly executed by the gaunt John Carradine, who gyrated briefly like a top and was suddenly horizontal. The behavior to which the legacy-hunters are driven is in all these instances expressive of the author's doctrine, which I shouldn't wish to downgrade; my point is, simply, that we profit through experiencing comic pleasure.

Our chief source of such pleasure is the fox himself. We delight in his delicious torments as he is steamed like a bath with Lady Would-be's thick breath. He drops hints, which have an effect opposite to that intended:

> *Volpone.*   The Poet,
>   As old in time, as PLATO, and as knowing,
>   Say's that your highest female grace is silence.
> *Lady.*   Which o' your Poets? PETRARCH? or TASSO? or DANTE?
>   GUERRINI? ARIOSTO? ARETINE?
>   CIECO *di Hadria?* I have read them all.
>
> (3.4. 76–81)

Above all, Volpone dazzles us as the quick-change artist. In his mountebank routine, as Scoto of Mantua, he is the ultimate carnival medicine-man, a type that has perennially amused. Disclaiming any kinship with such charlatans—"turdy-facy-nasty-paty-lousy-farticall rogues"—or any mercenary motive ("I have nothing to sell, little, or nothing to sell"), he offers his precious oil, "surnamed *oglio del* SCOTO," for six crowns, but will be pleased to settle for six pence. Volpone's most stunning (and uproarious) transformations, however, are from the lusty magnifico of Venice to a puling, decrepit old man, shivering in his caps and furs, dripping ointment and coughing out his signature of wheezes: "Uh, uh, uh, uh." The quickest change of all occurs when Celia is left alone with him, and the supposedly impotent invalid (no incantation can raise that spirit, her husband has been assured, a long forgetfulness having seized that part), suddenly leaps upright on his bed and, a Tamburlaine of the bedchamber, launches into his great seduction speech. I still remember this scene bringing down the house when I saw it acted, a quarter of a century ago, by José Ferrer in the City Center production. At the end of course Volpone receives his fearsome sentence, but we do well to remember that our emotions are quickly checked; for, after everyone else has departed, the fox remains on stage and, in the traditional fashion of comedy, begs applause—"fare jovially, and clap your hands."

Much of the fun of the play, as my remarks have suggested, requires performance to be appreciated. Moreover, costume, make-up, and gesture, by unmistakably identifying the various species comprising Jonson's bestiary, impart to the proceedings an air of grotesquerie which, however unsettling, leaves no doubt that we have not stumbled inadvertently into the precincts of tragedy. Even Knights, who uses such terms as "sombre," "bitterly derisive," and "grim" in his discussion of *Volpone,* must admit in another chapter and context that revivals have provided "some very good fun."

"Of the proper and normal material of comedy, extravagancies and absurdities, there is, in the main plot, nothing," write Herford and Simpson. "Its nearest approach to humour lies in the horrible simulations of the ludicrous effected by the misshapen creatures of Volpone's household."[15] *Extravagancies and absurdities.* It will not, I hope, be taken as disparagement of these learned gentlemen (or of Boas) to suggest that they belonged to a genteel tradition, and that their sensibility was limited accordingly. In recent years we have seen, in the work of a new generation of playwrights and film-makers, an expansion of the domain of comedy into areas formerly regarded by many as off-limits. As audiences we have learned that laughter may co-exist, uneasily perhaps, but co-exist nonetheless, with the perverse, the lurid, even the violent. I think of Joe Orton's *Loot* and *The Entertaining Mr. Sloane;* I think of Jerzy Skolimowski's film *Deep End,* with its controversial finale of death in the swimming bath. After black comedy we should no longer be surprised that audiences can find amusement in *Volpone.* When in the Prologue we are promised that he will rub our cheeks with laughter, the cunning old master knew what he was about.

Time remains only for a few remarks on one other play. Nobody questions that *The Alchemist* is a comedy, or describes it as somber, although some critics have worried about the dénouement as if it were somehow puzzling that Jonson's sympathies should go to the Lovewits of this world rather than to a Surly, who is after all a dishonest gamester. Criticism has however tended to preoccupation with Jonson's particularities (alchemy and Jacobean London), and with his classicism, to the neglect of other, no less compelling features. Thus Mares in his Revels introduction devotes a whole section to alchemy and a longish passage to the unities, while giving only brief mention to "stage funny-business," which he appreciates but is inclined to regard (with other commentators) as beneath the dignity of serious criticism. This to my mind smacks of an aesthetic Puritanism we could well do without. *The Alchemist* pleases not least because of its unabashed use of every mirth-provoking device in the comic dramatist's repertory.

Let me glance with you at a few. Jonson is a master of the art of derogation (did he not, to Drummond, define a schoolmaster as one who sweeps his living from the posteriors of little children?), and nowhere does derogation flourish more happily than in *The Alchemist.* I think of those little thumb-nail sketches of Jonson's gudgeons: Abel Drugger, "A miserable rogue, and lives with cheese, / And has the wormes"; or that child of wrath, Kastril, "come up / To learne to quarrell, and to live by his wits, / And will goe downe againe, and dye i' the countrey"; or Dapper, the lawyer's clerk,

> a speciall gentle,
> That is the heire to fortie markes, a yeere,
> Consorts with the small poets of the time,
> Is the sole hope of his old grand-mother,
> That knowes the law, and writes you sixe faire hands,
> Is a fine clarke, and has his cyphring perfect,
> Will take his oath, o' the *greeke* XENOPHON,
> If need be, in his pocket: and can court
> His mistris, out of OVID.
>
> (1.2.50–58)

We are less inclined to associate word-play with Jonson, but it is used in this play to equally deadly effect. So we have Face's mock tribute to Doll—

> at supper, thou shalt sit in triumph,
> And not be stil'd DOL Common, but DOL Proper,
> DOL Singular: the longest cut, at night,
> Shall draw thee for his DOL Particular.
>
> (1.1.176–79)

—a passage in which, as Professor Partridge has neatly demonstrated, the wit springs from the terminology of logic as well as of grammar.[16] Doll even becomes the vehicle for a kind of visual pun, as she is briefly seen jump upon Sir Epicure's use of the word *common:* a device that in English comedy goes back at least as far as John Heywood's *Four P's,* in which the Pedlar hops in a play on *hopes.*[17]

The climax of *The Alchemist,* the great off-stage explosion of the furnace, is justly admired, so it is fitting that we pause also to savor the anticlimax. As Surly temporarily turns the tables on the rogues, and Kastril and Drugger gang up against him, in the midst of general tumult and hubbub, enter the exiled Saint, Ananias: "Peace to the household. . . . Casting of dollers is concluded lawfull." We praise the dramatist's mastery of form—how closely he keeps tabs on the clock while the two hours' traffic of the stage ticks away!—but form is also function, and a primary function is laughter. So in Act 3, scene 5, Dapper, having dutifully put vinegar drops in his several orifices and thrice cried "hum" and "buzz" as often, and having cast off his gold half-crown (his leaden heart, a sentimental token, he is touchingly allowed to keep)—having done all this, he is presented with "a dead mouse, / And a piece of ginger-bread, to be merry withall," and bestowed in Fortune's privy lodgings, where "the Fumigation's somewhat strong." Time passes, and much happens. We forget about Dapper, but his creator forgets nothing. The ginger-bread gag crumbles in the gull's mouth, and he emerges dazed from the privy to receive his poignant reward: the honor of kissing the Queen of Fairy's departing part. There are (if you will permit a bad pun) no loose ends in *The Alchemist*. Nor does Jonson pass up any opportunity to invent mirth. When Lovewit suddenly returns to his house, he is surrounded by scandalized neighbors. The merest of bit parts, they appear only in this scene. A lesser playwright would have allowed them to remain ciphers. Not Jonson. And so we have the timorous Sixth Neighbor with a sad tale to relate:

> About
> Some three weekes since, I heard a dolefull cry,
> As I sate up, a mending my wives stockings.
>
> (5.1.32–34)

With these two lines, the Sixth Neighbor lives.[18] It is a tribute to Jonson's craft and anything but sullen art. I have once or twice referred captiously to Mares, but let me now, near my close, express gratitude. In his Revels introduction he performs a real service by dwelling on the theatricality of *The Alchemist*, an aspect which, as he remarks, has not been much talked about. The same holds true for Jonson's other plays, and for some more than for this one. The features of his art that I have been stressing today can be adequately expressed and responded to not in the classroom or on the podium, but in the theatre, and only in the theatre. As students, we do well to honor Jonson's birthday by conferences such as this, but we honor him best by producing his plays. It is a melancholy fact that while we are engaged in our ritual of scholarship, no complementary ceremony is taking place a few miles away in Stratford. Nor, so far as I know, is a quatercentenary production on the books this year for the Royal Shakespeare Company performing in the other, equally celebrated, Stratford, although they have in recent seasons varied their Shakespearean diet with other Elizabethan cates. While recognizing that amateurs can hardly aspire to the standards of professionals, we can as academics encourage, indeed browbeat, the drama departments of our universities to put Jonson on the boards; that is the serious plea with which I conclude my light-weight offering. This year I have used my best rhetorical powers to attempt to persuade the Northwestern Department of Theatre to revive *Epicoene*, a comparatively neglected play and one that I saw very entertainingly, if toothlessly, performed years ago by students in New York. Well, I didn't succeed. *Epicoene,* I was told, is fare too specialized for a university audience; but next winter Northwestern will do *Volpone.* That is a good deal better than nothing. It is my fervent hope that the great and master spirit we celebrate here this week will in the year ahead be celebrated in many campus theatres, and that a host of spectators will discover through their laughter the humorous Jonson.

NOTES

1. *The Alchemist,* ed. F. H. Mares (Revels Plays; London, 1967), p. 145n.
2. Jeannie Robison, "On Editing Jonson," *Satire Newsletter,* IX (1971), 75. I am obliged to my colleague, Professor Alan Dessen, for bringing this poem to my notice.
3. *Alchemist,* ed. Mares, p. 55. Herford and Simpson gloss "I fart at thee" (1.1.1) "like the Latin *oppedo* and the Greek καταπέρδω" (*Ben Jonson,* ed. C. H. Herford and Percy and Evelyn Simpson, 11 vols. [Oxford, 1925–1952]), X, 54.
4. *Ben Jonson,* ed. Herford and Simpson, X, 61.
5. John J. Enck, *Jonson and the Comic Truth* (Madison, Wis., 1957), p. 232.
6. Rufus Putney in his essay "Jonson's Poetic Comedy," *Poetry Quarterly,* XLI (1962), 188–204 (brought to my attention by Professor Brian W. Parker after this paper was written) is fervent in his appreciation of *Volpone* and *The Alchemist,* plays which he sees as having "power to charm us into a state of comic ecstasy." Such enthusiasm is always welcome, but I am afraid that in *Volpone* Putney sees the comic spirit as disporting itself more merrily than I can accept. I have also since seen two recent articles by William Empson on *Volpone* and *The Alchemist* in *The Hudson Review* (XXI [1968–69], 651–66; XXII [1969–70], 595–608). These vigorously argued essays, while protesting against "the pietistic strain in Eng. Lit.," give Jonson his due as a comic dramatist.
7. Charles Lamb, *Specimens of English Dramatic Poets,* ed. William Macdonald (London, 1903), I, 161.
8. *Coleridge on the Seventeenth Century,* ed. R. F. Brinkley (New York, 1968; reprint of 1955 ed.), pp. 647–48; *The Complete Works of William Hazlitt,* ed. P. P. Howe (London and Toronto, 1930–34), VI, 39; Algernon Charles Swinburne, *A Study of Ben Jonson* (Lincoln, Neb., 1969; reprint of 1889 New York ed.), p. 5. These passages have been conveniently brought to my notice by Ian Donaldson ("Ben Jonson," *Sphere History of Literature in the English Language,* vol. 3: *English Drama to 1710,* ed. Christopher Ricks [London, 1971], pp. 280–81).
9. T. S. Eliot, "Ben Jonson," *Selected Essays 1917–1932* (New York, 1932), p. 127. The essay was first published in 1919.
10. Jonson, *Selected Works,* ed. Harry Levin (New York, 1938), p. 1. Note that Jonson is referred to here again as a writer for the study rather than for the theatre.
11. Donaldson, "Ben Jonson," p. 281. In his summing up, Donaldson concludes that Jonson deserves remembering as "one of the two great poets of the English theatre," an estimate with which I am not inclined to take issue.
12. Frederick S. Boas, *An Introduction to Stuart Drama* (London, 1946), p. 106.
13. *Ben Jonson,* ed. Herford and Simpson, II, 49–50.
14. Quoted by L. C. Knights, *Drama and Society in the Age of Jonson* (London, 1937), p. 206.
15. *Ben Jonson,* ed. Herford and Simpson, II, 64.
16. Edward B. Partridge, *The Broken Compass: A Study of the Major Comedies of Ben Jonson* (London, 1958), pp. 124–25.
17. See T. W. Craik, "Experiment and Variety in John Heywood's Plays," *Renaissance Drama,* VII (Evanston, Il., 1964), 9.
18. This brief passage was delightfully commented upon years ago in an unpublished lecture by the late F. P. Wilson.

(1974)

15

A Chaste Maid in Cheapside and Middleton's City Comedy

In his early twenties, the exasperating juvenilia behind him, Thomas Middleton applied himself to a series of comedies portraying the contemporary scene and set, for the most part, against the background of Jacobean London. At first he stumbled. In *The Family of Love* (ca. 1602)[1] he combined satire with romance; but the satire is no more than tedious calumny of an insignificant Puritan sect, and fornication and blackmail—principal ingredients of the main action—perhaps do not afford the most promising basis for romantic comedy. In his next work, *The Phoenix* (1603), the dramatist gave his new monarch unexceptionable advice on the responsibilities of kingship.[2] The play itself is less satisfactory: an odd mixture of allegory, harsh satire, and good-humored farce. Middleton provided it, however, with his earliest distinctive verse—Prince Phoenix's soliloquy on "Reverend and honourable Matrimony"—and for the first time he employed the ironic method that stamps all his characteristic later writing. In *Your Five Gallants* (ca. 1605), he depicted, with unusual concern for detail, life in London's underworld circles; but a series of set scenes, however brilliant their execution, hardly constitutes an animated or cohesive play. These uncertain experiments were followed by three fine comedies, in which realistic settings and the natural rhythms of colloquial speech are united with ingenious, at times extravagant, narratives. With *Michaelmas Term, A Mad World, My Masters,* and *A Trick to Catch the Old One* (all ca. 1606–7), the playwright proved that he had mastered his medium. About 1613 Middleton produced his greatest comic achievement, *A Chaste Maid in Cheapside.*

Among the City comedies (which have on the whole received rather desultory critical attention),[3] the *Chaste Maid* enjoys a somewhat ambiguous status. Anthologists have preferred the less indecent *Trick*. Earlier critics, when not outraged, were pleasantly scandalized to find so little chastity in the *Chaste Maid*.[4] Of the more recent commentators, Miss Ellis-Fermor feels that it is "the finest of all Middleton's comedies,"[5] but her estimate, although not unique, is scarcely the prevalent one. The play is not mentioned by T. S. Eliot in his essay on Middleton;[6] to Frederick S. Boas it is objectionable;[7] to L. C. Knights it is "a typical comedy, neither one of Middleton's

worst nor his best," and he finds after several readings that "all that remains with us is the plot."[8] Actually, the *Chaste Maid* is the richest, most
impressive of Middleton's comedies, the culmination of a decade of creative experimentation and growth. With this play the themes, technique,
and point of view of the dramatist's City comedy attain their ultimate
form.[8] At the same time, the harsh mood of the *Chaste Maid*—its essential
misanthropy—prefigures the somber tragicomedies and tragedies to follow. Written by a great dramatist at the mid-point of his career, the play is a
crucial work that demands more searching study than it has received.

Middleton's early comedies, with the exception of the *Family* (possibly
written for the Admiral's men) and *Your Five Gallants* (a Blackfriars play),
were all produced by Paul's boys. Comedy, rather than tragedy or history,
was the dramatic commodity preferred by the sophisticated audiences patronizing the children's theaters,[9] but the first new comedies acquired by
Paul's—such ineptitudes as the anonymous *Wisdom of Doctor Dodypoll* and
Maid's Metamorphosis—could scarcely have been much superior to the
"musty fopperies of antiquity" with which the company resumed opera-
tion. Seen from this perspective, Middleton's City comedies constitute a
singular achievement. For the dramatist created, almost singlehandedly, a
repertory of original and distinctive plays for a major theatrical enterprise;
apart from *Eastward Ho,* which led to the closing of Paul's, the only truly
notable comedies extant from this company belong to the Middleton series.
They are quite unlike anything that the age knew. Parrott, almost half a
century ago, grasped Middleton's significance as an innovator:

> It [*Westward Ho*] is one of the first specimens of a new fashion in comedy
> which seems to have come into vogue shortly after the opening of the
> theatres in the spring of 1604. This new fashion was the realistic comedy
> of London life. . . . It seems probable that the first deviser of this fashion
> was Thomas Middleton, who after some years of experimental collabora-
> tion, opened in 1604, with *Michaelmas Term,* a vein that he continued to
> work for nearly a decade. Middleton has been well called 'the most abso-
> lute realist' in Elizabethan drama. He paints life as it is, but without the
> sympathetic interest that marks such work as Dekker's best. . . . His
> bourgeois comedies are undoubtedly clever, entertaining, and valuable
> as pictures of contemporary life, but they are anything but edifying. . . .
> His influence upon his contemporaries, however, is undeniable.[10]

Parrott's remarks are colored by a Victorian sensibility, but the essential
point is nonetheless valid.

Even innovations have their origins. For his City comedies Middleton
utilized, more adroitly than most of his fellow playwrights, the popular
conventions (multiple disguise and the like) that the theater of his time
conveniently provided. In the cony-catching pamphlets of Greene, Row-
lands, and others, with their sensational revelations of the indignities to
which rogues subjected gulls, the dramatist may have found inspiration for

scenes of metropolitan low life. No doubt, also, he was familiar with the current town scandal, heard tavern tales of the fetching over of young heirs and the merry tricks by which gallants cuckolded citizens and outwitted their creditors. More important, he looked about him and caught the accents of Jacobean speech firsthand in Holborn and on Goldsmith's Row, at Puddle-wharf and Cole Harbour, in the lodgings, shops, ordinaries, and playhouses of the great city.

An age in transition provided Middleton with the stuff of realistic comedy. As the traditional social superstructure, with its inherited privileges and obligations, moved rapidly toward dissolution, economic dislocations and shifting class alignments created the semblance, at least, of disorder and accentuated the discrepancy between social appearance and reality. (Thus, in *Your Five Gallants* the "gallants" of the title wear beaver hats, dice at the best ordinaries, and court a rich heiress; but all lack roots or status, and all owe their finery and pretensions to the grossest vices.) At the same time that "housekeeping" decayed,[11] there was emerging, out of the economic ferment of the day, a new order in which "wealth commands all." From the ranks of the citizen class rose the "money-men"—"they and some of their brethren . . . will not stick to offer thirty thousand pound to be cursed still: great monied men, their stocks lie in the poors' throats."[12] The woollen draper Quomodo, in *Michaelmas Term,* typifies Middleton's conception of these new men: flourishing, unscrupulous, insatiable. The gentry in the play, on the other hand, are more attractive and less affluent, as their names (Easy, Rearage, Salewood) suggest. But their land—"that sweet, neat, comely, proper, delicate land!"—is the citizen's sensual dream: For only by securing the gentry's holdings can tradesmen inspire the envy of the livery and ensure status for their descendants. "Gentry is the chief fish we tradesmen catch," declares Quomodo, and out of the clash between the two classes springs much of the dramatic tension of the City comedies.

The materials—literary, social, and economic—of these plays were equally accessible to Middleton's contemporaries. In the comedies of Jonson, Dekker and Webster, and Massinger, one sees reflections of the same world and manifestations of the same antiacquisitive attitude. But Middleton, more than the others, is concerned with the effects of the competitive struggle on family relationships—on ties of blood or marriage. The variety of relationships treated in his plays is wide, and the results of the ruthless quest for money and land are distinctly unsettling. In *The Phoenix* the Captain sells his own wife for five hundred crowns, and counts his gold as the scrivener reads the inventory of her virtues from the deed of sale. Falso, in the same play, attempts to seduce his niece, and is puzzled that she permits moral scruples to weigh against her obvious material interests:

A foolish, coy, bashful thing it is; she's afraid to lie with her own uncle: I'd do her no harm, i' faith. I keep myself a widower a' purpose, yet the

foolish girl will not look into 't: she should have all, i' faith; she knows I
have but a time, cannot hold long.

                                                              (2.3.33–37)

His daughter, the Jeweler's Wife, uses her father's house as a place of
assignation with her lover, an impoverished knight who significantly addresses her as his "sweet Revenue." In the *Trick,* Theodorus Witgood uses
all his ingenuity to cheat the uncle who has ingeniously cheated him; Dick
Follywit, in the *Mad World,* devises elaborate stratagems to rob his rich
grandfather of money, jewels, watch—anything of value—and for the old
man it is a capital jest to find that his whore has snared his grandson as a
husband. In *Michaelmas Term* the Country Wench sets up as a prostitute in
London, and takes into service her own father, who fails to recognize his
daughter in her rich new satin gown. Her lover Lethe, a toothdrawer's son
risen to sudden eminence, is likewise unrecognizable, and so can hire his
mother "as a private drudge, / To pass my letters and secure my lust." The
point made by the action is suggested as well by snatches of inconsequential
dialogue. "Are your fathers dead, gentlemen, you're so merry?" Fitsgrave
greets the five gallants, and his sally is applauded as "a good jest." "Is not
whole-sale the chiefest merchandise?" asks the Country Wench, "do you
think some merchants could keep their wives so brave but for their wholesale? you're foully deceived and you think so."[13] In focusing on marriage
and the family, Middleton conveys, perhaps more adequately than any of
his contemporaries, the breakdown or corruption of traditional values in
the wake of the new materialistic order.

The plays remain comedies, of course, and in them laughter is uppermost. But in spite of the moments of wild hilarity, the apparent detachment
of mood, the lightness of touch and incomparable irony, and the last-
minute reformations and reconciliations, one senses the dramatist's essential seriousness: his genuine concern with the contemporary scene. It is a
seriousness comedy must have if it is to attain, as do the best of these plays,
the permanence of art. In his City comedies Middleton in a sense fulfills the
high requirements for the artist as expressed by André Gide. "I will maintain," Gide writes in his *Journal,* "that an artist needs this: a special world of
which he alone has the key. It is not enough that he should bring *one* new
thing, although that is already an achievement; but rather that everything
in him should be or seem new, seen through a powerfully coloring idiosyncrasy."[14] Middleton brings the new thing, and also the coloring.

Although the *Chaste Maid* followed the earlier City comedies by over half
a decade, it clearly belongs with the group they comprise. "The Eighth
Epigram" of Chapter VI of Campion's *Art of English Poesie* may have furnished Middleton with suggestions for the character of Allwit,[15] and from
the chapter "The humor of a woman lying in Child-bed," in *The Batchelars
Banquet,* the dramatist may have taken hints for the festivities at the Allwits'

in Act 3, scene 2.[16] Otherwise his precise literary sources, if indeed there were any, have eluded investigation. But the world of the *Chaste Maid* is the familiarly sordid one of mercenaries, fools, religious fanatics, cuckolds, whores, and whoremasters: most of the characters, however animated or fantasticated, derive from stage traditions by then well established. Nor does the play reveal Jacobean society in a new light. Once again we see that the gentry are lecherous and economically precarious, that citizens are prosperous and thirst after social advancement, that the two classes do some brisk bartering of dowries and titles. The dramatist's astonishing advance over his earlier work lies not in his materials but in his shaping of those materials. The *Chaste Maid* testifies to the sudden advent of maturity, poetic and dramatic, in a major writer.

In his earlier City comedies Middleton preferred prose to verse. The stylistic evolution of the playwright's prose dialogue is yet to receive adequate, or even detailed, analysis; but it may, I believe, be said that what immediately impresses us about Middleton's best and most characteristic prose is that it is at once natural and stylized. It records faithfully, or with apparent faithfulness, the everyday speech of Jacobean London, and at the same time achieves the virtues of ease and buoyancy. In the realistic comedy of Middleton's contemporaries these qualities are rare. One does not seek or find them in such routine works as *Northward Ho* or *Westward Ho*, and one misses them even in the great plays of Jonson. The verse with which Middleton occasionally experimented in his early comedy is, on the other hand, less satisfactory: self-conscious, too much given to rhetoric and rhyme, distinctly immature. The *Chaste Maid* may well be the first of his acknowledged plays to be written almost entirely in verse,[17] and the transformation it reveals is a notable one. For Middleton gains the added dimension that only verse can confer, without sacrificing the qualities that distinguish his prose.

The contrast between Middleton's earlier verse and the mature verse of the *Chaste Maid* is more effectively demonstrated than described. The following passages afford some basis for comparison. Both are of some length and both are representative—neither the poet's best work nor his worst; moreover, they express similar emotions and mark similar turning points for the personages involved. Here is Penitent Brothel as he experiences the reformation his name promises:

> Where were thy nobler meditations busied,
> That they durst trust this body with itself;
> This natural drunkard, that undoes us all,
> And makes our shame apparent in our fall?
> Then let my blood pay for 't, and vex and boil!
> My soul, I know, would never grieve to th' death
> Th' eternal spirit, that feeds her with his breath:
> Nay, I that knew the price of life and sin,

What crown is kept for continence, what for lust,
The end of man, and glory of that end,
As endless as the giver,
To doat on weakness, slime, corruption, woman!
What is she, took asunder from her clothes?
Being ready, she consists of an hundred pieces,
Much like your German clock, and near ally'd;
Both are so nice, they cannot go for pride:
Besides a greater fault, but too well known,
They'll strike to ten, when they should stop at one.
                                        (*Mad World*, 4.1.7–24)

And here is Sir Walter Whorehound, similarly guilt-struck, as he repudiates his mistress:

                              Some good, pitying man,
Remove my sins out of my sight a little;
I tremble to behold her, she keeps back
All comfort while she stays. Is this a time,
Unconscionable woman, to see thee?
Art thou so cruel to the peace of man,
Not to give liberty now? the devil himself
Shows a far fairer reverence and respect
To goodness than thyself; he dares not do this,
But part[s] in time of penitence, hides his face;
When man withdraws from him, he leaves the place:
Hast thou less manners and more impudence
Than thy instructor? prithee, show thy modesty,
If the least grain be left, and get thee from me:
Thou shouldst be rather lock'd many rooms hence
From the poor miserable sight of me,
If either love or grace had part in thee.
                                        (*Chaste Maid*, 5.1.35–51)

The first passage is, like so much of Middleton's earlier verse, stiff and exclamatory. The tone of the second, on the other hand, is intimate; if the poet betrays his occasional tendency to continue a speech after the point has been made, he also shows impressive progress in fluency and naturalness—in awareness of the resources of his medium.[18]

Maturity is evident also in the structure of the play. The *Chaste Maid* is the grandest, most textured of the City comedies. Middleton forges three major actions, with three sets of characters and much incident, into a single dramatic entity, and at the same time is able to include a well-integrated minor intrigue (Tim's courtship of the Welsh courtesan), a topical digression on government informers, and the great naturalistic genre study that is the episode of the christening celebration. Yet the play never sprawls under the weight of its abundance, nor does it lapse into the loose ends that disfigure even the best of the preceding comedies.[19] Indeed, the gusto of the *Chaste Maid* is unparalleled in Middleton's comedy. Perhaps, as Miss Bradbrook suggests, its vitality is due to the fact that the dramatist was writing for the public stage of the Swan and not, as previously, for the less robust audiences of the private houses.[20] Perhaps it is also significant that the *Chaste Maid* was designed for an adult company, the Lady Elizabeth's men, rather than for the boy actors of Paul's. But circumstances alone could hardly account for the play's vigor. The *Chaste Maid* is clearly the work of a writer whose powers are at their height and who knows precisely what he wishes to do with them.

It is a disturbing vitality that informs the play. The "joyous animation" and "good-natured impartiality" which Miss Lynch discerns in Middleton's City comedies are in little evidence here:[21] no personable Witgood or "frolic" Sir Bounteous brightens the dramatist's mood. In his earlier plays Middleton sometimes used a spokesman—a Phoenix or Fitsgrave—to serve as an outlet for his moral indignation; but it is the wittol of the *Chaste Maid* who becomes the principal agent of retribution. Never has the playwright envisioned a world of more pervasive squalor.[22]

The London of the *Chaste Maid* is a harsh city. In the streets the abandoned Country Wench searches for a way to dispose of her bastard infant. The season is Lent; at the corners lurk "poisonous officers" who corruptly enforce the new "religious wholesome laws" prohibiting the consumption of flesh. Within doors, degradation and brutality exist on a scale unequaled in Jacobean comedy. At the Allwits', Sir Walter fathers Mistress Allwit's children and provides for the entire household. When the "good founder" arrives, the husband bows and scrapes, whispers "Peace, bastard!" to the boy who innocently addresses him as father, and smiles complacently while wife and lover embrace. At the Yellowhammers', Moll—the chaste maid of the title—tries to elope and in so doing brings down upon herself the wrath of her parents. It is a wrath which reveals the emotional bankruptcy that ensues when the only values recognized are those associated with social and material advancement. Middleton had expressed similar views in the earlier City comedies, but not to such chilling effect as in the scenes concerning Moll Yellowhammer and her family.

Imprisoned by her parents in a tiny room, Moll escapes, only to be overtaken by her mother on a Thames barge and, after a futile suicide attempt, dragged half drowned back to land. At the docks a brief, fierce exchange between the mother, Maudlin, and a bystander permits the dramatist to underscore the ugliness of the episode:

Maudlin [*to* Moll]. I'll tug thee home by the hair.
First Waterman.   Good mistress, spare her!
Maudlin.   Tend your own business.
First Waterman.   You're a cruel mother.

                                        (4.3.45–47)[23]

When afterwards it finally appears that Moll is dead and her presumably lifeless body is carried out, the preoccupations of the household are characteristic. Brother Tim, the Cambridge scholar, busies himself with a Latin epitaph, while Yellowhammer anxiously anticipates the reactions of his neighbors:

> All the whole street will hate us, and the world
> Point me out cruel: it's our best course, wife,
> After we've given order for the funeral,
> T' absent ourselves till she be laid in ground.
>
> (5.2.92–95)

His wife is at once consoled by the prospect of her son's marriage. "We'll not lose all at once," she hopefully concludes, "somewhat we'll catch."

Most of the dramatist's personages, major and minor, are involved in some form of duplicity, and most of them are venal; others—a Tim or Sir Oliver—are the necessary gulls. Sir Walter looking forward to his wedding day, when he will receive a dowry of "two thousand pound in gold / And a sweet maidenhead worth forty," is representative. So, likewise, is Touchwood senior, as he cures the sterility of the Kixes. He has Sir Oliver swallow a special potion, jump up and down several times, and then go off on horseback for five hours; meanwhile Lady Kix lies down to receive her potion from Touchwood himself. His therapy (which costs Kix a total of four hundred pounds) proves so effective that she conceives at once, to the indescribable elation of her husband. The notable exception to Middleton's pattern of the dupers and the duped is the virtuous Moll; but, like Castiza in *The Revenger's Tragedy* and Celia in *Volpone,* she seems to exist primarily to throw into relief the depravity around her.

The playwright's mood is mirrored in his language. Figures suggesting contempt and debasement color the verse. A mother about to give birth is "even upon the point of grunting"; a baby is "this half yard of flesh, in which, I think, / It wants a nail or two." Lady Kix refers to her impotent husband as "brevity." Bawds, we are told, will grow so fat that "Their chins will hang like udders by Easter-eve, / And, being stroak'd, will give the milk of witches." The government spies stand

>   pricking up their ears
> And snuffing up their noses, like rich men's dogs
> When the first course goes in.
>
> (2.2.55–57)

The idiom even of Middleton's young lovers may reflect the hardness of the world in which they furtively meet. "Turn not to me till thou mayst lawfully," Touchwood junior whispers to Moll in her father's shop, "it but whets my stomach, which is too sharp-set already."

But perversity reaches its ultimate form in the soliloquy Allwit delivers upon learning that Sir Walter has come to town. First the wittol prays for the preservation of the benefactor who has for ten years maintained him and his family, and he then goes on to enumerate the domestic joys he owes to his cuckolder:

> I'm at his table:
> He gets me all my children, and pays the nurse
> Monthly or weekly; puts me to nothing, rent,
> Nor church-duties, not so much as the scavenger:
> The happiest state that ever man was born to!
> I walk out in a morning; come to breakfast,
> Find excellent cheer; a good fire in winter;
> Look in my coal-house about midsummer eve,
> That's full, five or six chaldron new laid up;
> Look in my back-yard, I shall find a steeple
> Made up with Kentish faggots, which o'erlooks
> The water-house and the windmills: I say nothing,
> But smile and pin the door.
>
> (1.2.17–29)

After cataloguing the embossings, embroiderings, and spangles, the restoratives, sugar loaves, and wines that Whorehound provides when his mistress lies in, Allwit turns to the question of jealousy:

> And where some merchants would in soul kiss hell
> To buy a paradise for their wives, and dye
> Their conscience in the bloods of prodigal heirs
> To deck their night-piece, yet all this being done,
> Eaten with jealousy to the inmost bone,—
> As what affliction nature more constrains,
> Then feed the wife plump for another's veins?—
> These torments stand I freed of; I'm as clear
> From jealousy of a wife as from the charge:
> O, two miraculous blessings!
>
> (1.2.41–50)

Allwit's soliloquy is perhaps the most audacious example in Middleton of one of the dramatist's favorite devices: the deliberate inversion of traditional morality and customary emotional responses. Surely Miss Ellis-Fermor errs in seeing affinities between the *Chaste Maid,* with its disquieting cynicism, and *Tom Jones,* with its essential humanity.[24] One hesitates to regard the creator of Allwit in quite the same light as the creator of Allworthy.

To some extent Middleton's cynicism in the *Chaste Maid* is compensated by his irony, which here (as elsewhere in the City comedies) serves as an unobtrusive instrument of ethical comment. As the dramatist develops, his irony becomes deeper and takes more varied forms; in this respect, too, the play marks an advance over his earlier work. Middleton may convey his irony by means of a miniature story embodied in a simile:

> this shows like
> The fruitless sorrow of a careless mother,
> That brings her son with dalliance to the gallows,
> And then stands by and weeps to see him suffer.
>
> (5.1.61–64)

It may reside in the contrast between the Lenten season of self-denial, during which much of the action takes place, and the gross carnal self-indulgence of the participants. The narrative is enriched with ironic detail: Thus Touchwood junior orders his wedding ring, with the inscription "Love that's wise / Blinds parents' eyes," from the father of the very girl with whom he plans to run off, and maintains a discreet silence when the old man winks at him knowingly:

> You'll steal away some man's daughter: am I near you?
> Do you turn aside? you gentlemen are mad wags!
> I wonder things can be so warily carried,
> And parents blinded so: but they're serv'd right,
> That have two eyes and were so dull a' sight.
>
> (1.1.198–202)

"Thy doom take hold of thee!" Touchwood junior prays in an aside; and indeed ultimately it does.

In the larger reversals of the play, the dramatist's personages, vicious or foolish, find themselves unwilling recipients of an ironic dispensation. The Yellowhammers, who have failed with their daughter, succeed only too well with the son. Tim marries the Welsh gentlewoman; but the "heir to some nineteen mountains" is revealed to be Sir Walter's penniless cast mistress, and the Cambridge student is left to make good, as best he can, his previous boast that by logic he could prove a whore an honest woman. Whorehound himself is crushed in the play's supreme moment of irony. As Sir Walter lies bleeding and repentant at the Allwits', the cuckold thrusts wife and children upon him in a desperate effort to win back his favor. But Allwit's sole reward is a curse upon the entire household. The tide turns, however, when servants rush in to announce that Whorehound has killed a man in a duel and that he has lost his fortune, which he held only so long as the Kixes remained barren. (It is, as Miss Bradbrook observes, a suitable irony that the begetter of bastards should be undone by an equivocal conception.)[25] Sir Walter must now seek refuge with the family he has repudiated. But Allwit, realizing that he can hope for nothing from his ruined patron, turns upon him in a sudden assertion of virtue fully as impudent as his former defense of depravity. "I pray, depart, sirs," he orders the knight's men,

> And take your murderer along with you;
> Good he were apprehended ere he go,
> Has kill'd some honest gentleman; send for officers.

And to Sir Walter:

> I must tell you, sir,
> You have been somewhat bolder in my house
> Than I could well like of; I suffer'd you
> Till it stuck here at my heart; I tell you truly
> I thought y' had been familiar with my wife once.
>   (5.1.138–46)

Ironic understatement could scarcely be carried further.

Cruel, perverse, ironic—these qualities suggest the appalling comedy of *Volpone*. But the sinister decadence of Jonson's Venice has little in common with the spirit of the *Chaste Maid*. For Middleton's mood is, paradoxically enough, Rabelaisian as well as sardonic, and great gales of laughter sweep through the play. It is somewhat as though the author of *Gulliver's Travels* has contrived to relate his Fourth Book with uproarious good humor.

Laughter reaches its peak in the christening celebration at the Allwits'. In this, the central episode of the *Chaste Maid*, most of the principal characters—the Allwits, Yellowhammer and Maudlin, Tim and his tutor, Moll, Touchwood junior, Sir Walter, and Lady Kix—gather and mingle with a number of minor figures. At the door Maudlin and a gossip strain courtesies; the wives of an apothecary and a comfit maker clash briefly over precedence; the Puritans enter "in unity, and show the fruits of peace." Within all is movement, as charwomen, nurses, maids, and guests arrive, as Mistress Allwit receives gifts in bed and the midwife displays the "fine plump black-ey'd slut." Allwit, reveling in "recreation" that costs him nothing, modestly puts by compliments on his chopping baby. "They're pretty foolish things, put to making in minutes," he disclaims, "I ne'er stand long about 'em." Chief among the visitors is Sir Walter, who acts as godfather to his own infant to forestall scandal. Entering with his gifts (a silver standing cup and two large apostle spoons), he has a flattering word for the wives who, seated on needlework stools, shuffle up the rushes with their cork heels and heat the room with their thick bums. A nurse passes among the guests with wine and confections. The gossips, their tasseled handkerchiefs spread between their knees, greedily seize upon the sweetmeats with their "long fingers that are wash'd / Some thrice a-day in urine." Again and again the cups go round, and the wives fall into hiccups and intimate confessions. Maudlin thrusts comfits upon her son. "Come I from Cambridge," he protests, "and offer me six plums?" But he finds the kissing even more difficult to endure. "Let me come next," Mistress Underman shrieks, drunk:

Welcome from the wellspring of discipline,
That waters all the brethren.

She tries to kiss Tim, but staggers and falls.

Tim.   Hoist, I beseech thee!
Third Gossip.   O bless the woman!—Mistress Underman—[*They raise her
                   up.*]
First Puritan   [*Mistress Underman*]. 'Tis but the common affliction of the
                   faithful;
                   We must embrace our falls.

(3.2.161–66)

At last the guests reel off to the conduit, and Allwit and Davy Dahanna, Sir
Walter's attendant, survey the damage:

Allwit. What's here under the stools?
Davy.   Nothing but wet, sir;
           Some wine spilt here belike.
Allwit. Is 't no worse, think'st thou?
           Fair needlework stools cost nothing with them, Davy. . . .
           Look how they have laid them,
           E'en as they lie themselves, with their heels up!

(3.2.184–88)

The festivities are done; the scene closes.

For perhaps the only time in Middleton's career a single theatrical situation called forth simultaneously all his diverse talents as a comic dramatist:
his skill at conveying life and movement, his ability to faithfully set down
colloquial speech and visual detail, his capacity for ludicrous invention, and
his gift for effortlessly blending irony, innuendo, and open bawdry. The
playwright's mastery of the Jacobean stage, apparent throughout the christening episode, is notable even in the handling of properties.[26] Stage properties are employed far more extensively than was customary in the open-
air houses, and they perform an important role in evoking atmosphere and
heightening the audience's sense of familiar reality. Yet some critics are
uneasy. Knights feels that "the gathering of city wives . . . is presented with
imperfectly controlled disgust,"[27] and to Miss Bradbrook the episode stands
"among the rankest in all Elizabethan drama."[28] No doubt the Puritans are
subjected to merciless ridicule, and certainly the entire scene is quite unin-
hibited. But "disgust" would appear to be an imperfectly selected term, and
those of us who relish cakes and ale will scarcely be deterred from the
greatest triumph of Middleton's comic realism.

The *Chaste Maid* is not a simple play, and the powerful impression it
leaves is achieved, it seems to me, largely by means of a tension maintained
between disparate elements: The essential brutality of the content of the

play is counterpoised by the laughter which informs the dramatist's treatment of his chilling material. In effecting and sustaining this recalcitrant balance, Middleton is well served by his irony—an instrument peculiarly fitted to the expression of the cruel and the comic alike. Thus we laugh at what, under other circumstances, might well horrify us.

But there is another factor, as yet unsuggested, that contributes to the complex effect produced by this extraordinary play. As the action unfolds, we gradually perceive that Middleton's realism has taken on an added dimension—a dimension to which the Elizabethan comic dramatist does not often aspire. The life of the play overflows the artificial bounds of stage narrative; becomes, as it were, a fragment out of time. In the London of *Michaelmas Term* Easy meets Quomodo for the first time; Follywit in the *Mad World* and Witgood in the *Trick* set in motion their intrigues in the opening scenes. But situations introduced in the *Chaste Maid* existed before the play's beginning: Moll and Touchwood junior have already accepted one another, Mistress Allwit has borne Sir Walter six children in the course of a decade. In Elizabethan comedy the dramatist will of course provide necessary background information concerning his principal figures (Witgood's previous dealings with his uncle, for example) but in the *Chaste Maid* the characters' pasts have a concreteness beyond the immediate needs of the action. We learn much, for example, about the Yellowhammers. Maud was "lightsome and quick" two years before her marriage and took dancing lessons from "a pretty brown gentleman"; her husband is descended from the Yellowhammers of Oxfordshire, near Abingdon, and many years back had a child by Mistress Anne ("he's now a jolly fellow, / Has been twice warden"); for eight years Tim stumbled over *as in praesenti* in his grammar, only to go on to impress the gentleman commoners in the hall at Cambridge by eating his broth with a silver spoon. Even minor personages are portrayed with a scrupulous particularity. We are told of the Welsh courtesan's red hair, we hear her speak in her native tongue, we learn that she is from North Wales and lost her maidenhead at Brecknockshire.

As we follow the movement of the play, we are aware—as we were not with the earlier City comedies—of the passage of time and the changes wrought by the succession of events; finally, we can envision a future for some, at least, of Middleton's characters. Sir Walter travels his rake's progress to the Knights' ward. Mistress Allwit, "as great as she can wallow," longs for her lover's return and pickled cucumbers. Time passes: her infant is born and christened; the "good founder" casts her off and is himself cast off; in the end the Allwits look ahead to a different life as they prepare to take a house in the Strand and let out lodgings. The result of the dramatist's consciousness of time is an illusion of reality so persuasive that it is scarcely vitiated by the fantastic elements in plot and characterization.

In the years following the *Chaste Maid*, Middleton occasionally returned to comedy, but he never again attempted anything quite like the fantastic realism of the great earlier plays. In *No Wit, No Help Like a Woman's* (ca. 1615), he relied unimaginatively on his source, Della Porta's *La Sorella;* in *The Widow* (ca. 1616), he modeled himself on the popular Fletcherian formula. Both plays succeed on their own limited terms, but lack the vitality, concreteness, and depth of social implication of Middleton's previous comedies. The most distinctive writings of the dramatist's later years are his tragicomedies and tragedies, in which the corrosive view of humanity underlying the *Chaste Maid* takes disturbing new forms. In these plays Middleton becomes a subtle analyst of the mind—particularly the female mind—and of sexual passion; at the same time he achieves something of that "lofty impersonal power" which the young James Joyce admired as Ibsen's "highest excellence."[29] Perhaps when *A Chaste Maid in Cheapside* was completed, Middleton realized that he had written a masterpiece of City comedy and that his most compelling creative energies must thereafter find quite different expression.[30]

NOTES

1. G. J. Eberle argues, not entirely persuasively, that this play was written with the assistance of Dekker; see "Dekker's Part in *The Familie of Love*" in *Joseph Quincy Adams Memorial Studies*, ed. James G. McManaway, Giles E. Dawson, and Edwin E. Willoughby (Washington, D.C., 1948), pp. 723–38.

2. See N. W. Bawcutt, "Middleton's 'The Phoenix' as a Royal Play," *N&Q*, N.S., III (1956), 287–88; also Marilyn L. Williamson, "*The Phoenix*: Middleton's Comedy *de Regimine Principum*," *Renaissance News*, X (1957), 183–87, and William Power, "'The Phoenix,' Raleigh, and King James," *N&Q*, N.S., V (1958), 57–61.

3. The few studies one may cite are of a tentative, introductory, or cautionary nature. Wilbur Dwight Dunkel's *The Dramatic Technique of Thomas Middleton in His Comedies of London Life* (Chicago, 1925) leaves much to be investigated. Although to a degree undermined by a hopeless animus toward the plays, L. C. Knights's chapter on "Middleton and the New Social Classes" in *Drama & Society in the Age of Jonson* (London, 1937), pp. 256–69, contributes to an understanding of the dramatist's view of his society. Margery Fisher's "Notes on the Sources of Some Incidents in Middleton's London Plays," *RES, XV* (1939), 283–93, usefully reminds us of pitfalls in determining the exact sources of particular episodes. The most satisfactory introduction to the City comedies available to me, and one from which I gained valuable insights, was provided by Richard H. Barker in his *Thomas Middleton*, (1958). A good deal of work on this important group of plays is currently in progress, and one hopes that the comprehensive treatment may shortly emerge.

4. See, for example, A. W. Ward, *A History of English Dramatic Literature to the Death of Queen Anne* (London, 1899), II, 521; Thomas Middleton, *Works*, ed. A. H. Bullen (London, 1885), I, xliii; and Mermaid *Middleton,* introd. A. C. Swinburne (London, 1887), I, xviii–xix.

5. U. M. Ellis-Fermor, *The Jacobean Drama* (London, 1936), p. 135.

6. T. S. Eliot, "Thomas Middleton" in *Selected Essays* (London, 1951), pp. 161–70.

7. Frederick S. Boas, *An Introduction to Stuart Drama* (Oxford, 1946), pp. 224–26.

8. L. C. Knights, *op. cit.*, p. 259.

9. The statistics provided by Alfred Harbage are illuminating; see his *Shakespeare and the Rival Traditions* (New York, 1952), p. 85.

10. *The Comedies of George Chapman*, ed. Thomas Marc Parrott (London, 1914), p. 839. Parrott's date for *Michaelmas Term* is conceivable, but he is too positive: the play may be somewhat later than 1604. In the context, however, what is significant is that Middleton had

begun writing City comedy by that year. *The Family of Love, The Phoenix,* and possibly an early draft of *Your Five Gallants* were composed by 1604.

11. A helpful discussion of this phenomenon appears in Knights, *op. cit.,* pp. 108–17.

12. *Michaelmas Term,* 2.3.252–55. Line references are to the Bullen edition, which I have used throughout for quotations.

13. *Your Five Gallants,* 4.8.288–89; *Michaelmas Term,* 4.2.13–16.

14. Justin O'Brien, ed., *Journals of André Gide* (New York, 1947), I, 77.

15. Elisabeth Lee Buckingham, "Campion's *Art of English Poesie* and Middleton's *Chaste Maid in Cheapside,*" PMLA, XLIII (1928), 784–92. Allwit's catalogue of the advantages of cuckoldom (1.2) is closely paralleled by another wittol, Sophonirus, in 1.1 of the *Second Maiden's Tragedy* (1611), which several students attribute to Middleton; see S. Schoenbaum, *Middleton's Tragedies: A Critical Study* (New York, 1955), pp. 183–202.

16. *The Batchelars Banquet,* ed. F. P. Wilson (Oxford, 1929), pp. 20–35.

17. Verse is also the medium of *The Witch,* and Wilson follows Lawrence in conjecturally assigning the tragicomedy to the year 1609 or 1610 (*The Witch,* ed. F. P. Wilson, Malone Society Reprints [Oxford, 1950], pp.vi–vii). It seems to me, however, that *ca.* 1614–15 is the more plausible date of composition.

18. It is true that Brothel speaks in soliloquy, whereas Whorehound actually addresses his mistress. But the qualities that distinguish the latter passage are also to be found in the soliloquies of Middleton's mature period; see, for example, Allwit's speech, cited below, p. 211.

19. In *Michaelmas Term* the story of the Country Wench and her father is left unfinished, and the validity of Easy's marriage remains in question, conflicting statements being made by the Judge and Thomasine. In the *Trick,* nothing follows from the complications suggested in 2.1, in which Jenny Lucre sends off Freedom (her son by a previous marriage) to court the newly arrived widow.

20. M. C. Bradbrook, *The Growth and Structure of Elizabethan Comedy* (London, 1955), p. 161.

21. Kathleen M. Lynch, *The Social Mode of Restoration Comedy* (New York, 1926), p. 25.

22. Intimations of such a world appear, however, in those scenes of *The Phoenix* in which the Captain abuses and then sells his own wife (1.2; 2.2).

23. Later in the same scene the Waterman recounts the incident to Touchwood junior:

> Half-drown'd, she cruelly tugg'd her by the hair,
> Forc'd her disgracefully, not like a mother.
>
> (4.3.80–81)

In view of such comments, made by a minor personage regarded favorably by the author, one wonders how some critics have been able to characterize Middleton's mood in the play as lighthearted.

24. Ellis-Fermor, *op. cit.,* p. 137. Her analogy with Chaucer (pp. 135–36, 137) is open to much the same objection.

25. Bradbrook, *op. cit.,* p. 162.

26. I am obliged to W. A. Armstrong of Birckbeck College, London, for bringing to my notice Middleton's extensive use of properties in this scene.

27. Knights, *op. cit.,* p. 269.

28. Bradbrook, *op. cit.,* p. 162.

29. Stuart Gilbert, ed., *Letters of James Joyce* (New York, 1957), pp. 51–52.

30. I am grateful to the John Simon Guggenheim Memorial Foundation for a fellowship awarded me in 1956; this essay represents part of the work accomplished during that year.

(1959)

16
The Widow's Tears and the Other Chapman

More than half a century after George Chapman's death in 1634, Anthony Wood characterized him as "a person of most reverend aspect, religious and temperate, qualities rarely meeting in a poet."[1] The image of Chapman as a grave moralist has lingered. Investigation of his learning has served primarily as prelude to the study of his morality, and the criticism of the twentieth century has stressed the ethical intention underlying the poet's varied creative expression.[2] In so far as it is based upon the writings rather than traditions, our current and long-standing estimate of Chapman derives largely from his poems, his translation of Homer, and, above all, his tragedies. Chapman, however, produced another extensive body of work that has been regarded with comparative indifference. For a decade, from 1596 to ca. 1605, the poet put much of his energy into a series of unusual comedies, at least seven of which are extant.[3]

Perhaps it is the air of literary inconsequence that frequently marks these plays—designed, as they are, so clearly for the stage rather than the study—that has forestalled serious scrutiny of them. Yet, although the intellectual and rhetorical pretensions of the tragedies are absent, Chapman's comedies make a signal contribution to the drama of the age. In *The Blind Beggar of Alexandria* (1596), which survives only in a fragmentary and mutilated form, we may discern the elements of an inspired dramatic burlesque.[4] With *An Humorous Day's Mirth* (1597)—produced more than a year before *Every Man in His Humour*—the playwright introduced to the English stage that species of humours comedy of which Jonson was to become supreme master. In *The Gentleman Usher* (ca. 1602) he anticipates, as Parrott noted many years ago, the vogue of Fletcherian tragicomedy, which was to reign until the closing of the theatres.[5] And in the cascading dialogue of Monsieur D'Olive, in the play of the same name, Chapman reveals himself as the perfecter of a prose style of a fluency and vivacity equaled only by his rival Middleton in the repertories of the private houses. The comedies, it may be truly said, disclose another Chapman, and nowhere is this other Chapman more startlingly revealed than in the play with which the cycle reaches its culmination. That work is the strange comedy *The Widow's Tears*.[6]

The inconsequential air of the earlier comedies has vanished; it is clear that the author himself attached more than ordinary importance to *The Widow's Tears*. It is the only comedy that Chapman provided with a dedication. In it he makes a notable early assertion of the dignity of the maligned art of playwriting, and by implication he rests the merits of his case on *The Widow's Tears*. To be sure, the usual self-conscious expressions of literary modesty ("This poor play," etc.) make their appearance, but Chapman's pride of accomplishment is apparent from his opening sentence. "Sir," he writes, "If any work of this nature be worth the presenting to friends worthy and noble, I presume this will not want much of that value." *The Widow's Tears,* indeed, is stylistically the most mature of Chapman's comedies, the most serious of purpose, and certainly the most striking. It promises auditors and readers what the poet believes is "acceptable matter"—a phrase that Chapman does not use lightly—and to a greater degree than the earlier comedies the play seems to owe its being to some profoundly felt inner necessity. *The Widow's Tears* may, therefore, serve with peculiar applicability as a measure of our received image of Chapman.

I

In keeping with his commitment to the role of learned poet, Chapman thoroughly assimilated the theoretical psychology of his age. Indeed, Hardin Craig has gone so far as to suggest that Chapman is "the psychological dramatist *par excellence*," and that in his application of current scientific principles to the characterization of women, he looks ahead to the achievements of such later dramatists as Webster, Middleton, and Ford.[7] If the creators of Vittoria Corombona, Beatrice-Joanna, and Calantha owed anything—consciously or unconsciously—to their great predecessor, it is above all in *The Widow's Tears* that we might seek evidences of anticipation. For in *The Widow's Tears* Chapman anatomizes the character of the female sex. Women take several of the principal parts, and even when they are permitted to leave the stage, they are continually discussed. Yet the play is not essentially psychological, even in the limited doctrinal sense. Here, as elsewhere, Chapman's concern with women involves matters quite different from those dealing with the more subtle operations of the feminine mind.

In his earlier comedies Chapman tends to dwell primarily on his male personages, and the gallery of women these plays provide is necessarily a limited one, composed of perfunctory sketches rather than finished portraits. Still, a point of view toward the sex emerges. If the occasion should require, Chapman can strike a note of conventional—even somewhat excessive—romantic idealism. In *The Gentleman Usher* Margaret, whose grief over the presumed loss of her beloved prompts her to disfigure her face with a hideous ointment, is the pattern of the perfect mistress, just as Cynanche in the same play is the pattern of the perfect wife. But idealization of women flows uneasily from Chapman's pen, and one suspects that Lodovico in *May-Day* has the dramatist's sympathy when he observes: "He that holds religious and sacred thought of a woman, he that bears so reverend a respect to her that he will not touch her but with a kissed hand and a timorous heart, he that adores her like his goddess, let him be sure she will shun him like her slave" (1.1.260–65).

For the most part, Chapman regards his women with something less than reverence. They are, like so many of the women in the plays of the select theatres, lecherous hypocrites.[8] Love for them is an appetite in which they are prevented from freely indulging only by society's disapproval. They are concerned less with their virtue than with their reputation; their prudery serves to mask, and unconsciously to intensify, their lust. In *An Humorous Day's Mirth,* the young wife Florilla, who is described as "too religious in the purest sort," withstands the worldly and sensual allurements of jewels, rich clothes, and poetry—but her asceticism quickly evaporates when her passions are aroused, with cynical calculation, by Lemot. Elimene, in *The Blind Beggar,* has a sense of propriety so delicate that she disdains to refer to her husband as the count because his title sounds too nearly like a rude word; yet she is easily seduced by the usurer who offers gold and diamonds in return for her favors. The virtuous pretensions even of Aemilia, the orthodox romantic heroine of *May-Day,* must be punctured, and her modesty revealed as no more than "a superfluous nicety." Chapman's own attitudes are perhaps not far removed from those expressed in the bitter words of Rinaldo, the scholar of Padua in *All Fools.* Rinaldo's experience has taught him to regard the entire sex as

> Inconstant shuttlecocks, loving fools and jesters,
> Men rich in dirt and titles, sooner won
> With the most vile than the most virtuous,
> Found true to none; if one amongst whole hundreds
> Chance to be chaste, she is so proud withal,
> Wayward and rude, that one of unchaste life
> Is oftentimes approv'd a worthier wife:
> Undressed, sluttish, nasty to their husbands;
> Spung'd up, adorn'd, and painted to their lovers;
> All day in ceaseless uproar with their households,
> If all the night their husbands have not pleas'd them;
> Like hounds, most kind, being beaten and abus'd;
> Like wolves, most cruel, being kindliest us'd.
>
> $$(1.1.66-78)^9$$

It is from such a lineage and such a point of view that Eudora and Cynthia, the principal female personages of *The Widow's Tears,* trace their descent.

But the circumstances in which Eudora and Cynthia find themselves are exceptional. For in *The Widow's Tears* Chapman is concerned not with the ordinary run of women but with paragons. His Eudora (whose story is told first) is an "exquisite lady" who has resolved to emulate the noblest examples of virtuous widowhood: she has taken a solemn vow never to remarry. In dedicating herself to so austere a course, Eudora achieves a reputation that is remarkable. She is admired as an "impregnable fort of chastity and loyalty"; she has become a pattern for her sex and the "amazement of the world" (3.1.148–49).

Eudora, however, is no monument but a vital and still unfaded woman. She has, moreover, tasted the delights of the marriage bed; and, as her suitor Tharsalio shrewdly assumes, she will be reluctant to "make the noontide of her years the sunset of her pleasures" (3.1.165–66). To awaken Eudora's quiescent passions, Tharsalio commissions the procuress Arsace to approach her with a fabricated account of his extraordinary sexual prowess. In a brief, disturbingly gross scene,[10] in which the word "honor" occurs as an ironic comment no fewer than 26 times in the space of 127 lines, Arsace pretends to warn Eudora of the hazards of wedding Tharsalio. In so doing the bawd manages to disclose that Tharsalio is "the most incontinent and insatiate man of women that ever Venus blessed with ability to please them," and that he has made "nine in a night . . . mad with his love" (2.2.93–94). Obviously stirred by Arsace's recital, Eudora alternately flushes and goes pale. "What might a wise widow resolve upon this point, now?" she muses after the panderess has left her. "Contentment is the end of all worldly beings. Beshrew her, would she had spared her news!" (2.2.133–36). Later Eudora grows pensive and seeks solitude. When Tharsalio next visits her, a marriage contract is quickly arranged. Thus Eudora falls, and her collapse is represented as the betrayal, not only of a sacred oath and the ideals of widowhood, but also of the great principle of degree. For she is a countess, and Tharsalio, as we are pointedly informed, was the groom who waited upon her table and served as her husband's page.

In several respects the career of Eudora is strikingly similar to that of Aurelia, the Duchess of Milan in Middleton's *More Dissemblers besides Women* (ca. 1615). Like Eudora, Aurelia is a great lady who has sworn fidelity to her late husband's memory; like Eudora, she is celebrated for a virtue that is insistently extolled; like Eudora, she fails to understand her own nature and is betrayed by her awakened passion. But there resemblance ends, for Chapman's portrayal of feminine weakness is unsoftened by the sympathetic awareness of human frailty that makes Middleton's duchess a moving, almost tragic figure. "I confess I'm mortal," Aurelia cries, in her moment of truth:

> There's no defending on't; 'tis cruel flattery
> To make a lady believe otherwise.
> Is not this flesh? can you drive heat from fire?
> So may you love from this. . . .
>   I am lost,
> Utterly lost! where are my women now?

> Alas, what help's in them, what strength have they?
> I call to a weak guard when I call them;
> In rescuing me they'd be themselves o'ercome:
> When I, that profess'd war, am overthrown,
> What hope's in them, then, that ne'er stirr'd from home?
> My faith is gone for ever;
> My reputation with the cardinal,
> My fame, my praise, my liberty, my peace,
> Chang'd for a restless passion. . . .
>
> (1.3.107–11, 117–27)[11]

This is quite outside Chapman's sensibility. His Eudora never transcends her symbolic function to become more than merely a focus for the dramatist's misogyny. The essential insensitivity of Chapman's treatment of her is exceeded only by his handling of Cynthia, who emerges as an even more savage caricature.

II

For the story of Cynthia—the principal action of *The Widow's Tears*—Chapman turned to the ancient and renowned tale of the matron of Ephesus. As an illustration of the lechery, fickleness, and craft of women this Milesian fable has in its manifold guises enjoyed a truly remarkable popularity.[12] The most celebrated version of the tale, however, and the one actually used by the playwright, is of course that told by Eumolpus in the *Satyricon*. At times Chapman follows Petronius closely, and he succeeds—where others fail—in recapturing something of the temper of his source. Chapman's widow, like Petronius', is famed at home and abroad for her superlative virtue: "The world hath written . . . [her] in highest lines of honoured fame," an impartial bystander observes; "her virtues so admired in this isle as the report thereof sounds in foreign ears; and strangers oft arriving here, as some rare sight, desire to view her presence, thereby to compare the picture with the original" (2.1.65–69). (And in Petronius: ". . . tam notae erat pudicitiae, ut uicinarum quoque gentium feminas ad spectaculum sui euocaret.")[13] As in the source, the widow descends with her husband's coffin into the tomb, accompanied only by her devoted maidservant, and there for five days she weeps and fasts. Events take their inexorable course: The sentinel appears; the seduction in the vault is accomplished; the widow offers her husband's corpse as a substitute for the stolen body of the crucified criminal. But the matron of the *Satyricon* is, after all, merely the butt of an anecdote, while Chapman's widow is a principal figure in a major drama. Hence the playwright's expansions and innovations, which render his creation more vivid and, if possible, more appalling than its original.

It is of course with deliberate irony that the dramatist calls his widow, who is nameless in the source, Cynthia, and one remembers Chapman's use of the name, with all its traditional associations of purity and chastity, in the "Hymnus in Cynthiam," one of the two poems which constitute his brief volume of the previous decade, *The Shadow of Night*. The bitter passage (4.3.77–80) in which Cynthia's seeming virtue is exposed as vain and hollow ceremony is a Chapman touch. "If the world should see this!" she protests as the soldier embraces her on her husband's coffin. "The world!" her lover mocks. "Should one so rare as yourself respect the vulgar world?" And Cynthia replies: "The praise I have had, I would continue." (The hypocritical ostentation of Cynthia's mourning contrasts powerfully with the genuine sorrow of Chapman's widower, the Earl of St. Anne in *Monsieur D'Olive*, whose grief over the death of his wife is so intense that he cannot bring himself to inter her body.) Also a Chapman touch is the suggestion that the widow's degradation is social as well as moral, that in giving herself to a common "eightpenny sentinel" she has betrayed the venerable house whose honor it is her duty to uphold. But the dramatist's most telling indictment of Cynthia occurs late in the action, after she has proposed the exchange of corpses. "I cannot do't," the soldier suddenly declares, and he goes on to make a startling confession:

> my heart will not permit
> My hands to execute a second murther.
> The truth is I am he that slew thy husband.

Cynthia. The gods forbid!
Lysander. It was this hand that bath'd my reeking sword
In his life blood, while he cried out for mercy;
But I, remorseless, paunch'd him, cut his throat,
He with his last breath crying, "Cynthia!"

(5.2.25–32)

Cynthia registers shock—as well she might—but her qualm of honor quickly passes, and she resumes her grisly task. "For heaven's love, come," she urges her paramour, "the night goes off apace" (57).

Chapman's elaborations are scarcely calculated to render his widow more humanly persuasive than the matron of his source. Like her counterpart in the secondary action, Cynthia serves the exigencies of a thesis, and it was not essential to Chapman's purpose that he psychologize either character. The final unmasking of Cynthia is, however, so disturbing in its implications that the temptation to psychologize—and inevitably to soften—the portrayal is great indeed. Thus Miss Bradbrook discerns in Cynthia a subtle transformation of character. "She has undergone some horrible metamorphosis of an inward kind," Miss Bradbrook writes, "in which her previous self has been destroyed."[14] Such an observation might with justice be made of Beatrice-Joanna in *The Changeling*, but for Chapman's creation it is less suitable. The critic has, perhaps somewhat innocently, accepted Cynthia's virtuous protestations at their face value and has failed to see that the previous self was no more than a cynical sham. Chapman, it should be realized, is working directly within a time-honored tradition that antedates the humanism of the Renaissance by many centuries: it is the antifeminine tradition of classical satire and medieval fabliau. If in *The Widow's Tears* the dramatist had focused exclusively on his female personages, the play would, it seems to me, still engage our attention as representing the ultimate extreme to which the satirization of women is brought in the Jacobean theatre—a theatre in which the satirization of women is by no means an unusual theme. But *The Widow's Tears* offers a good deal more.

III

Chapman provides his play with several notable male characters. There is Lysander, Cynthia's uxorious husband, whose dotage takes the form of a strange obsession with his wife's reputation. The casual suggestion that she may be no different from other women and prove false to her husband's memory in the event of his death serves as the spark which sets afire his "dry, melancholy brain." Like Anselmus in the *Second Maiden's Tragedy*, whom he resembles in more than one respect, Lysander devises a "curious trial" of his wife's devotion. He has himself reported for dead, and when he next appears it is in the guise of the sentinel who visits the "widow" in the tomb. Thus, in a meaningful—and theatrically striking—variation on his source, Chapman has the husband seduce his own wife and in so doing discover the bitter truth that the former harmony of his marriage rested on nothing more substantial than an illusion.

Also significant is the Governor, who in his single, brief appearance contributes much to the final impression left by the play. In Elizabethan comedy the magistrate who brings the action to a close by disentangling the confusions of the intrigue and meting out appropriate punishments and rewards is a familiar figure. Master Baily in *Gammer Gurton's Needle* initiates a long succession that includes Justice Clement in *Every Man in His Humour,* the Prince in *The Phoenix,* and the Duke in *Measure for Measure.* If the dramatic function of such a personage is manifestly practical, it is symbolic as well: He signifies the triumph of wisdom and (depending upon the playwright's mood) good humor or stern morality over the forces of human folly, ignorance, and injustice. In Chapman's hands, however, the character of the magistrate undergoes a peculiar, indeed perverse, transformation; for the Governor who presides over the final judgment scene of *The Widow's Tears* deepens the confusion, makes a travesty of justice, and proclaims a series of astonishing reformations. Men (he declares) are to do good only where no need exists, braggarts and tavern haunters are to thrive, husbands are to embrace their wives' lovers. "I'll have no more beggars," the Governor goes on, carried away by his own vision of a better world,

> Fools shall have wealth, and the learned shall live by their wits. I'll have no more bankrouts. They that owe money shall pay it at their best leisure, and the rest shall make a virtue of imprisonment, and their wives shall help to pay their debts. I'll have all young widows spaded for marrying again. For the old and withered, they shall be confiscate to unthrifty gallants and decayed knights; if they be poor they shall be burnt to make soap-ashes, or given to Surgeon's Hall to be stamped to salve for the French measles. To conclude, I will cart pride out o'th' town.
>
> (5.3.310–20)

In introducing a lord of misrule during the closing moments of his play, the dramatist has established the atmosphere of, to use Miss Bradbrook's apt phrase, "a general saturnalia."[15]

But the Governor does not have quite the last word in *The Widow's Tears*. That belongs to the overwhelming figure of Tharsalio, into whom Chapman poured the full force of his creative energy. It is Tharsalio who opens the play, who sets its tone, who brings it to its sardonic conclusion. He is a prime mover in both stories. He dominates every scene in which he appears, and even when he is offstage—which is infrequent—his powerful presence is felt. Without question, Tharsalio is the most impressive creation in the entire cycle of Chapman's comedies. He is also the most sinister.

Descended from an ancient and honorable line, Tharsalio is a younger brother and therefore denied the lands to which he believes his spirits and parts were destined. Untrammeled by the obligations of wealth and status, he has permitted his career to be guided by impulse and opportunism. Tharsalio has served as a soldier and also as a groom in a nobleman's household. He has dissipated in tavern and brothel. He has traveled and felt the lure of that Italy which to so many Elizabethans was Circe's court. To Tharsalio's relations and associates the character which this unstable life has helped to formulate is a puzzling and disturbing one. "Brother, I fear me in your travels," his sister-in-law admonishes him, "you have drunk too much of that Italian air, that hath infected the whole mass of your ingenuous nature, dried up in you all sap of generous disposition, poisoned the very essence of your soul, and so polluted your senses that whatsoever enters there takes from them contagion and is to your fancy represented as foul and tainted, which in itself, perhaps, is spotless" (1.1.132–39). Tharsalio's brother believes that the damage was accomplished by dissolute companions. "I know him for a wild, corrupted youth," he recalls,

> Whom profane ruffians, squires to bawds and strumpets,
> Drunkards spew'd out of taverns into th' sinks
> Of tap-houses and stews, revolts from manhood,
> Debauch'd perdus, have by their companies

Turn'd devil like themselves, and stuff'd his soul
With damn'd opinions and unhallowed thoughts
Of womanhood, of all humanity,
Nay, deity itself.

(2.1.46–54)

The indictment of Tharsalio by his own family is seconded by the objective
testimony of Lycus, the ordinary man of decent intentions: "I marvel what
man," Lycus asks, "what woman, what name, what action, doth his tongue
glide over, but it leaves a slime upon't?" (4.1.142–44). The question is
purely rhetorical.

Tharsalio's soul is indeed poisoned. He has no illusions, no tenderness,
no conventional ideals. Virtue, he concedes, may have once existed in some
golden age; but like the goddess Astraea in Donne's *First Anniversary,* it has
long since fled the degenerate earth.[16] Tharsalio has faith only in his own
intelligence and energy and in the human capacity for faithlessness:

And this believe (for all prov'd knowledge swears)
He that believes in error, never errs.

(5.1.79–80)

Thus it is that he is led to make a religion of egoism and to worship a
curious deity of his own invention. It is significant that when we first see
Tharsalio he is holding a mirror in his hand. As he surveys his image in the
glass, he renounces Fortune, that "blind imperfect goddess," in order to
embrace

. . . a more noble deity, sole friend to worth,
And patroness of all good spirits, Confidence.

(1.1.11–12)

The crucial word *confidence* thus appears in Tharsalio's opening speech;
before the play closes it is to recur twenty-five times.

For the Elizabethans, as for us, *confidence* is a word rich in meanings and
overtones of meaning. It signifies trust or reliance; it suggests certainty and
serene expectation; it connotes the fearlessness born of self-assurance.
"Alas, my lord!" Shakespeare's Calphurnia pleads with Caesar,

Your wisdom is consum'd in confidence.
Do not go forth to-day. Call it my fear. . . .
                                              (*Julius Caesar,* 2.2.48–50)[17]

But for Chapman's age the word also has less favorable significances: It
may suggest complacence, or (more seriously) a presumption not far removed from *hubris* or—in Christian terms—pride. "These fervent repre-

henders of things established by publike authoritie are alwaies confident and bolde spirited men," writes Hooker in "The Epistle Dedicatorie" to the Fifth Book of his *Lawes of Ecclesiasticall Politie.* "But their confidence for the most part riseth from too much credit given to their owne wits, for which cause they are seldome free from error."[18] The confidence of Tharsalio springs, it would seem, from some perversion in him of the Renaissance ideal of *virtù.* He possesses the iron will that characterizes the great men of the Renaissance; he shares with them the conviction that "Men can do all things if they will"; but the uses to which he puts his will and intellect are profoundly different. Hence the ambiguous nature of Tharsalio's confidence: a compound of fearless frankness, ruthless determination, and cynical impudence. As is the case with most manifestations of *virtù,* it sweeps all before it.

The play is essentially the story of Tharsalio's triumphs. He courts and wins the haughty Eudora, takes possession of her household and her wealth, and to the great benefit of his line weds his nephew to her daughter. It is Tharsalio who leads Lysander, his own brother, to question for the first time the strength of his wife's love for him. Cynthia, as we have seen, falls; Tharsalio succeeds in shattering the false image on which his brother erected his domestic happiness. Only once in the play does Tharsalio relent, and that is when he fears, during Cynthia's long fast, that she may indeed perish for grief. It is a bitter and powerful irony that on the one occasion when Tharsalio is permitted to experience a twinge of human feeling, he is proved wrong by events. He peers into the tomb, sees Cynthia in the soldier's arms, and breaks into his impromptu song and dance of joy. "O the happiest evening," he exults, "That ever drew her veil before the sun!" (5.1.36–37). But perhaps Tharsalio's greatest victory is his last. With characteristic penetration he sees through Lysander's disguise, and he goes on to warn Cynthia that her husband is testing her. When the sentinel next appears, she is able to inform him, with splendid effrontery, that she has known his identity from the outset. Husband and wife are quickly reconciled, thanks to the good offices of Tharsalio. "Sister, give me your hand," he says to Cynthia, "So." And to Lysander, in the concluding lines of the play:

> brother, let your lips compound the strife,
> And think you have the only constant wife.
>
> (5.3.372–74)

Thus Tharsalio the destroyer becomes the restorer—with the full and delighted awareness that his brother's new felicity, no less than his old, springs from illusion.

As *The Widow's Tears* unfolds, we are brought to the gradual but inescapable realization that Tharsalio, the cynic, the debauchee, the implacable self-seeker, is also the play's only realist. The experience of his youth, he insists, "hath refined my senses, and made me see with clear eyes, and to judge of objects as they truly are, not as they seem, and through their mask to discern the true face of things" (1.1.140–43). And so it has. In perception and intelligence he towers above the hypocrites, fools, sentimentalists, and self-deluders who comprise the remainder of the dramatis personae. There is no force in the play to counter him; in being corrupted, Tharsalio has achieved a species of wisdom. He is the dramatist's spokesman, and his vision, terrible as it may appear, is also Chapman's vision.

Such a character, and one so starkly revealed, presents obvious inconveniences to students of the grave moralist and Christian humanist of the English Renaissance. Hence the temptation to sentimentalize Tharsalio, or to pass judgment upon him, or to ignore his existence. Even as sensitive a critic of Chapman as Jacquot fails to focus satisfactorily on Tharsalio:

> Tharsalio est plein d'audace et d'énergie, mais c'est un ambitieux sans rêves et sans foi, et par conséquent sans grandeur. Il a découvert la bassesse dont l'homme est capable, mais nul respect de lui-même ne l'empêche de descendre à son tour au niveau le plus bas. Il plaît d'abord par son aimable effronterie, mais l'on s'aperçoit bientôt qu'il n'aime que remuer la boue. . . . Il se refuse d'ailleurs à faire une distinction entre la vertueuse indignation d'une entremetteuse et les protestations amoureuses d'une femme mariée. . . . Le pseudo-réalisme de cet aventurier, qui ignore toute une partie de la nature humaine, ne peut conduire qu'à un appauvrissement de la vie.[19]

The difficulty with this estimate is that the disagreeable impression that Tharsalio understandably leaves upon the reader is not clearly separated from the playwright's own view of his creation. Thus Jacquot is led to censure Tharsalio for failing to make a distinction that does not exist. Nowhere in the play does Chapman acknowledge the existence of any more benign aspect of human nature than the one he chooses to portray; it is not Tharsalio but his detractors who are ultimately discredited.

IV

The pervasive cynicism of *The Widow's Tears* is, of course, anticipated in Chapman's previous comedies, just as is the related phenomenon of his antifeminism. One recalls the devastating parody of Marlovian aspiration that constitutes part of the very texture of the *Blind Beggar*. One recalls the figures in the earlier plays who presage, in one way or another, the triumphant appearance of Tharsalio: There is Irus, in the *Blind Beggar*, who marries two beautiful "nymphs of Alexandria," then in disguise merrily cuckolds himself with both, and finally foists them, pregnant, on a pair of kings he has captured. There is Lemot, in *An Humorous Day's Mirth*, the unmasker of Puritan hypocrisy and amused observer of human absurdity, whose name testifies to the ascendancy in him of intelligence over ordinary feeling. And finally there is Rinaldo, in *All Fools,* another aloofly disengaged intriguer, whose chief delight is the exercise of his own ingenuity in the affairs of others. One recalls, too, the open contempt for his audience that Chapman expresses in the prologue to *All Fools* and Valerio's speech on gullery, which, along with the title, amounts to a summing up of the intent of the play itself:

> Nay, never shun it to be call'd a gull;
> For I see all the world is but a gull,
> One man gull to another in all kinds:
> A merchant to a courtier is a gull,
> A client to a lawyer is a gull,
> A married man to a bachelor, a gull,
> A bachelor to a cuckold is a gull,
> All to a poet, or a poet to himself.

(2.1.359–66)

But the mockery of the earlier plays is, as a rule, light in tone and purpose. It is the intensity of *The Widow's Tears* that largely contributes to the disquieting effect left by this mirthless comedy. Beyond Tharsalio and *The Widow's Tears* Chapman could not continue in the same direction; the work marks as decisive a turning point in his career as, in a later age, "The Hollow Men" does in T. S. Eliot's. Henceforth the poet was to devote his major energies to his great translation of Homer and to that series of philosophical tragedies which reveals another and quite different Chapman.[20]

"Chapman's primary concern," writes Rees, "was with doctrine. He always wrote with the conscious aim of calling forth moral judgment, and an important part of an interpreter's task is to determine the precise judgments inherent in the dramatic material."[21] As counsel this seems to me somewhat questionable, and the interpreter who follows it by applying his faculties to *The Widow's Tears* may find his diligence rewarded with curious doctrine and curious morality. He may even be led to conclude that the received image of Chapman is not an entirely satisfactory one, and that the interesting and provocative thesis that Rees goes on to develop does not fully accord with the evidence.

> When *The Shadow of Night* appeared in 1594 [Rees maintains], the poet, then in his thirties, was well advanced in technical skill and had already arrived at a doctrinal position with which he was evidently satisfied. For poems, plays, and translations written over a period of more than thirty years are nothing if not consistent in doctrine and intention. . . .[22]

Every literary work, it may be said, is fraught with ethical significance; the very act of writing is, in a sense, a profoundly moral one. And of all creators of literature, the serious dramatist, preoccupied as he must be with the actions of men and women moved by passion or desire, is perhaps most deeply concerned with the moral implications of human conduct. But to suggest that he need be a didactic moralist or a systematic philosopher is quite another matter. Chapman, who *is* a serious dramatist, may on occasion assume the role of moralist, and he often philosophizes; but his primary concern is not with doctrine but with his art.[23]

As an artist Chapman is, I feel, more complex than his admirers have generally been prepared to concede. "Oh of what contraries consists a man!" declares Epernon in a memorable passage in *The Tragedy of Charles Duke of Byron:*

> Of what impossible mixtures! Vice and virtue,
> Corruption, and eternnesse, at one time,
> And in one subject, let together loose!
> We have not any strength but weakens us,
> No greatness but doth crush us into air.
> Our knowledges do light us but to err,
> Our ornaments are burthens, our delights
> Are our tormenters. . . .[24]

(5.3.189–97)

Idealist and cynic, classicist and romantic, conformist and iconoclast, Chapman wrote, one suspects, with some awareness of the powerful contraries of his passionately reflective nature. In the mysteries of literature, philosophy, and religion he sought the elusive resolution of his own contradictions. His literary career is the record of that troubled, heroic quest; a quest mirrored alike in the splendors and obscurities of his gnarled and sinewy line. Despite all that has been written on Chapman in recent years, the formulation of a coherent view of his development—one that will take into account the conflicting elements which do exist in his work—remains a principal task for criticism to accomplish.[25]

NOTES

1. Anthony à Wood, *Athenæ Oxonienses,* ed. Philip Bliss (London, 1815), II, 576.

2. "As Marlowe was the artist, and Jonson the critic," Havelock Ellis concluded, "so we might call Chapman the moralist of the English Renaissance" (*Chapman, with Illustrative Passages* [Bloomsbury, 1934], p. 74). In his Preface to a more recent volume on Chapman, *The Tragedies of George Chapman: Renaissance Ethics in Action* (Cambridge, Mass., 1954), Ennis Rees takes much the same view: " . . . poet and moralist are, in Chapman, one. Art without ethical significance as well as beauty was for him unworthy a poet, and few poets have had a higher regard for poetry as an art or, one is tempted to add, a more firm conviction as to what constitutes ethical significance. In Chapman we see an inherited and profoundly held moral philosophy as a mode of imagination."

3. In his *An Introduction to Stuart Drama* (London, 1946), p. 13, Frederick S. Boas remarks that "both the extent and the importance of . . . [Chapman's work in the comic field] are now

receiving increased recognition." Perhaps this is the case, but there is nevertheless little of consequence to cite. The essays on the individual plays included by Thomas M. Parrott in his edition of *The Plays and Poems of George Chapman: The Comedies* (London, 1914) may appear to the mid-century reader somewhat old-fashioned and unsophisticated in critical manner, but they are still the soundest treatment of the subject. Paul V. Kreider's *Elizabethan Comic Character Conventions as Revealed in the Comedies of George Chapman* (Ann Arbor, 1935) is, as its title suggests, rather mechanical in approach. The chapter on the comedies in Jean Jacquot's *George Chapman (1559–1634) sa vie, sa poésie, son théâtre, sa pensée* (Paris, 1951), pp. 81–121, is a helpful, if essentially superficial survey. The comprehensive study of Chapman's comedies remains to be published.

4. See Rees, "Chapman's *Blind Beggar* and the Marlovian Hero," *Journal of English and Germanic Philology*, LVII (Jan. 1958), 60–63. Chapman's parody of Marlowe in the play is more extensive and complex than Rees indicates. Helen Andrews Kaufman misses the burlesque in her recent article, "*The Blind Beggar of Alexandria*: A Reappraisal," *Philological Quarterly*, XXXVIII (Jan. 1959), 100–6, and her contention that the play is "simply Chapman's version of an actual commedia dell'arte" (p. 103) is otherwise not very persuasive.

5. Parrott, pp. 758–59. I have used Parrott's edition throughout for quotations.

6. The exact date of this play is not known, but it must have been produced before the Revels Company left Blackfriars in 1609. Students of Chapman are inclined to regard *The Widow's Tears* as the last of his extant comedies, and this seems to me a reasonable hypothesis. In the absence of any precise evidence for dating the piece, ca. 1605 may serve as a plausible guess—and no more than that.

7. Hardin Craig, "Ethics in the Jacobean Drama: The Case of George Chapman," in *Essays in Dramatic Literature: The Parrott Presentation Volume*, ed. Craig (Princeton, 1935), pp. 29, 38.

8. On the contrasting attitudes toward women and sexual conduct revealed by the repertories of the private and public houses, see Alfred Harbage, *Shakespeare and the Rival Traditions* (New York, 1952), pp. 186–258. Harbage performs a valuable service in treating Chapman, for the first time, in terms of a special theatrical environment.

9. It is true that Rinaldo's tirade is countered at once by the impassioned idealism of Valerio, who defends Love as "Nature's second sun, / Causing a spring of virtues where he shines" (97–98). But the same Valerio, we learn, is "Trusted in taverns and in vaulting-houses" (157), and it is he who delivers the great concluding oration celebrating the inevitability of cuckoldom. The effect of the idealism is thus perhaps tempered somewhat.

10. More than any other episode in Chapman's comedies, Act 2, sc. 2, has offended admirers of the venerable moralist. To Boas the scene is "repellent" (p. 27), and Parrott writes: "Nothing, at least, that I can recall prior to the worst excesses of Fletcher and his imitators is comparable for sheer animalism to the device by which Tharsalio . . . provokes the slumbering lust of his hitherto scornful mistress" (pp. 803–4).

11. *The Works of Thomas Middleton*, ed. A. H. Bullen, VI (London, 1885).

12. The vogue of the tale is the subject of Eduard Grisebach's monograph, *Die Wanderung der Novelle von der treulosen Wittwe durch die Weltlitteratur* (Berlin, 1889). A number of ancient and modern versions of the story are listed by Henri Regnier in his edition of *La Fontaine* (Paris, 1890), VI, 63–65.

13. *Le Satiricon*, ed. Alfred Ernout (Paris, 1950), p. 121.

14. Muriel C. Bradbrook, *The Growth and Structure of Elizabethan Comedy* (London, 1955), p. 176.

15. Ibid., p. 175.

16. Once in the play Tharsalio apparently *does* acknowledge the possibility of "true sorrow" (4.1.105). But such sorrow "evermore keeps out of sight": Tharsalio's observation is a shrewd response to Lycus' account of Cynthia's mourning, and serves less as an assertion of the existence of feminine virtue than as a comment on Cynthia's lack of it.

17. For my illustrations I am indebted to the *OED*.

18. Richard Hooker, *Of the Lawes of Ecclesiasticall Politie* (London, 1597), sig. A2^v.

19. Jacquot, pp. 102–3.

20. He may well have experimented with the first play in this series, *Bussy D'Ambois* (1604), before he wrote *The Widow's Tears;* but one cannot be certain because of the problematical dating of the latter. Elias Schwartz argues for an earlier dating of the tragedies in "The Dates

and Order of Chapman's Tragedies," *Modern Philology,* LVII (Nov. 1959), 80–82, but his arguments do not bear scrutiny; see Edmund K. Chambers' summation of the evidence in *The Elizabethan Stage* (Oxford, 1923), III, 253–54, 257–59.

21. Rees, *Tragedies of George Chapman,* Preface, unpaged.

22. Ibid., p. 1.

23. In a paper on *Bussy D'Ambois,* just published, Irving Ribner also takes exception to Rees' view of Chapman, and for much the same reason. Ribner writes: " . . . Rees is in danger of reducing the plays to mere moral *exempla* and of considering the entire corpus of Chapman's work as the reflection of an ethical system which the poet had fully evolved before he began to write and of which the various poems and plays merely reflect different facets. Chapman's career as a dramatic artist, on the contrary, must be viewed as one of continuous growth and development. . . ." See "Character and Theme in Chapman's *Bussy D'Ambois,*" *ELH,* XXVI (Dec. 1959), 482. Ribner's entire discussion of the play (pp. 482–96) indicates effectively the limitation of Rees' approach.

24. *The Plays and Poems of George Chapman: The Tragedies,* ed. Parrott (London, 1910).

25. I am grateful to the Huntington Library for a grant that made possible my stay there during the summer of 1958, when this essay was written.

(1960)

17

Wit's Triumvirate
A Caroline Comedy Recovered

The drama of the great age from the accession of Elizabeth I until the closing of the theatres has been studied so assiduously over a long period of time that the discovery of a simple fact—that a minor dramatist was born, sued for debt, or died at a certain date, or that a record exists of the title or subject-matter of some lost play—is sufficient to arouse interest. The actual recovery of a play or dramatic fragment is naturally more stirring, even when (as is too often the case) the survival is an amateurish entertainment in Latin designed for academic production or, worse, for the closet. But there is genuine excitement when one happens upon a complete five-act play which was produced for the professional London stage and which received the accolade of selection for Court performance; a play hitherto undescribed and unnoted by theatrical historians. Such a work is the anonymous comedy, *Wit's Triumvirate, or The Philosopher,* written, produced, and presented at Court in the year 1635.[1]

The play survives in a manuscript presented to the British Museum by Lord Howard de Walden in 1942. Catalogued as Additional MS. 45865, *Wit's Triumvirate* is described in the *Hand-List of Additions to MSS. in the British Museum,* vol. III, as "an apparently unpublished 17th cent. comedy, acted or intended to be acted at Court" (p. 51). Although the Manuscript Room of the British Museum is not the most remote hunting-ground for the literary investigator, one can understand why the play has gone unnoticed. The manuscript came into the possession of the Museum at a time when scholarly activities were curtailed because of wartime conditions. Secondly, the *Hand-List*—a temporary catalogue—is available only in the Manuscript Room, and, furthermore, it is impossible to tell from the few words of description that the comedy is pre-Restoration. Nor is it surprising, given the limitations of the available documentary sources, that even the title should be otherwise unrecorded. The dramatic records from the Lord Chamberlain's Office testify to a number of Court performances for the year 1635 (Malone Society *Collections,* vol. II, pt. iii, 375–77); but in keeping with customary procedure, so inconsiderate of the historian, titles are not specified. They are cited, of course, in the Office-Book of Sir Henry Herbert, Master of the Revels; but that crucial document has disappeared, and its contents are known only through a necessarily incomplete reconstruction. Herbert's records of Court performances for the season with which we are concerned, 1634–35, are missing.

A full description of the manuscript of *Wit's Triumvirate*, which is preserved in a much-soiled contemporary vellum binding, is outside the scope of this article; but some basic information may be provided. The text, a fair copy not intended for playhouse use, occupies ninety-six folio leaves measuring 11¼ by 7½ inches.[2] The flag watermark is number 1380 in Heawood.[3] Preliminary textual matter consists of a page providing title, *dramatis personae*, and scene location (London); a *"Prologue"*; and a *"Prologue, before the King & Queene."* Beneath the Court prologue appears the date 1635. The play itself is divided throughout into acts and scenes, the latter being determined on the Continental practice whereby a new scene is begun whenever a principal character enters. There is a brief *"Epilogue"* and an *"Epilogue* to the King & Queene."* Margins are ruled in red ink, the outer margins being used for stage-directions, exits, and re-entries. Act and scene divisions, along with the accompanying entries, are centered. The manuscript is in a handsome Italian hand, presumably scribal, with some use of a secretary "e." A number of revisions, involving such important matters as the substitution or addition of passages, seem to be clearly authorial. There are also, however, revisions of Act 5 in a third hand.[4] A sort of Gothic script is employed for speech-headings, marginal matter, and (with exceptions) proper names in the text. Catchwords are supplied irregularly. The decorative flourishes in the preliminary matter, as well as several other features of the manuscript, suggest that it may have been intended originally as a presentation copy.

It should be frankly acknowledged that, selection for Court performance notwithstanding, *Wit's Triumvirate* is by no means successful as a play. It consists almost entirely of talk, which is not, however, without intelligence, some happy turns of phrase, and several sharply satirical thrusts. But the play merits attention for other reasons. Written when Jonson, although still alive, had fallen into comparative obscurity, it testifies to the hold that the master, "our beste Poett," could still exercise on the imagination of an inexperienced but serious-minded and well-informed young writer. Of much greater interest is the range of discussion and reference in this extremely topical comedy. The matters alluded to or discussed at length are varied enough to include Donne's poetry, satire, Burbage in the parts of Hamlet and Hieronimo, contemporary playwriting and the status of the gentleman-amateur, the religious controversies of the day, and the new astronomy of Copernicus and Galileo. The quest for topicality extends to the revisions: a reference is inserted to Davenant's comedy, *The Platonic Lovers*, licensed November 16, 1635.

Yet, for his model, the author goes back to the twenty-five-year-old comedy *The Alchemist*. In an opening scene patently derived from Jonson's classic exposition, we are introduced to the three rogues, "wit's triumvirate." Their backgrounds are revealed, the articles of their imposture agreed upon, their false identities assumed. Clyster is to be the quack physician. His former classmate, Silence, with whom he shares a touching bond of common expulsion from the University, takes on, in the great tradition of Tribulation Wholesome and Zeal-of-the-Land Busy, the habit and the role of the Puritan divine. The crop-eared convicted forger, Bond, will serve as attorney. Thus the Caroline version of the "indenture tripartite" is established, and the clients, with their various humours, are soon knocking on the door in their quest for medical, spiritual, or legal counsel.

These clients are, in the fashion of the thirties, Jonsonian types lacking the vitalizing power of the Jonsonian imagination. They are more disposed to suffer from a palpitation of the eye than to be possessed (as Face remarks of Sir Epicure Mammon) of any "itch of mind." Thus Fright is troubled by night visions. His fantasy transforms everyday objects into strange monsters; the hideous noises assailing him in the dead of night are, upon investigation, revealed to be the snortings of an asthmatic owl. He is, moreover, a compulsive-obsessive type who cannot look at a window without counting the panes. With characteristic misfortune, Ominous, "A man fearefull of Superstitious Accidents," stumbles at the threshold upon his first entrance. His dreams, which he summarizes at length to Silence, foretell disasters; once he dreamt of dead folk, but (as ill-luck would have it) the next morning found his grandmother and mother-in-law alive. Love is the malady of Sir Cupid Phantsy, and the riming to which he is prone is "the very height of the disease." The hypochondriacal Sickly complains of such symptoms as an itching elbow and a red pimple on his nose. In the immemorial tradition of his kind, he has made the rounds of the physicians and tried in vain their nostrums. Clyster can do no more than dispense another "medicine"—actually harmless sugar-candy—and a paper with a charm against sweaty toes; but such remedies, as Clyster remarks, "with a strong Faith, may worke as great Miracles as the best." Signior Jealousia[5] is married and morbidly preoccupied with horns. Sir Conquest Shaddow is a timorous soul who in his reveries, described with circumstantial detail, accomplishes greater feats at sea than Magellan. The dupes of *Wit's Triumvirate*, then, with their oddities and not-so-strange obsessions, constitute a kind of Caroline casebook of the psychopathology of everyday life.

To the list of victims must be added, however, several in whom the interest is social rather than clinical. If the avaricious Caution has his own readily identifiable neurosis—he is "Riches slave, and run[s] on errands still for it"—he requires legal rather than medical advice, for the shady dealings by which he has assembled his fortune make him legitimately wary of the penal statutes. Dammy de Bois, of interesting name, is a roarer and

confidence man to whom "this Globe is butt Cheater's Hall"; it is appropriate that he should himself be victimized. Narrowitt, "A Precise Puritan,"
laments having suffered his son "to learne Prophane Philosophy, in the
University," while Bead—the "Scrupulous Papist"—regrets that he has not
shipped his offspring "to *Doway or S*ᵗ*: Omers,* to be well grounded in Catholi-
que Philosophy." In an entertainingly satirical episode (3.1), Silence, shifting rapidly back and forth between the roles of Roman priest and
nonconformist clergyman, strides between the two zealots, hearing the
confession of the one and listening with pretended sympathy to the conscientious revelations of the other. Bead is absolved and rewarded with a relic:
"a Tiburne Martyr's blood, upon a strawe, where you shall see that Holy
Martyr's Face, more exactly done, then had Van-Dike, with his rare Pencill
drawne it." To Narrowitt is given a purse with an elixir—"a peice of M^r
Prin's Eare, our blessed Saint," which he must boil "in the syncere Milke of
an Asse, hott from the Cowe." The parts of Narrowitt and Bead are
marked for excision in the *dramatis personae* and in 5.3, 4; one can easily see
how they might give offense. But the scene just described is one of the few
in the play which show a true awareness on the part of the dramatist that
the theatre is his medium. The customary formula is for the client to knock
and enter, discuss his problem at length with one of the impostors, receive
advice, make a donation, and depart—only to return a few scenes later to
go through the same cycle again. If the author is a disciple of Jonson, he
has profited from the example of the master only in regard to the general
scheme of his play. One need do no more than compare the Jealousia of
Wit's Triumvirate and the Kitely of *Every Man in His Humour*—characters
with similar "humours"—to be struck by the vastness of the gulf separating
the amateur, who describes character by means of conversation, from the
professional, who demonstrates character through stage action.

The philosopher of the alternative title is Algebra, who is introduced
arguing with Caution in 2.1. Against the materialism of the unscrupulous
miser, Algebra upholds knowledge as the greatest riches. To Caution, such
idealism smacks of preposterous naiveté. "Oh you Schollers wilbe wisemen
in time!" he admonishes Algebra. "You dreame of an Utopia, a
Philosophicall World, that never was, is, or shalbe; and soe long as you rule
your selves by that mysticall World, you cannot be Wise, in this wicked one."
But it is of course not Algebra but Caution who feeds upon illusion; the
philosopher sees at once through the ignorant pretensions of the supposedly "rare and learned Men." In the final scene of the play, as the dupes
besiege the house and Caution shares in the general discomfiture, Algebra
enjoys his triumph at the expense of "that prudent and rich Gentleman,
that thought so much of saveing, and could not save himself from being
gull'd." Cheaters and cheated agree to entrust the settlement of the entire
imbroglio to Algebra. In a striking anticipation of modern psychological
insight, he explains that the fears of a Sickly or an Ominous are implanted

in early childhood through the ignorance of nurses or governesses: "for when the waxe is soft and tender; Impression's easily enter; and after are seldome or never wip'd out, as the waxe hardens." With the rational counsel of Algebra, the spoils are redistributed to the satisfaction of all, and the rogues, now reformed, present him with gifts that even a philosopher contemptuous of mere possessions can hardly refuse: "a paire of *Hondius* Globes, a Glass of *Galileo's*, with brass Mathematicall Instruments of *Elias Allen's* makeing."

How academic it all is! Although it would be absurd to claim popularity for a play which never saw print and to which there are, so far as is known, no contemporary references, the fact alone of Court performance—or the intention of Court peformance—requires some explanation. One cannot conceive of such a play being produced on the professional London stage in an earlier decade. No doubt the fashionable up-to-dateness of *Wit's Triumvirate* on a number of matters of current interest recommended it to a theatrical audience which now provided a forum for the amateur. Despite the undeniable tedium of this protracted comedy, it holds much the same interest for us. Some of this appeal I hope I have conveyed in summarizing the action of an almost actionless play, but extracts from several of the more noteworthy discursive or allusive passages should help to make it clearer.

Here is Sir Cupid Phantsy commenting, in 1.4, on the poetry of Donne:

> In whineing Poetry to weepe, sigh, groane;
> And say thy Hart's hard Flint, or Marblestone,
> A frozen Statue of cold Ice, or snowe;
> I hate these æqually, I'l not say soe.
> Prythee as I then scorne these wittless Things,
> Wee'l fly a higher pitch, with unimp't wings;
> And see what Stuff doth make the bright hott Sun,
> And in our Similies damne Doctor Dunne.[6]

Earlier in the same scene, Clyster remarks that verse which hobbles and is rough is "the fashion now," and Phantsy—in character—replies, "I Sir, for those that can make no better." I do not recall any other direct references in the drama of the period to Donne and the vogue of metaphysical poetry.

Act 4.2 consists for the most part of a long and remarkable discussion of the new astronomy. In the course of it, Clyster makes the interesting suggestion that the hypothesis of the earth revolving about a stationary sun "was a drunken conceipt of *Copernicus* the Germane, & *Tycobrahe* the Dane, when wine made the Globe of their heades turne round, then they thought the World did soe." With equally invincible ignorance, Silence suggests that the sun is made of "Tallow, enlightened, by I cannot tell what; but I am sure every night, It is putt out with an Extinguisher, and lighted againe God knowes how, and thus they putt it out every Night, that it may be sure to last till Doomes-day." To which Algebra replies, "Hum! This is New Phylosophy." Algebra himself believes that the sun is a stationary fire, that "all the rest of the Planetts dance about it," and that the moon and planets are other worlds. But in a preposterous passage he also pursues to extravagant lengths the familiar doctrine of correspondences between macrocosm and microcosm. Invoking the authority of Campanella,[7] he maintains that the world is "a Great Animal, a Liveing Creature." Grass is its hair, and where there is none, as in the deserts of Arabia, the world is bald. Trees are stiffer bristles; minerals, veins; earth, flesh; stones, bones. Rivers are 'Urin that passes the Uritarys, & when they are come into the Bladder, there tis call'd the Sea." Clouds serve as the world's chamber pot, while rain is "Distill'd Urin, out of the Ayrey Alembeck." Snow and hail are rheum and phlegm, drawn up again by the sun as mists and vapors; dews are "Snuffes . . . left in the glass, and so throwne upon the Floore againe." Earthquakes result from colic in the world's belly, "and when he vents upward or downeward, that makes our great Windes." Lightning and thunder are "the Cloudes in a Burneing Feaver, and the noise, is the roreing of the Cloudes, for the paine of the stone in the Kidney, and when he parts with the Thunder-bolt, his Stone; Then you see what a deale of Urin comes downe with it." Finally, the living creatures that inhabit this world are "like Nitts, and Lice, and Flea's to us, And Townes in It, like Pimples to us; & a great Citty, but a greater Scabb." Later, however, a more modern, and more serious, note is struck. Asked what he thinks of "all the Spheres *Aristotle* spoke off," Algebra—as always, the dramatist's spokesman—replies that

> . . . *Aristotle* was a worthy Man, and so was his master *Plato;* and yet they differ'd; and I see noe reason, in reasoning of prophane things, Why Men that have braynes should not excercise them, and not alwayes follow weake authority; for so It were not possible to be wiser then they that went before us; and if they had done so, wee had beene just like Beasts nowe.

The confidence men are hopelessly outside their depth with the philosopher, but Clyster, who realizes that the game is up, nevertheless beseeches Algebra

> . . . not to tast *Copernicus, Tycobrahe,* or *Kepler,* but especially *Galileo,* hee ha's the Divell in a Glasse, and a greater Divell in his braine for perswations; a Man of infinite witt, Yet all this could scarce keepe him out of the Inquisition, marke that.

"It may be," Bond adds, "his witt brought him thither." But Silence has the last word on the subject: "And for his Booke although It was translated, It shall not be printed, here, Truth be with you Sir, and I will pray for you."[8]

Of greatest literary and (especially) theatrical interest is Act 4.4. On satire, Clyster remarks: "A Satyre is a dangerous thing now, and putts authority in mind of whipping." Phantsy gives his recipe for a successful play:

> . . . 'tis but to putt old Jest's in to Ballett rhyme, and then gett a new tune to it, and two or three of these songs well sunge, to three or foure peices of old Playes, will patch up a new one, at least seeme so, and then that's money both to the Poet, and the Players. . . .

> . . . if I but name any body, point at him, or her, or repeate the dullest part of the last Play, It setts the people on a roare, and that's a Jest, and sure to be call'd witt. . . .

He also discusses with Clyster some current attitudes, in fashionable circles, towards the gentleman-amateur playwright. The passage deserves quotation in full:

Clyster. . . . doe not you write a Play, 'tis dangerous.
Phantsy. Why I can name Good-men have done as much, What say you to *Julius Cæsar, Augustus,* and *Germanicus,* and most of the Emperors.
Clyster. I Sir, but that is now quite out of fashion, and what is out of fashion, will not please.
Phantsy. 'Tis true; Witt is now out of fashion, indeed.
Clyster. Besides to write for the Stage!
Phantsy. Why Doctor, as long as I am not mercenary, but give it them; Is it not as lawfull for mee, to give them witt, as Noblemen and ladies to give them Cloathes? Besides I thinke the Stage hath more need of one, then the other;
Clyster. Indeed, a Gentleman may sooner give them a Rich Shute, then a good Comœdy; but I say againe 'tis dangerous; besides some will say there goes the Play-maker, and then you're undune, that very no Jest, will æquall your Comœdy.
Phantsy. Will it; I hold him two to one of that.
Clyster. besides, If a few Gentlemen and Ladies, joyne togeather the witt Censurers of the Towne, they will doe—
Phantsy. What will they doe?
Clyster. That which they should not Sir, Cry downe your Play, and most because those Male Pretenders, cannot make one; besides the name of Poett, especially a witt, will hinder your Preferrment.

The reader who has struggled through a number of plays by Cavalier dramatists may be inclined to regret that Clyster's warnings so often went unheeded.

The following exchange, from the same scene, is perhaps the most interesting of all:

Clyster: How now! at verse againe?
Phantsy. No faith Sir, I was at my Prayers.
Clyster. What so lowd and acting as if *Burbedge's* soule had newly reviv'd *Hamlett,* & *Jeronimo* againe, or *Allen, Tamberlayne?*
Phantsy. Nay Sir, rather Feild, *in Love lyes a bleeding.*

That Field, who joined the King's men around 1615, performed (presumably the title part) in Beaumont and Fletcher's *Philaster* has not, I believe, been previously known.

What of the author? From the two prologues and the play itself, one gathers that he is a young gentleman recently down from the University. Collegiate reminiscence and loyalty to the values of the academy form part of the texture of *Wit's Triumvirate*. Just as clearly, the "Poëtt Incognitus" has immersed himself in the life of the town: he is interested in its places, keeps his ear open for gossip, and observes with relish the types of human eccentricity. As he himself puts it, "The Poett [has] left his Bookes, to study Men." With no theatrical apprenticeship and with little awareness of the essential elements of playmaking, he is nevertheless eager to try his hand at the endeavors of art. At the same time, he makes a point of his gentlemanly anonymity, and (one suspects from the fulsome praise of Charles and Henrietta Maria) looks hopefully towards Whitehall. He is, in short, one of the "modish scholars"—the apt phrase is Alfred Harbage's—who invaded the professional theatre in the 1630s.

Romantic drama rather than comedy was the favored form of these gentlemen-scholars, and the relatively few comedies they have left conform to a pattern. The representative examples are described succinctly by Harbage: "all are coarse and bourgeois in tone, all have to do with marriage and marriage portions, all contain a pair of romantic lovers, all are full of complex trickery involving among much else the humiliation of at least one character by a deceptive wedding ceremony, all feature a group of tavern-roarers or 'blades'."[9] It is noteworthy, therefore, that the author of *Wit's Triumvirate* consciously departs from a stereotype of which he is well aware. "Here," he boasts in his prologue,

> you will not see
> A Baud, or Whore, in all our Comœdy;
> Nor woman-kind. . . .
> With Marridge to conclude, shake hands, be freinds.
> And so aske blessing.

He rejects blank verse in favor of colloquial prose, and in so doing is apparently striving after a Jonsonian verisimilitude; his personages will "speake like those they act, like-men." He is, then, not content merely to echo those plays—themselves derivative—of Brome, Davenant, Nabbes, Glapthorne, and the rest, that constitute the popular comedy of the Caroline age. If what he does is undramatic and in its own way imitative, he manages nevertheless to touch upon so many lively topics that his work, completely forgotten for over three hundred years, will hold interest for anyone concerned with English literature in the earlier seventeenth century, and especially for the theatre historian.

It may be worth remarking, by way of a postscript, that despite the immensely useful researches of so many scholars, a number of manuscript plays belonging to the period before the closing of the theatres probably continue to lie unnoticed in public or private collections. Several of these I have come upon or learned about in the course of revising Alfred Harbage's *Annals of English Drama;* in the new edition, to be published shortly, they will be listed in the catalogue of manuscript plays that constitutes the appendix to the volume. I have little doubt that future investigation will bring others to light.[10]

NOTES

1. The title does not appear in M. S. Steele, *Plays and Masques at Court* (1926); G. M. Sibley, *The Lost Plays and Masques, 1500–1642* (1933); or in A. Harbage, *Annals of English Drama, 975–1700* (1940). Nor is the play described in W. W. Greg's *Dramatic Documents from the Elizabethan Playhouse* (1931) or in G. E. Bentley's *Jacobean and Caroline Stage* (1941–68). I have modernized the title, which appears in the manuscript as *Witts Triumuirate or the Philosopher.* In quoting I have italicized the Gothic script mentioned below; quoted passages affected by manuscript revision are given in the revised form.

2. Three leaves precede the text. F. i, which is stuck to the binding, bears the note, "Lord God of England & all ye world beside"; ff. ii and iii are blank. F. 97 is blank but ruled, and a final (unnumbered) blank leaf is pasted to the binding. The foliation, which is modern, was done at the Museum.

3. E. Heawood, *Watermarks Mainly of the 17th and 18th Centuries* (Hilversum, 1950), Pl. 203.

4. On the hands, see Cathryn Anne Nelson, "The Manuscript," pp. 53–73, in *A Critical Edition of "Wit's Triumvirate, or The Philosopher,"* Salzburg Studies in English Literature, 57 (Salzburg, 1975).

5. The name is altered to Doubtall in 5.3, 4; a marginal note alongside Jealousia's first speech in scene 3 reads: "he must be written Doubtall." There is a mark next to Jealousia's name in the *dramatis personae,* presumably to note the intended alteration.

6. The name is scored through in the manuscript.

7. The Calabrian philosopher, Tommaso Campanella (1568–1639), a follower of Bernardino Telesio and Nicolas of Cusa.

8. The events here referred to are of course very recent. The *Dialogo dei due massimi sistemi del mondo* was published in January 1632; Galileo recanted on June 22, 1633. The translation mentioned by Silence may well be Matthias Berneggerus' Latin version, published in Strassburg in 1635. The *Dialogue* was not printed in England until 1661, when it appeared in Thomas Salusbury's English translation.

9. Alfred Harbage, *Cavalier Drama* (New York, 1936), p. 73.

10. I wish to thank the staff of the Manuscript Room of the British Museum for their courtesy and helpfulness. I am obliged also to my friend, Professor Arthur Brown of University College, London, for one or two suggestions from which I have profited.

(1964)

18

A Question of Decadence

Some benefits may accrue from testing the validity of a term from the vocabulary of literary criticism—especially if the word is used pejoratively and not as a rule closely examined. For the term *decadence* or *decadent* one might reasonably expect such scrutiny to be conducted in a spirit of historical inquest.[1] True, the word retains its popular currency—an irate correspondent in the London *Times* (October 7) deplores the 1966 Christmas stamps as another sign of decadence in modern Britain—and it still appears occasionally in discussions on a somewhat higher plane;[2] nevertheless, a faint yet unmistakable aroma of the nineteenth century clings to the term. In the swinging Sixties one hears not so much about decadent comedy as about black comedy, or even blue-black comedy: the term applied by one reviewer to *Loot,* the last somewhat uncertain exercise in farcical brutality and calculated outrageousness by Joe Orton who came to so untimely and savage an end. Yet if *decadence* is definitely not a with-it word in the lexicon of today's more sophisticated professional dramatic critics, it survives in academic criticism, and in particular that criticism which is concerned with the drama before the closing of the theatres in 1642. There are more cultures than the two dreamt of by Lord Snow in his philosophy.

In his review of a book on Beaumont and Fletcher published in 1956, Professor Leech could observe, "it is with a feeling of expectation satisfied that we encounter the word 'decadent' in ch. II."[3] The concept of a decadence bulks large in T. B. Tomlinson's *Study of Elizabethan and Jacobean Tragedy* (1964). Tomlinson calls the third and final section of his work "The Decadence," and for the relevant chapters he provides such titles as "Decadence and Tragicomemdy" or "Decadence: The Hollowness of Chapman and Ford." The term, indeed, crops up in all sorts of places, expected and unexpected, in criticism and scholarship in the Elizabethan field.[4] It appears in writings that may fairly be said to represent the most dispiriting level to which students of the period have descended—Sherman's essay on "Forde's Contribution to the Decadence of the Drama,"[5] for example, or Bastiaenan's *Moral Tone of Jacobean and Caroline Drama* (1930)—but it finds a place as well in the work of such influential commentators as T. S. Eliot and Professors M. C. Bradbrook and L. C. Knights.

Usually the word *decadent* is employed without preliminary consideration of its meaning, although the critic may grant the advisability of attempting a definition. Thus Neilson remarks in the venerable Cambridge *History of English Literature:* "It is customary to instance Ford as typical of the decadence of the Elizabethan drama, and it therefore becomes important for a view of that drama as a whole, as well as for an estimate of Ford individually, to enquire what the term means and whether it can be justified."[6] Alas, no such disinterested enquiry follows. Given such a state of affairs, we need hardly wonder that judgments should conflict and confusion result. Is Ford, Fletcher, Massinger, or Shirley the high priest of the alleged decadence? All have been proposed. Is Tomlinson right in suggesting that this interesting condition has already made itself felt at the turn of the seventeenth century, in the chief dramas of Marston and Chapman?[7] Or do we first encounter it, as Simpson implies, in *The Revenger's Tragedy,* written at about the same time as *Volpone* and *Lear*?[8] Does it begin, as Saintsbury would have it, some fifteen years later than that?[9] Or are we, with McIlwraith, to see the rot as setting in only a year or two before the closing of the theatres?[10] Are *The Malcontent, The Revenger's Tragedy,* and *The White Devil* corrupting products of the decadent imagination or, rather, the authentic masterpieces that so many believe them to be? Was there, in truth, any phenomenon in the later Elizabethan, Jacobean, or Caroline drama that may legitimately be labeled a decadence? These are, I believe, questions of some interest, and that they still suggest themselves indicates at the very least a certain lack of precision in some of our criticism. Let us, then, seek clarification by looking into the background of the term and the uses to which it has been put.

I

As all students interested in the origins of modernism are aware, decadence as a movement flourished in France during the latter part of the nineteenth century. To think of decadence in this context is to think of Baudelaire (described by Paul Bourget as its theoretician); of Baudelaire's disciples, Verlaine and Mallarmé; and, above all, of Huysmans, author of the quintessentially decadent *A Rebours,* which provided "un programme involontaire, le loi et le code, le texte de ralliement, l'hymne des enrolés pour l'art neuf."[11] The decadents were in revolt against Romanticism, which had extolled the primitive and natural; instead they cultivated the artificial and unnatural. They became dandies. They suffered from ennui or neurasthenia or worse, pursued bizarre sensations, and embraced perverse varieties of religious experience. They renounced conventional bourgeois morality, and celebrated the virtues of vice, especially as it might be practiced in the fleshpots of the great modern cities produced by the advanced civilizations they despised. The Marquis de Sade was their god-father; they admired Poe. Their heroes were Nero and Caligula; their heroines included Messalina. Not surprisingly they scandalized less eman-cipated spirits. In "an attempt at a really scientific criticism," Max Nordau in his *Degeneration* (1892) sought to prove that "the tendencies of the fash-ions in art and literature . . . have their source in the degeneracy of their authors, and that the enthusiasm of their admirers is for manifestations of more or less pronounced moral insanity, imbecility, and dementia."[12]

In his preface to the 1868 edition of *Les Fleurs du mal* Gautier provided a definition of the movement that influenced decisively its future course. Taine attached the label of decadence to his own society—the Second Em-pire—and the sources of malaise were exhaustively dissected by Zola. With the establishment in 1886 of *Le Décadent,* edited by Anatole Baju, the move-ment gained a periodical of its own; but at around the same time it suffered defections from younger members who preferred to call one another Sym-bolists. At last the movement spent itself, vanquished by (as much as any-thing) the literary vice it least feared: repetition. Its last unreadable monument is Joséphin Péladan's *La Décadence latine,* in fourteen depressing volumes.[13]

In *Lafontaine et ses fables* (1853), *Essais de critique et d'histoire* (1855–60), and elsewhere, Taine analyzes the sources of modern decadence; but in the work by which he is best known to the English-speaking world, *Histoire de la littérature anglaise* (translated in 1871), he discerns no symptoms of the condition in the Jacobeans. To him Shakespeare, Heywood, Webster, Mid-dleton, Jonson, Beaumont, Fletcher, Massinger, and Ford together com-prise a single "génération nouvelle et favorisée."[14] The violent scene in which the pregnant Annabella, in Ford's *'Tis Pity She's a Whore,* is dragged by the hair and otherwise abused by her enraged bridegroom evokes evi-dent delight from Taine: "Elle rit, l'excès de l'opprobre et de la peur l'a relevée; elle l'insulte en face; elle chante; que cela est bien femme!"[15] Not until he comes to Dryden and the Restoration wits does Taine speak of a form "qui n'est plus inventée ni spontanée, mais imitée et transmise"; and in this section we encounter the word *décadence.*[16]

Application of the term to the theatre of the first Stuarts waited upon English men of letters of the *fin de siècle.* Professor Richard Ellmann has recently questioned whether we are justified in speaking of a Decadent Movement in Edwardian England; the note of levity and self-parody, alien to the decadent sensibility, enters irrepressibly into the work of these au-thors, and even Swinburne is not immune.[17] Ellmann's point is well taken. Still, English writers did strike decadent poses in the Nineties, they argued (e.g., LaGalliene and Symons) about a definition, and in general they adapted to their own uses formulae provided by the ferment in French letters. Swinburne seems to have been among the first to speak of a decadence in the Stuart drama; the term appears in an essay on Beaumont and Fletcher he contributed to the Ninth Edition of *The Encyclopaedia Britannica* (Vol. III) in 1875.[18] By the close of the first decade of the present century historians of literature had embraced as one of their commonplaces the idea of a Jacobean decadence. That concept represents perhaps the most influential single critical extension of the term, and it has been duly enshrined in those simplistic handbooks that cater for English Lit students. Thus, under *decadence* in A. F. Scott's *Current Literary Terms* (1965), we read: "This [phenomenon] is shown in the state of English drama after Shakespeare, and in the literary movement of the nineties in France." Note how the theory of a decadence in English drama is here stated as a fact of literary history; note too how the indisputably appropriate reference to the movement in France takes second billing.

Now, the idea of a decadence, as applied to a literary genre, implies a cyclical concept of growth and deterioration that takes its pattern from the birth-to-death cycle of a living organism. The concept is clearly akin to that of the development and decline of civilizations favored by certain modern historians and assailed by others less given to prophetic utterance. (It may be noted that nineteenth-century writers found the analogue for their decadent hour in the twilight of imperial Rome.) In the present instance the analogy would appear to go somewhat like this: Nourished by the fertile soil of the Renaissance, the Elizabethan drama budded with the University Wits, came to full bloom in the supreme masterpieces of Shakespeare and (perhaps) Jonson, then gradually (or rapidly) wilted, and finally died with the closing of the theatres. The decline is generally associated with poor health rather than with old age; decadent literature, as one student puts it, "bears the same relation to normal literature which a diseased or decaying body bears to one which is healthy and normal."[19] Contracted from the moribund host society, the disease manifests itself principally in the moral sphere: the playwright is censured (the judgment of "decadent" in this context is never complimentary) for his departure from what the critic regards as an acceptable treatment of human conduct. It is for this reason that Ford has been so often singled out as a decadent, for he delineates unconventional relationships, even incestuous ones, with extraordinary seriousness and sympathy. "Always the danger is that Ford is obviously in deadly earnest in these plays," writes Tomlinson:

> . . . His designs on the reader, whether they come off or not, are intended to carry as much tragic weight and import as Tourneur's or Webster's.
> Ford, then, is the real villain of the piece in Jacobean tragedy. He is untrustworthy.[20]

Mr. Tomlinson, it would seem, has little use for untrustworthy playwrights.

In passing his judgment on Ford, Schelling at the same time gives what amounts to a definition: "If decadency in art have anything to do with a loss, so to speak, of the sense of that moral direction which guides mankind, like the compass, in his perilous passage through life, and preserves for him an elemental conception at least of the right and honorable direction and the wrong, then Ford's is emphatically decadent art."[21] The formula, here expressed in terms of excruciating platitude, is dubious. One may readily grant exploration of the moral assumptions underlying a literary work to be part of the serious business of criticism: but that task cannot be accomplished merely by applying to the work in question a set of moralistic oversimplifications. Schelling and subsequent critics of standing have been satisfied to do no more when censuring "decadent" playwrights. The inadequacy of their criteria is shown (to cite but one instance) by investigations of Ford during the past decade; Oliver, Leech, and others have demonstrated persuasively that the dramatist's handling of the incestuous passion of Giovanni and Isabella in *'Tis Pity* has much greater moral complexity than earlier students appreciated.[22]

Rather less frequently the decadent traits are seen as defects of art.[23] These the critic may discern in a breakdown of the poetic (e.g., in Fletcher), in excesses of violence and sensationalism (Ford) in a febrile straining after novelty (Tourneur), or in a tired reliance upon overused conventions and themes (Shirley). Nielson on Shirley is characteristic: "It was, perhaps, hardly possible for any writer of his date to avoid the familiar types and situations which had been often employed. . . . If frequent conventionality in these matters implies decadence, then Shirley was undoubtedly decadent."[24]

The divergent evaluations made possible by the two approaches to decadence—moralistic and aesthetic—are nowhere better illustrated than in the critical response to Massinger. Massinger is serious of mind and purpose; he does not share his contemporaries' restrictive obsession with the erotic; he affirms the inherited ethical ideals of his age. Indeed, of all the later Stuart playwrights, Massinger is least susceptible to the charge of moral degeneracy. But to Eliot he is responsible for the "destruction of the old drama."[25] Massinger's verse (in Eliot's view) "suffers from cerebral anaemia; his "feeling . . . is simple and overlaid with received ideas," his imagination is "paltry."[26] Massinger's limitations are thus essentially those of intellect and sensibility, and it is with reference to these shortcomings that Eliot considers the dramatist's morality:

> What may be considered corrupt or decadent in the morals of Massinger is not an alteration or diminution in morals; it is simply the disappearance of all the personal and real emotions which this morality supported

and into which it introduced a kind of order. As soon as the emotions disappear the morality which ordered it appears hideous.[27]

While acknowledging Eliot's aversion to hollow men, and the unattractiveness of any dehumanized ethical code, I rather wish that he had given us a more precise idea of just what he finds hideous in Elizabethan morality as distinct from any other system of morality. Also—and this is more pertinent to the issue at hand—I think we may legitimately question whether Eliot has provided even by implication any real criteria for his judgment of decadence. Is he not merely saying, in his own remarkably suggestive fashion, that Massinger is not a very good writer? Such an estimate of Massinger may or may not be just, but there can be little question that the deficiencies Eliot stresses characterize the mediocre writer of any age, Shakespeare's included, and hence are not necessarily "decadent."

The validity of the idea of a decadence in the Jacobean drama cannot, it is clear, be established on the basis of narrowly moralistic protestations or vague appeals to implied aesthetic criteria. Nor will it suffice to focus exclusively on any single figure, for it is a phenomenon and not a particular writer—a "villain of the piece"—that is the subject of discussion. To be in a position to speculate on so far-reaching a phenomenon as a decadence, the dramatic historian may reasonably be expected to have a broad and sympathetic understanding of the Elizabethan and Stuart drama. Not all those who have pronounced on the real or fancied decadence have been qualified by knowledge and sensibility to do so.

Whether consciously aware of it or not, the critic may be swayed by a sense of the overwhelming preeminence of Shakespeare. Fletcher followed Shakespeare as principal dramatist for the King's men, and was in turn succeeded by Massinger, who did not enjoy anything like the popularity of either of his illustrious predecessors. It is a descending progression, and the critic may be tempted to say with Hamlet, "Look here upon this picture and on this" (3.6.53). But is a decadence signified? After all, no one before or since Shakespeare has been as good; what is unique can hardly serve as a yardstick. Although the analogy is inexact, one might with the same quality of reasoning argue that after *The Iliad* a decadence set in from which epic poetry never recovered. To use Homer as a club with which to beat Vergil is manifestly unfair, and by such a standard Milton, the last of the giants, dwindles into a pygmy. The Jacobean playwrights, no less than the epic poets, deserve to be judged on their own merits.

Yet profound changes in theatrical life—changes that affected the audiences, the companies, and the dramatic forms themselves—took place in the first decade of the seventeenth century, and the process of change continued without reversal until the closing of the theatres. The transformations wrought are of a kind as to stir unease in the historian and critic. It is in this context that the relevance of the idea of a decadence is best considered. Perhaps it would be useful at this point to clarify the issues of the discussion by looking at a few characteristic plays. Significantly, the three that I have selected all come late, belonging to the last decade or so before the final curtain fell.

II

On May 25, 1632, Sir Henry Herbert, Master of the Revels, licensed Philip Massinger's *The City Madam* for presentation by the King's men. This comedy, written by a playwright of outstanding professionalism for the foremost theatrical company of London, and hence of England, is frequently cited as one of Massinger's best plays.

For *The City Madam* Massinger drew his material from the contemporary London scene, and so it is scarcely surprising that the play should have much in common with the numerous City comedies that the age had already produced. Familiar character types reappear: decayed gentlemen, profligate younger brothers, whores, bawds, pimps, susceptible apprentices, rich merchants busily arranging for their daughters to be married to the sons of the old aristocracy. As in *Eastward Ho* (1605), a citizen's wife and her daughters figure prominently, and exhibit social pretensions and affectations very similar to those of Mistress Touchstone and Gertrude in the earlier play. What impresses one about *The City Madam*—what sets it apart from so many previous comedies of London intrigue—is a sober intensity of purpose and clarity of social vision. When, in concluding the story of Lady Frugal, Anne and May, Massinger tells us that his aim has been to "instruct / Our city dames, whom wealth makes proud, to move / In their spheres" (5.3.152–54)[28]—we are inclined to accept him at face value; this is no mere nod at the last moment towards the moral and social verities.

So, too, Massinger is serious about Luke Frugal, the most compelling figure of the drama. A bankrupt wastrel reduced to the condition of a servant in his brother's household, Luke dissembles—or seems to dissemble—the Christian virtues with insinuating rhetoric; he can be humble, devout, a persuasive pleader for charity to all unfortunates. But when told that he has inherited Sir John's estate, the former prodigal turns miser with a vengeance, tyrannizing over the sister-in-law and nieces who had humiliated him. In the last scene we see him magnificently attired and seated in state at his banqueting table, the rich delicacies spread out before him; while, to the strains of soft music, the victims of his avarice enter "as from prison" and "all kneel to Luke, heaving up their hands for mercy." Unmoved, he laughs. It is a stunning stage emblem of arrogant materialism personified. At times Luke reminds us of Tartuffe; on other occasions we think of the great hoarders of wealth on the Elizabethan stage: Barabas, Shylock, Volpone, but most often we are conscious that the pen which produced Luke also created the monstrous Sir Giles Overreach. In his perceptive introduction to *The City Madam* in the Regents edition, Cyrus Hoy is surely correct in seeing Luke's hypocrisy as paralleling the vanity of Lady Frugal and her offspring, whose antics constitute "an amusing piece of satiric portraiture."²⁹ But Luke is no mere "comic schemer"—Hoy's phrase; his effect is too disturbing to be accounted for entirely in terms of traditional theories of comic ridicule and incongruity. Sir John's final excoriation of his own brother has the accents of righteous indignation:

> Monster in nature!
> Revengeful, avaricious atheist,
> Transcending all example! But I shall be
> A sharer in thy crimes, should I repeat 'em.
>
> (5.3.134–37)

Massinger, there can be little question, is sporting with crimes, not follies. In *The City Madam* he is experimenting, as he had earlier in *A New Way to Pay Old Debts,* with what for want of a better term may be described as a species of melodramatic comedy.

Yet, while the play is full of interest, it ultimately disappoints expectation. The refreshing idea of the American Indian disguise, which introduces the impact of the New World into the Caroline milieu of *The City Madam,* does not in the execution live up to its promise. As T. A. Dunn points out, it seems incredible that Luke—a clever schemer and "a scholar / Well read, and travel'd"—should be so persistently naive and gullible.³⁰ The logic of character is being sacrificed to the requirements of plot and spectacle, especially in the last scene, where the magical effects provided by the "Indians" include a variation on the device from *The Winter's Tale* of the statue brought to life. One expects that Middleton, a master of fantastic realism, would have known how far to go. The lighter episodes of *The City Madam,* before the unleashing of Luke's acquisitive mania, lack the verve of first-class comic writing. There is a marriage contract scene in which the daughters set forth the articles of agreement to which their prospective bridegrooms must assent. "These toys subscrib'd to," Anne concludes,

> And you continuing an obedient husband
> Upon all fit occasions, you shall find me
> A most indulgent wife.
>
> (2.2.126–29)

Another interesting idea; this time, one that looks ahead to the Restoration stage. Anne, of course, is no Millamant, nor was she meant to be; but inevitably we think of Congreve, and to do so is to be brutally reminded of how wanting in grace and wit is Massinger's dialogue.

Nor does he have the imaginative resources to meet the Jonsonian requirements of the play's big serious moments. Instead he falls back on Jonson directly. When Luke is called upon to apostrophize his gold (3.3.18–25), he can only paraphrase Volpone. Two generations earlier, in the play that had ushered in the period of highest accomplishment in the English drama, Marlowe had equated deeds with words, and made inadequacy of language a powerful symbol of inadequacy of character.[31] "I find myself aggrieved," confesses the impotent King of Persia in the opening lines of *Tamburlaine:*

> Yet insufficient to express the same,
> For it requires a great and thund'ring speech.
>
> $(1.1.1–3)$[32]

It is a stroke of characterization that Massinger might hesitate to attempt, for he shares the insufficiency himself.

At the same time that Massinger was turning out a play or two each year for the King's men at the Blackfriars theatre, James Shirley, the most prolific dramatist for the second company of the age, the Queen Henrietta's men, was providing one each autumn and spring for performance at the Phoenix. On May 4, 1631, the Master of the Revels licensed Shirley's *The Traitor,* one of the more considerable late Caroline tragedies. In its own day "rewarded [according to the author] with frequent applause,"[33] the play was revived after the Restoration—Pepys saw it four times—and, in adapted form, held the stage until the latter part of the nineteenth century. Few tragedies by Shakespeare's contemporaries and successors can boast such a record of sustained popular acceptance.

An Italian court of the high Renaissance provides the setting for Shirley's drama. Lust, ambition, and the irrationalities of romantic passion set in motion tragic oppositions. Machiavellian intrigues wind a devious course through the corridors of power; emotions run high, and lead to crimes of violence which in turn beget equally violent retributions. The lecherous Duke of Florence attempts to bed the virtuous Amidea. Her brother Sciarrha tests her steadfastness by describing the sensual delights of the palace that await her if she will become the Duke's whore. But Amidea's honor is unassailable, and she even manages to cool the Duke's ardor by stabbing herself in the arm in his presence; the sight of blood is too much for him. Later, however, his libido reasserts itself, and Amidea must be stabbed again—this time fatally—by her own brother, who arrives on the scene fresh from the murder of her former and injudiciously fickle suitor. The Duke is finally brought to Amidea's bed. Unsuspectingly he kisses the cold lips of the corpse, and is then set upon and killed by his kinsman Lorenzo, an Iago-like villain who covets the throne. At the end, amid a "heap of tragedies," order is restored to Florence.

Thus summarized, the play sounds like pretty strong stuff. Tragedies of the previous decades throng to mind: we think of *Antonio's Revenge, The White Devil, Women Beware Women,* and the rest. But the most interesting parallels are with *The Revenger's Tragedy,* produced ca. 1606 by (so the title page informs us) the King's men. A number of elements recall the earlier work: the masques and forgetful revels of the palace; the brother commissioned to prostitute his own sister to a lustful duke; the test of that sister's virtue; the ghastly circumstances of the Duke's murder. There is, indeed, some likelihood that the author of *The Revenger's Tragedy* (whether he be Tourneur or Middleton) drew his inspiration from the same episode in Florentine history that provides the basis for Shirley's tragedy.

The later play is an efficient work of the theatre but, for a tragedy of blood, distinctly anemic. Although the dominant verbal imagery of the play has to do with fire, the dialogue seldom ignites. Terrible events occur, but somehow they do not seem very terrible; no atmosphere of malevolence is created, and the sources of evil in society or the individual are never probed. No doubt it did not occur to Shirley to have such ambitious aims. His characters are stock, and the drift of the play's feeling is towards sentimentality. Male and female characters weep copiously, and their tears provide matter for Shirley's worst excesses of frigid hyperbole. Here is Amidea consoling her brother after the slaying of Pisano:

> Though all my stock of tears were spent already
> Upon Pisano's loss, and that my brain
> Were bankrout of moisture and denied
> To lend my grief one drop more for his funeral,
> Yet the remembrance that you have made
> A forfeit of your dear life
> Is able to create a weeping spring
> Within my barren head. Oh, my lost brother,
> Thou hast a cruel destiny. My eyes
> In pity of thy fate desire to drown thee.
> The law will only seek thee upon land.
> Hid in my tears, thou shalt prevent the stroke
> Kills both our name and thee.
>
> (5.1.6–18)

All this is worlds removed from *The Revenger's Tragedy.* The latter is not nearly so well oiled a mechanism as Shirley's play, but it expresses powerfully its macabre vision of life. For Shirley the skull is a convenient prop to be referred to briefly in the moral masque of Act 3 and then forgotten; for the author of *The Revenger's Tragedy* a mocking skull is a literal and symbolic presence at the center of his great traditional themes of Death's Dance and *contemptus mundi.* The gulf separating the two works may be indicated by a single comparison. In *The Revenger's Tragedy,* as the Duke lies dying—his lips and teeth gnawed by poison, his tongue nailed down with a dagger— Vindice, the triumphant avenger, counsels Hippolito:

Brother,
If he but wink, not brooking the foul object,
Let our two other hands tear up his lids,
And make his eyes, like comets, shine through blood.

(3.5.201–04)[34]

Lorenzo in *The Traitor* thus addresses the Duke:

He smiles, he smiles upon me. I will dig
Thy wanton eyes out, and supply the dark
And hollow cells with two pitch-burning tapers,
Then place thee porter in some charnel house
To light the coffins in.

(5.2.45–49)

The threat is almost identical, but Lorenzo's words, considered simply as language, lack the horrific power of Vindice's. The dramatic context reinforces the point: Lorenzo is not addressing the Duke in person, but a portrait, which he stabs as he speaks. Action as well as language is thus neutralized, and the effect is that of rhetorical posturing: more hyperbole. This staginess characterizes the play as a whole. *The Traitor* neither expresses a private vision of evil nor any sort of social reality; it exists on no other level than that of theatrical artifice. In such a revenge tragedy it is entirely appropriate that the instruments of Websterian violence—the case of pistols and the poisoned saddle and prayer book—should in one of the Depazzi scenes (3.1) become the vehicle for lightly parodistic humor.

If the work of Massinger and Shirley sometimes reminds us of Browning's Andrea del Sarto, with his "low-pulsed forthright craftsman's hand," the same cannot be said of their contemporary, John Ford. In the half dozen plays on which his fame rests we recognize the presence of a talent—perhaps genius is not too strong a word—unsubdued by the prevailing clichés of stage language and action. At a time when plays on English history were out of fashion, Ford turned to the reign of Henry VII for material, and in the sympathetically conceived figure of Perkin Warbeck he created an impostor unlike any that the theatre had seen. With *The Lover's Melancholy*, *Love's Sacrifice* and, especially, *The Broken Heart*, we enter a strangely distinctive realm of chivalric idealism, sustained by the poet's grave and exquisite lyricism. Overcast by Burtonian melancholy, it is a world in which the heart's longings are frustrated by the force of a destiny ultimately merciful in the tragicomedies but implacable in the tragedies. The consummately Fordian note is struck by the lyric, sung to "soft sad music," that precedes the announcement of Penthea's death in *The Broken Heart*:

Love is dead: let lovers' eyes,
Locked in endless dreams,

> *Th' extremes of all extremes,*
> *Ope no more, for now Love dies,*
> *Now Love dies,—implying*
> *Love's martyrs must be ever, ever dying.*
>
> (4.3.148–53)[35]

In recent years Ford has received much attention, most of it appreciative, although critics have naturally differed on interpretative questions. The sheer volume of the work on Ford, as well as the perceptiveness of much of it, amply testifies that, of all the later Stuart playwrights, he exercises the most potent appeal to the modern sensibility.

Clifford Leech discerns in Ford's characteristic tragedies an "urge towards a cessation of movement."[36] In *The Broken Heart* the point of no return has been reached, and passed, before the play begins. Orgilus and Penthea love one another, but her brother Ithocles has forced her to marry the insanely jealous Bassanes. Himself experiencing love for Calantha, the King's daughter, Ithocles repents wronging his sister, but repentance alters nothing: Penthea's code requires her to remain faithful to her detestable husband. Orgilus, unreconciled to loss, must fulfill *his* code and murder Ithocles, thus imposing upon Calantha an analogous deprivation. Were we to give *The Broken Heart* a currently fashionable alternative title, we might well call the play *Eros Denied*. There is never a suggestion that escape is possible from this network of negations; the oracles of Ford's Sparta have spoken. All that his personages can do is to move like so many sleepwalkers through the drama. They grieve, and then they die. It is fitting that Ithocles should be slain as he sits immobilized in the curious engine designed for the purpose by Orgilus; fitting too that Penthea should be shown starved in her chair, that Orgilus should open his vein and bleed motionlessly to death, that Calantha's heart should silently break. Again and again action is arrested as we confront a moment of stillness. This phenomenon is viewed sympathetically by Professor Leech as an effort to overcome "the natural limitations of drama" by achieving "a form of spatial perception."[37] But if action (in the broadest sense) is a limitation of drama, it is also its primary strength; the kind of drama to which Ford seems to aspire may, in the last resort, be essentially antidramatic. Professor Leech is too sensitive a critic not to anticipate our reservations, but despite his illuminating discussion, we cannot readily discount Aristotle's powerful dictum:

> . . . most important of all is the structure of the incidents. For Tragedy is an imitation, not of men, but of an action and of life, and life consists in action, and its end is a mode of action, not a quality. . . . The incidents and the plot are the end of a tragedy; and the end is the chief thing of all.[38]

III

Were Massinger, Shirley, and Ford obscure stars in a brilliant firmament, the peculiar limitations I have pointed to in their work would seem less significant. But these men were not hacks—latter-day Chettles, Mundays, and Haughtons—straining their mediocre talents under adverse professional conditions to eke out an uncertain subsistence. All three were dedicated to their craft; all frequently enjoyed the luxury of working without collaborators; all had the opportunity to realize their potential. After publication of the great Jonson Folio in 1616, the once contemned art of playwriting had gradually gained in prestige as a literary profession. Massinger and Shirley, as we have noted, became established playwrights for the best metropolitan troupes. Ford, it is true, never achieved that very special status, but he did write for the King's men and for Christopher Beeston's companies at the well esteemed Phoenix theatre.

"In Shirley," Swinburne writes, in his inimitably florid style,

> the last if not the least of those in whom the lineal blood of the old masters was yet discernible, we find side by side with the fine ancestral indications of legitimate descent exactly such marks of decadence rather than degeneracy as we might have anticipated in the latest heir of a long line which began with the rise of Marlowe, "son of the morning," in the highest heaven of our song, to prepare a pathway for the sun. After Shakespeare there was yet room for Beaumont and Fletcher; but after these and the other constellations had set, whose lights filled up the measure of that diviner zodiac through which he moved, there was but room in heaven for the gentle afterglow of Shirley; and before this last reflex from a sunken sun was itself eclipsed, the glory had passed away from our drama. . . .[39]

Thus (in a likeness used by Gautier in his essay on Baudelaire) the decadence follows the great age as inevitably as the day the night. But does such an interpretation of Elizabethan dramatic evolution enjoin our assent?

When, some years ago, I was first drawn to this question, my answer was a qualified affirmative. At that time I defined the decadence as a decline signalized by a diminution, variously manifested in the several dramatists, of the force of the creative energy itself. The onset of this decadence, I thought, had some connection with the acquisition by the King's men in 1608 of the enclosed private theatre in Blackfriars, which offered production facilities different in kind from those obtaining at the Globe and which, by charging higher admissions, catered for an audience that was socially less heterogeneous.[40] While not now inclined to modify my estimate of the importance for subsequent stage history of this move on the part of the leading theatrical organization of the age, I am less certain that we are warranted in applying to the plays written in the following years the term *decadent,* with its fragrant associations.

In the first place, there is always danger in drawing a large generalization from a limited sampling of the available evidence, and even an investigator conscious of the perils does not necessarily escape them. In this paper I have dwelt on three Caroline dramatists, each represented by one play. Now, I hope it will be granted that I have not selected my authors capriciously or misrepresented the case by relishing the ineptitudes of their sorriest productions. But how can any single play adequately represent a dramatist of some range? The author of *The City Madam,* a comedy, also gave us the tragedy of *The Roman Actor,* the tragicomedy of the *Maid of Honour,* and (with Dekker) that unique late Miracle Play, *The Virgin Martyr;* Massinger, moreover, made a substantial contribution to the Beaumont and Fletcher corpus. For Shirley I chose *The Traitor,* which along with *The Cardinal* is responsible for whatever reputation that dramatist enjoys as a tragedian. But Shirley's distinctive achievement is as a writer of comedy. In *The Gamester, The Lady of Pleasure, The Witty Fair One,* and others, he shows himself (despite extravagances) a gifted observer and assessor of contemporary manners; these plays, as has been often noted, provide a link with the Restoration. As for Ford: *'Tis Pity She's a Whore,* unlike *The Broken Heart,* moves towards no somnambulistic trance but is in fact throughout vigorously dramatic; indeed, for some tastes excessively dramatic. Surely it is the play's exciting action, no less than its sensational theme, that has recommended it in recent years to the professional producers who have staged it in London, Paris, and New York. Ah, but (some may object) it is the absence of an ethical center—a helpful weathervane, like Kent in Marlowe's *Edward II,* to show the audience which way the moral wind is blowing—that renders this play decadent; Ford's Cardinal, who might conceivably have filled the bill, is less attractive than the incestuous lovers, and Friar Bonaventura disappoints us as both dialectician and counsellor. But to argue in these terms is to shift the grounds of discussion and to risk that confusion of moral and aesthetic criteria that has bedeviled past criticism.

Secondly, in arguing a decadence the investigator makes comparisons between individual plays and also between the character of one era (e.g., the Caroline) and another (e.g., the Elizabethan or Jacobean); and comparisons, we all know, are odious. Earlier I likened *The Traitor* to *The Revenger's Tragedy,* and one might easily draw up a list of particulars to justify setting the two plays alongside one another. But is such a comparison *entirely* fair? After all, *The Traitor* belongs not to some Caroline equivalent of the Theatre of Cruelty, but rather to the Theatre of Entertainment, which has existed wherever the commercial stage has flourished. Unquestionably *The Revenger's Tragedy* is the more impressive achievement, and more to present-day taste, but does not the fact that Shirley's play pleased audiences for two and a half centuries indicate that by his own lights he succeeded?

When we turn from particular works to the dramatic situation over a length of time, we run into other difficulties. To think in terms of neatly self-contained periods of literary development is, as we well know, to foster an illusion, but it is an illusion to which we sometimes still succumb. Recent scholarship has successfully explored the continuity of the medieval and Elizabethan dramatic tradition; I think, for example, of David Bevington's *From* Mankind *to Marlowe* (1962). Less stressed—although by no means ignored—are the powerful ties, despite the closing of the playhouses and the Interregnum, between the theatre of the first Stuarts and that of Charles II. Seen from one perspective, the art of Beaumont and Fletcher marks the aftermath of the Shakespearean culmination; seen from another, it is a beginning that points ahead to a different culmination in the heroic dramas of Dryden and the comedies of Congreve.

Within an age movements overlap, and distinctions blur. Fletcher's *Valentinian* (ca. 1614), a modish tragedy exemplifying the techniques of a gifted professional, may well have appeared in the same season as Webster's *Duchess of Malfi,* an immensely moving and profound work along traditional lines. Middleton and Rowley's powerful tragedy, *The Changeling* (1622) was licensed for the stage one week before Fletcher and Massinger's *The Prophetess,* a typical tragicomedy of the Twenties. Old plays like *The Jew of Malta* remained in the repertories. Some dramatists went on writing pretty much as they always had: Heywood's *The English Traveller* (ca. 1627?) in many respects closely resembles his *Woman Killed with Kindness,* produced a quarter of a century earlier. The marvelous diversities of art defeat the historian in his quest for tidy categories.

We may wonder what would have been the critical fortunes of Massinger, Shirley, and the rest if they had belonged to any other generation than the one that followed Shakespeare and Jonson. As it is, posterity has passed upon them the cruel censure of comparative indifference: Massinger has not been edited in toto since 1813, Shirley since 1833. It was their mischance to arrive not in the vanguard as did the University Wits, in whom we cherish the archaic virtues, but after the moment of most splendid accomplishment. They were the inheritors of fulfilled renown and thus predestined to careers of anticlimax. Yet these dramatists were endowed with native abilities; they profited from great models; they made distinctive contributions. Only a decade before the theatres were shut down, Caroline playwrights were still reaching out in new directions: Theodore Miles has drawn attention to the new vogue of place-realism in Shirley's *Hyde Park* (1632), Nabbes' *Tottenham Court* (1633), and Brome's *Sparagus Garden* (1635).[41] The last years produced some fine plays. Brome's striking farce, *The Antipodes* (1638), operates on a plane of fantasy inconceivable in later, more prosaic times. Davenport's *King John and Matilda* (ca. 1628–34) is an excellent late example of the English history play, and it is good to have a popular edition at last available in the Oxford World Classics. The list might be extended.

The great danger in labeling plays and playwrights as decadent is that in so doing we risk depriving ourselves of the fullest recognition of what they have to offer. Unfortunately, we cannot detach a word from its connotations. C. S. Lewis tried to do so when he categorized English writers of the sixteenth century as either "drab" or "golden";[42] but, despite the impressive erudition displayed in his book and the praise heaped on it by the reviewers, I do not believe that he succeeded; critics wield no such autonomous powers over the complex processes of language. So, too, we cannot redeem *decadent:* it remains pejorative. A quaint holdover from nineteenth-century deterministic thinking, the term does not help us in coming to grips with a great dramatic heritage. The task of the modern in reinterpreting and reassessing the literature of the past is continuous, and with respect to Shakespeare's successors much is still to be done. The critic will find himself in a better position to get on with the job if he ceases to cherish the illusion of the demonstrability of a decadence.

NOTES

1. This problem has interested me for some time. In 1958 and 1959 I published two exploratory notes on "'Decadence' in Jacobean Drama" in *The History of Ideas News Letter* (IV, 50–55, and V, 3–11), a publication, now defunct, which was not very widely circulated. For the present study I have made use of relevant material from my earlier discussion; but I have rethought the question afresh, incorporated much new matter, and revised my views as regards not only points of detail but also larger general conclusions.

2. I have, for example, encountered the term in reviews in *The New Republic* and *New Statesman.*

3. *Modern Language Review,* LII (1957), 256.

4. I here use the word *Elizabethan* loosely but conveniently to cover the period from the accession of Elizabeth I until the closing of the theatres in 1642.

5. S. P. Sherman, introduction to vol. XXIII of *Materialien zur Kunde des Alteren Englischen Dramas,* ed. Bang, (1908).

6. W. A. Neilson, "Ford and Shirley," *The Cambridge History of English Literature* (New York, 1910), VI, 219–20.

7. T. B. Tomlinson, *A Study of Elizabethan and Jacobean Tragedy* (Cambridge, 1964), pp. 218–23, 256–65.

8. Percy Simpson, *The Theme of Revenge in Elizabethan Tragedy* (London, 1935), pp. 33–34.

9. George Saintsbury, *A History of Elizabethan Literature* (New York, 1912), pp. 51, 394.

10. *Five Stuart Tragedies,* ed. A. K. McIlwraith (Oxford, 1953), p. xx.

11. "La Poésie nouvelle: A propos des décadents et symbolistes," *Revue Bleu,* 4 avril 1891; quoted by A. E. Carter, *The Idea of Decadence in French Literature 1830–1900* (Toronto, 1958), p. 135.

12. *Degeneration* (trans. 2nd German ed.; New York, 1895), p. viii.

13. In the foregoing summary paragraphs I am much indebted to Carter's able monograph, *op. cit.* The interested reader may also be referred to Mario Praz's well-known study, *The Romantic Agony* (2nd ed.; Oxford, 1951).

14. Hippolyte Adolphe Taine, *Histoire de la littérature anglaise* (Paris, 1863), I, i, 467.

15. Ibid., I, ii, 481.

16. Ibid., II, iii, 608.

17. Richard Ellmann, reviewing *Aesthetes and Decadents of the 1890's,* ed. Karl Beckson (1966), in *The New York Times Book Review,* to be published January 1967. The existence of a Decadent Movement in England is assumed by Jerome Hamilton Buckley in *The Victorian*

Temper (1951) and, more recently, by Barbara Charlesworth in *Dark Passages: The Decadent Consciousness in Victorian Literature* (1965).

18. The essay was reprinted with an additional final paragraph in Swinburne's *Studies in Prose and Poetry* (1894). I quote the relevant passage below, p. 254.

19. Herbert F. Allen, *A Study of the Comedies of Richard Brome, Especially as Representative of Dramatic Decadence* (Stanford, 1912), pp. 9–10.

20. Tomlinson, *op. cit.,* p. 268.

21. Felix E. Schelling, *Elizabethan Playwrights* (New York, 1925), p. 268.

22. See H. J. Oliver, *The Problem of John Ford* (Melbourne, 1955), pp. 86–98; Clifford Leech, *John Ford and the Drama of His Time* (London, 1957), pp. 41–64; also Ralph J. Kaufmann, "Ford's Tragic Perspective," in *Elizabethan Drama: Modern Essays in Criticism,* ed. Kaufmann (New York, 1961), pp. 366–71.

23. Some readers seek to correlate aesthetic and moral factors; thus, as regards Beaumont and Fletcher, Professor Bradbrook declares: "It is not surprising . . . to find a taste for the more extraordinary sexual themes (rapes, impotence, incest) combined with a blurring of the aesthetic difference between tragedy and comedy and the moral distinction between right and wrong." (M. C. Bradbrook, *Themes and Conventions of Elizabethan Tragedy* [Cambridge, 1935], p. 243). The correlation, as in this instance, is seldom very persuasive.

24. Neilson, *op. cit.,* p. 234.

25. T. S. Eliot, "Philip Massinger," in *Selected Essays 1917–1932* (New York, 1932), p. 190.

26. Ibid., pp. 187, 189.

27. Ibid., p. 189.

28. I quote from Cyrus Hoy's edition in the Regents Renaissance Drama Series (Lincoln, Neb., 1964).

29. Ibid., p. xiv.

30. T. A. Dunn, *Philip Massinger: The Man and the Playwright* (Edinburgh, 1957), pp. 70–72.

31. This point is nicely made by Harry Levin in *The Overreacher: A Study of Christopher Marlowe* (Cambridge, Mass., 1952), p. 44.

32. *1 Tamburlaine the Great,* in *The Complete Plays of Christopher Marlowe,* ed. Irving Ribner (New York, 1963).

33. James Shirley, *The Traitor,* ed. John Stewart Carter (Regents Renaissance Drama Ser.; Lincoln, Neb., 1965), Dedication, p. 2. All quotations are from this edition.

34. I have used R. A. Foakes' edition for the Revels Plays (Cambridge, Mass., 1966).

35. John Ford, *The Broken Heart,* ed. Brian Morris (New Mermaid Ser.; London, 1965).

36. Leech, *op. cit.,* p. 75.

37. Ibid., p. 74.

38. *Poetics,* Chapter VI; Butcher trans. Leech argues that "Aristotle appears to have overlooked the dramatist's need for a point of rest" (*op. cit.,* p. 72). This may be so; here, however, the primary issue concerns not "the moment of stillness" that may be required in a certain dramatic context, but rather a method of dramaturgy comprehending the total design of the play.

39. "Beaumont and Fletcher," in *The Complete Works of Algernon Charles Swinburne,* ed. Edmund Gosse and T. J. Wise (London, 1926), XII, 434–35.

40. The significance of this move is discussed by Gerald Eades Bentley in his important paper, "Shakespeare and the Blackfriars Theatre," *Shakespeare Survey 1* (Cambridge, 1948), pp. 38–50.

41. Theodore Miles, "Place-Realism in a Group of Caroline Plays," in *The Review of English Studies,* XVIII (1942), 428–40.

42. C. S. Lewis, *English Literature in the Sixteenth Century* (Oxford, 1954). See especially pp. 64–65.

(1967)

19
Old-Spelling Editions: The State of the Art

When I was invited to talk here about the current state of old-spelling editions of Elizabethan playwrights, it did not escape my own notice that I was possibly an odd choice to be called upon to deliver so responsible a statement. After all, most of my energies in recent years have gone into the biographical side of Shakespeare studies, which are sufficiently removed from the concerns of this conference. True, I have some editorial experience; but the only old-spelling text I ever prepared was that of the 1639 Quarto of *The Bloody Banquet* for the Malone Society. I can still recall, after almost two decades, the special tedium of collating ten copies without turning up a single variant; the gradually intensifying tension of frustration—which I am sure is familiar to all here—demonstrated, to my mind, the validity of the disputed psychoanalytic dictum that boredom is, paradoxically, a state of excitement. But of course preparing a Malone Society reprint is a very different cup of moveable type from tackling a full-dress critical old-spelling edition. I suppose it is a qualification of sorts that I kept tabs on editions, in both old- and modern-spelling, while revising Alfred Harbage's *Annals of English Drama* and assembling two subsequent supplements; also tabs on editions in progress when (for many years) I edited *Research Opportunities in Renaissance Drama*. But these experiences seem, in all candor, insufficient justification for my presence on this podium.

Perhaps I do best to present myself to you as one who has a special passion, not merely professional, for the plays themselves. That passion goes back to my youth in New York, when I began collecting such editions as were then available. These, most of them, had the disadvantage of being at once pretty bad and very expensive. So I then picked up, from the second-hand bookshops along Fourth Avenue, the so-called Pearson Reprint of *The Dramatic Works of Thomas Heywood now First Collected with Illustrated Notes and a Memoir of the Author in Six Volumes*. Also the *Brome* in the same series. These editions (if they may be dignified with that designation) are now a century old but remain unsuperseded, a source of communal lament to us here today. Publishers' lists of editions still in print offered slim pickings, but I ordered the ten volumes of the Glover and Waller

Beaumont and Fletcher in the Cambridge English Classics. Cambridge University Press were able to provide only nine of the volumes, assuring me that the sixth, then temporarily out of print, would in due course be supplied. It never came, and for years afterwards, every time I glanced at my Beaumont and Fletcher shelf, I entertained dark thoughts about Cambridge, although these were mitigated by the fact that each volume had cost 12*s* 6*d,* that being the price to which they had been lately raised. While reviewing my collecting past for this morning I also recalled being told by the late Alfred Harbage, my mentor at Columbia, that he understood Lionel Trilling had a set of the Parrott *Chapman* he no longer had any use for and which he would willingly sell. I was to phone Trilling if I was interested. This I did. He was (as I only later realized) embarrassed: as the humane inheritor of the liberal imagination, he must have felt some awkwardness about parting with books, from his own library, representative of the values of poetry and intellect, and embodying the tradition of literary scholarship—values and a tradition which his own career exemplified. And furthermore he was parting with them, for money, to an impecunious graduate student he had never laid eyes on. "I suppose you have a great lust to read these books," the great man said. "Well, no," came the reply, as without thought I delved into some deep inner resource of callowness, "No, I just want to have them around." A difficult silence followed; but I procured the Parrott *Chapman,* which, with Trilling's signature on the flyleaves, remains as part of my library. That was the only contact I ever had with Lionel Trilling.

Clearly a speaker who reaches back for such reminiscences to regale you with is going to come up with a light-weight performance. That that will be the case I cheerfully grant. At least it is deliberately so; but there is darker purpose behind my recollections of the editions of my youth. Recently, in the Founders Room of the Folger Shakespeare Library, I was exchanging chitchat with another reader, one who had produced a weighty and generally well-received tome on an aspect of Shakespeare's intellectual development. We talked about conferences, and I mentioned that my paper, in Toronto, would be on old-spelling editions of Elizabethan playwrights rather than something critical for one of the Shakespeare Association of America meetings to follow later in the week. A puzzled look came over his face, the brow furrowed; he nodded, and declared with some confidence, "*That* should be pretty boring." The thought fleetingly passed through my mind that *his* book was pretty boring, but I said nothing; I've saved it till now. I suppose it all depends on what you are interested in—or bored by.

Distrust for the textual critics on the part of the interpretative or historical critics who dominate Elizabethan studies, while more subdued than in the past, yet persists, and is exceeded only by the alarm generated by the electronic computers, with their fancied magical potencies, those computers sometimes enlisted by the textual critics. The ghost of Edmund

Wilson still stalks the corridors of MLA. This despite the notable example of those, like Professor Philip Edwards (here with us today), who have valid passports to both cultures. On the whole, editors have a harder time getting foundation support in the form of fellowships than do those pursuing other varieties of humanistic research. The mistrust is, I expect, partly owing to inadequate comprehension of the demands of the editor's task, partly to a familiar resentment of the exclusivity of a special knowledge or discipline; but the makers of the editions too must shoulder part of the responsibility for the situation. This is a matter to which I will return.

It is beginning to look as though my paper will consist entirely of pre-liminaries, but I'll risk one more. Editorial conferences in Toronto, albeit in another university setting, have been going on now for almost fifteen years; ever since a group of scholars actively involved in editorial tasks decided that it would be a useful undertaking to get together with others of like interests to discuss their projects, exchange experiences, and in general pool their intellectual resources and expertise. The first such conference, sponsored by the University of Toronto, took place in 1965. That year the subject was the editing of sixteenth-century texts. I had the privilege of offering the first address, which was on the editing of English dramatic texts. So it is a special honor to be invited back to this handsome city to speak on a related, if not identical, topic. The occasion naturally invites a retrospective glance at the past (hence my initial reminiscences), some con-sideration of the present state of affairs, and cautious anticipations of things to come.

Past, present, and future converge in a recent decision of the Oxford University Press. Slowly, volume by volume, the Herford and Simpson *Ben Jonson* is going out of print, to be replaced by a new four-volume edition, based on the Herford and Simpson text. The new edition, which will bear the Clarendon Press imprint, will have modernized spelling and light anno-tation on the page. The editor is Gerald Wilkes; the first two volumes are expected next year, with an Oxford Paperback edition of five of the plays coming out around the same time to replace the old World's Classics selec-tion of five plays which (unlike some others in that series) has no annotation at all. These developments we register with interest. The replacement of the World's Classics *Jonson* especially comes as agreeable news, despite the pleasure volumes in that convenient and well designed series have given us over the years: certainly readers will welcome the notes. But to the passing of Herford and Simpson we respond with sadness, tinged (I dare say) with resignation.

Familiar as the Oxford *Jonson* is, however often we have dipped into the riches of these bulky volumes, this seems an appropriate occasion to stand back from them for a few moments and contemplate, with admiration still awed after the passage of a quarter of a century, the sheer scale of the achievement; a scale we perhaps lose sight of when we turn to the edition, as generally we do, with some specific, ulterior purpose in mind. Let us therefore now praise Herford and Simpson. As the editors state in their preface to the first two volumes, those installments comprise

> the Life; Introductions to the several Plays, to the Masques, the Poems, and the Prose works; and a series of Appendices, in which the whole of the extant and accessible documents bearing upon Jonson are reproduced *in extenso*. These comprise the Drummond *Conversations,* now reprinted in a critical text with full commentary; the authentic Letters of Jonson, including several hitherto unknown or unpublished; a catalogue of the books which can be shown to have been in Jonson's library; and a number of extracts from public records, furnishing evidence for conclusions advanced, or new facts embodied, in the text.[1]

This is the matter of the first two installments. Volumes 3 through 8, the heart of the enterprise, furnish texts of Jonson's plays, masques, and poems, including those uncollected by Jonson or found among his papers after he died; also the prose writings: the *English Grammar, Timber, or Discoveries, Leges Convivales,* and Jonson's epitaphs and inscriptions. An introduction on the state of the text, the early editions, etc., precedes each item. Volume 9 gives an historical survey of the text and a stage history of the plays. In the same volume the commentary begins, and continues through volumes 10 and 11, the latter also incorporating Jonson's literary record (which the editors loftily distinguish from the allusion-book species of compilation), supplementary notes on the life, and sections on portraits of Jonson, his library, and musical settings for his songs. Finally, the index. I have not yet mentioned the numerous appendixes scattered through the edition, twenty-four in all, the last (in two parts) being on Jonson and Inigo Jones, and Chapman's "invective against Mr Ben: Johnson."

Such an edition is long in the making. Percy Simpson teamed up for it with Charles Harold Herford in 1902. The first two volumes appeared in 1925. Herford, born in 1853, died in 1931. Mrs. Evelyn Simpson, who had previously given invaluable help with the collations, came on board as a collaborator with the sixth volume in 1938, her name duly appearing on the title page. The eleventh and last volume (originally ten were contemplated) was published in 1952. By then the edition had taken, from inception to completion, a full half century. It replaced the 1816 Gifford *Jonson,* the last previous edition in a century. One must reckon these projects in something like geological time. It is fortunate that they are undertaken by the Oxford University Press, which, having just celebrated its half millenium, may be reasonably expected to stick around to see them through.

Also to see them through in proper style. The quality of the production befits the majesty of the conception; excellent, heavy-stock paper (heavier in the earlier volumes than in the later), plentiful illustrations (including some hitherto unpublished), an exemplary performance by the Oxford printers, most stringently tested by the sixth volume of masques, with their many complicated marginal notes.

Any design so vast must in places be vulnerable to criticism. New information came to light as the edition progressed, and had to be incorporated in later volumes, producing some awkwardnesses. The punctuation, following Jonsonian idiosyncrasy, has made some readers unhappy, as have the act-and-scene divisions (again Jonsonian), which hinder ease of reference. By current standards the edition is insufficiently committed to textual criticism; for example, of the original version of *Every Man in His Humour*, the 1601 Quarto, the editors collated only three copies, whereas the *Short-Title Catalogue* (published the year before this section) lists seven. The commentary notes optimistically assume a knowledge of the classical languages, including rather more Greek than Shakespeare presumably commanded.

Let that pass. The notes offer unparalleled resources of diverse information presented with leisurely amplitude. "Egges, in *Egypt!*" in *The Alchemist*, rates half a page, mountebanks in *Volpone* a page and a half. Here are the editors on that common domestic object, the umbrella, in *The Devil Is an Ass:*

> Coryat, *Crudities*, 1611, pp. 111–112: 'Also many of them doe carry other fine things . . . that will cost at least a duckat, which they commonly call in the Italian tongue *umbrellaes*, that is, things that minister shadow unto them for shelter against the scorching heate of the Sunne. These are made of leather something answerable to the forme of a little cannopy, & hooped in the inside with divers little wodden poopes that extend the *umbrella* in a pretty large compasse. They are used especially by horse-men, who carry them in their hands when they ride, fastening the end of the handle upon one of their thighes, and they impart so large a shadow unto them, that it keepeth the heate of the sunne from the upper parts of their bodies.' Fynes Moryson, *An Itinerary*, 1617, part III, i, ch. ii, p. 21: 'On the contrary, in hot regions, to avoide the beames of the Sunne, in some places (as in *Italy*) they carry Umbrels, or things like a little Canopy over their heads, but a learned Physician told me, that the use of them was dangerous, because they gather the heate into a pyramidall point, and thence cast it downe perpendicularly upon the head, except they know how to carry them for avoyding that danger.'[2]

Jonson's learning finds, in his editors, answerable learning.

So it is just that we mourn the departure of this title from the catalog of books in print. In a famous passage in the *Worthies of England* Thomas Fuller described the wit combats between Jonson and Shakespeare, in which he beheld the former as a Spanish great galleon, solid but slow in his performances, although built far higher in learning than Shakespeare, who reminded Fuller of an English man of war, lesser in bulk but lighter in sailing. The Herford and Simpson edition has perhaps some of the quality of that Spanish galleon, and so must give way to the man of war. Or, to vary and update the nautical comparison: The retirement of the great Oxford

Jonson is not unlike the withdrawal of one of those super ocean liners, like the *France*, with its many decks, elegant accommodations, spacious public rooms, swimming baths, and cinemas; marvelous creations but uneconomical to maintain under the pressures of new-guise, when the day of the steamer trunk is past, energy is prohibitively expensive, and mass bookings replace individual itineraries. The ocean empresses give way to the jumbo jets, catering for a different clientele. They get us there fast, without comfort but relatively cheaply. The day of the Herford and Simpson *Jonson*, predicated on ample space on the shelf and ample money in the pocketbook, a willingness to put up with archaic spelling and punctuation, and competence in the classical languages, not yet discarded as so much excess baggage; the day of such editions too is past. We will have instead four volumes, modern spelling, and a cheap paperback version.

Lest the mood become unduly elegiac, let me hasten to add that of course my analogy breaks down. Whether consigned to the scrap heap or fitted out as a garish tourist attraction, the liner *France* and others like it now truly exist only in the memories of those who sailed on them. On the other hand, the Herford and Simpson *Jonson* will always remain part of our libraries. The nature of humanistic scholarship being evolutionary, this edition will influence future editions of Jonson; Wilkes is basing his on Herford and Simpson. Like Everest it is there, and capable of withstanding the puny assaults of the textual mountaineers. Those of us who feel strongly about our educational mission will applaud the publication of a cheap paperback edition (cheap being, as always, a relative term) which will make a great writer available to an audience for whom the intimidating—and intimidatingly expensive—Herford and Simpson would always be a closed book. The real source of melancholy must reside in our sense that the future for editions of the old dramatists conceived and produced with comparable magnificence now looks bleak.

Jonson is only one of these dramatists. In my previous harangue in Toronto I said:

> The most signal achievement of editing in our field is, of course, the authoritative edition of a writer's entire *œuvre*. In this line much has been promised and little, thus far, delivered. The fourth and final volume of the Bowers *Dekker*, which will serve as a model for prospective editors, appeared in 1961. The edition as it now stands is limited to texts and textual introductions but will eventually be supplemented by a volume of commentary which Professor Hoy has in hand. Announced as in preparation are Beaumont and Fletcher, Chapman, Greene, Thomas Heywood, Lyly, Marlowe, Marston, Massinger, Middleton, and others. Some of these editions have already been in the works for many years. The slow progress is not surprising in view of the magnitude of the editorial task presented by these dramatists, many of whom were discouragingly prolific.[3]

Where do we stand thirteen years later? As for the Dekker commentary, it is fair to say (varying a witticism of the late F. P. Wilson) that Hoy has turned out to be *mañana*. Now, *mañana* appears to be close at hand. Rather than indulge in speculation (of which there is a sufficiency in our business) I decided to put in a telephone call to Cyrus Hoy, who is not with us this week. He told me that the Dekker commentary will run to four volumes, one to each volume of text. After many years of laborious application he has delivered three of the volumes, in typescript, to Cambridge, and is now finishing up the fourth. All will be issued simultaneously.

In this context the old Glover and Waller *Beaumont and Fletcher* of over half a century ago has an instructive history. "When the publication of the entire text is completed," Waller wrote in his prefatory note to the second volume in 1906, "it is intended to print, by way of a commentary thereon, a companion volume containing a series of explanatory notes upon the text, a glossary and whatsoever supplementary material may be deemed to be of use to the student or to the general reader." Six years later, the preface to the tenth volume contains a mournful announcement:

> The present volume sees the end of the task. In 1906, it was announced that a volume or, possibly, two volumes of notes would follow the text. These, together with a critical text of the scattered poems, must be left to other hands. I hoped, at one time, to undertake this additional burden myself, but that seems now to have become impossible.[4]

In the event, other hands failed to take up the burden. Such promises carry risks. As regards plans for the *Beaumont and Fletcher,* the Great War intervened, although it is perhaps doubtful that we would ever have had the volumes of commentary anyway. For another Cambridge project, the *Dekker,* we now have assurance that within a few years we will indeed have the commentary which we have so long awaited. I expect it will have been worth the wait.

As for the others. Cambridge University Press have so far given us three volumes—fifteen plays—of a critical old-spelling edition of the works customarily assigned to the Beaumont and Fletcher corpus, under the general editorship of Fredson Bowers, and with contributions by various hands. A prefatory section, on "The Text of this Edition," reflects mature reconsideration of the principles set forth in the same editor's *Dekker;* principles which have, as predicted, served as a model for prospective editors. The two statements, often word-for-word the same, deserve careful collation by those accustomed to making careful collations. In the *Beaumont and Fletcher* the editors expand speech prefixes and modernize the Elizabethan use of *i* for *j*, initial *v* for *u*, and medial *u* for *v*, these practices remaining unmodernized in the *Dekker.* We have also had, from Professor Bowers, in 1973, a two-volume Marlowe, the somewhat controversial reception of which you know. With Allan Holaday as General Editor, the University of Illinois Press has given us a volume of Chapman's comedies. That was in 1970; a companion volume, comprising the tragedies, is in the works. The Clarendon edition of *The Plays and Poems of Philip Massinger*, prepared by Philip Edwards and Colin Gibson, appeared in five volumes just two years ago. Meanwhile Greene, Heywood, Lyly, Marston, Middleton, and others remain still in the wings. "The others" include most notably a new Clarendon *Shakespeare Apocrypha* and new Clarendon *Kyd*. The *Apocrypha*, which has been on the drawing board for some years, is now well advanced, and the editor, Richard Proudfoot, has given urgent priority to its completion. In the interim Mr. Proudfoot has picked up the reins, as General Editor, of the Malone Society. For long in the doldrums, the Society has taken a new lease of life, with members enjoying the novel experience—or so it has come to seem—of receiving publications in return for their subscriptions. Tasks of the sort performed by Mr. Proudfoot are usually described as thankless, so I'd like here, publicly, to thank him. As for the Heywood edition, I will remark only that it would be premature for anyone to place an advance order with Blackwell's.

Of the Illinois *Chapman* it may at least be said that we have it. This handsomely printed volume of almost six hundred pages presents texts of the seven comedies, from *The Blind Beggar of Alexandria* through *The Widow's Tears*, with (as a bonus) *The Memorable Masque* performed by the Middle Temple and Lincoln's Inn on the occasion of the marriage of Princess Elizabeth to the Palsgrave. The editorial team assembled by Professor Holaday consists mainly of experienced hands with impeccable credentials, including the distinguished textual editor of *The Riverside Shakespeare*. Much work has transparently gone into the undertaking. In his General Introduction, Professor Holaday makes the case for a new edition of Chapman's dramatic works. Granting the importance of his immediate predecessor's achievement a half century earlier, he goes on to observe that

> current readers recognize in Parrott's edition serious limitations, the most conspicuous of which result from our changed editorial standards. The inadequacy of Parrott's textual apparatus, for example, often exasperates scholars, many of whom, for quite sound reasons, also object to his modernized text. But even more serious than these shortcomings are his numerous errors, several of which directly resulted from a decision to correct for the printer a copy of Shepherd's second edition [*The Works of George Chapman: Plays*, 1875]. He [Parrott] also chose to collate only two or three quarto copies, thereby missing numerous press-variants. And, inevitably, he overlooked some cruxes, misinterpreted others, and sometimes misread. Thus, though he carried Chapman scholarship a great step forward, Parrott left unfulfilled the critical need for sound texts.[5]

This is a fair argument, fairly stated. One can scarcely quarrel with the editors' determination to build a new text on a firmer foundation.

Moreover, the increased interest in Chapman's comedies evinced in recent criticism enhances the desirability of a new edition.

The Illinois *Chapman* follows a by now predictable pattern. An introduction to each play discusses the text and analyzes the evidence respecting the nature of the underlying manuscript. Thus Lloyd E. Berry, responsible for *The Blind Beggar,* favors Greg's speculation—that the play, as it survives, represents a reported text—over Parrott's suggestion that the manuscript was a "stage copy"; Lloyd's argument, if inconclusive, is not urged beyond the evidence. The other introductions are similarly responsible. Each is followed by the text of the play, with notes (at the page bottoms) recording both accidental and substantive emendations. After the text comes a three-part apparatus: the historical collation, a table of press-variants, and textual notes supplying (as the General Editor puts it) "a terse commentary on special cruxes and a defense of editorial decisions." These methods, familiar from recent practice, seem hardly calculated to raise hackles. Why, then, does this edition leave some of us with such a strong sense of unease?

Well, for starters, there are the inconsistencies and anomalies. "Only substantive and semi-substantive variants are recorded; obvious errors are not recorded"—this sentence appears, without variation, in the headnote to all eight historical collations; but in fact obvious errors are sometimes listed. Although the editorial program requires the silent emendation of turned letters where no ambiguity exists, in a number of instances unambiguous emendations are signaled. Other inconsistencies apply to punctuation and capitalization. Some elisions are modernized, others not. Digraphs— whether to conflate or not to conflate—are inconsistently handled. The editors refrain from normalization where that seems evidently appropriate. These, and other, anomalies T. H. Howard-Hill has illustrated with much detail in his notice of the Illinois edition of Chapman's comedies in *Shakespeare Studies.*[6] This review, which has really the substance of a review-article, prospective editors ignore at their peril. Professor Howard-Hill, incidentally, on the basis of his specimen checks assumes the text itself to be reasonably accurate. It all depends on where the checks are made. Other specimen collations have revealed a fair number of errors. As we well know, old spelling and elaborate editorial paraphernalia do not by themselves insure accuracy. I rather guess that some of these problems go back to the way in which the General Editor has exercised his prerogative. Reluctant to monarchize, he has allowed his contributors leeway where consistency is preferable. Inconsistency and unevenness of performance often bedevil group enterprises. Even Professor Bowers, known to run a tight ship, has allowed his Beaumont and Fletcher team questionable lateral drift, for example as regards which modern editions (such as textbook anthologies) to include in the historical collation of often reprinted plays.

These matters of detail much engage the serious reviewer, but the unease engendered by the Illinois *Chapman* has a larger resonance. That has to do not with the skill with which the editorial program has been implemented, but with the desirability of the program in the first instance. Do we, in fact, lust after a critical old-spelling edition without exegetical materials? Chapman is notoriously a difficult writer: intellectual, learned, sometimes confused, often obscure or enigmatic. He allows as much. "Obscuritie in affection of words, & indigested concets," he wrote in his dedication of *Ovid's Banquet of Sense,* "is pedanticall and childish; but where it shroudeth it selfe in the hart of his subject, utterd with fitnes of figure, and expressive Epethites; with that darknes wil I still labour to be shaddowed: rich Minerals are digd out of the bowels of the earth, not found in the superficies and dust of it."[7] Well, if Chapman did *his* digging, we must be prepared to do some also, and we look to the editors to labor in our behalf with their pickaxes, shovels, and pails. Meanwhile I will continue to turn to my Trilling copy of Parrott's *Chapman,* while wishing it were in old spelling, and realizing that the notes are insufficient, that the editor probably erred in basing his *Bussy D'Ambois* on the "much corrected and emended" 1641 Quarto rather than the first, 1607, Quarto, and that probably he had no business including *The Ball, Alphonsus Emperor of Germany,* and *Revenge for Honour* at all.

But that's Chapman, a special case. What about Dekker, Heywood, Beaumont and Fletcher, and the rest, who are less learned, obscure, or confused? For almost a generation our most important collected editions of the Elizabethan dramatists have appeared *sans* commentary. For whom are they intended? Not, surely, for the general reader, but he may not exist anyway. For undergraduates reading English? Hardly. Nor, I think, for most post-graduates, unless they are preparing editions as their dissertation projects. Well, then, for the scholars, specifically for those attending conferences on old-spelling editions. But even this clientele, not noteworthy for numerosity, will be concerned with understanding a text as fully as possible, not just with having it established, as though those two tasks were separable. Let's face it; even if we have devoted most of our reading lives to the literature of this period, we now and then still need help. Even with Beaumont and Fletcher. Of Volume 2 of the Cambridge *Beaumont and Fletcher,* a reviewer has written:

> It need hardly be said that such notes [*i.e.* explanatory] would greatly increase the value of the edition. One wonders, indeed, whether it is really possible to establish a reliable text without being able to explain every line of it; and it seems a pity that the knowledge so acquired should not be shared with the reader.[8]

The point is shrewdly made. He goes on to say: "In *Cupid's Revenge,* for example, there are five or six words for which the reviewer would have liked assistance, and there must be other Elizabethan scholars almost as ignorant."[9] The author of these words is Kenneth Muir. If *he* would have appreciated help with some of the words, it is a fairly safe bet that most readers require considerably more.

Professor Muir is not the first to express, publicly, reservations about such editions. But mostly we have had rumblings rather than the manning of the barricades. Fair enough. We are churlish to give even the appearance of ingratitude for self-denying efforts taken, surely without ambition either of self-profit, or fame; only to keep the memory of these worthy dramatists alive with laboriously produced editions of their works. At the same time we have a responsibility to send out clear signals about the sorts of editions we most want to have. The Cambridge *Dekker* (it is, I believe, agreed) started the ball rolling for the kind of edition we have been receiving in 1953, when the first volume appeared. But the editor always had as his intention to furnish a commentary, which he originally entrusted to the late John Crow. Although, for reasons which we can only guess, he makes no mention of such plans in his foreword to the first volume, those of us who have followed the progress of the edition have always known of their existence. Professor Bowers' statement in his last installment, "With this fourth volume the textual editor's assignment is completed," would seem to imply another assignment to be completed by another kind of editor. Of course Professor Bowers abandoned this strategy for his subsequent editions of Beaumont and Fletcher and of Marlowe, but still it is curious that this costly experiment in scholarly publishing has taken its cue, or so it seems, from an inadvertence. I have heard these unannotated editions rationalized on grounds that subsequent editors will build upon them and supply the deficiencies. Thus the Revels editor of *The Shoemaker's Holiday* will assimilate the contribution of the Cambridge *Dekker*. That is a good thing. Still I expect we will have to wait for a while for *The Coxcomb* in the same series. Anyway, the Revels Plays are in modern, not old, spelling, and as a Frenchman practicing his English once said to me, that is not the same *même*. On the whole, collected editions, whatever their special features—however good, bad, or indifferent—inhibit the investment, of scholars' time and publishers' money, in other collected editions of the same writers, at least for the short term. Let us by all means register appreciation for labors already expended, while hoping that standards formulated and refined with laborious methodologcal care will take their place as part of a larger design which will minister to the requirements of the great variety of readers.

Thus far I have talked only about collected editions, for that is where the principal thrust of editing resides. But I should not wish to pass over the work on single plays. Not that there is all that much to report. Apart from the Malone Society, once again serving us so well, most of the individual plays surface in doctoral thesis editions, by means of which neophytes are initiated into these more removed mysteries. About the propriety of such exercises a difference of views is possible; I know of one distinguished Ivy League institution that looks upon them as suitable undertakings for (relatively speaking) the dummies, the brighter lights being encouraged to get on with the serious business of the profession, which is, needless to say, interpretative criticism. The familiar arguments need not detain us here; but I think that dissertation editions are rarely a dead loss for the candidate (even a first-class candidate), and that, by and large, they make a more persuasive bid for our notice than the general run of lit-crit dissertations. I must confess that I am not really interested in knowing what a doctoral candidate at Bowling Green State University has to say about the meaning of *King Lear*, but I would gladly have a look at an edition of Brome's *The English Moor*, from the manuscript in Lichfield Cathedral Library; a project which I understand a student at Bowling Green has in fact undertaken. Even experienced hands may sometimes profit from apprentice spadework, and meanwhile there is a handy edition. Sometimes these pupil exercises find their way into print in the Salzburg Studies in English Literature, a series about which almost everybody has a bad word.

One such recent comment has made an impression disagreeable enough to move me to share it with you, especially since the view expressed no doubt has some currency. The opinion belongs to a colleague who has published deservedly well received critical studies of *A Midsummer Night's Dream* and Shakespeare's pastoral plays. In a roundup article in *Studies in English Literature* in 1976, the reviewer touched passingly on an anonymous Caroline play, *Wit's Triumvirate*, edited in two volumes by Cathryn Anne Nelson for the Salzburg series. About the quality of the editing he says nothing, but he does venture the opinion that *Wit's Triumvirate* is such "an astonishingly bad imitation of *The Alchemist* [that] one cannot help but wonder whether it were better left unexhumed." Now I do well to admit a personal stake of sorts in *Wit's Triumvirate*. I didn't supervise the thesis, which was done at the University of Arizona, but I am the vandal who dug up the manuscript in that large public graveyard, the British Library. That was fifteen years ago, and to my best knowledge no previous stage historian had ever been aware of the existence of *Wit's Triumvirate*. It *is* an amateurishly bad play; no argument on that score. But one may argue with the criterion of aesthetic excellence as a necessary justification for editing a seventeenth-century manuscript play. The interest of *Wit's Triumvirate* lies in its extraordinary topical allusiveness; an allusiveness that finds room for Van Dyke, Copernicus, Galileo, Donne's poetry, and the fashionable gentleman-amateurs of the Caroline stage. To adapt a remark of W. C. Fields, any play that allusive can't be all bad. But even without this special historical interest, *Wit's Triumvirate* invites editorial attention as a dramatic manuscript. Every manuscript play of this period, without exception, repays our study. The reviewer's remark, indicative of vulgar error, reminds us once again of the two cultures that still exist in Elizabethan studies.

It is proper that we take exception to vulgar error, especially now when a new cache of dramatic manuscripts has unexpectedly become available. I refer to the collection belonging to the Earl Compton that only a few months back came to light "in the back of an old drawer" at Castle Ashby, Northamptonshire. These are the manuscripts known in the eighteenth century to Bishop Percy, and in a list in an interleaved copy of Langbaine's *Account of the English Dramatick Poets* attributed by Percy to Cosmo Manuche, the author of two plays published in 1652, *The Just General* and *The Loyal Lovers,* as well as of manuscript plays, *The Feast* (in the library of Worcester College, Oxford) and *The Banished Shepherdess* (at the Huntington Library). The new accessions make it possible to correct and supplement the information about Manuche in G. E. Bentley's *Jacobean and Caroline Stage.* The recovery, first publicly noticed by William P. Williams in a letter to the *Times Literary Supplement* (December 9, 1977), includes a previously unknown comedy, *Love in Travail,* in Manuche's hand. The Castle Ashby collection comprises in all sixteen manuscripts, ten of which are not in Manuche's hand. Identification of this hand is an obvious desideratum. The whole lot was acquired, for auction, by Christie's, which graciously invited me to have a look when I was in London. This I did, with Richard Proudfoot in tow, and came away more impressed than I had expected to be. The Castle Ashby collection went on sale a month ago, and was acquired, without an opposing bid, by the British Library. So these manuscripts should before long be available to anyone who cares to study them. A body of dramatic writing which bridges the Caroline and Restoration ages must hold interest. I hope that we may look forward to an edition of some, at least, of these plays, and especially of *Love in Travail,* which bears evidence of having been intended for performance.

I have just touched upon a hope, and it is agreeable to be able to conclude my remarks on an optimistic note by saying a word about a major edition to which we can now reasonably look forward, and another which has only lately come our way.

Well and good to survey the shape of things as regards Chapman, Jonson, and that crew; but, after all, our hierarchy is not John Webster's, and for us the "right happy and copious industry" of Master Shakespeare earns him a place rather different from those "lastly (without wrong last to be named)." How do we in fact stand with respect to a critical old-spelling edition of our greatest dramatist? We have been waiting for a long time. For years seemingly moribund, the New Variorum has lately returned to the ranks of the living wih an impressive *As You Like It* edited by Richard Knowles.

The Variorum is a special case, though. It is now half a century since the

Delegates of the Clarendon Press invited R. B. McKerrow to prepare a complete old-spelling Shakespeare, an undertaking which, by happy coincidence, he had himself commenced as far back as 1910, after the triumphant completion of his *Nashe*. By 1937 McKerrow expected to see the introduction and first two volumes of nine plays in print the following year, but illness intervened. He brought out his *Prolegomena for the Oxford Shakespeare* on the eve of the Second World War, and in 1940 died. The commission passed to Alice Walker. Now retired and in fragile health, she has withdrawn. There will be an Oxford *Shakespeare*, in both the English Texts and Standard Authors series; but after careful deliberation the Delegates have opted for modern spelling, I believe appropriately under the circumstances. But we still need an old-spelling Shakespeare, and before long we should have the initial installments of one. This is The International Shakespeare, originally baptized the South Carolina Old-Spelling Shakespeare but now rechristened, with a new publisher, Burt Franklin & Co., at the font. It is good news that the General Editor, J. Leeds Barroll, has managed, by resisting despair, to place this ambitious—and costly— undertaking on a secure financial footing. Professor Barroll informs me that the first plays—a group comprising *Julius Caesar, The Tempest,* and *Twelfth Night*—should be coming our way in due course.

Two aspects of the editorial program require special remark here. The General Editor has called for the collation of all pre-1623 quartos, an undertaking as worthwhile as it is wearisome. Members of the Advisory Council for the edition have been asked to help in the tracing of any copies not listed in the Bartlett *Census*. This initiative has already yielded results. Paul Werstine has found ten previously unobserved, or unrecorded, variants among copies of the 1598 Quarto of *Love's Labour's Lost*. (Perhaps, in this context, you will permit a brief digression. A large number of Elizabethan, Jacobean, and Caroline plays—102 altogether—are to be found in the Royal Library in Stockholm. Although the Hamilton Collection, as it is known, boasts no Shakespeare quartos, it does contain Chapman, Heywood, Middleton, Shirley, and others of special interest to us. Isak Collijn in 1927 described and itemised the collection in *Nordisk Tidskrift für Bok-och Biblioteks-väsen*. I shrewdly suspect that this journal, published in Uppsala, is not excessively familiar.)

The International Shakespeare will also give particular attention to linguistic problems, especially as these pertain to illustrative definition. Professor Barroll has observed that, when we turn to the O.E.D., often enough we find that the context cited to justify a definition is the very one for which we are seeking help. True. Surely he is right to see here a possibility for his edition to make a special contribution.

That edition lies ahead. Meanwhile we already have the five volumes of the Clarendon *Plays and Poems of Philip Massinger,* by Philip Edwards and Colin Gibson: the first truly new collected edition since the revised Gifford

Massinger of 1813. The Oxford *Massinger* has been in the works since the early Thirties. It is refreshing to have the whole at once: General Introduction (including sections on Massinger's life and theatrical career and Massinger's reputation), texts of fifteen plays and the poems, appendixes on running corrections to the texts and Massinger spellings, commentary, and a glossary and index to the commentary. This edition is very much in the new mode, no luxury liner but a neat trim vessel. The editorial principles remind us, if we need reminding, that we still live in the Age of Bowers. No doubt we can expect discussion, even debate, about some of the ways in which the editors have carried out their mandate, for example the emendation of accidentals (which I understand that Professor Turner will be discussing at the conference). But, on the basis of my own specimen collations, I wish to applaud the generally high standard of textual accuracy. The glossary is an especially welcome feature which future editors will do well to think about for their dramatists.

The Clarendon *Massinger* has also, to my mind, a negative virtue worthy of note. When I talked about old-spelling editions here in Toronto in 1965, I questioned the desirability of interpretative introductions in which the editor indulges in "fancy criticism, . . . in effect having a free ride at the expense of a captive audience that has paid its money for the plays."[10] Such interpretative embellishments tend, besides, to be ephemeral. The elaborate critical introductions of the Herford and Simpson *Jonson*, I venture to think, rank nowadays among its least profitable features. Completion of that edition spurred a large-scale critical revaluation of Jonson which left Herford and Simpson behind. Edwards and Gibson have resisted a similar temptation (it must have been strong) to accommodate Massinger's art to the sensibility of the Seventies. Soon enough the Seventies will give way to the Eighties; the sensibility inevitably will change. Meanwhile we have the edition. Critical revaluation, to which Edwards and Gibson are splendidly equipped to contribute, will follow. That is one of the humanistic functions editions encourage. May Middleton, Shirley, and others in the wings make their entrance before very long, to enhance the pleasures of literature for us all.

POSTSCRIPT

Rather than revise my address for publication and thus risk falsifying the historical record of what was for me—and I dare say others—a memorable occasion, I thought I would simply add a brief factual update.

Two of the four volumes of the Wilkes *Jonson,* corresponding to vols. III–VI of Herford and Simpson, were published in 1981, and the other two in 1982. Cyrus Hoy's four volumes of commentary to the Bowers *Dekker* duly appeared in 1980. A fourth volume of Beaumont and Fletcher plays, under Bowers' general editorship, was published in 1979. The next year Mark Eccles' *Measure for Measure* joined the list of available New Variorum titles. Oxford plans now call for an original-spelling *Shakespeare* as well as modernized texts.

NOTES

1. C. H. Herford, and Percy and Evelyn Simpson, eds. (Oxford, 1925–1952), I.v.
2. Ibid., X. 248.
3. "Editing English Dramatic Texts," in Richard J. Schoeck, ed., *Editing Sixteenth Century Texts* (Toronto, 1966), p. 18.
4. (Cambridge, 1906), p. vii; (Cambridge, 1912), p. v.
5. (Urbana, 1970), pp. 1–2.
6. 7 (1974), 420–31.
7. (Menston, 1970), A$_2$–A$_2$v.
8. Kenneth Muir, in *Shakespeare Studies,* 7 (1974), 391–92.
9. Ibid., 392.
10. "Editing English Dramatic Texts," p. 20.

(1984)

Index